Windows
on the Psalms

an anthology to amplify the Psalms
for Years A, B and C of the Lectionary

Ronald W. Dale

Kevin Mayhew

First published in 2001 by
KEVIN MAYHEW LTD
Buxhall
Stowmarket
Suffolk IP14 3BW
E-mail: info@kevinmayhewltd.com

9 8 7 6 5 4 3 2 1 0

ISBN 1 84003 748 2
Catalogue No 1500440

Cover design by Jonathan Stroulger
Edited by Elisabeth Bates
Typesetting by Louise Selfe

Printed and bound in Great Britain

About the author

The Reverend Ron Dale entered the ministry after seven years in the electrical wholesale business and two years as a military dog handler in Libya. He has worked on a variety of Methodist circuits as pastor, superintendent and preacher, combining this with part-time teaching, industrial chaplaincy, broadcasting with the BBC regional network in Birmingham, Derby, Devon, Cornwall and the Channel Islands, prison chaplaincy and a considerable involvement with ecumenical work. He is married with two adult children.

Contents

Foreword   9

Psalm 1   11
Psalm 2   14
Psalm 4   18
Psalm 5   21
Psalm 8   25
Psalm 9   29
Psalm 13   34
Psalm 14   38
Psalm 15   41
Psalm 16   45
Psalm 17   49
Psalm 19   54
Psalm 20   57
Psalm 22   60
Psalm 23   63
Psalm 24   66
Psalm 25   69
Psalm 26   72
Psalm 27   75
Psalm 29   78
Psalm 30   82
Psalm 31   85
Psalm 32   89
Psalm 33   93
Psalm 34   96
Psalm 36   99
Psalm 37   102
Psalm 40   105
Psalm 41   108
Psalms 42 and 43   110
Psalm 45   113

Psalm 46	117
Psalm 47	120
Psalm 48	123
Psalm 49	126
Psalm 50	129
Psalm 51	132
Psalm 52	135
Psalm 54	139
Psalm 62	142
Psalm 63	145
Psalm 65	148
Psalm 66	152
Psalm 67	155
Psalm 68	158
Psalm 69	162
Psalm 70	165
Psalm 71	168
Psalm 72	171
Psalm 77	174
Psalm 78	176
Psalm 79	179
Psalm 80	182
Psalm 81	184
Psalm 82	187
Psalm 84	190
Psalm 85	193
Psalm 86	195
Psalm 89	198
Psalm 90	201
Psalm 91	204
Psalm 92	207
Psalm 93	211
Psalm 95	213
Psalm 96	216
Psalm 97	219
Psalm 98	222

Psalm 99	225
Psalm 100	229
Psalm 103	232
Psalm 104	235
Psalm 105	238
Psalm 106	242
Psalm 107	246
Psalm 110	248
Psalm 111	251
Psalm 112	253
Psalm 113	257
Psalm 114	261
Psalm 116	264
Psalm 118	268
Psalm 119	271
Psalm 121	277
Psalm 122	280
Psalm 123	283
Psalm 124	286
Psalm 125	289
Psalm 126	292
Psalm 127	294
Psalm 128	296
Psalm 130	298
Psalm 131	301
Psalm 132	305
Psalm 133	308
Psalm 136	311
Psalm 137	314
Psalm 138	317
Psalm 139	319
Psalm 143	322
Psalm 145	324
Psalm 146	327
Psalm 147	330
Psalm 148	333

Psalm 149   336
Psalm 150   339
Index of Sundays and Special Feasts   343
Index of Authors and Translators   351
Acknowledgements   355
Addresses of Copyright Owners   367

Foreword

The powerful relevance of the psalms came home to me a few years ago when visiting Israel. I was guiding a group of BBC Radio Devon listeners around some of the ancient sites and we had arrived at Caiaphas' palace. We had seen his garden with places to store wine and grain and we were in what is called the Bottleneck Cell. It is believed that Jesus spent his last night before his trial in this cell. The cell is cut out of solid rock about 40 feet high and about 20 feet square. The original circular entrance is at the top and prisoners were lowered into the cell and into total darkness.

A new entrance has been cut to allow pilgrims in and there is a small altar on which is a printed card with the words of Psalm 88 which I read to my fellow pilgrims. Before I read the psalm I asked everyone to magine how Jesus, in total darkness, must have prayed and pondered over his imminent trial and death. The closing words of the psalm are: 'You have caused friend and neighbour to shun me; now darkness is my one companion left.' After a short prayer I led the group into the sunlight outside and was amazed to see how many were in tears, one or two sobbing uncontrollably. That made me realise how the psalms continued to speak to people. I have discovered that the psalms seem to cover the whole gamut of human experience; the sorrow of exile and being a refugee; fear of death; loss of the sense of God's presence; reassurance of God's care as Good Shepherd and so on. From the depths of sorrow to the heights of joy, all find a place in the psalms.

It is thought that the psalms were regularly used in the Temple to worship God. Because of some of their themes they are ideally suited for that purpose. The psalter contains psalms of thanksgiving, see Psalm 103; penitence, see Psalm 51; adoration of God, with a call in Psalm 150, 'Let everything that breathes praise the Lord,' and Psalm 148 calls all creation to join in the praise.

Even today in Christian worship many churches make use of psalms as chants or to read reponsively. So they continue to be relevant to our world, our lives and the worship we offer today.

Windows on the Psalms contains first of all an exposition, both old and new in scholarship terms, of most psalms, and then a quote that in one way or another illustrates some aspect of that psalm.

I hope preachers, teachers and anyone interested in the psalms will find enlightenment as to the text and thought-provoking quotes about each psalm.

As with my other books in the 'Windows' series, I have based *Windows on the Psalms* on material commended by the Revised Common Lectionary. This gives a three-year cycle for the Book of Psalms, tying in each psalm with lections for the Old and New Testaments, giving a comprehensive coverage of material that I find liturgically helpful.

For the first 20 years of my preaching I never used a lectionary, basing my sermons on what arose out of a daily methodical study of mainly commentaries based on the Greek text. In the end I found that unsatisfactory because I kept returning to old famililar themes to the neglect of much Old and New Testament material. For me the RCL has been a real blessing and an excellent tool in the proclamation of the Gospel.

RON DALE, 2001

Psalm 1

Sixth Sunday of Epiphany/Proper 2/
  Ordinary Time 6: Year A
Proper 25/Ordinary Time 30: Year A
Seventh Sunday of Easter: Year B
Proper 20/Ordinary Time 25: Year B
Proper 18/Ordinary Time 23: Year C

I see and approve the better things of life, but the evil things I do.

Psalm 1 teaches that life is a journey through time: living chooses a particular route for existence. It uses the great biblical metaphor of the 'way', a road or path that one follows. Within all the individuality that particular lives express, there are ultimately only two ways for the journey to take, the way of the righteous and the way of the wicked (verse 6). The first way leads to the fulfilment of life, depicted by the favourite simile of a tree that bears fruit (verse 3). That way is incorporated in the providence of God (verse 6a), because it follows the direction given through the Torah of the Lord. The fulfilment is not so much a reward as a result of life's connection with the source of life. The second way is really an illusion. It has no more substance than chaff that the wind drives away (verse 4) and no future among the righteous who are vindicated by the judging of God who watches over human life. The wicked are grounded and guided within themselves, a way that has no connection with the source of life. That way will perish. Let the readers understand and ask in what way their feet are set.

The first psalm teaches without qualification that each way has its distinctive destiny. The claim is the claim of faith, not experience. It will be reiterated at other points in the psalms (e.g. Psalm 37), but it will also be qualified in many ways. The prayers testify that the righteous meet affliction rather than fulfilment in life. Some psalms wrestle with the enigma of the prosperity and power of the wicked (e.g. Psalm 73). A few perceive that only the forgiveness of God can sustain life because of the sinfulness of the human condition (e.g. Psalm 130). . . . Nevertheless, qualified in all these ways, the doctrine endures and is heard again in the New Testament from another teacher who uses Beatitudes and warns that the outcome of life depends on one's guidance by the Torah (Matthew 5-7). 'Blessed,' he says, 'are those who hear the word of God and keep it.' (Luke 11:28)

James L. Mays
Psalms

Whenever you set out to build a creative temple, whatever it may be, you must face the fact that there is a tension at the heart of the universe between good and evil. It's there: a tension at the heart of the universe between good and evil. Hinduism refers to this as a struggle between illusion and reality. Platonic philosophy used to refer to it as a tension between body and soul. Zoroastrianism, a religion of old, used to refer to it as a tension between the god of light and the god of darkness. Traditional Judaism and Christianity refer to it as a tension between God and Satan. Whatever you call it, there is a struggle in the universe between good and evil. Now, not only is that struggle structured out somewhere in the external forces of the universe, it's structured in our own lives. Psychologists have tried to grapple with it in their way, and so they say various things. Sigmund Freud used to say that this tension is a tension between what he called the id and the super-ego.

But you know, some of us feel that it's a tension between God and man. And in every one of us this morning, there's a war going on. . . . It's a civil war. . . . I don't care who you are, I don't care where you live, there is a civil war going on in your life. . . . And every time you set out to be good, there's something pulling on you, telling you to be evil. It's going on in your life. . . . Every time you set out to love, something keeps pulling on you, trying to get you to hate. . . . Every time you set out to be kind and say nice things about people, something is pulling on you to be jealous and envious and to spread evil gossip about them. . . . There's a civil war going on. There is a schizophrenia, as the psychologists or the psychiatrists would call it, going on within all of us. And there are times when all of us know somehow that there is a Mr Hyde and a Dr Jekyll in us. And we end up having to cry out with Ovid, the Latin poet, 'I see and approve the better things of life, but the evil things I do.' We end up having to agree with Plato that the human personality is like a charioteer with two headstrong horses, each wanting to go in a different direction. Or sometimes we even have to end up crying out with Saint Augustine as he said in his Confessions, 'Lord, make me pure, but not yet.' . . . We end up crying out with the Apostle Paul . . . 'The good that I would, I do not: And the evil that I would not, that I do.' Or we end up having to say with Goethe, 'There's enough stuff in me to make both a gentleman and a rogue.' . . . There's a tension at the heart of human nature. . . . And whenever we set out to dream our dreams and to build our temples, we must be honest enough to recognise it.

. . . In the final analysis, God does not judge us by the separate incidents or the separate mistakes that we make, but by the total bent of our lives. In the final analysis, what God requires is that your heart is right. . . . Salvation isn't reaching the destination of absolute morality, but it's being in the process and on the right road. . . .

Oh, we have to finally face the point that there is none good but the Father. . . . But if you're on the right road, God has the power . . . and he has something called Grace. . . . And he puts you where you ought to be.

'A Knock at Midnight'
from *The Great Sermons of Martin Luther King, Jr*

Psalm 2

*Last Sunday of Epiphany/Transfiguration
Sunday: Year A*

In a mad, mixed-up world, suffering love is the only form of power which can do men good without an inevitable backlash of harm.

Power and non-power

Power – that's the word for our day . . . Black Power, Student Power, Nuclear Power, Power-politics. The title of that television series which starred the late and much lamented Patrick Wymark – *The Power Game* – is a good short-handed description of life in the modern world. The struggle for power underlies almost every conflict of our day, from the clash of great nations, through industrial disputes to family and marital bust-ups.

A dangerous thing, power, which in our life-time has devastated the world, torn nations apart and in the process destroyed the personalities of those who have used it wrongly. Yet we can't do without it, for power is the ability to get things done, so we've got to learn to use it.

And it's worth noting that power in essence is ethically neutral. In itself it's neither good nor bad. It all depends who uses it and how it is used. The cobalt bomb in the hands of a medical specialist can be used to cure cancer; its cousin, the hydrogen bomb, in the hands of a maniac, could destroy the world. Few of us have got *that* degree of power, but all of us have some power in our personal relationships, at work, or in the community. And all of us are on the receiving end of someone else's power. You can make someone else's life miserable by the misuse of power, and you don't have to look far for someone who has the power to turn your life into a fair semblance of hell.

There's one thing we've got to get straight. Power is not an absolute. It is only power*ful* if it is consistent with the declared purpose for which it is intended. The hydrogen bomb is an effective form of power if the purpose is to destroy the world; it is impotent as a means of feeding the hungry. An axe is a power*ful* instrument for chopping down trees but it is slightly less than useful for shaving. Dynamite is a powerful device for blasting rocks, but when it comes to lulling a baby to sleep, it is *non*-power. What Paul called 'the power of the Cross' – suffering love – was sheer weakness in the bustling world of Roman power-politics, but it proved immensely power*ful* in changing men's hearts – in melting those who would not break.

In the last resort, there are only two forms of power in this world. Power *over* people (compulsion) and power *with* people (persuasion). And civilisation could be described as man's attempt to replace power *over* people by power *with* people – compulsion by persuasion, regimentation by education.

The classical example of the clash of these two forms of power is seen in the Judgement Hall when Pilate confronts Jesus. Pilate had the power to command men's bodies – the power of death. Jesus symbolised the power to win men's hearts – the power of life. And Pilate was to discover that what he had always believed was the ultimate form of power was really impotence. He could break a thousand men's bodies but could not break one man's spirit.

But as the centuries have rolled on, that poignant lesson has been wasted on us. We still try to use power *over* people to do what can only be achieved by power *with* people. The overbearing parent can use superior force to impose his will on a child, but that power proves impotent to inspire the child to do the right thing willingly. That takes a different form of power, made up of affection, trust and respect – in a word, power *with* the child.

So if power is the ability to accomplish purpose, then we ought to look closely again at the Cross as the ultimate form of power in doing what God intends for the world – winning the loyalty of men without violating their freedom.

And I suspect that when we get down to the thorny question of deciding what our ultimate purposes are – such as creating a just and peaceful society, and of passing on to our children a world in which they can be more fully human and where all men can take their place at the Feast of Life, we shall discover that what we have regarded as the power to achieve these ends turns out to be *non*-power, and what some men sneer at as the ultimate weakness – the way of suffering love, will prove to be the ultimate power.

Certainly, in a mad, mixed-up world, suffering love is the only form of power which can do men good without an inevitable backlash of harm.

Colin Morris
What the Papers Didn't Say and Other Broadcast Talks

In his wonderfully imaginative book *Telling the Truth: The Gospel as Tragedy, Comedy and Fairy Tale*, Frederick Buechner describes many points of contact between the Gospel and fairy tales. In the following passage he expands on this theme: 'Maybe the first thing to say is that (the world of fairy tale) is a world full of darkness and danger and ambiguity. Almost the first thing that Lucy's brother Edmund sees when he too steps through the wardrobe into Narnia is a sleigh being pulled through the deep snow by reindeer and seated in the sleigh, wrapped in furs, a queen with a face white as death who holds the whole land under her icy sway.

There are fierce dragons that guard the treasure and wicked fairies who show up at royal christenings. To take the wrong turning of the path is to risk being lost in the forest for ever, and an awful price has to be paid for choosing the wrong casket or the wrong door. It is a world of dark and dangerous quests where suitors compete for the hand of the king's daughter with death to the losers, or the young prince searches for the princess who has slept for a hundred years, or the scarecrow, the tinman and the lion travel many a mile in search of the wizard who will make them whole, and all of them encounter on their way great perils that are all the more perilous because they are seldom seen for what they are. That is another mark of the fairy tale world. The beautiful queen is really a witch in disguise, and to open the lid of the golden casket is to be doomed. Not only does evil come disguised in the world of the fairy tale but often good does too. Who would guess that the little grey man asking for bread is a great magician who holds in his hands the power of life and death . . .

Beasts talk and flowers come alive and lobsters quadrille in the world of the fairy tale, and nothing is apt to be what it seems. And if this is true of the creatures that the hero meets on his quest, it is true also of the hero himself who at any moment may be changed into a beast or a stone or a king or have his heart turned into ice. Maybe above all they are tales about transformation where all creatures are revealed in the end as what they truly are – the ugly duckling becomes a great white swan, the frog is revealed to be a prince, and the beautiful but wicked queen is unmasked at last in all her ugliness. They are tales of transformation where the ones who live happily ever after, as by no means everybody does in fairy tales, are transformed into what they have it in them at their best to be . . . The scarecrow gets his brain from the great and terrible Oz, the lion his courage, the tinman his heart. Even in Hans Christian Anderson's *The Steadfast Tin Soldier*, one of the darkest of his tales, the theme of the transformed hero is repeated. With only one leg to stand on and battered by his misadventures, the tin soldier remains so steadfast in his love for the paper doll that even after the little boy hurls him in the stove and the flames have melted him, what the servant girl finds in the ashes is a piece of tin in the shape of a heart. For better or worse, in the world of the fairy tale transformations are completed, and one thinks of the angel in the book of Revelation who gives to each a white stone with a new name written on it which is the true and hidden name that he was named with even from the foundations of the world . . .

It is a world of magic and mystery, of deep darkness and flickering starlight. It is a world where terrible things happen and wonderful things too. It is a world where goodness is pitted against evil, love against hate, order against chaos, in a great struggle where often it is hard to be sure who belongs to which side because appearances are endlessly deceptive. Yet for all its confusion and wildness, it is a world where the battle goes ultimately to the good, who live happily ever after, and where in the long run everybody, good and evil alike, becomes known by his true name.

Frederick Buechner
Telling the Truth: The Gospel as Tragedy, Comedy and Fairy Tale

Psalm 4

Third Sunday of Easter: Year B

It is easy enough for an Aeolian harp to whisper music when the winds blow; the difficulty is for the music to come when no wind is blowing.

Psalm 4 is an individual prayer for help. Its occasion is the trouble caused by falsehood. The honour of the one who prays has been damaged by a lie (verse 2). In spite of distress, the prayer's dominant mood is confidence. In that confidence the prayer petitions God to hear and help (verse 1), rebukes those who cause humiliation (verses 2-5), and declares trust in God (verses 6-8). In the culture of ancient Israel, honour was of the greatest value; it is in most societies. Honour is the dignity and respect that belong to a person's position in relation to family, friends, and the community. It is an essential part of the identity that others recognise and regard in dealing with a man or a woman. In Israel its loss had tragic consequences for self-esteem and social competence. Shaming and humiliating a person was violence against them worse than physical harm. Job's lament over his lost honour (Job 29) is eloquent testimony to the suffering caused. The fourth commandment shows the importance of the notion in the family. Though the terms and the notion are not prominent in our culture, the reality and the experience of it are inherent in the roles and expectations that belong to all social relations.

The prayerful and theological significance of this psalm is that God is the ultimate basis of the 'honour' of the faithful. The psalmist has a basis of identity that transcends the judgements of others – the relation to God. He calls the Lord 'God of my right', that is, the one on whom his 'rightness' as a person depends. One's righteousness is finally a matter of God's judgement. See Isaiah 50:8f and Romans 8:31.

Indeed, the language of the psalm suggests a situation in which the psalmist has already appealed to God and been answered, probably in sacral proceedings, by a word or sign that God has identified and claimed the psalmist as one of the faithful (verse 3) and by doing so has freed the one who prays from the constraints of distress (second line of verse 1). That would explain the exhortation addressed to the detractors (verses 2-5) calling on them to be in trembling awe before this evidence of divine acceptance and to desist from the sin of their falsehood. Instead, they should bring sacrifices to express their own devotion to righteousness, trust themselves to God, and forsake their malicious intentions.

The prayer concludes with a declaration of the psalmist's

experience of grace (verses 6-8). It contrasts the mood of some at the time with that of the one who prays. Many in restless dissatisfaction with what they have pray a version of the ancient prayer of Numbers 6:25, 'Let the light of your face shine on us, O Lord!' (verse 6), hoping for an increase of corn and wine. But the one who prays has been given more joy by the signs of God's acceptance than would be gained from an abundance of meat and drink. The gift of trusting in God transcends the value of any material good. That gift brings with it *SHALOM*, a sense of completeness in relation to God, self, and others. No sleepless anxiety erodes the night. The psalmist is content to find security in God.

Verse 8 has prompted believers through the ages to use Psalm 4 as an evening prayer or hymn. Whether or not one's honour has been injured by misunderstanding, lack of appreciation, scorn, or lie, it is good at the close of the day to repair to the marvellous vindication given to faith in the sign of Jesus Christ and to know with Paul that 'the peace of God which surpasses all understanding will guard your hearts and your minds in Christ Jesus' (Philippians 4:7).

James L. Mays
Psalms

Singing in times of trouble

Any fool can sing in the day. When the cup is full, a person draws inspiration from it. When wealth rolls in abundance round about him, anyone can sing to the praise of the God who gives a plenteous harvest or sends home a loaded argosy. It is easy enough for an Aeolian harp to whisper music when the winds blow; the difficulty is for the music to come when no wind is blowing.

No one can sing a song in the night by themselves. They may attempt it, but will feel how difficult it is. Let all things go as I please – I will weave songs, weave them wherever I go, with the flowers that grow upon my path. But put me in a desert, where no flowers are, and wherewith shall I weave a chorus of praise to God? How shall I make a crown for him? Let this voice be free, and this body full of health, and I can sing God's praise; but stop this tongue, lay me upon the bed of languishing and it is not easy to sing from the bed and chant high praises in the fires. Give me the bliss of spiritual

19

liberty, and let me mount up to my God and get near the throne, and I will sing, aye, sing as sweet as seraphs. But confine me, fetter my spirit, clip my wings, make me exceeding sad, so that I become old like the eagle – ah! then it is hard to sing.

It is not natural to sing when in trouble, 'Bless the Lord, O my soul, and all that is within me bless his holy name,' for that is a daylight song. But it was a divine song that Habakkuk sang when in the night he said, 'Though the fig tree shall not blossom . . . yet will I trust in the Lord, and stay myself in the God of Jacob' . . . songs in the night come only from God; they are not in human power.

Charles Haddon Spurgeon
Songs in the Night

Psalm 5

Proper 6/Ordinary Time 11: Year C, verses 1-8

Here is the great dilemma of the prophets, and indeed the dilemma of us all to this day. Which comes first, mercy or justice?

The Book of Psalms begins by affirming that 'happy' are those whose 'delight is in the instruction [NRSV 'law'] of the Lord' and 'who take refuge in' the Lord (1:1-2; 2:12). Psalms 3 and 4 make it clear that this happiness does not guarantee an easy, carefree life. The psalmist, surrounded by 'foes' (3:1-2) and in 'distress' (4:1), 'cry' (3:4) and 'call' to God for help. In Psalm 5 also, the psalmist is not unopposed (see 'enemies' in verse 8) and so must 'cry' and 'plead' and 'watch' (5:2-3). As is usually the case, the precise nature of the opposition and the identity of the enemies are unclear, but the psalmist seems to be the victim of some sort of false testimony (5:6, 9-10). His or her plight is reminiscent of the kind of opposition experienced by Jeremiah and Jesus, as well as by Naboth in the Old Testament lesson for the day.

The psalm falls most naturally into five sections, as follows:

- Verses 1-3 Petition and affirmation: the 'I' and God

- Verses 4-6 Affirmation: God and wickedness

- Verses 7-8 Affirmation and petition: the 'I' and God

- Verses 9-10 Affirmation and petition: God and the wicked

- Verses 11-12 Petition and affirmation: 'all' the 'righteous' and God.

In language typical of the prayers for help, the psalmist asks in verses 1-3 to be heard (see for example, 'give ear' in Psalms 17:1; 55:1; 'listen' in 61:1; 86:6; 'cry' in 28:2; 31:22). The addressing of God as 'my King' is significant, since this is the first occurrence of the Hebrew root *mlk* (to reign, be king) in the psalter. . . . This title for God relates Psalm 5 and other prayers for help to what has been identified as the theological 'heart' of the psalter – God rules the world. . . . In Psalm 5, as is always the case, this fundamental affirmation is made amid opposition. Indeed, the affirmation of God's sovereignty has the effect of *inviting* opposition, as the life and death of Jesus illustrates. In other words, to call God 'my King', is eschato-logical. It articulates the present reality that our lives belong to God, but it also anticipates a future when God's sovereignty will be fully manifest. The psalmist's posture is the persistent posture of the people of God; that is, it is always necessary to 'watch' (verse 3). This posture also explains how the psalmist

– beset by opposition, 'sighing' (verse 1), and crying out for help (verse 2) – can call for rejoicing and singing (verse 11). Because the sovereign God is a 'refuge' (verse 11), the people of God will always be able to proclaim joyfully, 'Thine is the kingdom,' even as we pray, 'Thy kingdom come'.

Verses 4-6 of Psalm 5 elaborate on the character of the one addressed as 'my King and my God', and explain why it makes sense to 'plead my case' (verse 3) to God. The rationale is simple: as ruler of the world, God opposes wickedness and the wicked. Seven words or phrases describe wickedness, perhaps suggesting God's complete opposition. . . . Wickedness will finally lead to its own destruction, because the wicked cut themselves off from God, who is the source of all life.

In contrast to 'the boastful' (Psalm 5:5) the psalmist humbly attributes the opportunity to 'enter your [God's] house' to 'the abundance of your steadfast love' (verse 7). Verse 7 represents the first occurrence in the psalter of the crucial word *hesed* 'steadfast love'. . . . The meaning of this Hebrew word is difficult to capture fully in English; it includes God's graceful and faithful dealing with sinful people (see especially Exodus 34:6-7). The appropriate human response is gratitude and service, which the psalmist displays as he or she states the intention to 'bow down . . . in awe of you' . . . The central petition also bespeaks humble gratitude and openness to God's help rather than a reliance on the self (see Psalm 23:2). In effect, the psalmist prays what Jesus taught disciples to pray: 'Lead us not into temptation, but deliver us from evil.'

J. Clinton McCann, Jr
Texts for Preaching, Year C

Loving-kindness

This is a biblical word, invented by Miles Coverdale, and carried over into the EVV (Authorised and revised versions of the Bible). It is one of the words he used in the psalms (23 times, plus Hosea 2:19) to translate the Hebrew *chesed* when it refers to God's love for his people Israel. Otherwise he used 'mercy', 'goodness' and 'great kindness' in the psalms for God's attitude to man, and, outside the psalms, such words as 'mercy', 'goodness', 'favour' for God's attitude to man and 'kindness' for man's attitude to man . . .

The word is used only in cases where there is some recognised tie between the parties concerned. It is not used indiscriminately of kindness in general, haphazard, kindly deeds; that is why Coverdale was careful to avoid using the word 'kindness' in respect of God's dealings with his people Israel. The theological importance of the word *chesed* is that it stands more than any other word for the attitude which both parties to a covenant ought to maintain toward each other . . .

God's loving-kindness is that sure love which will not let Israel go. Not all Israel's persistent waywardness could ever destroy it. Though Israel be faithless, yet God remains faithful still. This steady, persistent refusal of God to wash his hands of wayward Israel is the essential meaning of the Hebrew word which is translated as loving-kindness . . .

The widening of the meaning of the Hebrew *chesed*, used as the covenant word and especially of the covenant between God and Israel, is due to the history of God's dealings with his covenant-people. The continual waywardness of Israel has made it inevitable that, if God is never going to let Israel go, then his relation to his people must in the main be one of loving-kindness, mercy, and goodness, all of it entirely undeserved. For this reason the predominant use of the word comes to include mercy and forgiveness as a main constituent in God's determined faithfulness to his part of the bargain. It is obvious, time and again, from the context that if God is to maintain the covenant he must exercise mercy to an unexampled degree . . .

The loving-kindness of God towards Israel is therefore wholly undeserved on Israel's part. If Israel received her proper treatment for her stubborn refusal to walk in God's way, there would be no prospect for her of anything but destruction, since God's demand for right action never wavers one whit. Strict, however, as the demands for righteousness are, the prophets were sure that God's yearnings for the people of his choice are stronger still. Here is the great dilemma of the prophets, and indeed the dilemma of us all to this day. Which comes first, mercy or justice? Rashi (eleventh century AD Jewish commentator) said that God gave 'precedence to the rule of mercy' and joined it 'with the rule of justice'. But this much is clear: when we try to estimate the depth and the persistence of God's loving-kindness and mercy, we must first remember his passion for righteousness . . . so strong that he could not be more insistent in his demand for it, but God's persistent love for his people is more insistent still. The story of God's people throughout the centuries is that their waywardness has been so persistent that, if even a remnant is to be preserved, God has had to show mercy more than anything else. It is important to realise that though the Hebrew *chesed* can be translated by loving-kindness and mercy without doing violence to the context, yet we must always beware lest we think that God is content with less than righteousness. There is no reference to any sentimental kindness, and no suggestion of mercy apart from repentance, in any case where the Hebrew original is *chesed*. His demand for righteousness is insistent, and it is always at the maximum intensity. The loving-kindness of God means that his mercy is greater even than that. The word stands for the wonder of his unfailing love for the people of his choice, and the solving of the problem of the relation between his righteousness and his loving-kindness passes beyond human comprehension.

Article by N. H. Snaith
in *A Theological Word Book of the Bible*

Psalm 8

Holy Name: Years A, B, C
Trinity Sunday: Years A, C
New Year: Years A, B, C
Proper 7/Ordinary Time 12: Year B
Proper 22/Ordinary Time 27: Year B

We believe . . . that God is prepared to let the whole universe run itself while he attends to the needs of one human soul.

'When I consider thy heavens . . .' What happens when we consider the heavens? Some people never consider the heavens; they never consider anything very much above eye-level. As far as they are concerned, the heavens are there, that's all, and unless they come tumbling down, why bother about them? Suppose we do consider the heavens, look at them, study them, search them and consider their place in the total scheme of things. What happens then?

One possibility is that we end up feeling rather small, smaller than a grain of sand on the ocean floor. The mind staggers at the sheer size of the heavens. On a clear night the stars seem close enough to touch, yet astronomers tell us that they are unbelievably far away; in fact, so far that their light, which travels at 186,000 miles per second, takes hundreds of years to reach us. And there are so many millions of stars; they cover the heavens like a snowstorm in reverse. Even God, surely, would not miss a little star, like the one on which we live, if suddenly it passed out of the picture. That's one reaction when we consider the heavens.

Then there is the reaction of the person who wrote the eighth Psalm. He also considered the heavens. In fact, he probably thought about them more often and more deeply than we do, because they were the roof under which he worked. Tradition assumes that he was King David, a poet and musician, and that this was one of the psalms that he composed when he was a young man taking care of his father's sheep on the hills near Bethlehem. When he knew that the animals were bedded down for the night he would lie on his back and look up at the heavens before falling asleep. He saw them as God's heavens, the work of God's fingers. They spoke to him of the glory of God and they didn't make him feel small; on the contrary, they made him feel rather great. He poured out his feelings in a prayer: 'When I consider thy heavens, the work of thy fingers, the moon and the stars, which thou hast ordained; what is man, that thou art mindful of him? and the son of man, that thou visitest him? For thou hast made him a little lower than the angels, and hast crowned him with glory and honour. Thou madest him to have dominion over the works of thy hands, thou hast put all things under his feet . . .' Our generation needs to recover some of the tremendous truths about man that came to the psalmist as he considered the heavens.

One truth is that *man is God's special concern*. 'What is man, that thou art mindful of him . . .?' To be mindful of a person means to think about him, care for him, consider him and have his interests at heart. A loving father is mindful of his children. In his attitudes, his conversation, his conduct and in his demands of life he will do nothing that causes his children to suffer. He will sacrifice his own pleasures for their sake. He makes no decision without taking them into account.

The Bible asks us to believe the same about God. Though he holds the stars in their courses and presides over his vast universe, yet he is mindful of the very least of his human creatures. They are his special concern, more precious to him than all the glittering galaxies in heaven above. That may be difficult to believe when we consider the heavens, but we should look very silly saying our prayers if we didn't believe it. We go to God because we believe that he is concerned more about worth than about size. We believe, as Jesus said, that God is prepared to let the whole universe run itself while he attends to the needs of one human soul.

'. . . and the son of man, that thou visitest him?' Modern Bibles change that to read 'care for him'. Yet there is a truth in the old translation, and it comes very close to the truth of the Gospel. The father of John the Baptist blessed the Lord God of Israel 'for he hath visited and redeemed his people' (Luke 1:68 AV). In Jesus Christ God visited the human race, came to stay with us, made our home his home, our life his life. He may have visited other planets in his vast universe, but we don't know about them. We do know that he visited our planet and became, as the prophets foretold, 'Emmanuel . . . God with us', God beside us, among us and for us (Matthew 1:23 AV). He showed that we are his special concern.

The psalmist, who lived hundreds of years before Christ, could not share that insight or even perceive its possibility. Yet he did perceive the hand of God in human affairs, the presence of God in human experience, the role of God in human history. He did have the spiritual insight to know that man is infinitely precious to God, so precious that God does for him what he does not do for any of the planets and solar systems; he is mindful of him and visits him, he loves him with an everlasting love.

Another truth that came to the psalmist as he considered the heavens is that *man is God's highest creation*. 'For thou hast made him a little lower than the angels . . .' The Epistle to the Hebrews suggests that man may be higher than the angels. In a passage commonly read on Christmas Day, the New Testament writer asks, 'For to what angel did God ever say, "Thou art my Son, today I have begotten thee"? Or again, "I will be to him a father, and he shall be to me a son"'? (Hebrews 1:5 RSV). That accords with a later translation of the psalm which does not say that man is a little lower than the angels but that man is 'little less than God.' (RSV)

However we translate the Old Testament poet, he must have soaked his mind in the first chapter of the Book of Genesis. He believed that man, created in God's image, differs from all other creatures not only in degree but in kind. His affinity is with the Maker, not with the made. He has reason, intelligence, the faculty of creating and appreciating beauty, the ability to distinguish between right and wrong and the freedom to choose right or wrong. Man is like God, he has eternal personality. He can think God's thoughts after him and rejoice in that in which God rejoices. The stars in their courses are wonderful, and astronomy opens up the greatness of the universe, but greater than astronomy is the astronomer. In fact, the greatest of all wonders, short of God, is the mind of man . . .

There are two more truths that came to the psalmist as he considered the heavens, and each truth interprets the other. The first is that *man is God's most honoured creature*. 'For thou hast made him a little lower than the angels, and hast crowned him with glory and honour.' Those are words usually reserved for kings. They denote a royal status and by themselves scarcely seem applicable to ordinary people. They make sense, however, in the light of the second truth which declares that *man is God's deputy in the world*. He is a king by virtue of the lordship which God has given him over all creation. 'Thou madest him to have dominion over the works of thy hands; thou hast put all things under his feet. All sheep and oxen, yea, and the beasts of the field; the fowl of the air, and the fish of the sea, and whatsoever passeth through the paths of the seas. O Lord our Lord, how excellent is thy name in all the earth!'

If the psalm were written today, the writer would not stop there . . . He would rejoice in the achievement of Sir Edmund Hilary who stood on the summit of Mount Everest and said afterwards, 'I had the world lie under my clumsy boots.' He would exalt in man's dominion over the forces of nature, his splitting of the atom, and harnessing the sun's rays and making the ether waves his messengers. The Old Testament poet spoke in a much larger sense than he realised.

Here, then, is one of the earliest psalms in the Old Testament pointing to its fulfilment in the New Testament . . . Jesus is the Man par excellence, the Representative Man, the Pattern Man, the measure and stature of manhood as God created it without sin. God crowned him with glory and honour and in so doing gave a royal status to the whole human race.

Leonard Griffith
Reactions to God: Man's Response to God's Activity in the Psalms

Psalm 9

Proper 7/Ordinary Time 12: Year B, verses 9-20

And, as for me, my foolish love will not stop where my reason stops. I will love him . . . simply because it pleases him.

These verses . . . assume a triangle of social power and social reality . . . One member of that triangle is the 'enemy' or adversary, who is variously identified as the 'wicked' or the 'nations.' The second member of the triangle is the speaker of Psalm 9, who is portrayed as oppressed (verse 9), afflicted (verse 12), suffering (verse 13), needy (verse 18), and poor (verse 18). The superscription of the psalm, as well as the lectionary connection to 1 Samuel 17, suggests that this speaker is the king in dire straits. That identification, however, is not necessary for the actual words of the text, and there is nothing that requires such an identification. More importantly, whoever the speaker is (and it may be any needy believer), is weak and helpless before the adversary. That is, the relations between the two are unequal. If these are the only two layers in the drama, then the adversary will surely prevail, and the speaker will be further disadvantaged.

The psalm, however, concerns the third member of the triangle, the Lord, who is the powerful 'equaliser.' This equaliser adjusts the dynamics of social power so that the strong adversary cannot prevail and the weak petitioner can have a good outcome to life. In various voices of praise and petition, the psalm insists that social power is not a drama between two unequal parties, but always includes this Third Party, who thereby transforms all social reality. Everything depends on this Third Party, a character who decisively reshapes reality.

Psalm 9:9-12, verses of doxology, serve to identify and enhance the Lord as a party to social reality. They have the practical, liturgical effect of 'singing' the Lord into a decisive role in the conflict about to be enacted. The Lord is abruptly and tersely identified as the safe place for the oppressed who have no other safe place. Those who are otherwise without refuge or resource can count on and trust in this one whose name is known, because the Lord is faithful and will stand by. The singing of the praises of verse 11 is not simply a liturgical experience, but in fact is a profoundly political act.

In the midst of this buoyant doxological affirmation, verse 13 voices a petition. The speaker asks God one more time, this time, right now, to be the God who 'avenges blood' (verse 12), who will protect the honour and well-being of one who suffers and is victimised. The language might be taken to refer to those close to death in battle (see 1 Samuel 17), but more likely it is characteristic psalmic rhetoric, whereby any situation of distress is spoken of as the threat of death. In the context of doxology, the petition can be offered in great confidence.

After the brief petition of verse 13, the poem immediately returns to the doxology in verses 14-18. Indeed, a motivation for God to answer the petition of verse 13 is that if the petition is answered, the ones in trouble will promptly and eagerly return to the great choir that spends its energy recounting, reciting, resaying all the praises, all the transformations, all the deliverances whereby God has reordered power, diminished threat (see the Gospel reading) and made new life possible.

Verses 15-18 seem to be an actual example of the 'recounting' that is anticipated in verse 14. What is to be recounted as a celebration of God is that the very nations who dug a pit and hid a net for the speaker (perhaps the king) have fallen into their own pit and have been trapped in their own net. The speaker (the king or any poor believer) leads a charmed life, escaping the pit and the net. Though not explicitly stated, it is clear that it is the Lord who has kept the speaker from these dangers and turned the traps against the trapper. The Lord is indeed a 'wild card' in the social process, so that outcomes do not follow the expected, prearranged sequence of the powerful. While the Lord is absent in verse 15, and matters turned out in understated oddity, in verses 16-17 it is explicitly the Lord who inverts the social process.

The needy have a powerful defender and advocate, who keeps the social process open on their behalf, so that they are not the inevitable victims of the designs of the powerful. By the fidelity of God, the public life is indeed kept open for the weak, poor, and oppressed.

On the basis of that bold, tireless affirmation, the rhetorical unit ends in a strident petition in verses 19-20, escalating the request of verse 13. The speaker does not doubt the capacity of the Lord. The Lord only needs to be aroused and motivated to action. The Lord is to 'rise up' and get moving, in order to do the Lord's characteristic thing. When the Lord acts on behalf of the forgotten and marginated, it is clear that the pretentious and powerful are not as strong as they imagined, not gods and not godlike. The Philistine giant is a cipher for such pretentious human power. When faced by the inscrutable purposes of the Lord, such pretentious power is 'only human.' The word used twice (in verse 19 'mortals,' in verse 20 'human'), means humanity in its futile weakness. The power of the Lord yields a new perspective on human pretension. As with the Philistine, such human pretension is almost all hot air. And when the hot air evaporates before the real power of God, the weak are safe and have room for the living of their life. The very ones who are vulnerable and exposed now can be buoyant and celebrative. The difference in their situation is the powerful move of God which staggers human history (see Psalm 9:10; 1 Samuel 17:45).

Walter Brueggemann
Texts for Preaching, Year A

When experiencing a time of distress, the writer of Psalm 9 says: 'The Lord is a stronghold for the oppressed, a stronghold in times of trouble. And those who know thy name put their trust in thee, for thou, O Lord, hast not forsaken those who seek thee' (verses 9-10 RSV). So now a quote from a twentieth-century believer who suffered imprisonment and torture during many years of Romanian communist rule:

Certainly I believe that God is the maker of heaven and earth. I could not explain the existence of the universe otherwise. This is called theism. But really it is unimportant to me how this universe came to be. God made it. Fine. Reason is satisfied with this. But what about the rest?

My reason categorically refuses to believe that God is love. Your interrogators tie you to a chair. Your head has been shaved, and at intervals of one minute, tup-tup-tup, a drop of water falls on you, always in the same spot. And this happens in the world ruled by the God of love! Luther called reason a beast because it gave him arguments against the faith. But I treat it as a beast when it puts forward arguments to convince me that belief is the right thing. Reason tells me fairy tales: that I have free will and that I, and others, have chosen to sin. Hence all sorrows! Suffering is the unavoidable outcome of sin. (Something unavoidable in the universe of an almighty God! It makes me laugh!) But why then do babies suffer? What have they done to deserve it?

. . . The whole story of a God of love is madness. It is madness that God should love, not only the good people, but also those who use the Chinese drip torture, and make jokes while you suffer. And how can he love the dictator who sits quietly in his office and never touches anybody himself, but orders these things to happen? Equally mad is the story of redemption by the blood of Christ. My reason rejects it. And if I don't keep my reason, the purpose of the Communists will have been attained. I shall begin to yell, and to bang on the door. I shall be put in a straitjacket. I shall end up in an asylum.

But could I not be mad in a reasonable way – reasonably mad? In the conflict between Galileo and his inquisitors reason was on the side of the inquisitors. It was obvious, a simple fact proved by the senses since humanity existed, that the sun moves round the earth. Galileo's assertion was mad. But observations, experiments, calculations were made, and what was madness became reasonable. Galileo was reasonably mad. It is reasonably mad to believe that I am surrounded not by strong walls, but only by whirlwinds of electrons, with huge spaces between them.

And if the earth is in fact circling without any reason for doing so, and all this time has been mocking our sense, if elementary particles are dancing round as unpredictably as madmen, then the ultimate truth in religion is contained in a very strange Biblical expression. While other religious writings flatter God and speak of him in the most reverent language, the Bible speaks of 'the foolishness of God' (1 Corinthians 1:25). Maybe he does love, but not as a reasonable being would. He loves to the point of folly, in the truest sense of that word. The Chinese drip cannot come from the love of a reasonable God. St Paul speaks in the same verse about both the foolishness and the weakness of God. If God is almighty he must also have the capacity for weakness and madness. Nothing is impossible for him, not even this . . .

There is a foolishness in God, and a corresponding foolishness in the saints. My reason stops short of theism. But Einstein demanded that we relinquish convictions that we have held for so long that they have become synonymous with common sense. I will give up common sense in religion, too. If Einstein consigned to the flames the classic laws of physics, we must do the same with the classic notion of love. God loves in a sense of this word which is different from our use of it. And, as for me, my foolish love will not stop where my reason stops. God loved us without any deserving on our part. I will love him, and believe in him and in his plan of redemption, without any reasonable cause, simply because it pleases him.

And having once given up reason, I will go all the way with madness. I will love my torturers, too, though to do so is sheer folly. And when you, Jesus, come to take us to yourself, I will make it difficult for you. I will refuse to go with you. I will keep my arms firmly around the worst of hangmen, and I will say to you, 'I go to heaven only if he comes too.' You will have to yield.

Richard Wurmbrand
If Prison Walls Could Speak

Psalm 13

Proper 8/Ordinary Time 13: Year A

*He may reveal
himself to you in
the beauty of a
sunset; through
the pages of a good
book; through a
film or a play or a
friend . . .*

Hide, hidden

These words are employed in the EVV to represent about a dozen different words in the original. This amazing wealth of synonyms for 'hide' in the vocabulary of Hebrew is an index of a distinctive attitude of mind: the mind of Israel was characterised by a profound sense of the hiddenness of things, in marked contrast to Greek thought with its sanguine belief in the capacity of reason to probe the inmost secrets of reality.

No comment is required on the use of 'hide' for the ordinary and familiar act of men (e.g. Genesis 3:8; Joshua 7:22). The distinctively biblical usage appears where the subject of the verb is God: God hides certain things (2 Kings 4:27; Proverbs 25:2); he hides his face (Deuteronomy 31:17; Psalm 13:1). The hiddenness of God in the Bible must be carefully distinguished from agnosticism in the modern sense; it is correlative with revelation; it is the obverse of the fact that God is known only when and where he chooses to reveal himself. And even in his revelation God remains hidden, for while he makes himself known, he does not explain himself to men. He is hidden in respect to his ways which are 'past finding out'. (Romans 11:33; Isaiah 55:9)

Article by G. S. Hendry
in *A Theological Word Book of the Bible*

Psalm 13:1b: 'How much longer will you hide your face from me?' moans the psalmist and the prophet Isaiah cries out: 'Truly, thou art a God that hidest thyself, O God of Israel, the Saviour.'

Let's take a look at three ways in which God hides himself:

He hides power in weakness. To me it is so often misleading to speak of God as being All Powerful . . . Omnipotent naked force; if you believe in a God who has power to do all things, some very awkward questions call for an urgent response.

For example, if God has all the power, why doesn't he stop wars? Why doesn't he feed the hungry? Why doesn't he heal cancer, prevent suffering, disease and death on a massive scale as witnessed in the summer of '99 in the Turkish earthquake?

Yes, God does have power, but a power always related to his purposes of love, at one and the same time both hidden and revealed in the Babe of Bethlehem and in a broken man suffering death on a Cross. In the Musée des Beaux Arts in Brussels there is a painting by Peter Brueghel depicting the massacre of the Holy Innocents. The soldiers are not Herod's but the King of Spain's. The killing is going on whilst mothers weep in bitter helplessness, whilst others frantically try to protect their children against the cynical soldiers. Others in the picture simply carry on with their work, and others are skating on a frozen pond. It is an indictment of indifference; the indifference of those who tried to turn their backs on the murder, carrying on as if nothing were wrong; of the soldiers who did the killing; and of God who allowed such barbarity to happen. The one baby that escaped death that day was later to prove the one who alone truly and finally answered the violence in the slaughter of the Innocents. Jesus knew only too well that retaliation and force, used against violent men only breeds more violence. The marvellous truth about the Babe of Bethlehem and Christ crucified, is that he still has power to change human lives. God's power is here disclosed in weakness.

God hides his wisdom in folly. Listen to some words of an early Christian preacher[1]: 'The Jews ask for signs and the Greeks search for wisdom, but we proclaim Christ upon his Cross, to the Jews a stumbling block; to the Greeks a thing of foolishness; but to those who have been called, both Jews and Greeks, Christ the power of God and the wisdom of God . . . (St Paul in 1 Corinthians 1:23). "He that is hanged on a tree is accursed of God", so the Jew believed. Therefore Jesus could not possibly be the Son of God. And when they looked for signs and miracles, asking Jesus, "Show us a sign," Jesus refused.

Shortly after the crucifixion of Jesus, 30,000 people followed a man who said he would miraculously make the walls of Jerusalem fall down on his word of command. As for Greeks, they only had time for the Sophist, the wise man; the man with a clever mind, cunning tongue and persuasive speech.

1. G. A. Studdert-Kennedy; 'The Psychologist', from *The Unutterable Beauty:* Hodder & Stoughton, 1957. Page 121.

He would spend hours splitting hairs . . . It is said, for example, that when Adrian the Sophist appeared in Rome to lecture, the Roman Senate emptied and the games were abandoned as people flocked to hear him. No wonder the message of the Cross was ridiculed. And of course, things have not changed much in our day. To the modern, highly educated person with many technical skills, the Cross is against all reason, it is folly, it makes no sense. But as "Woodbine Willy" wrote many years ago about the Psychologist:

"His reasoning is perfect,
his proofs as plain as paint,
he has but one small weakness,
he cannot make a saint."'

The Christ of the Cross can and does.

God hides his goodness in severity. My favourite story concerning Elizabeth the First, Queen of England, tells of her concern for Lord Burghley who was on his deathbed. Elizabeth, severe, prim and gorgeously dressed, ropes of pearls around her neck and a very tall headdress studded with diamonds on her head, determines to visit the great statesman. Her arrival causes pandemonium because, due to her tall headdress, the Queen cannot enter the low doorway leading into Lord Burghley's sick-room. The courtiers panic, the ladies-in-waiting flutter about and nobody seems to know what to do. That is, until a courtier makes a suggestion that no one else dared to propose to her severe majesty. He courageously says: 'Your Majesty, would it be possible to stoop?' There's a long silence, all eyes are upon the Queen. Elizabeth responds by saying: 'Fellow, for the King of Spain we would not bow our head – but we will do so for your master.'

How many people still imagine God to be the severe and stern lawgiver who says, 'Break my laws and you die.' For them, God is remote, hard to please and unbending. The cry of their hearts is the question of the courtier: 'Your Majesty, would it be possible to stoop?' And the Christian Gospel says that this is exactly what he has done in Jesus his only Son. He came as a baby to the smallest corner of the vast Roman Empire; he grew up in obscurity, identifying himself with the poor and lowly, most of whom were totally unacceptable to the ruling classes; and finally he died a death of horrible pain between two bandits.

'Your Majesty, would it be possible to stoop?' . . . Could he stoop any lower? Behind the seeming severity of the Ten Commandments carved in stone, stands the son of God with a bleeding heart of love. He comes not to destroy but to fulfil.

God hides his power in weakness; his wisdom in folly; his goodness in severity. But the big question mark remains. Where will you find this hidden God? There are many answers to that question. For he may reveal himself to you in the beauty of a sunset; through the pages of a good book; through a film or a play or a friend; and in your work as well as play. Maybe above all in broken bread and poured-out wine during Holy Communion . . . 'Here in thine own appointed way, we come to meet thee, Lord'. So your prayer and mine must be: 'Holy Father, open my eyes to see you, open my ears to hear you, open my heart to receive and love you and open my hands to serve you, through Jesus Christ our Lord. Amen.'

Ron Dale
Unpublished sermon

Psalm 14

Proper 12/Ordinary Time 17: Year B
Proper 7/Ordinary Time 12: Year C

Don't be a fool . . .
As the days
become dark and
the nights become
dreary, realise that
there is a God who
rules above.

Folly, fool, foolish, foolishness

In the Old Testament several Hebrew words denote 'folly', 'fool', etc. They do not usually imply mere stupidity or actual insanity, except in certain cases where the context makes this clear. There is generally a religious and ethical content in them. Folly is the opposite of wisdom, which is always regarded as a gift of revelation. Hence the Gentiles, who do not possess revelation, are 'a foolish nation' (Deuteronomy 32:21 etc.); when Israel disregards the divine revelation which she has received, she also is 'foolish' (Deuteronomy 32:6 etc.). Since the content of wisdom is detailed in the Law, disobedience to the Law is the essence of folly; it leads to the denial of God – not so much theoretical atheism, but that overlooking of the divine righteousness which leads inevitably to disaster (Psalm 14:1, 53:1; Isaiah 9:17, etc.). In Romans 1:18-32, St Paul shows how the corruption of such knowledge of God as the Gentiles should have possessed leads to every kind of superstitious, idolatrous and immoral foolishness: 'professing themselves to be wise, they became fools' (verse 22) . . .

It follows from the general Old Testament use, described above, that amongst the Jews to call a man a fool is much more derogatory than merely to call him stupid or mad. . . .

It is a serious matter to be a fool in the biblical sense, and the word virtually means 'apostate' or 'damned'. Hence folly is contrasted with that 'wisdom from the Lord' which is spoken of so highly in the New Testament as well as in the Wisdom Literature (cf. especially James 3:13-18). But there is a 'wisdom of the world' (James 3:15) which is wise only in its conceit (cf. Romans 11:25; 12:16) and which is in truth folly in the eyes of God. This is the wisdom which confounds God's strength with weakness and its own weakness with strength (1 Corinthians 1:26-2:14). 'The wisdom of this world is foolishness with God' (1 Corinthians 3:19; cf. context, and compare 4:10; 2 Corinthians 11:16ff). Paul is here using the language of paradox, but it is the paradox of the cross – 'the divine foolishness' – which has inspired him to write in this way. He returns to the normal biblical usage in Ephesians 5:15-17: 'Be ye not foolish, but understand what the will of the Lord is.' From this verse we may deduce the full biblical meaning of 'wise' and 'foolish'.

A Theological Word Book of the Bible
ed. Alan Richardson

Continuing the theme of foolishness mentioned in Psalm 14:1 and in both the Old Testament and the New Testament, here is a part of Martin Luther King's sermon on the same theme:

I'd like for you to look at this parable with me (the parable of the wealthy farmer) and try to decipher the real reason that Jesus called this man a fool. Number one, Jesus called this man a fool because he allowed the means by which he lived to outdistance the ends for which he lived. You see, each of us lives in two realms, the within and the without. Now the within of our lives is that realm of spiritual ends expressed in art, literature, religion and morality. The without of our lives is that complex of devices, of mechanisms and instrumentalities by means of which we live. The house we live in – that's part of the means by which we live. The car we drive, the clothes we wear, the money that we are able to accumulate – in short, the physical stuff that's necessary for us to exist.

Now, the problem is that we must always keep a line of demarcation between the two. This man was a fool because he didn't do that.

The other day in Atlanta, the wife of a man had an automobile accident. He received a call that the accident had taken place on the expressway. The first question he asked when he received the call: 'How much damage did it do to my Cadillac?' He never asked how his wife was doing. Now, that man was a fool, because he had allowed an automobile to become more significant than a person. He wasn't a fool because he had a Cadillac, he was a fool because he worshipped his Cadillac. He allowed his automobile to become more important than God.

. . . And so this man was a fool because he allowed the means by which he lived to outdistance the ends for which he lived. He was a fool because he maximised the minimum and minimised the maximum. This man was a fool because he allowed his technology to outdistance his theology. This man was a fool because he allowed his mentality to outrun his morality. Somehow he became so involved in the means by which he lived that he couldn't deal with the way to eternal matters. . . .

Now, number two, this man was a fool because he failed to realise his dependence upon others. Now, if you read that parable in the book of Luke, you will discover that this man utters about 60 words. And do you know in 60 words he said 'I' and 'my' more than 15 times? This man was a fool because he said 'I' and 'my' so much, he lost the capacity to say 'we' and 'our'. He failed to realise that he couldn't do anything by himself. This man talked like he could build the barns by himself. And he failed to realise that wealth is always the result of the commonwealth.

. . . You know, a lot of people are forgetting God. They haven't done it theoretically, as others have done through their theories – postulated through the God-is-dead theology – but a lot of people just get involved in other things. And so many people become so involved in their big bank accounts and in their beautiful expensive automobiles that they unconsciously forget God. So many people become so involved in looking at the man-made lights of the city that they forget to think about that great cosmic light that gets up early in the morning in the eastern horizon and moves with a kind of symphony of motion, like a masterly queen strolling across a mansion, and paints its technicolour across the blue as it moves – a light that man could never make. Some people have become so involved in looking at the skyscraping buildings of the cities that they've forgotten to think about the gigantic mountains kissing the skies, as if to bathe their peaks in the lofty blue – something that man could never make. So many people have become so involved in televisions and radar that they've forgotten to think about the beautiful stars that bedeck the heavens like swinging lanterns of eternity, standing there like shining silvery pins sticking in the magnificent blue pincushion – something that man could never make. So many people have come to feel that on their own efforts they can bring in a new world, but they've forgotten to think about the fact that the earth is the Lord's and the fullness thereof. And so they end up going over and over again without God. . . .

Don't be a fool. Recognise your dependence on God. As the days become dark and the nights become dreary, realise that there is a God who rules above.

'A Knock at Midnight'
from *The Great Sermons of Martin Luther King, Jr*

Psalm 15

Fourth Sunday of Epiphany/Ordinary Time 4:
  Year A
Proper 17/Ordinary Time 22: Year B
Proper 11/Ordinary Time 16: Year C

To worship God in an authentic manner, one must first be compassionate and just.

Psalm 15 was originally used as an entrance liturgy by pilgrims entering the sanctuary. Paralleling the reading from Deuteronomy, Psalm 15 offers a series of qualities characteristic of the ideal worshipper.

The psalm opens with a question, perhaps asked by pilgrims as they reached the temple gates: Who can enter the sacred precincts? It is asked here in a graphic and metaphorical form, as if access was to be permanent (verse 1). Admittance to the courts of the temple is the concern of the questions.

The remainder of the psalm is an answer to the question, probably spoken by cultic officials (the Levites? the Priests?) inside the precincts. The requirements for entry are given in a series of ten characteristics. It should be noted that, in antiquity, temples did not operate on the principle 'everyone welcome, all come.' Certain persons (cripples and the deformed, those with improper parentage) and persons at certain times (when unclean from contact with some pollutant, women during menstruation, persons with certain skin ailments) were not admitted into the sanctuary (see Deuteronomy 23:1-8).

The characteristics of those who might enter were probably proclaimed to the worshippers as the proper qualities of life; pilgrims couldn't be checked on an individual basis, and some of the characteristics noted are as much attitudes as action. Two features about the requirements in the psalm are noteworthy. First, the requirements articulated all fall into the category of what we would today call moral qualities and interpersonal attitudes. None of the characteristics would fit into the category of purity laws and regulations, such as having recently touched a dead body or eaten unkosher food. (Note how the two are intermingled in Ezekiel 18.) Second, the qualifications given in the psalm are ten in number. Ten was a round figure, and lists of ten could be memorised by ticking off the list on one's fingers. The Ten Commandments may once have been used in such gate or entrance liturgies, perhaps being written on two stone slabs or the posts of the temple gates.)

The following is a listing of the ten requirements:

- Walks blamelessly and does what is right (behaves according to the accepted morals and standards of the society)

- Speaks truth from the heart (shows integration of the internal will and external actions; does what one says and what one thinks)

- Does not slander with one's tongue (does not attack others verbally and falsely so as to destroy them)

- Does no evil to a friend (does not physically harm a fellow human being)

- Does not take up a reproach against a neighbour (does not participate in or perpetuate gossip or spread rumours)

- Despises a reprobate (dislikes those who turn their back upon God or society)

- Honours those who fear God (the positive counterpart to the preceding negative)

- Swears to one's own hurt and does not change (one's word and oath are kept, even if keeping them brings injury and cost to oneself)

- Does not put out money at interest (does not use another person's need to one's advantage; see Deuteronomy 23:19-20)

- Does not take a bribe against the innocent (would not do wrong even if paid; see Exodus 23:8; Deuteronomy 16:19)

Those who live up to such standards are declared blessed, unshakeable, immovable (verse 5c). This final formulation is interesting. The focus of the conclusion is no longer on such a person who has access to the holy place but on such a person who has the quality of life and integration of social characteristics that make for stability of life.

John H. Hayes
Preaching Through the Christian Year: Year A

In verse two of Psalm 9, the psalmist says, 'I sing praise to your name, Most High', thus acknowledging the importance for him of worship, so here is Walter Rauschenbusch, a twentieth-century American Baptist, a firm advocate of the Social Gospel, on the meaning of worship for him:

The real worship, the only thing that God really cares for, is a Christ-like life. To live all the time in the consciousness of the love and nearness of God, to merge all our desires and purposes to his will, to walk humbly before him and justly and lovingly with everyone, this is the real Christian worship. Without that no prayer, no song, no 'divine service' on Sunday is more than discordant noise in the ears of God. That is what Paul means when he tells us to offer our bodies, our own selves, as a living sacrifice and says that will be our 'reasonable service' (Romans 12:1), that is, our rational form of worship. He was well aquainted with many irrational forms of worship. When James says that a pure and undefiled 'religion' consists in helping the helpless and keeping ourselves unspotted from the world (James 1:27), the word 'religion' means liturgy or ceremonial. A loving and pure life is the true liturgy of Christian worship.

The life of Jesus was as full of religion as a nightingale is full of song or a rose full of fragrance, but the bent of his life was away from the inherited forms of worship, and he can scarcely have said to have taught new forms. He taught a prayer when his disciples asked for it, but that prayer was meant to teach utter simplicity. In our common worship we shall come closest to the spirit of true Christianity if every act is full of joy in God and his fellowship, love for one another, hatred of all evil, and an honest desire to live a right life in the sight of Christ. Our worship should eliminate as far as possible all selfish greed, all superstition, and all untrue and unworthy ideas about God. It should clear our conception of the right life by instructing our moral nature, it should give our will strong, steady, lasting impulses toward righteous action; and it should breed and foster habits of reverence and the faculty of adoration.

Walter Rauschenbusch
'Why I am a Baptist'
Colegate-Rochester Divinity School Bulletin, Vol. XI, no. 2

Perhaps the really remarkable thing about Psalm 15 is that this concern for commitment to compassion and justice on the part of the true worshipper is framed within a liturgical setting. It is clear that, in the history of worship, liturgy and personal renewal have often been polar opposites. It is so easy to feel that when one has fulfilled the liturgical niceties ('bulls on the altar' or 'gone to church'), one has paid one's dues to God. And so a love of formal liturgies and an attachment to the status quo have sometimes been the best of friends. But ancient Israel's prophets knew that should not be so, and so did Israel's priests! (Or at least some of them.) Here, right in the midst of a formal, question-and-answer liturgy about what it takes to enter God's sanctuary, we find a very non-liturgical affirmation: to worship God in an authentic manner, one must first be compassionate and just.

Walter Brueggemann
Texts for Preaching, Year A

Psalm 16

Second Sunday of Easter: Year A
Easter Vigil: Years A, B, C
Proper 13/Ordinary Time 18: Year A
Proper 28/Ordinary Time 33: Year B
Proper 8/Ordinary Time 13: Year C

*Contentment
is a state of mind;
it flows from the
inside out, not
from the outside in.*

God suffices

The sixteenth psalm is one of those Hebrew poems which is so candid in character that the poet's personality shines through every verse. Its mood of sheer delight climbs to such a crescendo of exuberant joy that you realise that it could have been written only by a supremely happy man. You have the feeling that he must be the happiest man in the Bible.

> Preserve me, O God, for in thee I take refuge.
> I say to the Lord, 'Thou art my Lord;
> I have no good apart from thee.

It recalls a light-hearted song from George Gershwin's *Porgy and Bess*; 'I've got plenty of nothing . . . but I've got my Lord.' This Hebrew poet had plenty of nothing – no money, no property, no status and no security – but he had God, and that made him happy. Like all the psalmists of Israel he learned from his own experience an important truth about God, and in this case it was the truth that God suffices. If a man has God he can be happy, though he may not have much else. Without God, nothing else can make him happy. God alone gives him the ingredients of happiness, and the psalm shows what those ingredients are:

> The Lord is my chosen portion and my cup;
> thou holdest my lot.
> The lines have fallen for me in pleasant places;
> yea, I have a goodly heritage.

What a sharp contrast to the prevailing mood of our day! An Englishman began a letter to the editor of *The Times* by saying, 'I have recently returned after an absence of ten months to this lovely and beloved country to find, as it seems to me, a nation of grumblers.' The writer catalogued some of the grumbles: 'There is too much rain. There is not enough rain . . . The rates are too high. The roads are too full. The beaches are filthy . . . and the telephone service! And the trains! And the shop assistants!' Trying to diagnose the mood of discontent the writer suggested that it might be the psychological aftermath of finding ourselves a second-class power or partly the result of being an 'affluent society'. He was very certain that 'if we do not have the sense – if only the sense of humour – to snap out of it soon, a more dismal fate will overtake us.' He closed with a bit of advice from the immortal wisdom of Bruce Bairnsfather, 'If you knows of a better 'ole, go to it!'

But that's the trouble. Many people are, in fact, looking for a better 'ole. They are not satisfied with the present one. They believe that life has handed them a raw deal. They wish they had been born in some other century and some other country, of different parents and different social background, with greater gifts and better opportunities. They do not feel that the lines have fallen for them in pleasant places and that they have a goodly heritage. On the contrary, they feel cheated, badly used and deprived, thoroughly dissatisfied and therefore utterly unhappy.

They may not believe it, but a change of scenery won't make them feel any better. There is no illusion more pathetic than the idea that, if we can just juggle a few things around and jockey ourselves into the perfect situation, we shall find the contented feeling which has hitherto eluded us. To begin with, there is no perfect situation. Then also, contentment is a state of mind; it flows from the inside out, not from the outside in. That is why men have found contentment in some very imperfect places. Paul found it in a prison cell where he wrote to his friends at Philippi, 'I have learned, in whatever state I am, to be content.'

Describing the hardships and dangers of his life during the Nazi occupation, a leader of the Norwegian underground said in a kind of wonderment that one day it came to him that even in this hellish existence he was what men would call a happy man.

The psalmist felt satisfied because he had God – 'The Lord is my chosen portion and my cup . . .' A cynic may murmur something about 'compensation' and religion being an 'opiate', and he may declare that, if this pious poet had only possessed a few of the good things of life which are within man's power to provide for himself, he would not have needed God. The cynic, whatever doctrinaire axe he has to grind, betrays a naïve ignorance of human nature. He supposes that the so-called 'good things of life' can in fact meet man's deepest needs. He does not know that, when God created man, he left him unfinished within and gave him thirsts which God alone can quench and hungers which God alone can satisfy. Augustine saw more deeply into human nature when he confessed to God, 'Thou hast made us for thyself, and our souls are restless until they find their rest in thee.' The psalmist found his rest in God. Therefore he was content and he asked nothing more of life. That was the effect of God in his experience. . . .

Some years ago a man said to me, 'I have never been happier in my life!' That was a strange thing to say under the circumstances, because he had just resigned a highly paid job to enter a new line of work that would never give him more than a quarter of his former salary. The change would make most people quite miserable. Yet he really meant it when he said, 'I have never been happier in my life!' The reason for his new-found happiness was that he had discovered God and had offered his life in obedience to the purpose of God. He really believed that for the first time in his life he was doing what God wanted him to do. And he was happy. That made him a kindred spirit with the writer of the sixteenth psalm who learned from his own experience that, when a man has God, he does not need much else, because God alone can give him contentment, guidance, stability, hope and fulfilment – the ingredients of happiness.

Leonard Griffith
God in Man's Experience: the Activity of God in the Psalms

If ever I was asked about the deepest moments of joy that I've experienced in over 40 years of Christian ministry, I could not point to any single experience and say that it was *the* exclusive one. Because the deepest joys I have known, whilst having, I believe, their true source in the being of God the Holy Trinity, have been many and various and in many and various facets of life.

Some of the richest experiences of joy for me have come in my pulpit ministry, in the act of preaching the Good News of God's love in Christ. So great was the joy after one service I conducted in a small Devon village, that it remained with me for days afterwards. Then there have been moments of great joy in family life, and quite often in the sharing of ordinary life. The one occasion that still lives with me is sharing a family holiday. We had a small Devon resort beach to ourselves on a late autumn day. At the suggestion of the children we carved out a zoo on the wet sand and peopled it with visitors looking at all the different animals. As we were all engaged in this a deep joy flooded into me. Again, it was so powerful that it remained with me many days.

But perhaps the most mysterious joy has been that which has been given me when sharing someone else's sadness and pain; or going through my own personal time of trial. In the midst of all the pain a mysterious joy has filled my heart, sustaining me through some very rough and tragic times. And always during those moments, some words of George Mattheson's hymn spring to mind: 'O joy that seekest me through pain'. That joy for me, always the pure gift of God, is mysterious, wonderful, sustaining and glorious. A foretaste, if you will, 'of glory divine'.

Ron Dale, 1999

Psalm 17

One of the secrets of Christian living is to thank God for everything, for all things bright and beautiful and the valley of the shadow. For he is to be found in both.

Proper 13/Ordinary Time 18: Year A, verses 1-7 , 15
Proper 27/Ordinary Time 32: Year C, verses 1-9

My theology tutor used to say in his lectures that 'murmuring', i.e. complaining, grumbling against God who had always been gracious to his people, was to his mind, *the* great sin of the whole Bible. (But cf. Psalm 17:3: 'No murmuring from me'.)

The ancient Israelites 'murmured' against God and Moses (cf. Exodus 16:7; 17:1-7). In the time of Jesus, in John 6:41f, the Jews murmured at him (Jesus) because he said, 'I am the bread which came down from heaven.'

Instead of murmuring there ought to have been a deep sense of thankfulness for all their Lord's deliverance and care. Hence now, some readings from the twentieth century on the theme of grumbling.

First, an excerpt from *Noah* by Andre Obey; a witty play about Noah and the flood. Michel Saint-Dennis in his introduction, says of *Noah* that it shows 'how such an ordinary family will behave under extraordinary conditions: the children revolt against their father, the best of them show themselves to be frivolous, lazy and ungrateful; Mother goes off her head for life on board, with its quarrels and tempests, is too much for an old woman who can't help clinging to dreams of a little kitchen and a garden as she knew them before the flood swallowed them up; Noah alone emerges a finer man from an adventure he does not attempt to understand; he is content to obey, to follow the commandments of a God whose purpose escapes him, but whom he fears and in whom he has placed a blind trust.'

In the play, one day Noah gets fed up with the behaviour of his children and tells some of the animals about it all:

'It's the children, you see, it's the children. . . . And then Mother too, she's beginning to give way – she's beginning to fail me. I never knew that happen before. All this happening at once, you know, it's taken me by surprise. It's worn me out, bowled me over. They all keep asking questions: 'Why this? Why that? What now? What next?' Well, I don't know everything, I'm only an old farmer after all. If it was only their natural curiosity . . . because they're young, I mean . . . but it isn't. There's only one thing they're after . . . to catch me out. . . . And then there is another thing. . . .

God isn't with us any more. . . . Well, put yourselves in his place. Every day, all day long, hearing his existence doubted, even at times when it is most apparent. It was all mankind before, now it's these children. Always asking him for proofs and miracles; demanding – ah, it's too much – guarantees! 'If you are God, take away my toothache.' 'If there was a God, he wouldn't have let me bang my head coming upstairs this morning.' Yes, my friends, that was what one of the little girls dared to say today. So he's gone off on a holiday, you see. Well, you can't really blame him; all I can say is, it's a wonder he didn't do it long ago. Goodness knows he's had patience enough. Well, he hasn't any more, that's all. . . . He's gone to have a little rest, that's all. He's just shut up shop for two or three weeks. All right, we'll wait till he opens up again.

Andre Obey
Noah

The journey

Dr William Sangster, the great Methodist minister and scholar died 21 years ago. He was one of God's truly gifted people, a marvellous man.

When he lived in Conway, in the 1920s, he was visited by a friend from London, who travelled by rail on a very beautiful summer's day, but the only thing he noticed during the whole journey was that Stafford was a bit grimy. Try and imagine that journey.

The train left Euston, passed through Watford and was soon hurrying through the pleasant fields of Hertfordshire and Buckinghamshire. Then came Rugby, Tamworth and Lichfield before going through the Potteries and Crewe. From there it raced across the Cheshire Plain bathed in beauty and sunshine, and then through Chester with its old walls and Cathedral. Next it roared along the North Wales coast and passed by the sands of the Dee. Then the Welsh hills, the glorious sweep of Colwyn Bay, the Little Orme, and so to Conway, one of the most beautiful towns in the British Isles. The gateway to lovely Snowdonia.

All Sangster's friend could say on arrival was: 'I'm glad that's over. It was so grimy in the Potteries.' He's had over

200 miles of sunshine and beauty, and only 25 were a bit gloomy. But all he noticed was the dirt.

On our journey through life it can never be all sunshine and beauty, for it's always a mixture of light and shade, good and bad, all mixed up.

But one of the secrets of Christian living is to thank God for everything, for all things bright and beautiful and the valley of the shadow. For he's to be found in both.

Ron Dale
Never on Sunday: Broadcast Talks

God lives with us

Mum and Anna shared many likes and dislikes; perhaps the simplest and the most beautiful sharing was their attitude towards Mister God. Most people I knew used God as an excuse for their failure. 'He should have done this', or 'Why has God done this to me?', but with Mum and Anna difficulties and adversities were merely occasions for doing something. Ugliness was the chance to make beautiful. Sadness was the chance to make glad. Mister God was always available to them. A stranger would have been excused for believing that Mister God lived with us, but then Mum and Anna believed he did.

(Interestingly enough, Psalm 17:3 says, 'No murmuring from me.')

Mr God, this is Anna

The flyleaf of the book tells how Fynn, on one foggy November night, picked up Anna literally from the gutter, bruised, battered and terrified. He took her home to his Irish 'Mum'. Anna's main occupation in life was being a personal friend and helper of Mr God. She knew the purpose of being and the meaning of love. At six she was a theologian, mathematician, philosopher, poet and gardener. At seven she died after a terrible accident with a grin on her beautiful face, saying: 'I bet Mister God lets me get into heaven for this.'

Fynn
Mister God, This Is Anna

I shall behold your face

Psalm 17 is a prayer in which a person who trusts in God and has been faithful to God in his conduct appeals for deliverance from wicked, hostile adversaries. The psalm is one of the prayers for help in first person singular style. . . . It is composed of petitions for deliverance (verses 1-2, 6-9), a plea of innocence (verses 3-5), a description of the adversaries and a petition for their defeat (verses 10-12, 13-14), and a concluding assertion of trust (verse 15). The prayer typically uses language that draws on different spheres of experience and culture in Israel. The opening petition employs legal language and appeals to the Lord as judge. The second petition employs the image of asylum or sanctuary in which the persecuted takes refuge at a shrine. The enemies are described as predatory animals. God is asked to overthrow the enemies, acting as the divine warrior who intervenes on behalf of his own. . . .

The concluding statement of confidence (verse 15) makes it clear how important the relation to God is in the theology of these prayers. Their purpose is not simply to gain relief from dangers and difficulty. The real trouble with the trouble reflected in these prayers is that one's relation to God is troubled. Deliverance not only brings relief but restores a sense of acceptance and communion. Acceptance bestows righteousness. Communion occurs in the experience of the presence. The prayer anticipates an answer given as a vision of the form of the presence (face) of the Lord. The vision will convey justification; it will be a sign of the acceptance that makes the relation to God right. 'The upright shall behold his face' (11:7; see Matthew 5:8). Just how the vision of the presence occurred is not known. Israel was forbidden to make any likeness of the Lord in the form of an image (Exodus 20:4; Deuteronomy 5:8). But Moses and the elders 'saw the God of Israel' in the ritual meal that concluded the Sinai covenant. . . . In the psalms there are references to seeing God or the face of God in the temple (e.g. Psalm 42:2; 63:2; 36:7-9).

There is a seeing that comes with prayer and a waiting that transcends what the eye can behold.

In Christian interpretation there is a long tradition that sees a reference to the resurrection in verse 15. 'When I awake from the sleep of death, my life will be finally fulfilled when I see God.' In the context of Israel's religion, 'when I awake' may have referred to a ritual of spending the night at the holy place after prayer for help, waiting for the propitious time of the morning. But the verse can be read with a second sense, because it is only the resurrection to be with the Lord that brings the final and full justification of the life of the faithful.

James L. Mays
Psalms

Psalm 19

Easter Vigil: Years A, B, C
Proper 22/Ordinary Time 27: Year A
Third Sunday of Lent: Year B
Proper 19/Ordinary Time 24: Year B
Proper 21/Ordinary Time 26: Year B
Third Sunday of Epiphany/Ordinary Time 3: Year C

Even people who do not call themselves religious are willing to believe that nature with its laws declares the glory of God.

He feels warned

A motorist, driving along a city street from east to west, comes to a busy intersection where the traffic light turns green. He continues driving, knowing the north and southbound traffic have a red light and must stop. He is protected by the law. At the next corner he stops at a red light, because if he keeps on driving, the law will not protect but condemn him. As he approaches the third intersection the light flashes yellow, as it usually does in Canadian cities. Now he has a split-second choice either to accelerate or slow down and stop. If he is wise he will apply the brakes. Now the law is warning him.

Those are three functions of the law – to protect, to condemn and to warn. Often the law acts on people like a yellow traffic light, deterring them from conduct which is criminal or dangerous or anti-social. The law warns them, and they are grateful for the warning. They realise that a society without laws would be like a busy street corner without traffic lights – a scene of confusion and chaos. The laws are there for our good. They are essential to a well-ordered society.

The writer of the nineteenth psalm saw the whole universe as a well-ordered society. He believed that when the Father God created it he wrote into its structure certain natural and moral laws for the well-being of his children. Those laws serve the same purpose as the laws of the land: they protect, they condemn and they warn. They warned the psalmist. He said, 'By them is thy servant warned.' That was his reaction to the laws of God. It's an old-fashioned reaction in these days when people rebel against any kind of moral authority, especially the authority of religion, but it could contain the secret of life which we are in danger of losing. Examine the psalmist's thought more closely.

First, he insists that there is a moral order which declares the glory of God no less than the natural order declares the

54

glory of God. The natural order fills him with wonder and awe, as it fills many people with wonder and awe. They marvel at the beauty, the vastness and the steadfast order of the created universe and at the laws which are the basis of its continued existence. I marvelled at those laws when I visited the Manned Spacecraft Centre in Houston, Texas, and saw an astronaut walking on a wall. Suspended by wires at an 18 degree angle, he was training for survival on a planet where his body would be governed by only seven-tenths of the earth's gravity. The presence and dependability of such laws as the law of gravity make possible the exploration of outer space and all scientific advance. We did not create those laws. They were here before we came, and we must live within them in order to survive.

Even people who do not call themselves religious are willing to believe that nature with its laws declares the glory of God. They may not recognise God in the Bible or the church or the Sacraments or in personal piety but they share the reaction of the psalmist who said, 'The heavens declare the glory of God; and the firmament sheweth his handiwork. Day unto day uttereth speech, and night unto night sheweth knowledge. There is no speech nor language, where their voice is not heard.' If ever there was a statement of universal religion – there it is. Above the confusion of conflicting cultures and civilisations nature speaks to man its universal language and it speaks to him of God. . . .

Actually two things filled the psalmist with wonder and awe. Alongside the natural order he saw a moral order governed by laws which to him seemed just as marvellous as the laws of nature. They also declared the glory of God. His reverent spirit was shared by the German philosopher, Emmanuel Kant, who said that two things filled him with wonder and awe – 'the starry heavens above . . . and the moral law within'.

Leonard Griffith
Reactions to God: Man's Response to God's Activity in the Psalms

About three years ago I went with my wife to the Imax cinema in Bradford to see a film concerning the launch of the Hubble telescope. It proved a mind boggling experience to see the earth from space on a screen somewhere in the region of 70 feet square. So vast were the scenes I saw, so black the darkness of space, and so small the astronauts, that it made me feel very small indeed; and the silence of outer space proved mysterious and awesome.

Such experiences as I had that day can make us feel totally alone in a huge universe, with no God either to understand, or care, or come alongside us to share our life. Hence my love of the following quotation. What Gorky says of Tolstoy, 'I am not an orphan on the earth as long as this man lived on it', I would want to say of God coming to us in Christ to share our lot and redeem us eternally.

Ron Dale

God's Grandeur

The world is charged with the grandeur of God,
It will flame out, like shining from shook foil;
It gathers to a greatness, like the ooze of oil
Crushed. Why do men then now not reck his rod?
Generations have trod, have trod, have trod;
And all is seared with trade; bleared, smeared with toil;
And wears man's smudge and shares man's smell: the soil
Is bare now, nor can foot feel, being shod.

And for all this, nature is never spent;
There lives the dearest freshness deep down things;
And though the last lights off the black West went
Oh, morning, at the brown brink eastward, springs –
Because the Holy Ghost over the bent
World broods with warm breast and with ah! bright wings.

Gerard Manley Hopkins
Quoted in the Oxford Library of English Poetry, Vol. 3

Psalm 20

Proper 6/Ordinary Time 11: Year B

Though the sea roar and the waves rise high, they cannot overwhelm the ship of Jesus Christ.

Save the King, O Lord

The practice of praying for rulers, presidents and governors is an ancient and enduring tradition. These prayers express the deep awareness of the people that their destiny is bound up with the success of the one who has been invested with power for the sake of the whole. Psalm 20 is such a prayer. It concludes with the petition, 'O Lord, save the king (verse 9; NRSV, 'give victory to'). Like Psalms 18 and 21 it was composed for the ceremonies and services concerned with the king's offices as a military leader and defender of the nation.

1. The theme of the whole is set in the first measure, 'The Lord answer you', and is repeated in the psalm's last measure, 'answer us'. The first part is an extended bidding prayer in which the congregation expresses its wish that the king's prayers made in Zion's sanctuary and accompanied by sacrifices be answered (verses 1-5). Then a representative individual proclaims confidence that, the king having prayed and the people having joined their prayers to his, the Lord will answer with mighty saving help for his anointed (verses 6-8). The psalm concludes with the congregation's direct prayer for the king and appeal to be heard (verse 9). The king and the people who call the Lord 'my God' have the right to call upon the Lord in a time of trouble and have the promised privilege of the Lord's answer. The psalm is a liturgy in which the people support the prayers of the king and add their intercession for him.

2. The basic theology of the psalm is the confessional cry, 'Salvation belongs to the Lord' (3:8). Every line assumes, expresses, and confesses this belief that the Lord will deliver those who call upon him. That confidence is particularly focused on the theologoumenon of 'the name of the Lord' (verses 1, 5, 7) . . . The 'name' is appealed to, confessed, and praised as the manifestation of the God who bears the name. The name not only identifies but becomes the identity of God. The name bears the presence, power, and person of God. . . .

As Scripture, the psalm teaches the Church to pray for those who hold the power of office because they, like us, are dependent on the Lord. It warns against ever letting our dependence on their service turn into the trust we owe to God alone. It warns against allowing their fascination with military strength to make us support policies based on trust in military might.

As liturgy, the psalm leads us into the strange position of praying for the saving victory of our Messiah, who has already been given the victory over sin and death for our sake. But we worship and pray while the end has not yet come, 'when he delivers the kingdom to God the Father after destroying every rule and every authority and power' (1 Corinthians 15:24). Through the psalm we may join our prayers to the intercessions of Christ for us in hope and anticipation of the consummation of his victory.

James L. Mays
Psalms

There once lived a monk called Jordon who, whilst travelling to the Holy Land in 1237, was shipwrecked. He was drowned and his body was washed ashore and interred in a Dominican church at a place called Akka, modern Acre in Israel. A young Carmelite, troubled about his vocation said, 'This Friar Jordon was a good man . . . and all he got for it was to be drowned.' It begs the question, 'What, if any, are the rewards of God's faithful people? What are the rewards of the good life? Is faith in God worthwhile?

Let one of the greatest figures in the history of Christendom point to some kind of answer. John Chrysostom, known as Golden Mouth because his preaching was so wonderful, was once falsely accused of treason and malpractice when he was Archbishop of Constantinople. He replied, 'Violent storms encompass me on all sides; yet I am without fear, because I stand upon a rock. Though the sea roar and the waves rise high, they cannot overwhelm the ship of Jesus Christ. I fear not death which is my gain; nor banishment, for the whole earth is the Lord's, nor the loss of goods, for I came naked into the world, and I can carry nothing out of it.' Chrysostom knew that because God was with him, no matter what pain and suffering came his way, he was secure. God was his only reward, but with him came the gift of fellowship with all his people in light and love.

Mother Julian of Norwich, the fourteenth-century mystic, said once of God, 'He did not say, "You shall not be tempest-tossed, you shall not be workweary, you shall not be discomforted." But he said, "You shall not be overcome." God wants us to heed these words so that we shall always be strong in trust, both in sorrow and in joy.'

Ron Dale
First part of unpublished sermon

Psalm 22

Good Friday: Years A, B, C
Fifth Sunday of Easter: Year B, verses 25-31
Second Sunday of Lent: Year B, verses 23-31
Proper 23/Ordinary Time 28: Year B, verses 1-15
Proper 7/Ordinary Time 12: Year C, verses 19-28

Even in the death camps, God was remembered and celebrated.

Like Psalm 51, this psalm has become traditional for use during Holy Week. The reasons for the association of this psalm with Good Friday are threefold: (1) its content bears striking resemblance to the events of Jesus' trial and crucifixion (so much so that the psalm may be seen as one of the 'sources' used by the Church in describing the events surrounding the crucifixion); (2) according to Mark 15:34, Jesus quoted at least the opening lines of this psalm while hanging upon the cross; and (3) John 19:24 quotes from this psalm to illustrate the belief that actions and events in the life and career of Jesus were to fulfil Scripture, in this case Psalm 22:18.

In this psalm, we find an opening address infused with a strong complaint against God for divine inactivity (verses 1-2), a statement of confidence (verses 3-5), a description of distress (verses 6-8), a second statement of confidence (verses 9-10), a plea for help (verse 11), a second description of distress (verses 12-18), a second plea for salvation (verses 19-21a), a vow to God to offer testimony (verses 21b-22), a little sermonette to the human audience calling upon the people to offer God praise (verses 23-24), a short prayer of thanks to God (verse 25a), and proclamation to the human audience of the consequences of the salvation that has been experienced (verses 25b-31).

. . . In Psalm 22, two themes run through the statements about the person's distress; a sense of alienation from the Deity and hostile opposition from opponents.

The theme of God's distance and correspondingly the person's sense of alienation are sounded in the opening lines. A sense of divine forsakenness pervades the words – God is too far away to hear the sufferer's groanings; day and night move through their ceaseless revolutions, but for the worshipper there is neither answer nor rest from God but only dismay at the divine silence and the loneliness of feeling forsaken.

The theme of human opposition parallels that of divine alienation. If God is too far distant, humans are too near.

Human opposition and enmity are described in various ways. People mock, wagging their heads and making faces, ridiculing the person's dependence and seemingly futile reliance on God (verses 7-8). Powers described as bulls, lions, dogs and a company of evildoers assail the worshipper (verses 12-13, 16). The depiction might suggest that the speaker was a king and the enemies foreign powers. In any case, the opponents are portrayed as menacing, life threatening, and life destroying. They seize the person's abandonment by God as the occasion for attack.

. . . In spite of the dismal picture that the descriptions of distress paint, the psalm is shot through with statements and confessions of great confidence in the Deity. Verses 3-5 affirm that God is holy and that in the past the faith and trust of the fathers were rewarded with divine favour. . . . The confidence in God displayed throughout the psalm moves in verses 22-31 to pride of place and suggests that the worshipper received from God some oracle or sign affirming that a reversal of fate was in store, that tears and pains would be replaced by songs and celebration. Good Friday ends with the pain and tribulation but like the psalm looks forward to Easter with its victory and triumph.

John H. Hayes
Preaching Through the Christian Year: Year A

Whenever I have led a group of people on pilgrimage to Israel, I have always taken them to the Holocaust Museum at Yad Vashem.

It is a place where I have to force myself to view the various displays and photographs depicting Nazi brutality visited so terribly upon European Jews. The experience always moves me to tears.

Some verses in Psalm 22 have become more meaningful to me when I read them in the light of the Holocaust. Lines such as, 'My God, my God, why have you deserted me? (verse 1). 'I call all day, my God, but you never answer' (verse 2). 'All who see me jeer at me' (verse 6). 'A pack of dogs surrounds me, a gang of villains closes me in' (verse 16). 'They divide my garments among them' (verse 18).

But even in the death camps, God was remembered and celebrated and Psalm 22 has its themes of trust in God and also hope in him; hope also that one day all nations would acknowledge him to be the Lord, cf. 22:7: 'The whole earth, from end to end, will remember and come back to the Lord, all the families of the nations will bow down before him.' (All quotes from the Jerusalem Bible.)

Something of what the Jews suffered in the Holocaust is movingly told by Michele Guinness in her autobiography *Child of the Covenant*. Here is part of what she wrote:

'No Jew can come to terms with being Jewish without coming to terms with the Holocaust. I could look at it objectively as a historic event, be appalled at the degradation of human behaviour, even grieve for the relatives I never met, but that was not enough. Amongst Jews genetic bonds are very strong. Each Jew seems to carry in his bones the tragedy and sufferings of his entire race. It was not enough to wonder what it would have been like if I had been there, then bury the feelings in the depths of my subconscious when they became unbearable. One thing was certain, if I had been born twenty, even ten years earlier, in Germany, Poland, Holland, Czechoslovakia or France, I would have been transported to a concentration camp. In that it happened to my people it happened to me, and I had to allow myself to experience the absolute hell of it. Nightmare followed nightmare for several months, as my emotions wrestled to resolve their inner turmoil. I felt the terror of that uncertainty in the overcrowded cattle-trucks, the ache and pain of bereavement, the humiliation of becoming a faceless, nameless piece of human flesh, the stench of hatred and loathing exuding from the bodies of our persecutors. Then the dreams stopped. I had reached a total acceptance of what it meant to be Jewish, the conscious awareness that time after time again throughout history one has had less value than horse manure. How one uses that knowledge is crucial. It has produced the dedicated Zionist, convinced that a homeland is the only solution, the aggressive Israeli who has discovered that for the first time a Jew can actually fight and win, the materialistic entrepreneur, seeking security in acceptance in wealth, and the extraordinary cultural and intellectual achievement of the Jewish people in recent years born of centuries of brokenness and rejection. I too had a choice to make. I could allow my Jewishness to have a negative influence, read anti-Semitism into every meaningless word and gesture, or I could use it positively, learning to trust and forgive. Ironically, it was my experience of the Church which drove me to the crisis point and forced me to a definite decision.'

Michele Guinness
Child of the Covenant

Psalm 23

Fourth Sunday of Lent: Year A
Fourth Sunday of Easter: Years A, B, C
Proper 23/Ordinary Time 28: Year A
Proper 11/Ordinary Time 16: Year B

Wilderness becomes home, isolation becomes companionship, scarcity becomes generosity. That is how the life of faith is.

As you know, this psalm begins, 'The Lord is my shepherd.' The very first word is 'The Lord' or, better, 'Yahweh'. The first word in Lenten talk is the peculiar name of the God of Israel, the one who makes heaven and earth, and who liberates and heals and commands. The psalmist is focused upon this peculiar God and the memory we have of the ways of this God. And then he says of this God: 'Yahweh is my shepherd.'

To think 'shepherd' might suggest an idyllic pastoral scene. In fact, however, the term *shepherd* is political in the Bible. It means king, sovereign, lord, authority, the one who directs, to whom I am answerable, whom I trust and serve. In this simple opening line, the psalm is clear about the goal and focus, the centre and purpose of life: Yahweh and no other. There is no rival loyalty, no competing claim – not economic or political, not liberal or conservative, not sexist or racist, nor any of the other petty loyalties that seduce us. It is a mark of discernment and maturity to strip life down to one compelling loyalty, to be freed of all the others that turn out to be idolatrous.

Then the poet draws a stunning conclusion from this statement about God: I shall not want.

I shall not lack anything. I shall not have any other yearnings or desires that fall outside the gifts of God. What God gives will be enough for me. This is a statement of enormous confidence in the generosity of God, the one who knows what we need and gives well beyond all that we ask or think. But notice at the same time that this phrase, 'I shall not want', is a decision made against the greed and lust and satiation and aggressive ambition of a consumer society. Our consumer society is driven by the notion that we always must want one more thing, and we are entitled to it, and we will have it no matter what.

And now comes this Lenten invitation: I will refocus my desire. I will not entertain all those other lusts and greeds and yearnings that keep me busy and make me selfish and cause me not to notice my neighbour. Here, I suggest, is a

Lenten project for all of us who are competent and affluent and driven and anxious and greedy. Faith in this God requires a refocus of all our desires, because most of our wants are contrived and imagined and phoney. This Lord will be Lord of our wants and our needs, and we need much less when we are clear about the wonder and goodness of God. No substitutes allowed or required.

To unpack this statement of focused trust, the poem invites us to two images. The first is this: Imagine that you are a sheep. As you may know, sheep are really dumb. They do not know how to take care of themselves or even to come in out of the rain. Left to their own devices, they would soon be in trouble, hurt, and likely destroyed. A sheep needs a shepherd, and must learn to trust its life to the shepherd. But it matters a lot what kind of shepherd a sheep is able to have. There are all kinds, some good, some bad. Then this sheep, according to the poet, says, 'Let me tell you about my shepherd, like whom there is no other. Yahweh, the maker of heaven and earth, the liberator of Israel, is my shepherd whom I trust completely. Let me tell you specifically about why I trust so completely.

This reliable, strong, generous shepherd has done three things for us sheep:

> He has led us into green pastures. He has sought out the best grazing ground, so we have plenty to eat. Without such a shepherd, we might have gone hungry on thin pasture lands.

> He has led us beside still waters. He has found gentle streams of fresh water where we can drink. Without such gentle streams, we might try fast, rushing streams, and be swept away to our death.

> He has led us in paths of righteousness, which means safe, straight paths. There are dangerous paths on which the sheep may walk in treachery, crooked and narrow and stony, or through dark places where wild animals lurk. But we have been safe.'

Indeed, this good shepherd has given us all that is needed – good food, good water, good paths. What else could an average sheep need?

Notice that all the verbs of action are for the shepherd. The sheep has no verbs. The sheep does nothing. The sheep waits and receives and enjoys the gifts. Because the shepherd is generous, the sheep lives a safe, trust-filled life, surrounded by generosity. No hunger, no thirst, no fear, no anxiety, no danger. All is well, because there is one shepherd who is trusted.

The poem shifts abruptly to a second metaphor. Now it is the image of a traveller going through dangerous territory. Remember, this ancient terrain is not all superhighway and police patrolled. It is more like the man with the Good Samaritan who went on a journey and got mugged (Luke 10:30). The journey is one pervaded by threat and danger.

But remember, Yahweh is my shepherd. Yahweh is my guardian and protector. In the most dangerous place, 'I fear no evil'. This traveller has confidence, even in ominous places, because the travel is accompanied. 'Thou art with me.' It is precisely the reality of God who is the antidote to our consuming anxiety. The poet has discovered that things on the journey are not as they seem when God is present. We are safer, more cared for than we imagined. It is the presence of God that transforms dangerous places and tough circumstances.

So, says the psalmist, let me tell you about the valley of the shadow of death, when God is present:

There, on the journey, we are comforted by God's protective rod and staff, instruments of guidance. We are not on our own, but guided, guided by God's presence and God's Torah, safe from all that would rob us of life.

There on the journey, we thought there were no resources, but in the very presence of need, fear, and hunger, God sets a table of generous food. It is like coming around the corner of deep threat and there in the middle of the road a lavish table of marvellous food, water from the rock, bread from heaven.

There on the journey, where we thought there was only scarcity, the God of generosity pours out precious oil on our heads, into our cup. Our lives brim over because of God's inexplicable generosity, just where we thought God had no gifts to give.

The journey, with the power and the purpose of God, changes the circumstances in which we live. Wilderness becomes home, isolation becomes companionship, scarcity becomes generosity. That is how the life of faith is. It is, to be sure, very different from the life where Yahweh is not at its core.

You already know this psalm well. There is nothing soft or sweet or easy or sentimental here. This is the voice of a reorganised, refocused, reorientated life. Such a refocus means to see differently, to trust differently, and to obey differently.

Walter Brueggemann
'The Threat of Life'; *Sermons on Pain, Power, and Weakness*

Psalm 24

Proper 10/Ordinary Time 15: Year B
All Saints: Year B
Presentation: Years A, B, C, verses 7-10

No other religion
makes joy a virtue
and its absence
a sin!

Humbug of holiness

A too exclusive preoccupation with holiness itself distorts, and may even pervert, this precious teaching. Sanctification is not meant to be isolated from the rest of the Christian theme. It is both an end and a means to an end, and is not only the climax of God's purpose with man but also the essential commencement of his work through man thereby fitted to further the best interests of mankind. Even then it is part of a completer purpose, namely the glory of God. In any case it demands people of great insight and strength of character to enter frequently any holy place. Familiarity soon breeds contempt, or a concealed cynicism, or a stylised complacency, each of which is a defensive evasion of candid assessment. It is reported that a conversation once took place between Thomas Cook (the then Principal of Cliff College) and Samuel Chadwick (at the time a tutor, and later Principal) in which one remarked to the other, 'Have you found it more difficult to be a Christian at Cliff than anywhere else?' The other agreed. Some people would be puzzled by this, but there is really no mystery about it; anything else would have been the subject of puzzlement. Where any movement or group forms a self-enclosed community, abstracted from life as it ordinarily has to be lived, an element of artificiality seeps in. In the confined limits every whisper echoes like the shouts of boys in the public indoor baths. The wide-ranging human mind has its attention riveted on far too narrow a range of interests. Where there is also a very lofty ideal (especially when it is isolated from the antiseptic of rational investigation and is unrealistic-ally interpreted, unrelated to the scriptural attitudes hitherto outlined) there is a more obvious inclination to odious compari-sons and unreasonable disappointments. The very concern with holiness assumes and develops a sensitiveness of spirit which therefore feels deeply and is easily pained. In the Jewish Temple of Holies, entered once a year by the High Priest, there was nothing beyond the cubic content of the place, except possibly a spider or two and some dust. It required a person of exceptional spiritual insight and maturity of understanding to undertake such a role successfully. The same types of reaction can be predicted in any group or institution in the world devoted to the specialised cultivation of spiritual excellence, whether within Christianity or any other religion.

Tests of sanctity

. . . Some general guidance on the kind of attitudes which might be expected from any true Christian. The Roman Catholics have accepted officially a two-standard Christian life, which Wesley saw from another point of view, and which has much in general experience to justify it, even though the New Testament does not encourage such a division. Consequently it has had to work out a system of assessment for sanctity. Baron von Hugel, writing to the Quaker Stanley Jones, reminded him of the four requisites laid down for such a purpose. First the candidate must have been loyal to the Faith. Second, he must have been heroic under trial. Third, he must be able to do the impossible, humanly speaking. Fourth, he must be radiant in the stress of life. Von Hugel concludes, 'The Church may conceivably be wrong in insisting on the first three of those conditions, but it is gloriously right about the fourth.' No other religion makes joy a virtue, and its absence a sin! Equally we must beware of synthetic joy, a pathological inability to suffer grief as Jesus suffered. At every point genuineness is the test. 'Buy the truth, and sell it not' (Proverbs 23:23). 'Test everything, hold fast to what is good, abstain from every appearance of evil' (1 Thessalonians 4:22). Beware substitutes, larded unction, conspicuous humility, the greasy alternative to real tact whereby the religious get their own way at the expense of declaring their hand. Nevertheless the advertisement on the rear of buses poses a proper question: Is your oil up to standard? The smooth working depends on and produces the oil of joy.

T. D. Meadley
Top Level Talks: The Christian Summit Meeting

A man, very hungry, was caught stealing food from the King's storehouse and ordered to be hanged. He accepted the sentence but said he wanted to give the King a magic secret of great value rather than have it die with him. The King was intrigued and went with his court to the place of the gallows. The thief took a small bag from his belt. 'These are magic pomegranate seeds,' he said, and dug a small hole in the earth by his foot and then looked up. 'If one seed is put in this hole by a man who has never in his life taken anything that didn't belong to him, the seed would grow overnight into a tree, bearing fruit. I cannot do it because I am a thief.'

The King took the little bag. 'I also am not fit,' he said, and went from one to another of his Court, every single one of them drew back. Only the High Priest hesitated, and the King waited, but honesty is catching, and the High Priest also shook his head.

The King went back to the thief. 'You are free,' he said. 'For you showed us not magic but a mirror.'

David Kossoff
A Small Town is a World

Psalm 25

Proper 21/Ordinary Time 26: Year A, verses 1-9
First Sunday of Lent: Year B, verses 1-10
First Sunday of Advent: Year C, verses 1-10
Proper 10/Ordinary Time 15: Year C, verses 1-10

The thing is to understand myself, to see what God really wishes me to do; the thing is to find a truth which is true for me, to find the idea for which I can live and die.

Heartache and alienation are such universal human experiences that many psalms from the liturgies of ancient Israel appear to have been composed, not for any specific occasion, but for use by any worshipper who felt himself or herself to be out of touch with God in 'general', or for no particular reason whatsoever. Psalm 25 seems to be such a prayer for any season of distress, in that there are no concrete references of any sort to relate this petition to a particular crisis of the spirit, other than the psalmist's sense of human sinfulness (verse 7; compare verse 11).

And why should there not be such hymns and prayers? Just as the people of God have felt the need to speak in self-revealing ways about their individual faults and offences, so there is the need to speak of those ways by which each of us is joined to the other members of the human race through our shared sinfulness. Psalm 25 recognises this need and provides the necessary words that permit the pray-er to acknowledge his or her sense of estrangement from God through the universal experience of human sin.

In a manner typical of a classic lament, the psalm begins with a statement that, at the same time, identifies the object of the prayer – the Lord – and affirms that because the psalmist trusts the Lord, there are grounds for hope (verse 1, 2a).

O my God, in you I trust;
do not let me be put to shame;
do not let my enemies exult over me.
do not let those who wait for you be put to shame;
(but do) let them be ashamed who are wantonly treacherous.

This is nothing less than a plea for justice; it is nothing less than the cry, 'Let what ought to be, be!'

A second cluster of petitions is framed in verses 4-5, where the poet acknowledges a need for the Lord's instruction. It is not entirely clear that the Torah is in mind here, but that is likely, since both 'ways' and 'paths' are elsewhere used as synonyms for Torah (Psalm 18:21; 119:15 – translated 'ways' in both instances in NRSV). But what is quite clear is that 'ways' and 'paths' are metaphors for 'truth,' – 'your truth,' to be precise – and the centrality is rendered all the more obvious in that it is the focus of two verbs, 'lead me' and 'teach me'.

Justice, then, and truth are the agenda of the psalmist, and to these are now added mercy and steadfast love. Verses 6 and 7 highlight these qualities, and, in a somewhat bold statement, the Lord is admonished not to forget that these are qualities that characterise the Lord's own life. 'They have been from of old' does not mean that these qualities have some existence apart from the Lord, but they have been reflected in the Lord's deeds from the very beginning. . . . It is because the Lord is merciful and constant in love that the psalmist claims the right of appeal, in cadences that echo Psalm 51:1.

Finally (for that part of the psalm that constitutes the lectionary text), the basic goodness and moral rectitude of the Lord are affirmed, and because the Lord is the kind of God [he] is, people of God are taught to be 'good and upright themselves' (verses 8-10). . . . As the paths of the Lord are steadfast love and faithfulness, so should they be the same 'for those who keep his covenant and his decrees'.

The bringing together in this passage of so many qualities by which the Lord is known, as a means of making an important statement about the faith and the moral commitment of the people of God, is reminiscent of the prophets. Indeed the vocabulary of the psalmist is profoundly reminiscent of Amos, Hosea, and others in the prophetic tradition who also emphasised justice, truth, steadfast love, faithfulness and righteousness, and who, like Psalm 25:1-10, went to great pains to point out that the life of God's people is most appropriately lived when these qualities prevail. Hosea 2:18-20 comes to mind. . . . God's ways will ultimately prevail. Of that the psalmist is convinced, and for that the psalmist prays.

James D. Newsome
Texts for Preaching

My own truth

What I really lack is to be clear in my mind *what I am to do*, not what I am to know, except in so far as a certain understanding must precede every action. The thing is to understand myself, to see what God really wishes *me* to do; the thing is to find a truth which is true for *me*, to find *the idea for which I can live and die*. What would be the use of discovering so-called objective truth, of working through all the systems of philosophy and of being able, if required, to review them all and show up the inconsistencies within each system; what good would it do me to be able to develop a theory of the state and combine all the details into a single whole, and so construct a world in which I did not live, but only held up to the view of others; what good would it do me to be able to explain the meaning of Christianity if it had *no* deeper significance *for me and my life*: what good would it do me if truth stood before me, cold and naked, not caring whether I recognised her or not, and producing in me a shudder of fear rather than a trusting devotion? I certainly do not deny that I still recognise an *imperative of understanding . . . but it must be taken into my life*, and *that* is what I now recognise as the most important thing. That is what my soul longs after, as the African desert thirsts for water. That is what I lack, and that is why I am left standing like a man who has rented a house and gathered all the furniture and household things together, but has not yet found the beloved with whom to share the joys and sorrows of his life.

The Journals of Kierkegaard, 1834-1854
ed. and trans. Alexander Dru

Psalm 26

Proper 17/Ordinary Time 22: Year A, verses 1-8
Proper 22/Ordinary Time 27: Year B

Times may and do come when we need the help of remembering that God knows the mind and heart, even if others don't, and believing that God will vindicate faithfulness even if the world does not.

Judge me, O Lord

'Vindicate me, Lord, for I am righteous.' That is the theme. The prayer is written for people who need the 'judgement' of God. That is the existential occasion of the prayer. The theme sounds theologically wrong and the occasion unlikely. To pray for vindication on the basis of one's own righteousness contradicts what we have learned from Jesus and Paul. It sounds like the prayer of the Pharisee (Luke 18:11f). It conflicts with Paul's doctrine that 'all have sinned' (Romans 3:23). Surely it is incredibly presumptuous to pray that God investigate and vindicate us. Perhaps the only use we can make of Psalm 26 is to take it as a negative example, an Old Testament contrast to proper prayer and faith.

Before we relegate the psalm to that use, we need to be sure we have understood the language and purpose of the psalm in its own terms. It may be that there are positive things to be learned about the project of living and the uses of prayer.

1. First, what is prayed for? The petitions come in verses 1, 2, 9-10 and 11. The thematic supplication that all the others develop is the opening appeal that in Hebrew says literally, 'judge me' (NRSV, 'vindicate'; REB, 'uphold my cause'). In Israel's social life, this appeal would have been made by an innocent party who had been unjustly accused or had been injured by another and sought a decision to set things right, to order the matter justly. The situation assumed is like that of the widow in Jesus' story who kept petitioning a judge to right a wrong done to her by an adversary. (Luke 18:3). Naturally, the innocent party would make the appeal and a relieving decision would be redemptive (verse 11). The prayer turns to God as the supremely authoritative judge of nations and individuals because he is the arbiter who knows not only the facts but what lies in heart and mind, what is felt and intended (verse 2). The decision sought is put in the plea of verse 9; 'Don't withdraw my life, don't deal with me as though I deserved to die.' God is asked to order the situation of the one who prays so that things work out for life instead of death.

2. When would such a prayer be made? The petitions assume

a situation in which one needs the ordering decision of God to restore the circumstances of life. But as usual in the Psalms, the language is so formulaic and traditional that it is open rather than restrictive about the setting of such a prayer. There is a series of texts that describe a procedure that could be followed by people falsely accused or involved in cases where evidence was inconclusive; they could come to shrine or temple to seek a clarifying verdict from God given through an oracle or an ordeal or by lot (1 Kings 8:31-32; Deuteronomy 17:8; Exodus 22:6-8; Numbers 5:1-11ff). Perhaps prayers like Psalm 26 were composed for use in these proceedings. Jeremiah, accused and attacked by opponents of his prophetic activity, prayed like this for God's providence to vindicate his mission and message. So such prayers could be used outside formal proceedings in hope of an answer that would take shape in the course of experience. In any case, this psalm and others like it are not concerned with the final judgement and the ultimate destiny of the soul but with proximate and specific problems of life in which justice and right are not created by what human beings know and do but seems to depend on what God knows and can do. Then one prays, 'Judge me, give me justice.'

3. But one prays to be judged only if one is *saddiq* – a word that means 'right, righteous' in the broadest sense and in judicial contexts means 'innocent' in the case to be decided. A large part of Psalm 26 is self-description of the one who prays (verses 1, 3-8, 11). The term 'righteous' is not used in this description, but that is what the description comes to. The self-description is not individual, the identification of a particular person; it is, rather, the portrait of a type, the recitation of what is typical and characteristic of a manner of living.

When the remainder of the description is examined, it is apparent what gives the life described its integrity: a devotion to the Lord that governs all of life. . . . Unwavering trust (verse 1), living in the light of the Lord's steadfast love and faithfulness (verse 3). The love of the psalmist's life is the temple because that is the place and space where God lets his glory be known (verse 8). He keeps his hands free of acts inimical to God's will and way (verse 6), so that when he praises God by reciting what God has done, the deeds of his life will be coherent with his praise (verse 7). As an act of devotion he has refused to let his thinking and doing be formed and guided by the falsity, hypocrisy, and wickedness prevalent among some in the society (verses 4-5). Finding the nurturing social context in the great congregation is a matter of faith for him (verse 12). In this description the areas of what we call religion and morality are regarded as one, believing and doing are understood as an undivided whole. Integrity is a quality of life lived out of that understanding where the love of God orders will and work.

Such an integrity is not self-righteousness, a conviction of autonomous moral superiority based on one's independent achievements. It is not legalism, conduct based simply on a checklist of requirements. It is, rather, the offer of God in prayer of a wholeness of religion demanded by the prophets (e.g. Amos 5:21-24) and taught by Jesus (e.g. Matthew 23). Perhaps what gives us pause before the psalm is a serious hesitancy about describing ourselves favourably to God. But we need to remember what the prayer seeks – the vindicating decision of God in circumstances where life or vocation is accused or suspected by others. Jeremiah prayed like this on occasion. Paul, suspected and challenged in his mission and faith, claimed a good conscience before God (2 Corinthians 1:12; 4:2; Acts 23:1; 24:16). Luther interpreted this psalm personally in the context of accusations against him of disloyalty to the church and perversion of doctrine. Times may and do come when we need the help of remembering that God knows the mind and heart, even if others don't, and believing that God will vindicate faithfulness even if the world does not.

James L. Mays
Psalms

Jesus our righteousness

Methought I saw, with the eye of my soul, Jesus Christ at God's right hand, there I say, was my righteousness; so that wherever I was, or whatever I was doing, God could not say of me, he wants my righteousness, for that was just before him. I saw also, moreover, that it was not my good frame of heart that made my righteousness better, nor yet my bad frame of that which made my righteousness worse; for my righteousness was Jesus Christ himself, 'the same yesterday, and today and for ever.' Now did the chains fall off my legs indeed.

John Bunyan
Grace Abounding.

74

Psalm 27

Second Sunday of Lent: Year C
Third Sunday of Epiphany/Ordinary Time 3: Year A

*Religion must
be a personal
testimony, it must
be an experience
that happens to
us, like falling in
love or being
cured of an illness,
before we can
relate it to our
concerns and
worries and fears.*

God heartens

A picture in a popular magazine showed hundreds of people on a busy street corner going about their daily affairs. You could see a mother with two children, her arms filled with parcels, and worry written on her face. You could see a business man rushing into a bank, evidently annoyed at missing the first section of a revolving door. You could see a youth leaning against a building, apparently with no place to go, whose eyes betrayed a sense of boredom and discontent. The caption read, 'Of what are these people afraid?'

It was a fair question, because most people, even those with strong and aggressive personalities, harbour some secret fears. They may be afraid of the dark, or of dizzy heights or of big crowds or of small spaces. Psychology has coined a whole new jargon to describe our fears, endless variations on the Greek word *phobia*. Consult the phobias listed in a modern dictionary. They total more than 75, ranging all the way from erythrophobia, the fear of blushing, to phobophobia, the fear of fear itself – and that is not imaginary, because, as President Roosevelt declared during the Second World War, 'The only thing we have to fear is fear'.

Addressing the National Association of Mental Health in London, a distinguished psychologist, Professor G. M. Carstairs of Edinburgh University, said that fear is the great threat to mental health in our generation. He catalogued some genuine fears that unnerve us and play havoc with our peace of mind. First and most obvious, there is the fear of the bomb. Said Professor Carstairs, 'We live in a world where the lunatic dialogue of 'if you blow me up, I will blow you up' has become a serious reality. Our children are living in a folklore of bombs.' Then there is the fear of unemployment which becomes increasingly acute as machines do the work of men, and the fear of failure which haunts a child from the day when he writes his first examinations in school. Many people in middle-age fear a breakdown in health, and most people, as they grow older, have some fear of death. Thus the litany of fear might be extended indefinitely; the cry, 'Good Lord, deliver us!' gathering intensity with each item.

Fear is not a sign of cowardice; it does not denote an absence of courage. When a demolition officer had removed the fuse from a land mine and rendered it harmless, a friend gasped in admiration, 'How can you do that kind of thing without being afraid?' The officer wiped the perspiration from his face and said, 'Every time I am called to one of these jobs I am afraid.' Of course he was afraid. His fear kept him alert to the danger. Fear is an essential emotion that plays a preventive and constructive role in life. It is part of the process of growing up. Unless a child develops a few healthy fears like the fear of speeding cars, boiling kettles, deep water and bottles labelled 'poison', he may not have a chance to grow up. Nor is fear the same thing as anxiety. Anxiety is an abnormal state of mind which exists without a specific cause and may turn a man into a neurotic. The anxious man has a supply of anxiety stored up inside him; it may focus for a time on some acceptable object but, even if the object were removed, the anxiety would still be there. Fear, on the other hand, does have specific causes which can be faced, analysed, attacked, eliminated or endured. A man can deal with his fears.

Psalm 27 is the personal testimony of a man who learned to deal with his fears. Despite the strange alternation of moods, which support the theory that it may be a composite poem by more than one author, the psalm as a whole does have a unifying theme in the relation of God to man's fear. Whoever he was, the psalmist knew the meaning of fear. He had suffered all the symptoms – dry mouth, trembling hands, weak knees and fainting heart. These symptoms had not been brought on by any spectre of the imagination but by terrifying circumstances which were as real as an air raid, an earthquake, an armed robbery or a cancer operation. When his nerve failed him, the psalmist did what many people do – he turned to God and, in so doing, made a tremendous discovery. He discovered that, though God does not always remove the causes of fear, he does give us the inward resources to deal with them. God puts courage into a man, strengthens his heart, stiffens his backbone and gives him a sense of spiritual guts. The God with whom we have to do is *a God who heartens*. Such was the effect of a living religion in the experience of the writer of Psalm 27.

. . . 'Though an host should encamp against me, my heart shall not fear: though war should rise against me, in this will I be confident.'

In reading the psalm we must place our emphasis on the personal pronoun – 'The Lord is *my* light and *my* salvation . . . the strength of *my* life . . .' The psalmist is not preaching a sermon, not outlining a set of general propositions about religion. He is not trying to prove anything or speak for anyone except himself; and in this he provides a refreshing contrast to some agnostics who insist on generalising their own doubts, like a blind man who says that there is no moon because he can't see the moon. Psalm 27 is a personal testimony, nothing more, nothing less. The author shares with us his own conviction about God and tells how his religion has helped him to deal with his fears.

Religion *must* be a personal testimony, it must be an experience that happens to US, like falling in love or being cured of an illness, before we can relate it to our concerns and worries and fears. I always like to meet someone who wants to read books and listen to lectures and join in discussions and generally be informed about religion. However, I tell that person that, if he expects religion to be anything more than a subject of academic enquiry, if he wants it to make a real difference in his life and be a means of solving his problems, he will have to make the transition from second-hand knowledge to first-hand experience. He will have to stop talking about his religion and begin practising it.

John R. Mott, a great Christian layman who was the first Honorary President of the World Council of Churches, said that in his early years at university he began to have some serious doubts about the effectiveness of prayer. He didn't see how prayer could work, how it could change people or events outside the person who prays. To deal with his doubts Dr Mott decided to read some books on prayer. He read 43 in all and, though he found them enlightening, they did not resolve his doubts. At last he decided to try a different approach. He stopped reading and gave up his wearisome discussions on prayer and actually began to pray. He prayed regularly and fervently and discovered for himself the truth of Scripture, that 'the prayer of a righteous man has great power in its effects'. Dr Mott made the transition from a second-hand knowledge of religion to a first-hand experience of religion; and that is what *we* must do if we want our religion to make a real difference in our lives and be an effectual means of dealing with our fears.

Leonard Griffith
God in Man's Experience: the Activity of God in the Psalms

Psalm 29

Baptism of the Lord: Years A, B, C
Trinity Sunday: Year B

Words are not taken as seriously as they should be; and we have forgotten that our words can change the world, for good or ill.

The open heavens, the voice of God, and the imagery of water are all features in the narratives of Jesus' baptism and play roles in this event depicted as the affirmation of his messiahship. A similar set of images is found in Psalm 29 and explains the choice of this psalm for this Sunday throughout the three years of the cycle.

When the ancient rabbis read this psalm, they noticed the 18 occurrences of the divine name Yahweh ('the Lord' in the NRSV) and saw these as paralleling and even providing the basis for their 18 benedictions used in synagogue worship and private devotions.

The repetitive quality of the psalm is further evidenced in the sevenfold repetition of the term 'voice' (of the Lord). Such repetitions indicate an artistic effort and a desire to overwhelm the hearer with a certain emotional impact, an emotion focused upon God and the divine voice.

The hearer of this psalm, like the listener to the account of Jesus' baptism, is not asked to become part of the scene or a participant in the account. The significance of the action asks that the worshipper simply affirm what has been said and then live in the certainty of what has been affirmed.

John H. Hayes
Preaching Through the Christian Year: Year A

Because 'the voice of the Lord' is stressed so much in Psalm 29, here is a quote concerning the Logos (word) made flesh in Christ, a quote that uses the psalm in its exposition.

The 'Word of God'. When the evangelist (John) uses the term 'Logos' or 'the Word' in the opening sentences of his Gospel, whatever else he has in mind, he is most certainly thinking of the Creation story in Genesis 1. 'In the beginning was the Word.' It would have been impossible for anyone, writing to a Christian Church which had accepted the Old Testament as a

Christian book, to say 'In the beginning was the Word', without intending to carry back the minds of his readers to the opening words of Genesis. The 'Word' of which they would immediately think was 'Let there be light, and there was light'. God speaks and there comes into being the 'firmament'; the waters are 'gathered together'; earth appears, and both 'water' and 'earth' bring forth living creatures. The evangelist is thinking of the creative Word of God. It may therefore be assumed that the Johannine Logos conception has its roots in Hebrew thought. . . .

It means not only spoken word, but the spirit of reason immanent in the world, the ultimate principle of things, a spiritual continuum in and behind the material world. Logos was used in the Septuagint to translate the Hebrew *Dabar* ('word'), which always means the spoken word.

It is essential to understand that a spoken word to the Hebrew is not a mere sound uttered through the lips in order to express a meaning. A word is a living *thing* and has power to effect things. Goethe knew this when he translated 'In the beginning was the word' by 'In the beginning was the Act'. The idea of the spoken word as a living thing applies both to the word of God and the word of man. Even a human word carries with it inherent power. We see this illustrated in the story of Jacob's stolen blessing in Genesis 27. Isaac's blessing actually lights on Jacob, yet he cannot revoke it, much as he longs to do so. It must belong to Jacob for ever. . . . It is the projection of a spiritual power inherent in the person of him who utters it. Similarly, the Word of God is personal and goes forth charged with all the power of God himself. 'So shall my word be that goeth forth out of my mouth: it shall not return unto me void, but it shall accomplish that which I please, and it shall prosper in the thing whereto I sent it' (Isaiah 55:11). This word takes shape in the mouth of the prophet. The prophet's word not only predicts, but has, if God has really inspired him, the power to bring to pass what it foretells. 'Lo, I have put my words in thy mouth. See, I have commissioned thee this day over the nations and over the kingdoms, to pluck up and to pull down, and to destroy and to overthrow' (Jeremiah 1:9f). The prophetic word is a constant creative factor in history. As the context of Isaiah 55:11 shows, this Divine 'Word' not only created the material world, but sustains it hour by hour. The Hebrew has no idea of natural law. God himself creates ever anew all the phenomena of nature. The Word of God is the agency that produces frost and snow, floods, the wind, the melting of the ice. 'The voice of the Lord breaketh the cedars' (Psalm 29:5). It 'splits the rocks with flashes of fire' (verse 7). It keeps the stars in their courses (Isaiah 40:26). The universe to the Hebrew is not maintained by an all-pervading immanent reason, but by the Word of God. Should that word be withdrawn, all things would relapse into the primeval chaos, and the waters would once again cover the whole earth. (Psalm 104:9; 33:6f)

R. H. Stachan
The Fourth Gospel

With the advent of propaganda and 'spin doctors' and people being 'economical with the truth', language has lost a lot of power. Words are not taken as seriously as they should be; and we have forgotten that our words can change the world, for good or ill.

If, as the Christian faith teaches, we humans are made in the image of God, then that means among other things, that our words are God's gift. For he is supremely the God who speaks the powerful creative word.

The Book of Genesis opens with the story of creation and in that story a constant refrain is 'And God said'. From his speech all creation flows; light and the firmament, water and dry land, trees and fruits, sun, moon and stars and every living creature. Even human beings are created by his Word but differentiated in that man is the crown of creation and made in God's image.

Now if that is so, it follows that human beings have been given attributes and gifts that reflect God himself. The ability to create, think, relate to creation. And one of those gifts is the gift of speech. Just as when God speaks things always happen, so also with mankind. When we speak, our words do create new worlds; worlds that are new and different and that did not exist before the word was spoken.

During my seven year stint in the electrical trade I picked up the telephone and used it every day for business purposes. But, as a direct result of my calls, new worlds, new events, new activities and work were created. I would for example order thousands of pounds worth of equipment and ask that it be delivered to a ship or a factory, so setting in motion a chain of events that made work for many other people. Work to collate the order, to deliver it, to install it, to complete a ship or a building, that many people might sail the ship or use the building in an endless variety of ways.

When in 1962 the minister conducting my marriage said, 'Will you take this woman to be your lawful wedded wife?', and I responded, 'I do', those two little words created a whole new world for me and for my wife, and a world of experience that is ongoing today.

The more I ponder all of this, the more I am amazed at the endless power of speech, and so I have learned to be careful what I say and try always to mean what I say. Words to me are still powerful instruments in creating new life and experience for myself and many other people.

Ron Dale, 1999.

Psalm 30

Sixth Sunday of Epiphany/Proper 2/
  Ordinary Time 6: Year B
Proper 8/Ordinary Time 13: Year B
Third Sunday of Easter: Year C
Proper 5/Ordinary Time 10: Year C
Proper 9/Ordinary Time 14: Year C

*I will thank him
for the pleasures
given me through
my senses, for
the glory of the
thunder, for the
mystery of music,
the singing of birds
and the laughter
of children.*

Mourning turned to dancing

Here we have one of the best illustrations of thanksgiving of an individual. The psalmist's prayer for healing has been granted, and he thanks God for his restoration. The part of the title which reads, 'A Song at the dedication of the Temple' (literally, 'house'), shows that the Psalm came to be used on the anniversaries of the rededication of the Temple in 164 BC by Judas Maccabaeus. The Jewish community thought of itself as repeating the experience of the psalmist in its suffering under Antiochus Epiphanes and its deliverance under the Maccabees.

The occasion for thanksgiving (30:1-5). The psalmist was about to die with a serious illness. His death would have pleased his enemies, but God heard his cry and brought him up from the realm of the dead into which he was already sinking as his life ebbed away. He calls upon other saints to join him in his thanksgiving. They are persons who are recipients of God's steadfast love and respond to that love in devotion to God and his people. God's anger which brings weeping is short-lived, but his favour which brings joy is enduring.

Autobiographical narrative (30:6-12). In his prosperity the psalmist was guilty of self-sufficiency and a false sense of security. Yet it was God who had established him. Then, as a result of his self-sufficiency and perhaps other sins as well, God removed his favour and the Psalmist was sorely troubled (compare Deuteronomy 8:10-20). In his illness he cried to God for help. With childlike simplicity he reminded God that his death would mean what he could not praise him further, since those in the Pit could not praise God. . . . But God has granted his petition and turned his mourning into dancing (cf. 26:6-7; 118:27-28; Lamentations 5:15), the sackcloth of sorrow into the festal garments of praise. Faith in God, communion with God, and joyful thanksgiving to God are the keynotes of this Psalm.

A. B. Rhodes
Psalms

'Mother's own marriage made her a stickler about one thing,' Gran confided in me at another of our late-night encounters in the kitchen. The stillness of the hour and a strong cup of tea always had a strangely liberating effect on our conversation. 'Any marriage could be made to work, whatever the circumstances.' She paused, the steaming kettle in her hand poised over the teapot, and turned to look at me, as if debating whether to continue her story or not. Then her face relaxed into a grin and she giggled. 'You'll never guess what I did on my wedding night. I ran away!' 'You what? Why?' 'Well I wasn't having any of . . . that, was I?' 'You mean, for all her apparent broad-mindedness Great-grandma never actually told you about the facts of life?' 'She wouldn't have dreamed of it, but she did that night, when she found me on the doorstep.' 'What did she say?' 'She sent me home to Grandpa. Told me to get on with it, that I was lucky it wasn't an arranged marriage like hers or some of her friends'.' 'What did you do?' 'Did as I was told, just as we all did and always have done, until she died. As brothers and sisters we've had our differences, but she kept the family together. Now I seem to be falling out with everyone. If only one of us had been more like her.'

I waited in silence, not daring to interrupt her flow, desperately hoping that Gran would explain what she meant. What was so special about [my great-grandmother]? Gran sighed, swirled the teabags round in the pot with her spoon in a distracted sort of way, pouring the steaming black liquid into a cup and then sipped thoughtfully.

'You see, she was a good Jew. I mean she was a really good woman.' I must have looked quizzical.

'Well, for example, after she died and we were sitting *Shivah* for her, you know, the ritual one week of mourning, one evening just before prayers your mother happened to tell us that whenever she went to the house [my] mother sent her down the road with a hot meal for a certain Miss Weinberg, an old lady who was infirm and bedridden.'

'You took hot meals to Miss Weinberg? So did I!' 'Me too!' [responded the other sisters].

Well, it turned out that each of the grandchildren had taken meals to Miss Weinberg every time they called and that in all probability Miss Weinberg had had a good hot meal every day of her life. That was Mother all right, that was her Judaism, she lived and breathed it. Gran stared wistfully into her empty teacup.

'I'm not like that,' she said slowly. 'I try, God knows I try. I keep the festivals. I keep the laws, well most of them. I keep a strictly kosher kitchen, just as she taught me to. Have you ever had meat with dairy products in this house? Of course not. But somehow it's not the same. She and Father, they were on familiar terms with the Almighty. They spoke to him like you speak to a friend. But I've never seen him like that. I can't. Life's too complicated. My brother, your uncle Joe, he's a clever man, he reads, he studies the Torah, the Talmud and other holy Jewish writings; perhaps he can make sense of it all. Well,' Gran started suddenly, 'none of us has inherited their simple kind of faith and there's an end to it.' She rinsed her cup and saucer without a word and then headed for the door. She stopped and turned round slowly. 'Perhaps,' she said thoughtfully, 'perhaps it's something you're given when you specially need it, you know, in all the troubles they had to face. And perhaps with all this,' she waved vaguely at her beautifully fitted kitchen, 'we no longer need it, well not in the same way. Who knows?' She shook her head and disappeared into her bedroom. The door clicked shut and the still house seemed very cold and empty.

Michele Guinness
Child of the Covenant

Gifts through the senses

I will thank him for the pleasures given me through my senses, for the glory of the thunder, for the mystery of music, the singing of birds and the laughter of children. I will thank him for the pleasures of seeing, for the delights through colour, for the awe of the sunset, the beauty of flowers, the smile of friendship and the look of love; for the changing beauty of the clouds, for the wild roses in the hedges, for the form and beauty of birds, for the leaves on the trees in spring and autumn, for the whiteness of the leafless trees through the winter, teaching us that death is sleep and not destruction, for the sweetness of flowers and the scent of hay. Truly, oh Lord, the earth is full of thy riches! And yet, how much more will I thank and praise God for the strength of my body enabling me to work, for the refreshment of sleep, for my daily bread, for the days of painless health, for the gift of my mind and the gift of my conscience, for his loving guidance of my mind ever since it first began to think, and of my heart ever since it began to love.

Edward King
Sermons and Addresses

Psalm 31

Holy Saturday: Years A, B, C, verses 1-4, 15-16
Palm/Passion Sunday: Years A, B, C, verses 9-16
Fifth Sunday of Easter: Year A, verses 1-5, 15-16
Proper 4/Ordinary Time 9: Year A, verses 1-5, 19-24

Yes, we have a dogmatic Christianity, but its dogmas are inconsequent, vague, contradictory. God is light. Physicists will tell you that light behaves in an inconsequent, contradictory manner.

This psalm is a lament, interspersed with thanksgiving, composed to be prayed by one in trouble or distress. The following is an outline of the psalm: opening address and appeal (verses 1-2), a statement of confidence in God by the worshipper (verses 3-6), an anticipatory thanksgiving based on confidence in a favourable response from God (verses 7-8), a description of personal distress and trouble (verses 9-13), a plea for help interspersed with statements of confidence and trust (verses 14-18), a further statement of confidence (verses 19-20), a proclamation blessing God addressed to a human audience (verse 21), thanksgiving addressed to God (verse 22), and a sermonette admonishing the human audience to love and trust Yahweh (verses 23-24).

In spite of the misery and suffering of the worshipper, the psalm nonetheless expresses a sense of security and a strong faith in the outcome of an appeal to God. Luke (23:46) has Jesus quote verse 5 [of the psalm] as his last words from the cross.

In the opening appeal and statement of confidence (verses 1-5), images used to express the distress of the complainant draw from warfare ('fortress', 'refuge'), trapping ('net hidden'), and personal self-evaluation and public judgement ('shame'). The troubles suffered articulated in verses 9-13 suggest that the person suffered from social isolation and personality disturbances. Perhaps the problem was some illness such as 'leprous' disease (see Leviticus 13), which required living apart from society and under social ostracism and condemnation (see Leviticus 13:45-46).

The worshipper prays for divine protection, that God would offer consolation and prove to be a hiding place. The willingness to commit oneself to the Divine (verse 5) would indicate not only a piety toward the Deity, but also a sense of the person's own innocence and confidence.

Perhaps in a service of worship focused on the individual, or after spending the night in the temple, the worshipper, through priestly word or personal dream, became convinced that a good outcome was granted by the Deity. In verse 22, the psalm describes the earlier panic and plight but is confident that salvation awaits because God has heard the plea.

Verses 23-24 may have been spoken as words of encouragement to the complainant by the priest or to friends and family by the sufferer. It affirms the two attitudes that one may take – that of faithfulness or that of acting haughtily.

John H. Hayes
Preaching Through the Christian Year: Year A

Richard Wurmbrand was a Christian minister living and working in Rumania when governed by communism. Here is part of a sermon called 'Imprecise Thought', taken from If Prison Walls Could Speak, *published, according to the author, as an attempt to make others feel the storms of doubt and rebellion against God that assailed him in his prison cell:*

How terrible is a God who strips himself naked, because Roman soldiers armed with whips order him to do so! He stripped himself not only of his clothes, but also of his ability to perform miracles, he stripped his immaculate human nature of its immortality. This God cannot be put into words. We can only be changed into his likeness. The people, looking at us, will believe in this strange God.

During an interrogation, a Christian was asked by a Communist officer, 'Where is your God? Why doesn't he perform a miracle?' Our brother answered, 'You have a great miracle before your eyes, but you are blind. That is the miracle.'

We have to speak like this to the Communists. It may even convert them. We ourselves are not satisfied. We would like to see quite another miracle: that there should be no more beatings, no more suffering. But God is what he is, not what we want him to be. This is why we call the Beloved terrible.

I have said that my Christianity is undogmatic. Again I use a human word, and it may mislead. Christianity can no more do without dogmas than natural sciences can do without laws.

But in many sciences the notion of the 'natural law' has changed. Science has ceased to be consequent. The atom is considered, according to the needs of a given experiment, as a particle or as a wave. Nobody has seen it, and it cannot be located. So it makes no difference. Or try to imagine what geometry calls a point – an entity without dimension. It is impossible. Or, take Max Planck. He says that matter *per se* does not exist. Matter appears and remains only thanks to an energy which brings particles of the atom into orbit. This energy is the ultimate basis of matter.

This means that the scientist must live in different spheres. He has an object in his house which he can handle and sit on, and which he calls a chair. When he begins to think about it in his laboratory, he knows it to be a whirlwind of elementary particles. When he draws philosophical conclusions from his science, the chair becomes an unreal object. Planck says that it is not the seen, transitory matter which is the real, the true, the existent, but the unseen, the immortal spirit, without which matter could not even exist. And having said this, he sits down on a chair with full confidence. On a practical level, he knows it to be matter.

So we have to live our life with God on different levels. There is practical religion, in which God is very like a man. He has eyes with which he looks on us. He can stretch out his arm to help us. He speaks to us in our language. He enjoys our songs and prayers.

When we meditate about him, all these things disappear. No human word exists to explain him. The French say, 'a god who is defined is finished'. You cannot define his image.

Yes, we have a dogmatic Christianity, but its dogmas are inconsequent, vague, contradictory. God is light. Physicists will tell you that light behaves in an inconsequent, contradictory manner.

Imprecision is the only precise manner of thinking about God and about his rules. The leap of faith is a leap into the vague, the indefinite, the equivocal, the uncertain, the undetermined.

'He hangeth the earth upon nothing' (Job 26:7). Hang your faith upon nothing. Jesus 'offered up prayers and supplications with strong crying and tears unto him that was able to save him from death' (Hebrews 5:7). But he was not saved. He had to endure death. And on the cross he asked in vain, 'My God, my God, why hast thou forsaken me?' There came no answer and no help, but only a new mockery. To this mysterious, terrible God he said, 'Father, into thy hands I commend my spirit.'

My last sermon before my arrest was on the terribleness of God. My congregation did not understand much of it. Neither did I, and I wondered about what I said. Now I begin to understand. Because I understand less and less about what God is doing with me.

How beautiful is the bride of Christ when she does not try to understand the Unintelligible, but follows him blindly, and embraces him in love. Amen.

Richard Wurmbrand
If Prison Walls Could Speak

Psalm 32

First Sunday of Lent: Year A
Fourth Sunday of Lent: Year C
Proper 6/Ordinary Time 11: Year C
Proper 26/Ordinary Time 31: Year C, verses 1-7

Like a radical and excruciatingly painful operation God's forgiveness had cured him not only of sin but of sinfulness.

He feels happy

'Blessed is he whose transgression is forgiven . . .' The keyword is 'blessed'. It has a larger, deeper, richer, more spiritual meaning than 'happy' (NEB), yet blessedness contains happiness as a red-hot iron contains fire. That gives the psalm a very human appeal and brings it right into our experience. Most people want to be happy. They dream of happiness, they plan for it, and will often pay any price to achieve it. In the search for happiness one man makes a lot of money, and another gives all his money away. In the same search one woman has half a dozen babies, and another goes into a convent. Ask the average person what he wants most out of life, and the chances are that he will reply without hesitation, 'I want to be happy.'

Psalm 32 contains the spiritual case-history of a man who discovered a way to happiness. To him that was a vitally important discovery, because he had not been happy; in fact, he had been quite miserable. He tells about three stages in his experience, the first a stage of *abject misery*. It was the misery of a painful and serious illness. He does not specify its exact nature but he does describe the symptoms. He says, '. . . my bones waxed old through my roaring all the day long . . . my moisture is turned into the drought of summer.' It is a terrible thing for any person to see his own body wasting away and to realise that some day there will be nothing left and he will die.

There could be no doubt in anybody's mind about the cause of his illness. According to the settled opinion of the times he was guilty of some sin, else he would not have fallen ill. The Jews connected all sickness with sin. They argued inexorably that if a man suffered he must be a sinner. Openly or secretly, knowingly or ignorantly he must have broken God's laws, and God was punishing him for it. Job's so-called 'comforters' pressed that point almost brutally, 'Whoever perished, being innocent?' (Job 4:7 AV). Job himself had a more enlightened view. He insisted that his suffering might have nothing to do with sin, a view that Jesus confirmed when he answered the question of his disciples concerning the man born blind, 'It was not that this man sinned, or his parents . . .' (John 9:3). Even today there is nothing fanciful about the connection between suffering and sin. It may not be as direct and automatic as people assumed in Old Testament times but it is still present in varying degrees. The sense of guilt lays a burden on the soul, and the soul passes part of the burden to the body, and the patient becomes physically ill. . . . High blood pressure, toxic goitre, migraine headaches, arthritis, apoplexy, heart trouble, peptic ulcers, and many others – may be caused by our failure to obey God's laws. Modern medical science acknowledges a very definite connection between suffering and sin.

The psalmist, conditioned by orthodox theology, knew that there was such a connection but in his own case he refused to admit it. Like the suffering Job he persuaded himself that no sins could be charged against him. For he admitted that God was the author of his suffering: 'For day and night thy hand was heavy upon me . . .' But he refused to believe that he deserved it. God was punishing him unjustly. His friends may have begged him to search his conscience and pour out a prayer of confession, but he 'kept silence'. That was a very human thing to do. Not many people, suffering from emotional or physical illness, are prepared to admit that they have brought it upon themselves by their disobedience of God's laws. More likely they make the rounds of the medical profession, hoping that a new drug or a series of treatments or even an operation will give them back their health. They would be surprised if some kindly doctor said what Shakespeare's doctor said concerning Lady Macbeth, 'More needs she the divine that the physician.'

Perhaps someone gave similar advice to the psalmist in his illness. He may even have said it to himself but he did nothing about it. He kept silence. Meanwhile his pain became more intense, his body more emaciated, and his chances of survival more faint. Abject misery was the first stage in his spiritual history.

The second stage can be described as *moral honesty before God*. Came the day when the poor fellow could suffer no longer. He had to break his silence or die. 'I acknowledged my sin unto thee, and mine iniquity have I not hid.' He didn't simply break down like a torture victim and confess a guilt he did not feel. He actually searched his conscience and found the particular sin which he had committed and confessed it to God. 'I said, I will confess my transgressions to the Lord; and thou forgavest the iniquity of my sin.' That was probably the most painful thing he ever did but also the most liberating because it marked the turning point in his experience. From that moment his condition began to improve. Whether the sin he confessed had actually caused his illness or not, the very act of moral honesty before God became a healing force in his body and soul.

Augustine in the fourth century made the same thrilling discovery. It is reported that he had Psalm 32 inscribed above his bed so that he could read it first thing every morning. He had made the psalmist's experience his own.

. . . Having found a way to happiness, he wants to share it with the young and inexperienced. He says specifically, 'I will instruct thee and teach thee in the way in which thou shalt go . . .' He calls upon all who are godly to cultivate and practise the habit of prayer and return to God, not as animals who have to be bridled but as human beings who can come by choice. His words may be paraphrased: 'If you are ill and suffering any kind of physical or emotional misery, consider the possibility that you brought it upon yourself by your disobedience of God's laws. Go into the secret place of your heart. Unlock the hidden door. Take out the unresolved guilt, the unforgiven sin. Be morally honest about it before God, confess it to him, repent. It won't be easy, but you will recover your health of body and mind and you will set your feet on the way to happiness.'

Happiness is the third stage in the psalmist's spiritual history. After he had been morally honest with God, his whole mood changed as the whole earth changes when the sunlight comes out after a storm. Yet it was not he himself but God who made him happy. His happiness was an emotional response to God's forgiveness which he describes in four memorable phrases.

'Blessed is he whose transgression is forgiven . . .' Transgression implies wilful disobedience against some kind of legal or moral authority. Forgiveness is a personal act whereby the transgressor, because of his penitence, is freely restored to the relationship in which he stood before he defiled that authority. . . . 'Blessed is he . . . whose sin is covered.' There is a moving example of that in Charles Dickens' novel *David Copperfield*, where little Emily runs away from home, leaving a note confessing that she is pregnant. Her uncle, Mr Peggoty, resolves to find her. He tells the woman whose son seduced Emily, 'I'm a-going to seek her, fur and wide . . . If I should bring her back again, my meaning is, that she and me shall live and die where no one can reproach her.' He does exactly that. He finds Emily in a life of shame, takes her out of it and emigrates with her to Australia to a new life where no one can reproach her. He covers her sin. God's forgiveness is like that.

'Blessed is the man unto whom the Lord imputeth not iniquity . . .' That means that the Lord lays no guilt to his account. Nothing stands against him even in the unforgiving region of law. There is no eternal dossier that contains an indelible record of all his misdeeds and failures. Some people fear that there is. They cannot suppress the feeling that their sins, although forgiven and covered, are somehow chalked up against them like traffic offences on the back of a driver's licence. If they pile up too many offences, they might even lose their licence. Perhaps they will never know the truth until they stand before the great King on his throne and he shows them the page on which the offence was written and they see that it is a clean page. The record may have been there once but it has been erased and the page wiped clean. . . .

'Blessed is the man . . . in whose spirit there is no guile.' That means no deceit, no possibility of the sin's recurrence. A surgeon can give the greatest happiness to a person who has undergone a cancer operation by telling him that all traces of the malignancy have been removed. The disease has been cured, and the symptoms will not recur. That's what made the psalmist happy. Like a radical and excruciatingly painful operation God's forgiveness had cured him not only of sin but of sinfulness, that inner falsehood, that deceit, that guile which, exposed to temptation, could start the whole vicious circle all over again. . . .

Psalm 32 points to the Cross. It holds out the promise of God's forgiveness which the Cross makes actual and inserts into human experience. Whoever comes to the Cross of Jesus Christ in absolute moral honesty will receive from God a total and complete forgiveness that restores his health of body and soul and opens for him a new way to happiness.

Leonard Griffith
Reactions to God: Man's Response to God's Activity in the Psalms

Psalm 33

Proper 5/Ordinary Time 10: Year A, verses 1-12
Proper 14/Ordinary Time 19: Year C, verses 12-22

*The language
of the psalms
permits us to be
boldly anticipatory
about what may
be, as well as
discerning about
what has been.*

The word and work of God

Psalm 33 is a hymn which brings together the work of God in creation and the word of God in history. Some number it among the psalms sung at the New Year Festival.

The call to worship (33:1-3). Joy, praise, music and song are all united in this call to worship. The 'righteous' or 'upright' are not the morally perfect but are the worshipping congregation who acknowledge themselves to be God's Covenant people. The expression 'new song' refers to the psalm itself because it is a fresh composition for a particular occasion.

The word of God (33:4-9). God's word and work are one in creation and history. For God to speak is for him to accomplish. For God to work is for him to speak. In the parallelism of Hebrew poetry, to say 'the word of the Lord is upright' is to say 'all his work is done in faithfulness.' This is in accord with Hebrew psychology. All of God's activity in creation and history is characterised by uprightness, faithfulness, righteousness, justice, and steadfast love. Verses 6-7 are a poetic reflection of Genesis 1. 'The breath of his mouth' is another way of denoting God's word. The 'bottle' in which the waters of the sea are gathered is thought of as a bottle made of skin. The power of God manifested in creation is sufficient cause for all men to reverence God (verses 8-9).

The purpose of God (33:10-12). Up to this point the psalmist's concentration has been largely upon God's work in creation. He now begins to concentrate upon his work in history. The word 'counsel' means 'purpose'. God's purpose is set over against the purpose of the nations. He rules and overrules in individual and national affairs. The Chosen People are counted happy, the reason being their participation in the privilege of election.

The providence of God (33:13-19). The phrase in this section of the psalm which best expresses the meaning of providence is 'the eye of the Lord' (verse 18). God sees the deeds of all men, who in some way serve his purpose (verses 13-15). Physical might is not the ultimate security (verses 16-17), for the destiny of men and nations is in the hands of God (verses 18-19), who provides food and saves from premature death.

The ground of hope (33:20-22). The psalm begins on the note of joyous praise and ends on the note of joyous expectation, composed of quiet waiting, simple trust, and persistent hope. The ground of hope is the sovereign Lord of creation and history (compare Romans 8:25).

A. B. Rhodes
Psalms

Psalm 33:6 speaks about the creative word that God speaks: 'By the word of the Lord the heavens were made, their whole array by the breath of his mouth.' This of course echoes the account of creation in Genesis 1. But here is a piece of writing that picks up that theme from a different perspective (see also my own comments on Psalm 29).

A language adequate to experience. Let us begin with a presupposition about language that is necessary to enter into the psalms. In our culture, we imbibe a positivistic understanding of language. That is, we believe that the function of language is only to report and describe what already exists. The usefulness of such language is obvious. It lets us be precise and unambiguous. It even lets us control. But it is one-dimensional language that must necessarily be without passion, and without eloquence, and indeed without boldness. It is useful language, but it is not the language we have in the psalms. Indeed, it is not the language in which we can faithfully pray. Such language is useful for managing things. But it makes no impact on how things really are, for things would be the same even if there were no speech.

In the psalms, the use of language does not *describe* what is. It takes what has not yet been spoken and *evokes* it into being. This kind of speech resists discipline, shuns precision, delights in ambiguity, is profoundly creative, and is itself an exercise in freedom. In using speech in this way, we are in fact doing on a smaller scale what God has done in the creation narratives of Genesis. We are calling into being that which does not yet exist (cf. Romans 4:17).

Now in contrasting these two kinds of language, we need to be clear about the social function of each. The first mode of language is appropriate to science, engineering, and perhaps the social sciences. When it is used in the arena of human interaction, however, it tends to be conservative, restrictive, and limiting. It can only describe what already exists and, by its very use, deter anything new from coming into being. It crushes hope, for it cannot 'imagine' what is not already present. By contrast, the bold, symbolic use of language in the psalms is restive with what *is*. It races on ahead to form something that never was before. This language, then, with its speech of liberation, is dangerous and revolutionary, for its very use constitutes a threat to the way things have been. It is for this reason that totalitarian regimes, even when they control all the hardware, are most fearful of the poet. The creative speech of the poet can evoke new forms of human life that even the power of arms and repression is helpless to prevent. Such speech, which is the proper idiom for prayer, is the language of surprise. It means that in such speech both the speaker and God may be surprised by what is freshly offered. The language of the psalms permits us to be boldly *anticipatory* about what may be, as well as *discerning* about what has been.

A great danger in praying the psalms is that we shall mistakenly take their language in a positivistic, descriptive way as nothing more than a report on what is. Taken that way, the psalms can probably be managed, comprehended, and rendered powerless. That is a hazard of the repeated use of any important words. We assume we already know what they mean. But if the language of the psalms is understood impressionistically and creatively, then it holds surprise and in fact creates new realities where none existed before.

Walter Brueggemann
Praying the Psalms

Psalm 34

All Saints: Years A and B, verses 1-10, 22
Proper 14/Ordinary Time 19: Year B, verses 1-8
Proper 15/Ordinary Time 20: Year B, verses 9-14
Proper 16/Ordinary Time 21: Year B, verses 15-22
Proper 25/Ordinary Time 30: Year B, verses 1-8, 19-22

Nobody can be
'argued' into belief
in God.

This song of thanksgiving is in the mouth of one who had been in a situation of threat, who had appealed to God, who as a result of the appeal had now been rescued by God, and who now witnesses to the powerful rescue of God. The psalm is on the side of trouble resolved, only now looking back to the trouble through the lens of resolution. Thus the psalm nicely corresponds to the reading from Job, which is also about a generous restoration and rehabilitation wrought by God.

The beginning of Psalm 34 is one of praise to and celebration of the Lord. The praise is unending. This is the voice of one who is so elated about rescue that he cannot stop speaking of the wonder and miracle of what has been given. A clue to the social location of this psalm is the summons to the 'humble' (*anawim*, i.e. poor, abused, v. 2) to hear the message and join in the act of exaltation. That is, the psalmist suggests that in his trouble, he was one of the powerless who had no hope of rescue. And then, belatedly, he found that the Lord was attentive even to, and especially to, the abused who are without hope of rescue. Thus the inversion of circumstance wrought by God is even more astonishing.

Verses 4-7 are arranged in an antiphonal pattern, so that verses 4 and 6 are personal testimony, answered in verses 5 and 7 with statements of confidence and praise. As is characteristic in such a psalm, this one moves from quite concrete experience to large liturgical generalisation.

In a standard formula of thanksgiving, the speaker remembers having prayed to the Lord and being delivered by the Lord (verse 4). In verse 6 the speaker refers to himself in the third person as 'this poor *one*' (ani), who cried out and was saved. Thus verses 4 and 6 are closely parallel. Both describe the transaction whereby God was mobilised into saving action. . . . This 'humble one' addressed other 'humble ones,' who may share confidence in the God who hears, answers and acts.

The counterpoint to the personal testimony is given in

verses 5 and 7. In verse 5 the witness of verse 4 is turned into a summons to trust God. The affirmation that 'your faces shall never be ashamed', that is, those without power who are depreciated by society. The personal testimony becomes ground for hope for action by God, hope for all the others in a similar state.

Verse 7, by way of generalising from personal experience, moves in a very different direction. Now a new character is introduced into the narrative plot. It is God's angel who bivouacs with the faithful, who is present and who intervenes to save (yet a third, different term for 'deliver'). The effect of verses 1-7 is to insist from personal experience that God is available and is prepared to act for those who need rescue.

Verse 8 [is] . . . a summons to the faithful and an affirmation that God is 'good', that is, loyal, faithful, friendly, capable of bestowing blessing. The imperative 'taste' is an odd one, which is thus far unanticipated in the text. It is most probable that 'taste' here means to eat and enjoy the fruits of God's blessings. In Christian usage, this verse has been taken over as a eucharistic invitation, but in the Old Testament usage the verse does not suggest 'tasting God', but rather enjoying God's good gifts.

The last line of verse 8 introduces something like a military image. The one who 'takes refuge' is a *Geber*, a bold, brave warrior. Thus the image is created of a man in battle who seeks protection from God; God is a protective fortress.

Verses 19-22 are a reprise on the main themes of the psalm.

James D. Newsome
Texts for Preaching

Psalm 34:8, 'O taste and see that the Lord is good' was uppermost in my mind one Friday night in Exeter prison. I was conducting my Bible class with about a dozen or so inmates. At one stage of the discussion things became a little heated.

We were discussing whether or not God existed and the meaning of faith, and on such occasions I had learned never to try and win arguments (nobody can be 'argued' into belief in God). There was one inmate who was a bit of a know-all and who produced a counter argument to everything that the other inmates said. One of them turned to me in anger and asked me to 'win' the argument, and prove that God 'is'.

I refused and said to him that he and his colleagues must carry on the debate 'for' belief in God.

So the debate raged on for another ten minutes or so and the 'devil's advocate' inmate continued with his negative comments until suddenly, his main opponent looked straight at him and said, 'The trouble with you is that you don't really want to believe in God. You're hiding behind arguments all the time.' To my surprise, every other man in the room believed in God and wanted their fellow inmate to do so also.

Later on I was able to say that in the end, to 'taste and see that the Lord is good' is for many the only way forward. For only as we invite God into our lives, only as we surrender ourselves to him, do we begin to 'taste him', to experience him for who he is: our Creator and Redeemer. And as the quotation from James Newsome reminds us (see above), we taste God supremely as we celebrate Holy Communion in broken bread and poured out wine. During my nine years service as a prison chaplain I soon learned that the best attended of any act of worship in the prison was always Holy Communion.

Could it be that all those who faithfully partook of Holy Communion in the prison chapel dimly realised that whilst they could not argue the case for God intellectually, they nevertheless experienced him in mystery and love through the bread and wine; tasting for themselves that the Lord is good.

Ron Dale, 1999

Psalm 36

Second Sunday of Epiphany/Ordinary Time 2: Year C,
verses 5-10
Monday in Holy Week: Years A, B, C, verses 5-11

The thirst of the
spirit is chiefly of
two kinds, the
desire of light and
the desire of love.

The character of the righteous God (36:5-12). In contrast to the wicked man, God is characterised by steadfast love, faithfulness and righteousness – terms used almost synonymously. These attributes of God characterise him not only in his relationship to his Covenant people but also in relation to the universe (verses 5-6), to animals (verse 6), and to all men (verse 7). 'The mountains of God' may be an allusion to the ancient Near Eastern idea that the abode of the gods was in the mountains, but the psalmist does not accept the polytheistic theology associated with the expression. He is saying that God's righteousness is dependable. The expression of his righteousness in judgement is unfathomable like the great deep sea (see Genesis 1-6, 7-11; compare Romans 11:33). God reveals his attributes in saving man and beast alive (verse 6). He protects men under the shadow of his wings (cf. Psalm 17:8; the figurative expression, 'shadow of thy wings' . . . is of uncertain origin. It may have been prompted by the winged solar disk of the Egyptian sun-god Horus, or by the care of a mother bird for her young, or by the wings of the cherubim in the Temple). 'The abundance of thy house' and 'the river of thy delights' are figures to describe God's provision for man's needs (compare 65:1-13). God is the source of life (see Jeremiah 2:13) and light (see Psalm 27:1); to have one is to have the other. As the Christian reads verse 9, he thinks of the light – life of the Incarnation of Jesus Christ: 'In him was life, and the life was the light of men.' (John 1:4)

The psalmist concludes with a prayer that God continues his steadfast love and salvation to his true people, and that he protects him from wicked men (verses 10-12). To know God (verse 10) is to commit oneself to him in steadfast love and faithfulness (see Hosea 4:1-6; 6:6; Isaiah 1:1-4).

A. B. Rhodes
Psalms

Thirst of the spirit

All our spirits are born of God's Spirit; the likeness of God's own nature is planted in every one of us; and therefore our spirits can never be at rest till they reach the heavenly fountain from which they came. Unhappily we do not understand our own selves; we feel the thirst within us, but we are long before we learn what alone will quench it.

The thirst of the spirit is chiefly of two kinds, the desire of light and the desire of love. No one surely is without the desire of light. We all are constantly meeting with things which provoke us to ask within ourselves, what is this? how is this? why is this? If we are not curious about such things as books might tell us, we still are troubled with much greater questions. We cannot help seeing what is going on around us among our friends and neighbours, and then we ask how it is that this or that event happens to them. We are still more troubled by thoughts about ourselves and our present and future life. We wonder how a world so full of evil and sorrow can be the work of a good God. This is a longing for light. It is partly satisfied every time that a word spoken by anyone else, or a verse from the Bible, or any other cause gives us a hint which throws light upon what was dark before. And the more we know, the more we desire to know, and then we soon find that there is no teaching like God's own: and all his words and works seem to give forth ever fresh light so long as we remember that they do indeed proceed from him. At last we find that nothing less can satisfy us than God himself to shew us all truth, and we fall on our knees before him, and pray him to scatter all our darkness, and fill us wholly with his own light.

The desire of love is a still deeper thirst of the spirit. There is to us a delight in the presence and affection of those who are dear to us, which we would not exchange for anything that a person could give us, whether it be child, or father, or mother, or husband, or wife, or brother, or sister that we love. They partly satisfy the thirst of our hearts, as God meant that they should. But they are not always the same to us: sometimes, it may be, fretful, sometimes cold: and then, it may be, they die from among us, and our eyes can behold them no more. The more tenderly we love them, the more we shall feel that they cannot exhaust our love, that there is something within us which longs after one who cannot change like poor weak mortals, whose love is as deep and constant as the everlasting heavens, from whose presence death itself cannot cut us off. Our love is therefore never fulfilled till it lays hold upon God himself, and renews itself from that never-failing source.

F. J. A. Hort
Village Sermons

Psalm 37

Seventh Sunday of Epiphany/Proper 3/
Ordinary Time 7: Year C, verses 1-11, 39-40
Proper 22/Ordinary Time 27: Year C, verses 1-9

Crime continues to flourish, and for a time criminals seem to get away with their crimes, but life has a nemesis for every sin, and sooner or later justice catches up with them.

This question still vexes the human spirit – does it pay to be good? Despite the insights of the men who wrote the Bible, many people feel tempted to answer with a resounding 'No!' They see the glaring inequalities of life, the success of sinners and the suffering of the saints, and they exclaim bitterly, 'Virtue obviously has no reward and vice no punishment. It makes no difference how you live. It does not pay to be good.'

Doesn't life prove it? I know a woman who has turned sour because her husband does not make very much money and she cannot keep up with her more affluent friends. What galls her is that once she could keep up with the best of the them. Her husband used to be the sales manager in a large private corporation. He drew a big salary, and they lived in a big house. One day the president of the company asked him to endorse certain household appliances that were not new but were defective products rebuilt and being sold as new products. The sales manager protested, 'This is dishonest! I can't do it!' 'Well, you had better do it,' warned his employer, 'if you want to keep your job.' So now he draws a small salary and lives in a small house, and his wife is bitter about it. She doesn't think that it pays to be good.

That is what bothered the Hebrew poet, and to deal with his problem he put his thoughts into writing. His poem is not the greatest in the Bible nor is it the most sophisticated treatment of this particular problem. The authors of Job and Psalm 73 found a more mature solution, but this man had at least the advantage of speaking out of a lifetime of personal experience. His own words, 'I have been young, and now I am old,' suggest that he wrote with the wisdom that belongs to old age. . . . . He says in effect, 'When you see crooks and scoundrels enjoying more than their fair share of the good things of life, don't be jealous of them, don't get all hot and bothered and don't make it your excuse to imitate them and do something stupid.' Many people do exactly that. Convinced that there is no justice in the world, they exclaim, 'Oh, what the hell!' and promptly lapse into licence, dishonesty or infidelity. 'Why shouldn't I let the producers make love to me?' cried the young actress. 'The others do, and they are happier and more successful than I am. Sure, I have ideals, but they don't get me anywhere.' The psalmist speaks to the young lady and others like her and counsels a more serene, philosophical attitude: 'Fret not thyself because of evildoers, neither be thou envious against the workers of iniquity.' He adds, 'Cease from anger, and forsake wrath: fret not thyself in any wise to do evil.' Behind this homely advice lies deep religious conviction which has grown out of a lifetime of experience with God. The Psalmist has lived close to God for many years and reached the conclusion that, whatever else he may be, he is a just God. His justice controls all of life, so that the world is like a responsible and well-ordered society. Crime continues to flourish, and for a time criminals seem to get away with their crimes, but life has a nemesis for every sin, and sooner or later justice catches up with them. . . .

Sometimes the justice of God does operate most dramatically within a single lifetime. Years ago a real-estate agent on the west coast of the United States had a pamphlet printed which he sent to every American millionaire. . . . The pamphlet carried a story which was so fantastic that it has to be true. It seems that in 1923 eight of the world's most successful men met at the Edgewater Beach Hotel in Chicago. Present were the president of the world's largest independent steel company; the president of the world's largest utility company; the greatest wheat speculator in the United States; the president of the New York Stock Exchange; a member of the Federal Cabinet; the greatest financier in the history of Wall Street; the president of the Bank of International Settlements; the head of the world's largest monopoly. Collectively these men controlled more wealth than there was in the United States Treasury. For years the newspapers had featured their success stories and held them up as examples to the youth of the nation. Look at their story 25 years later. The president of the world's largest independent steel company, Charles M. Schwab, lived on borrowed money for the last five years of his life and died penniless. The head of the world's largest utility company, Samuel Insull, died in obscurity in Canada. The greatest wheat speculator in the United States, Arthur Cutten, died abroad, insolvent. The president of the New York Stock Exchange, Richard Whitney, served a term in Sing Sing. The member of the Federal Cabinet, Albert Fall, was released from prison so that he could die at home. The greatest financier on Wall Street, Jesse Livermore, committed suicide. The president of the Bank of International Settlements, Leon Frazer, committed suicide. The head of the world's largest monopoly,

Ivor Kreuger, the so-called 'Match King', leaped from a plane crossing the English Channel and committed suicide.

Leonard Griffith
God in Man's Experience: the Activity of God in the Psalms

Commit thy ways to the Lord

This wisdom poem of quiet confidence in God was the inspiration of Paulus Gerhardt's hymn translated by John Wesley as 'Commit thou all thy griefs and ways into his hands' (*Methodist Hymn Book* 507, now 672 in *Hymns and Psalms*). It has been called 'a mirror of providence' and 'an antidote to murmuring'.

The psalm is an acrostic. The verses are in pairs and the first word of each pair begins with a different letter through the whole Hebrew alphabet. It has been suggested that this rather artificial structure was used as an aid to the memory. More probably it was thought of as expressing completeness . . . this psalm being the 'A to Z', as it were, of trust in God. . . [The psalm]:

1. warns against envy of the prosperity of the wicked or righteous indignation at their sinfulness, since this may lead to a discontent which doubts God's loving care and ends by abandoning its own integrity (verse 8; cf 73:2-14);

2. is certain that the good prosper and the wicked will soon suffer disaster. . . .

3. This confidence is the outcome of faith that God is active in the world. He watches over those who trust him, raising them up when they fall, rescuing them from the wicked, and proclaiming their innocence when they are falsely accused (verses 5-6, 17, 24, 28, 33, 39-40).

4. In spite of his frequent promises of prosperity and material welfare for the righteous, he knows that goodness is valuable in itself, even if it brings no tangible rewards (verse 16). It is to have God's law in one's heart (verse 31), to wait eagerly for him and keep his way (verses 7, 9, 34), and to act graciously to those in trouble (verse 21).

5. He urges his hearers to commit themselves to God and discover the same serene faith which he possesses (verses 3-5, 7, 27, 34).

Cyril S. Rodd
Psalms 1-72

Psalm 40

Second Sunday of Epiphany/Ordinary Time 2:
Year A, verses 1-11
Annunciation: Years A, B, C, verses 5-10 (Alt)

Work . . . could be deeply satisfying when done by the grace of Christ who himself was a worker, a carpenter from Nazareth.

It is important to note that the first part of the psalm tells about the past (verses 1-10). It begins with a report of deliverance (verses 1-3). The singer was in death-threatening trouble. He prayed for help. The Lord delivered him. The deliverance was the subject of a 'new song', a hymn of praise that is a witness and summons to others to fear and trust the Lord. The witness continues in a 'beatitude' (verse 4) that teaches that trust in the Lord is a better course of life than resorting to other gods. . . . The psalmist sees his deliverance as one more example of the innumerable wonders by which the Lord has preserved his people; the salvation of the psalmist is set within the continuity of salvation history of Israel (verse 5).

Now the difficult verses 6-8. When a person came to a shrine or temple to perform the public rituals of thanksgiving for deliverance, the rituals included the offering of a sacrifice of thanksgiving along with the song of praise for help (see 50:23; 56:12; 107:22; 116:14, 18; etc). But in verse 6 a surprising thing happens. The psalmist praises the Lord because the Lord did not desire or require any kind of sacrificial offering! The psalmist knew this because 'you bored ears for me'; that is, the Lord had given him the capacity to hear the Lord (hearing always involves responding and obeying; note Isaiah 50:4-5 and the similar gift of hearing to the servant of the Lord). If sacrifice were not to be brought, what was the alternative? Verses 7-8 can be understood in this way. The psalmist came to the temple with a scroll on which was written an account of his trouble, prayer, and deliverance, and his praise of the Lord for his salvation. The content may have been more or less what is said in verses 1-5. The writing would have been recited and deposited in the temple as witness and praise to the Lord. . . . Besides the document, the psalmist brought himself – a person whose desire is to do what pleases his God and in whose inmost parts is the Lord's instruction (verse 8). He presents himself as a person who wants what the Lord wants and who feels and thinks with and through the *Torah* of the Lord. It is important to remember what the function of this statement about the self is. It is not the self-righteous claim of a confident legalist. It is an offering of praise for salvation, and what is even more important, it is the confession of a transformation of the self worked by salvation. Where human desire and will are conformed to divine pleasure and instruction, the purpose of praise through sacrifice and song has been incorporated into the very processes of the self. The true thanksgiving for salvation is witness and will.

In verses 9-10 the psalmist tells his God that he has been a faithful witness. The theme of the telling is stated in the first sentence: 'I brought tidings (*bisser*) of your setting-right deed (*sedeq*) in public assembly.' One way to do that was through singing praise to the Lord (96:1; Isaiah 60:6). In the rest of the statement, the whole vocabulary used to speak of God's saving action is used to expand on the theme: righteousness, salvation, loving-kindness, and faithfulness. The psalmist has done what the saved are supposed to do – proclaim the good news of God's salvation to others, that they may be led to trust in the righteousness of God. Verse 11 is best read as a statement of trust (with NJPS) rather than as a petition (with NRSV). The psalmist trusts himself to the gospel he has proclaimed in the situation in which he now is. He does what is usually so difficult to do – live by the gospel you preach.

James L. Mays
Psalms

Psalm 40:9a, 10b

I have told the glad news of deliverance in the great congregation. . . . I have made no secret of your love and faithfulness in the Great Assembly.

Some of the deepest joys in my life have been given me when I have been engaged in the same activity as the psalmist; that is in proclaiming the saving help and faithfulness of God from the pulpit 'to the great congregation', as the psalmist puts it.

However there are other places, not in a church setting, that I have enjoyed sharing the good news of God, and in these places a rather different method has to be used.

The three main areas I think of are broadcasting on the radio, industrial chaplaincy and prison chaplaincy.

Any preacher of God's work of redeeming the world has to deal with sincerity and truth and this is particularly so on the radio. For in a most mysterious way, any listener is

106

immediately aware of hypocrisy and cant. One listener to one of my broadcasts, a person who had no real faith, reported to a mutual friend that she had listened to me. When asked about her response she said, 'I didn't believe a word, but his words had the ring of truth.'

Apart from all the above, radio broadcasting really demands picture language for most of the time so that the listeners imagine everything. But as an industrial chaplain you have to wrap up the 'God speak' in industrial terms. Time and time again for me the Gospel has come alive, and powerfully so, through what I have observed happening on the shop floor. To take but one example. I once met a man operating a big milling machine. I stood by him whilst he performed one part of a complex piece of engineering. Picking my moment I asked him how he was. His response was that he was absolutely fed up and 'brassed off'. He was sick and tired of work. So I asked him when was the last time he was off sick. He answered that it was only a couple of weeks ago. Then he suddenly said, 'And was I glad to get back to work.' Suddenly he realised the funny side. For there he was complaining about work one moment and the next saying how much he appreciated his work.

Now all this led to a long discussion about work and its meaning and purpose and importance. I ended the conversation by saying that God made us in his own image, and God was a worker; in creating and sustaining everything and everyone. Therefore work helped to remind us of all this and could be deeply satisfying when done by the grace of Christ who himself was a worker, a carpenter/builder from Nazareth.

However, the prison formed a very different context for preaching and witnessing to the Gospel. For some reason, in my own experience I found that the only meaningful service for inmates was Holy Communion. I have pondered long and hard as to why this should be, and the only reason I can think is that the brokenness of the bread relates to the brokenness of their lives and the agony symbolised by the wine, the blood of Christ, somehow relates to the agony of life in prison. All right, there may have been those who came just to get out of their cells, but it is my belief that because the service was not compulsory, inmates came because they wanted to and because in some mysterious way and however dimly, each one saw the relevance of liturgy and the broken body and blood of Christ to their everyday situation.

Ron Dale, 1999

Psalm 41

Seventh Sunday of Epiphany/Proper 3/ Ordinary Time 7: Year B

And he is your example and mine, in trouble and in joy, because he knows how to deal with both.

A beatitude for the merciful

The happiness of the righteous man is celebrated in Psalm 1, the happiness of the forgiven sinner in Psalm 32, and the happiness of the compassionate man in Psalm 41. If the time sequence were reversed, the psalm might be considered a commentary on one of Jesus' beatitudes: 'Blessed are the merciful for they shall obtain mercy' (Matthew 5:7). It is the thanksgiving of a man who has been delivered from a critical illness and from the reproach of malicious enemies.

The blessedness of the merciful (41:1-3). The heart of the psalmist's teaching is found in these verses, for they are the conclusion at which he arrived as a result of the experience he later narrates (compare 32:1-2). The blessedness of the man who considers the poor (see 35:13-14; James 1:27) consists in deliverance from trouble, preservation of life, esteem in the community, protection from enemies, support in illness, and healing of disease.

Narrative of past distress (41:4-10). The psalmist reconstructs his past distress so vividly that he seems to be passing through it as he writes. He appeals to God's grace for healing and, by implication, for forgiveness, since he considers his illness the punishment for sin (verse 4). His enemies speak of him maliciously, desiring his death and the obliteration of his name. Even when one of them visits him, his words are empty, for all the while he is plotting mischief to spread abroad when he leaves. In fact, all the psalmist's enemies carry on a whispering campaign against him and imagine the worst with uncharitable satisfaction (verses 5-7).

They say a magical curse (deadly thing) has been fastened upon him by a sorcerer, so that he cannot get well. Even the psalmist's 'bosom friend' (literally 'man of my peace'), who is bound to him by the tie of hospitality, has turned against him (compare 55:12-13). Verse 9b is quoted by Jesus in John 13:18 as being fulfilled in the treachery of Judas. Again the psalmist prays that by God's grace he may be healed, and gives as a reason for his healing that he may requite his enemies. We may understand his feelings, but we can hardly share them, for vengeance belongs to God alone (Leviticus 19:18; Deuteronomy 32:35; Romans 12:19).

Request granted (41:11-12). The psalmist knows that God is pleased with him because he has healed him and thereby prevented the triumph of enemies over him. God has vindicated him and placed him in his abiding presence on account of the psalmist's undivided commitment to his will. In the light of verses 1-3 this means among other things that the psalmist habitually showed mercy to the poor and weak. It does not mean that he was sinless, for he has already appealed to God to be gracious to him as a sick sinner (verse 4).

Verse 13 is the editorial doxology which closes Book 1 of the Psalter; it is not part of Psalm 41.

A. B. Rhodes
Psalms

Shortly after the train crash near Paddington Station on 5 October, 1999, I broadcast the following script on my local radio station. It could be seen as a comment on Psalm 41:1b and 2a that speak about the protection and deliverance of God.

One of the survivors of last Tuesday's train crash near Paddington station is called Patrick Welcome. All he suffered was a cut face and injured knee. Amazingly he'd also survived a plane crash last month in Bangkok.

He said, 'My guardian angel must be working overtime'. But that made me ask myself about the other guardian angels of those who died and were injured. Were they not working overtime? Does a so-called guardian angel keep human beings safe from all harm or not? For some kind of answer I turned to the story of Jesus in Gethsemane. Knowing that he was about to die on a cross, Jesus prays hard for help from his Heavenly Father. St Luke tells how, after that, in all his agony, an angel from heaven appeared to strengthen him. Not to escape suffering and death, but to face it, endure it, and, on Easter Day to triumph over it. He could have called on legions of angels to save him, but he refused to. And he is your example and mine, in trouble and in joy, because he knows how to deal with both.

Ron Dale
Broadcast talk on Stray FM Radio

Psalms 42 and 43

Easter Vigil: Years A, B, C
Proper 26/Ordinary Time 31: Year A
Proper 7/Ordinary Time 12: Year C

From all sides comes the piercing question 'Where is thy God?' That becomes our question too. Sometimes it makes us feel despondent. We may even shed tears.

He feels despondent

One of the most distinguished novels in recent years is a book entitled *Roots*. The author, Alex Haley, traced his ancestral roots to a man whose African name was Kunta Kinte. Mr Haley went to Africa and visited the tribe from which Kunta came and there he reconstructed the story of the youth growing up among a people whose culture and civilisation were remarkably advanced. They educated their children, had strong family loyalties and stern moral standards and were devout Muslims. In 1767 slave traders captured the young man as they would capture a wild animal and transported him to America where he was enslaved and treated like a wild animal. In that foreign land his enemies taunted and brutalised him. Several times he tried to escape and was finally punished by having the front part of his foot chopped off with an axe. No one could get through to him for a long time. He became sullen, withdrawn and despondent. He longed for his home and his God. He tried to pray, but God seemed very far away.

The author of Psalms 42 and 43, which originally were a single piece, felt despondent for much the same reason. He too was separated from his country and therefore felt separated from his God. Wistfully he recalls the sheer joy of worshipping God in the temple, and his soul thirsts for God as a wild animal thirsts for water when overtaken by hunters or by drought. 'As the hart panteth after the water brooks, so panteth my soul after thee, O God. My soul thirsteth for God, for the living God: when shall I come and appear before God?' Now, instead of the joyous temple music, he is deafened by the thunder of waterfalls and mountain torrents as 'deep calleth unto deep at the noise of thy waterspouts'. They seem to symbolise his calamities; and he calls them God's 'waves and billows which are gone over me'. The scoffing of the heathen deepens his despondency. They are idolaters, worshipping gods which they can see and touch, ridiculing him for his simple faith in the living God who seems invisible and indifferent and far away. Their mockery feels like a mortal wound in his body, and their derisive question, 'Where is thy God?' reduces him to tears and becomes the question of his own tortured soul.

Devout believers have often asked themselves that question, and many are asking it now. They feel exiled in a foreign country, where the very language and customs are strange to them and where all the old familiar landmarks are gone. They feel lost in a secular society where churches are empty and sports stadiums filled, where modern idolaters have turned from the living God to worship the gods of money, pleasure, science and sex that they can see and hear and touch. From all sides comes the piercing question, 'Where is thy God? Why doesn't he show himself, if he exists at all? Why doesn't he save you from your troubles and why doesn't he do something about the tragedy of the world?' That becomes our question too. Sometimes it makes us feel despondent. We may even shed tears.

The psalmist, however, did more than torture himself by asking, 'Where is thy God?' He reacted to the absent God in a positive and constructive way and in so doing dealt with his despondency. Stage by stage he raised himself from the depths of despair to fullness of trust and peace of soul. Any devout person who feels despondent for the same reason can well afford to imitate his pattern of behaviour. Actually he looked in three directions – past, present and future.

First, he looked to the past. He searched the archives of his memory and brought out pictures of the great religious festivals. 'When I remember these things, I pour out my soul in me: for I had gone with the multitude, I went with them to the house of God, with the voice of joy and praise, with a multitude that kept holyday.' That memory steadied and heartened him.

. . . As a second stage in dealing with despondency the psalmist looked at the present. Actually he looked at himself. In fact, he talked to himself and rebuked himself. 'Why art thou cast down, O my soul? and why art thou disquieted in me?' It's a good thing a psychiatrist didn't come along and interrupt him, else he might have been made to feel like an eccentric.

There is nothing eccentric about talking to yourself. Shakespeare's characters do it all the time; their most famous speeches are their soliloquies. Soliloquy can be a helpful form of self-analysis, a means of lifting yourself out of your depressed moods. 'So I feel spiritually down. Why? Am I suffering pain or nervous tension or passing through a personal crisis? Those are common causes of spiritual depression, but once they have been dealt with, I needn't feel depressed any more.'

111

The psalmist was having his troubles. He felt homesick and physically ill and beaten down by the taunts of his enemies. That didn't mean that God had deserted him. It didn't really justify the question, 'Where is thy God?' . . .

Having looked to the past and present, the psalmist looked also to the future. Three times he asked his soul, 'Why art thou cast down?' and each time said to his soul, 'Hope thou in God: for I shall yet praise him, who is the health of my countenance, and my God.' Hope, as a creative way of looking at the future, does hold the secret of health; it can make all the difference between life and death.

Viktor Frankl, the psychiatrist, writing from his experience as an inmate in a concentration camp, tells that hope was the one thing that kept the prisoners alive. They might lose their freedom and dignity, but as long as they kept their hope they survived. When they lost hope they were doomed. He tells how the death rate increased dramatically between Christmas and New Year at the end of 1944. The cause did not lie in harder working conditions or inadequate food or change of weather or new epidemics. It was simply that the majority of prisoners had been kept alive by the naive hope that they would be home again by Christmas. When Christmas came and went, they lost hope. That lowered their powers of resistance, and a great number of them died.

Leonard Griffith
Reactions to God: Man's Response to God's Activity in the Psalms

Psalm 45

Annunciation: Years A, B, C, (Alt)
Proper 9/Ordinary Time 14: Year A, verses 10-17
Proper 17/Ordinary Time 22: Year B, verses 1-2, 6-9

Why can we not see that, massive as our contemporary problems are, God's almighty act in Christ is infinitely greater?

The king's wedding

This is a song for a royal wedding. Although it has probably been preserved in the Psalter because it was applied to the messianic king and his bride Israel, it belongs to the marriage of a historical king. Who this king was is quite uncertain. Ahab has been frequently put forward, because the bride in the psalm seemed to be a princess from Tyre. Other suggestions are Solomon, Joram of Judah and even Aristobulos I. The last of these is extremely unlikely, and there is really no evidence to make any name more than a guess. . . .

'Thy throne, O God, is for ever and ever'(45:6). This cannot be an aside addressed to the Lord, as the Aramaic paraphrase understood it, but, like the rest of the section, must apply to the king. According to the RV, the king was called God. This would be unique in the Old Testament, for although the king occupied a very exalted position in ancient Israel, and as the Lord's anointed and adopted son was his representative, his person being sacrosanct and inviolable (cf. Psalm 2; 1 Samuel 26:11; 2 Samuel 7), he is never more than first among men. This interpretation therefore, would have to be explained as poetic enthusiasm perhaps influenced by the court songs from other countries of the ancient Near East. . . . If the present reading is accepted, the analogy of 'Thine eyes are doves' (i.e. 'like those of doves', Song of Songs 1:15) suggests that a literal 'Thy throne is God, for ever' is to be interpreted as 'Thy throne is everlasting like that of God'.

After expressing his eagerness to compose his song (verse 1), the poet praises the king. He possesses the bodily beauty and eloquent speech that mark a king. A mighty warrior, may he be victorious in the cause of righteousness, maintaining true justice at home. Joy and splendour adorn him (verses 2-9). Turning to the princess, he urges on her the duty of allegiance to the king, her new lord, and describes her bridal attire (verses 10-15). His final wishes are for many descendants and great renown (verses 16-17).

The strong Israelite emphasis on righteousness and justice marks this ideal of kingship (see Psalm 72). Moreover, the inclusion of this song in the Old Testament shows that nothing is secular to the Bible, save sin. Religion enters every part of life. In the same way the Song of Songs, those love poems whose eroticism was once held to be beyond the cultivated taste of western readers, bears witness to the divine acceptance of human love.

The psalm was regarded as a messianic prophecy from early times. The aramaic translation paraphrased verse 2 as, 'Thy beauty, O King Messiah, exceeds that of the children of men; a spirit of prophecy is bestowed upon thy lips,' while Hebrews 1:8-9 quotes verses 6-7 to show the superiority of Jesus to the angels. In Christian liturgical tradition it is sung on Christmas Day. Such interpretations, so far removed from the intention of the author, repel many, striking them as utterly forced and false. Yet to take this psalm and then to sing:

> My heart is full of Christ and longs,
> Its glorious matter to declare!
> Of him I make my loftier songs,
> I cannot from his praise forbear;
> My ready tongue makes haste to sing
> The glories of my heavenly King.
> (*Methodist Hymns & Psalms:* 799)

is not to cling to what is written with a blind determination which will distort and twist rather than relinquish. Rather it is to seize upon living symbols to express the light which is in Christ.

Cyril S. Rodd
Psalms 1-72

Balaam stood there looking down on the tents of Israel in the valley, this host he had been bribed to ruin. 'No,' he said to Balak, 'I cannot do it. No spell-binder or necromancer in the world could do it. For the Lord their God is with them.' And then suddenly he added this lightning word – 'And the shout of a king is among them.'

Is that not magnificently apposite for the new Israel, the Church? First, the presence of God; and now – *the victory of Christ*.

Who that knows the story of the new Israel, whose King and head is Christ, has not heard some echo of that shout reverberating across the centuries? Always it has kept breaking out anew in the great triumphant days when a Francis, a Luther, a Wesley has given the Church back its soul; always that ringing joyful confidence, like the chant of a marching host, always that shout of a King!

'Well,' you say, 'it does not seem to me that there is very much of that in the Church today. It seems to me that any such resounding triumphant conviction is conspicuous by its absence.' And then you go on to diagnose the dilemma. You say – 'There is this mounting crisis of belief of which we hear so much, hanging like a miasma over the Church's life and witness. There are the discouraging statistics providing ample material for every self-appointed prophet of pessimism and gloom. There are all the contemporary bewilderments and uncertainties, the haunting doubt about relevance and reality . . . and in the meantime the less said the better about the possibility of saving a secular society. Not much of the shout of a King there.'

If that is true – and I am not denying that there is an element of truth in such a diagnosis – it is because we have been allowing the magnitude of our problems to blind us to the majesty of our Master. Why can we not see that, massive as our contemporary problems are, God's almighty act in Christ is infinitely greater? Why do we persist in living as if 'Immanuel, God with us' were some sort of psychological self-suggestion or rhetorical mysticism, and not – as indeed it is – the most exciting and irrefragable of facts? Why are we not glorying in the Lord?

But there is also a different kind of attitude current today, equally mistaken. There is the attitude that frowns on anything like what it calls 'triumphalism' in religion. It has no desire, it will tell you, to hear in its religion the shout of a King. Anything savouring of triumphalism – from the confident and unabashed assertion of a once-for-all salvation, universally valid for ever, down to much lesser things, down even to the ordered dignity of a church procession, or a General Assembly's psalm-singing that makes the rafters ring – it labels an offence. It maintains that the really radical thing about Christianity is not the shout of a King but the cry of dereliction. It tells us that Jesus was not a sceptre-bearing monarch but the 'man for others', not the conqueror renowned but the servant girt with a towel washing men's feet; and that therefore Christianity must soft-pedal its victory songs, and tone down its soul-winning glad heroics, and mute or stop its rhapsodising about invincible world salvation. Instead of that, let it get on and be practical, with the humbler duties of secular involvement and political, economic and social humanitarianism.

There is just enough truth in this half-truth to make it dangerously misleading. It is nowhere near measuring up to the full-orbed truth of the New Testament. Certainly the apostles are not above using triumphal language when they talk of Christ. 'Every day I live,' cried Paul to the Corinthians, 'he leads me in triumph in his victory march.' 'In the world you shall have tribulation,' said Jesus, 'but I have overcome the world.' If we cannot hear the shout of a King in that – that 'I have overcome', so much more radical than the song of the modern, revolutionary 'We will overcome' – we must be deaf indeed.

James S. Stewart
King for Ever

Psalm 46

Easter Vigil: Years A, B, C
Proper 4/Ordinary Time 9: Year A
Proper 29/Ordinary Time 34: Year C

Much may fall
apart, but we
are not finally
in jeopardy.
God is faithful,
God is present,
God is powerful.
Nothing else
matters in the face
of that sure reality.

This much-loved psalm is a statement of confidence and trust, which especially counts on God's protective presence in the city of Jerusalem. Thus it was probable that it was used in the liturgy of the Temple. One of its spin-off effects is that it served to legitimate the Jerusalem political/liturgical establishment, with the Davidic dynasty understood both as the protector and the beneficiary of this place of God's sure presence.

Psalm 46 begins with an affirmation of God's protective presence, though without explicit reference to the Temple (verses 1-3). We may take verse 1 as the thesis sentence of the entire poem. God is a reliable presence and help in every trouble. Such an assertion may in part be based on the experience of the city, such as the astonishing deliverance of Jerusalem from the Assyrians in 701 BC (Isaiah 37:33-38). And no doubt the assertion is in part based on the theological claim of God's abiding presence in the Temple, which is much older than the reports of deliverance. . . .

The consequence is that worshippers in the Temple are free of anxiety, unafraid even when life becomes disordered and unstable. In this the first example of the city under threat, the anticipated assault on the city is cosmic and geological, for the Temple is understood as not only a historical but a cosmic reality (verses 2-3). The fourfold threat (the earth changing, the mountains shaking, the waters roaring, and the mountains trembling) portrays a destabilised earth. It is indeed an awesome account of the palpable threat of chaos when the creation is undone. These images may be understood literally or metaphorically and liturgically. In any case, those who trust in God's presence are unflappable. They find God's reliability more compelling that the threat that can undermine all else, all of creation, but cannot impinge on the faithfulness of God. The text is a profound assurance when life becomes unglued.

The first unit of the psalm has focused on the large picture of creation and chaos (verses 2-3). The second focuses on a military-political threat, for the fortress city of Jerusalem was endlessly exposed to such assault (verses 4-9). Verse 5 is an affirmation, not unlike verse 1. God is in the midst of Jerusalem, that is, in the Temple, so the city is safe. The city has an adequate water supply, a stream that makes the city 'glad,' a stream that has special significance for God's presence and for the sacred dimension of royal power, cf. 1 Kings 1:33-45 . . .

This time it is the raging nations that threaten; they are in fact, however, no more threat than the chaos of verses 2-3, because God's sovereign word is more than adequate to command the nations, to ensure a decree that overwhelms armies and compels the earth to obey. The Lord of creation is also the Lord of history and the nations that occupy it.

. . . The military metaphor of verse 7 is extended in the next unit of the poem (verses 8-11). The Lord does extraordinary acts of power ('works'). These acts serve to savage any enemy of Jerusalem. Thus the Lord of the troops has a capacity of halting wars (verse 9). The way of stopping wars, however, is not peaceable or benign, or simply by decree. Rather, the graphic image is of requiring a surrender, confiscating all enemy weapons (bow, spear, shield) and burning them all, so that the threatening enemy is completely disarmed (cf. Isaiah 9:5). Conflict ends because the Lord prevails and the enemy is rendered helpless and impotent.

At the conclusion, the Lord now speaks in a solemn, sovereign, first-person voice, the first time in the psalm (verse 10). The Lord now addresses the enemy nations and orders them to desist ('Be still!'). This phrase is not a pious, romantic, or spiritual utterance, as it is often construed. It is rather a harsh, imperative command, which tells the attacking enemies and the forces of chaos to stop their foolish, inappropriate, and ineffective assault on God's city and God's people. The Lord here asserts that the Lord's governance will be obeyed, acknowledged, and exalted by the very nations that must stop their misguided resistance to God's rule (see the more directly political reference to the same matter in Psalm 2:4-11). As long ago as the Pharaoh in the book of Exodus, the nations have refused to 'know' the Lord (see Exodus 5:1-2). Now, however, they will come to acknowledge the Lord as ruler; the Lord will prevail and defeat every threat.

This first-person oracle of God is answered by worshipping Israel, by the refrain repeated from verse 7. God's power and resolve evoke profound trust and confidence on the part of the Jerusalem worshipping community.

This psalm is a crucial one, given our cultural situation of dismay and anxiety. The disappearance of old structures and signals of cultural order causes us to experience the world as falling apart. A keen sense of God's powerful protective presence (of whatever constitutes our precious 'Jerusalem') permits us to experience and embrace even that disorder with freedom and equanimity. Much may fall apart, but we are not finally in jeopardy (Romans 8:37-39). God is faithful, God is present, God is powerful. Nothing else matters in the face of that sure reality.

James D. Newsome
Texts for Preaching

Faust, in the old story, gambled with his soul: and an artist has painted a picture – a game of chess, Faust at one side, Satan at the other. The game in the picture is almost over, and Faust has only a few pieces left, a king, a knight, one or two pawns; and on his face there is a look of blank despair, while at the other side of the board the devil leers in anticipation of his coming triumph. Many a chess-player has looked at the picture and agreed that the position is hopeless; it is checkmate. But one day in the picture gallery a great master of the game stood gazing at the picture. He was fascinated by the look of terrible despair on the face of Faust. Then his gaze went to the pieces on the board. He stared at them absorbed. Other visitors in the gallery came and went, and he still studied the board, lost in contemplation. And then suddenly the gallery was startled by a ringing shout: 'It is a lie! The king and the knight have another move!' This we know to be true of the human struggle; this is implicit in our proclamation of God as the Father of Jesus Christ. No matter how hopeless apparently the position, *the king and the knight have another move*.

Thus when Kierkegaard pictures Barabbas becoming a Christian, will anyone say it is fantastic and unreasonable? Even Judas – if at the eleventh hour he had gone to Calvary, if he had waited to see the Resurrection, if he had encountered the risen Christ – might have heard the word that came redeemingly to Peter: 'Lovest thou me?' This is the word which obliterates and masters and makes free. And by Christ's authority, this is the word we preach.

James S. Stewart
A Faith to Proclaim

Psalm 47

Ascension: Years A, B, C

The Lord has made a place for his people among the nations so that the nations may be included among his people.

King over all the earth

1. Psalm 47 is a hymn that praises the Lord as king. . . . The theme of the whole is: The Lord is king over all the earth (verses 2, 7 specifically). One way to describe the logic of the hymn is: The Lord has made a place for his people among the nations so that the nations may be included among his people. . . .

2. The occasion for the hymn is an event. Something has happened to which the psalm is a response. The Lord has 'gone up' (verse 5) and has assumed his throne (verse 8). In the liturgical drama of the temple the event may have been portrayed by a procession bearing the ark (24:7-10). In the royal ceremonies of the ancient Near East, when a king had mounted the dais and assumed the throne, whether on the day of his coronation or on a great state occasion, the surrounding court would acclaim the king's rule. Assuming the throne was always a symbolic assumption of rule. Representatives of his subjects would acclaim his royal identity and acknowledge his authority. The psalm provides a way for the congregation to acclaim the Lord as sovereign above all other sovereignties.

3. The hymn combines two traditions. One is the memory and interpretation of the way Israel gained its land (verses 3-4). The land is a heritage that the Lord himself chose and gave to Jacob/Israel by helping them to overwhelm the nations and peoples who were already there. The Lord did it as an expression of his love for Jacob. 'Love' is to be understood in the sense the term had in ancient Near Eastern suzerainty covenants, the favour shown vassals dependent on the great king. The other tradition is the narrative plot of Near Eastern myth about the way one god acquired sovereignty. The pattern involved subduing and defeating chaos, the assumption of kingship, and acquiring a royal place, a palace for a throne. . . . In the psalm the two are merged. The conquest of Palestine's peoples becomes the basis for the Lord's kingship, and in turn the Lord's kingship becomes the basis for his claim on all nations and peoples of the earth. The particular is the basis for the universal, and the universal draws out the meaning of the particular. The myth interprets the meaning of history.

4. The psalmic vision of the kingship of God is multidimensional. It involves history, liturgy, and myth, and so memory of the past, experience of the present, and hope for the future. Remembering the conquest as the initiative of God is the tangible point of reference. Viewing that point as a revelation that the Lord is the king of all the earth gives cosmic and eschatological meaning to it. It becomes a manifestation of what is going on behind and above the chaos of history. Celebrating the Lord's assumption of a universal rule in liturgy actualises memory and meaning for present experience. In these respects, this hymn is a paradigm for authentic understanding and celebration of the reign of God. The reign of God is never there apart from an event in the human world, but never fully there in any event. It is not purely eschatological, and yet it will be fully there in final fulfilment. It cannot be perfectly represented by any human proceedings, but it can be experienced by human beings as actuality only in praise and prayer of liturgy.

5. Notice the implicit understanding of the 'the people of God' in verse 9. The people of God are constituted, not by ethnic or national identity, but by recognition of the rule of the Lord. The notion goes back behind Sinai to Abraham and to the promise that in and through his seed all the nations of the earth would be blessed (Genesis 12:1-4). The theology of God's universal kingship in the psalm reaches back and makes contact with the universal purpose of God in the election of the ancestors. The extension of the reign of God becomes the mode of fulfilling the promise.

6. The exilic Isaiah connected the return of the Babylonian exiles to Zion to the announcement of the reign of the Lord (52:7-10). Jesus of Nazareth connected his career with the announcement of the reign of God (Mark 1:14-15). Both show how the celebration of God's rule can acquire and has acquired new historic points of reference to inform hope and liturgy. According to Jewish tradition, Psalm 47 was sung in the temple seven times before the trumpet blast inaugurating the new year. The early church used the psalm to celebrate the ascension of Jesus, a practice that is commonly followed still in the liturgy of many churches. In these liturgical contexts, the psalm declares that the reign of God is the transcendent truth about what is inaugurated in the new year and in the new era.

James L. Mays
Psalms

The Lord's rule is first of all the double work of creation and salvation. The divine king is a warrior who has overcome the unruly chaos to establish the world and has subdued the hostile powers of the world to gain a place and a people in the world. The marvellous deeds of creation and salvation make the Lord the judge of gods, nations, his people, and every life in the world. In these marvellous deeds, the holiness, power, justice and righteousness, and steadfast love and faithfulness of the Lord's kingship are made known . . .

The campaign to consummate the reign of God in the world continues. Nations rage against it; people ignore and subvert it. Opposition and conflict, enemies and adversaries are part and parcel of its present and prospect. All who seek to live in the reign of the Lord are caught in the conflict and endure the incompleteness. The people of God are afflicted. The messiah is humiliated and rejected. The faithful are undone by hostility and done in by the powers of death. The voices and roles in the psalms are defined by the situation of the conflicted reign of the Lord. The *servants* of God are those who acquire their identity in having the *Lord* as Lord. The *enemies* are their counterpart. The *righteous* are those who live and speak in ways that affirm the reign. The *wicked* are the opposite. The *lowly* (poor, needy, humble) are those who know that they are dependent on the Lord for deliverance from alienation, sin, and death. Their counterpart is composed of the arrogant, the ruthless, and the proud.

The time of the psalms is the interim. The hymns proclaim among the nations, 'The Lord reigns'. The prayers of the people of God are based on the confidence that the proclamation is true. The instruction lights the darkness of the before-times with the assurance that life and experience will ultimately vindicate the proclamation.

James L. Mays
Psalms

Psalm 48

Proper 9/Ordinary Time 14: Year B

The pilgrims make
a tour of the city
in order that they
may the better tell
their children not
only of the city
itself but of the
God of the city.

The City of the great King

This is one of the songs of Zion (see 137:3), which celebrates Jerusalem as the Holy City to which the people of God made pilgrimages for the great religious festivals. It is very closely related in thought to Psalm 46.

Mount Zion in the far north (48:1-2). Ultimately a song of Zion is always a song in praise of the God of Zion, for he gives the city its significance, and his people worship him there. Jerusalem is thought of as God's holy mountain and as a source of joy to the Jewish people scattered in so many lands. It is identified as 'Mount Zion', in the far north. Of course Jerusalem is not geographically in the far north. The phrase 'in the far north' is a reference to an ancient Babylonian and Canaanite idea that the gods assembled on a mountain in the far north (see Isaiah 14:3; Ezekiel 38:6, 15; 39:2). The psalmist throws the pagan mythology out of the window and, by his use of the expression, says that Zion is God's mountain. In other words 'in the far north' gives Jerusalem its theological location. Jerusalem is also called 'the city of the great King' (see 95:3; Matthew 5:35). 'The great King' was a title used of the kings of Assyria (see 2 Kings 18:19,28; Isaiah 36:4), but to the psalmist there is only one Great King.

God's defence of his city (48:3-8). In time past God has revealed himself as the defender of his city. Attacking kings have become panic-stricken. Probably the psalmist has in mind God's deliverance from Sennacherib in the time of Hezekiah (Isaiah 36:1-37:38) and other less spectacular events. God's delivering power is comparable to the destructive east wind as it demolishes the sturdiest vessels which sail the Mediterranean, namely, the Phoenician ships that make the journey to Tarshish in Spain. The enthusiastic reports which the pilgrims have received about Jerusalem from others are now confirmed by a visit to the Holy City. Past deliverance is a token of future security.

God's steadfast love (48:9-14). The pilgrims, as part of their worship in the Temple, have meditated on the ways in which God has shown his Covenant love to his people. God's praise extends to the ends of the earth, at least in part through the pilgrims who tell their story when they return home. It is God who has given his people victory in times past. Jerusalem and her daughter towns and cities throughout Judah are called upon to rejoice on account of his judgements that have brought deliverance to his people. The pilgrims make a tour of the city in order that they may the better tell their children not only of the city itself but of the God of the city. 'He will be our guide for ever.'

A. B. Rhodes
Psalms

He feels proud

The prevailing mood of Psalm 48 is one of unfettered pride. The psalmist sings about Jerusalem and he sings with patriotism and love. That is his reaction not only to Jerusalem itself and its glorious history but to the presence of God and to God's care and protection of the holy city. His words expressed the feelings of all the worshippers of God toward the city where God dwelt. They became a hymn of praise on the lips of pilgrims who journeyed through deserts and across seas to join in the sacred festivals.

There have been two occasions when the words of Psalm 48 came tumbling into my mind. I sensed the spirit of the psalmist the first time I caught a glimpse of the Holy City. It was in 1962 when I guided a pilgrimage of Christian people through the lands of the Bible. We started in Galilee, then drove south along the Mediterranean coast to Tel Aviv, and from there went inland. Suddenly in the distance we saw Jerusalem high on a hill. 'Stop the bus!' I shouted, much to the driver's consternation. He pulled over to the side of the road, and we became a worshipping congregation as we opened our Bibles and read in unison the familiar words, 'Beautiful for situation, the joy of the whole earth, is Mount Zion, on the sides of the north, the city of the great King.' Spiritually we were preparing ourselves to enter the beautiful city; and God seemed to be saying to us, as he said to his pilgrims long ago, 'Walk about Zion, and go round about her: tell the towers thereof. Mark ye well her bulwarks, consider her palaces; that ye may tell it to the generation following.'

Again I thought of Psalm 48 when I saw a fascinating film that was produced as part of the campaign for the restoration of Canterbury Cathedral. Prince Charles is the star of the film. With him we walk about 'Zion' and go round about her. We stand in the chancel and listen to the exquisite choir, we rest in the cloisters and talk with the Archbishop of Canterbury, we pause at the tombs of kings, we see the place where Beckett was martyred, we ascend the stone steps worn down by the feet of Canterbury pilgrims. With Charles we tell the towers thereof. He takes us up in the towers and shows us the incomparable stonework that was fashioned by the hands of dedicated craftsmen. We mark well her bulwarks, the walls, foundations and buttresses that have stood the storms of fourteen centuries. We consider her palaces as we join the worshipping congregation and listen to the young Prince read a lesson from Proverbs. The whole film tells the story of historic Canterbury to a new generation. 'Tell it to the generation following.'

Christians are proud of Jerusalem and Canterbury, yet their most sacred pride is directed not to a single city or to a single building but to the whole structure of God's Church on earth. In that sense they share the reaction of the psalmist.

Leonard Griffith
Reactions to God: Man's Response to God's Activity in the Psalms

Psalm 49

Proper 13/Ordinary Time 18: Year C, verses 1-12

Treasure is in knowing that you are loved and that you love because you are loved.

Foolish confidence and true confidence

A wisdom psalm, akin to 37 and 73, considers the problem of the prosperity of the rich. After an introduction (verses 1-4), in which the psalmist calls on all men to hear his discussion of life's riddle, the psalm falls into two sections, each ending with a refrain (verses 5-12, 13-20). The writer has pondered much upon this problem, and now he has set to music thoughts which came to him as if by direct inspiration. . . .

Psalm 49:6

Compare Psalm 52:7; 62:10; Job 31:24-24; Ecclesiasticus 11:18-19; Mark 10:17-27; Luke 6:24; 12:13-21; 16:19-31; James 5:1-6. The frequent emphasis in the Scriptures on the dangers of riches gives little comfort to those in the West, for we are the rich, at whose gate Lazarus lies, and who have so exalted the bourgeois virtues that envy, avarice and greed are not even recognised as sins. Property tends to be ranked above persons, finance governs most policies, and the comforts of wealth are a sore drag on the spiritual quest.

Cyril S. Rodd
Psalms 1-72

In a sermon called 'When Too Much Is Not Enough', Peter Gomes, described by *Time* magazine as one of the top seven preachers in modern America, meditates on wealth. He uses in part Jesus' parable of the wealthy farmer in Luke 12 who, after a superb harvest, decides to tear down his barns and build greater ones. Then he proposes to eat, drink and be merry.

Peter Gomes says that the farmer made two mistakes. First, he assumed that his good fortune would continue. For the second, he assumed that his good fortune would not only continue, but that it would also increase so that every day that passed would make him even wealthier. Here is Peter Gomes:

Now that second error is compounded when [the farmer] believes that he himself has done all the work that produces this prosperity, and thus he can now live off the profits; yesterday's profits yielding tomorrow's ease. 'Soul, you have ample goods laid up for many years; take your ease, eat, drink, be merry' (Luke 12:19). Notice that there is a phrase missing, one that you heard in that wonderfully secular classical aphorism: 'Eat, drink, and be merry, for tomorrow we must die.' This is no Epicurean enterprise; he doesn't expect to die tomorrow, he expects to live on forever and forever, eating and drinking and being more merry and living off more income compounded daily. What he has he believes he has earned; it belongs to him and is for him to enjoy and to dispose of as he will. He can now afford to relax and to rest for he is what he has accumulated. The work and the worker and the results of the work have all become one and the same. That is where his identity is, that is where his enterprise is, and that is where his reward is, here and now. None of this postponing pleasure until tomorrow, none of this waiting for heaven to be rewarded; no, 'I have done it, and here it is.'

Here Jesus says, 'Fool,' and in the Bible 'fool' means one who does not acknowledge the existence of God. 'Fool!' he says. 'This night your soul is required of you . . .' You will be foreclosed upon tonight even though you don't have a mortgage. You will be foreclosed upon tonight, 'and the things you have prepared, whose will they be?' (Luke 12:20).

These things that you have accumulated and laid up and invested in, whose will they be? Here is where the silence of the text speaks vividly, because they will not be yours. What will become of those bonds and those surpluses? You are rich in the world but when the world ends and you with it, what will you have if you are not rich toward God?

The one who is rich toward God, Jesus says, is the one who recognises here and now that treasure is not in what one has, or even in what one leaves or gives away, or even in what one does. Those are not riches. Treasure is in who one is, and ultimately that treasure is defined in terms of the relationship one has with God. Treasure is knowing that one belongs not to self, or to work, or vocation, or ambition, but that one belongs to God. You don't belong to your talent or to your skill or identity in the world. Treasure is knowing that you belong to God; treasure is knowing that therefore you are not alone. You are not isolated, you are not on your own. Treasure is in knowing that you are loved and that you love because you are loved, and that knowledge of self and relationship and purpose is what treasure is all about. Treasure means rich in relationship to God, that which the world cannot give and which therefore the world and all of its adversities and all of its trials and tribulations cannot take away. The one who would then be truly rich is the one who cultivates that treasure, that knowledge, and who does so with all the effort that other people use to cultivate earthly but perishable goods. So that when you leave 'everything' as we all most certainly will leave everything, you can take 'it' with you, for it is the only thing you ever truly had, and that is the love of God.

Peter J. Gomes
Sermons: Biblical Wisdom for Daily Living

Psalm 50

Last Sunday of Epiphany/Transfiguration: Year B,
*   verses 1-6*
Proper 5/Ordinary Time 10: Year A, verses 7-15
Proper 14/Ordinary Time 19: Year C, verses 1-8,
*   22-23*

Even when he spoke, Jesus created silence. Many of his sayings were so cryptic that no response was possible, while others were so offensive that replies were withheld.

The opening verses of this psalm (verses 1-6) form part of a call to worship that constitutes an affirmation of the coming of the Lord to judge the people. The remainder of the psalm is composed of speeches of the Lord to the worshippers, placing them under judgement and condemnation. The psalm thus appears clearly to have been part of a liturgy of judgement carried out in the context of worship, perhaps a service of covenant renewal or of national lamentation. Some officiating priest perhaps spoke verses 1-6, and a prophet proclaimed the judgement of God in the remainder of the psalm. The psalm speaks of the presence of awesome phenomena as attendant upon the coming of God – devouring fire and mighty tempest. Such descriptions were at home in speech about the Lord's presence in theophanies, especially about the theophany at Sinai (Exodus 19:16-19). Just as God appeared at Sinai when the law was given with the accompaniment of unusual phenomena, so in similar terminology Psalm 50 describes the appearance of the Deity to judge his people.

The psalm opens with a piling up of divine names – El (Mighty One), Elohim (God), Yahweh (The Lord). This three-fold ascription of names, which stresses the honorific power of the Divine, is followed by a threefold summons to assemble for judgement. God summons the earth (verse 1), then the heavens and the earth (verse 4), and finally 'my faithful ones' (verse 5), the members of the covenant community. The heavens and the earth are to appear as witnesses to the proclamation of judgement that follows, for they, as permanent features of the world, are also witnesses to the initial giving of the law and the demands for obedience.

John H. Hayes
Preaching Through the Christian Year: Year A

'*Our God comes, he does not keep silence*' (Psalm 50:3a). The 1997 Lyman Beecher Lectures on Preaching were given by the Reverend Barbara Brown Taylor and published under the title *When God Is Silent*. This short passage from the flyleaf helps set the scene: 'Silence has become God's final defence against our idolatry. By limiting our speech, God gets some relief from our descriptive assaults. By hiding inside a veil of glory, God eludes our projections. God deflects our attempts at control by withdrawing into silence, knowing that nothing gets us like the failure of our speech.'

Later on in the book Barbara Taylor says: 'It is no coincidence, I think, that so much of the literature on the silence of God has been written by Jews. *The Exile of the Word; From the Silence of the Bible to the Silence of Auschwitz* by Andre Neher. *The Disappearance of God* by Richard Elliott Friedman. *In Speech and in Silence: The Jewish Quest for God* by David Wolpe. *The Eclipse of God* by Martin Buber. Each of these writers is a Holocaust survivor, even if he never set foot in a camp. Each writes with the knowledge that the sky can grow dark with smoke from burning human bodies without so much as a whimper from God.

For some survivors, this knowledge has resulted in a relinquishment of God. For these particular writers, it has resulted more in what I would call a relinquishment of certain language about God. As Buber makes clear, the divine eclipse does not mean that God is dead, as rumour had it in the sixties. 'An eclipse of the sun is something that occurs between the sun and our eyes,' he explains, 'not in the sun itself.' He goes on to suggest that what blocks the sun from our eyes is the radical subjectivism of our age, in which our knowledge of God is limited by our language. As 'pure Thouness,' he says, 'God is not objectifiable. Words serve only as mute gestures pointing to the irreducible, ineffable dimension where God subsists.'

If he is right, as I believe he is, then what about the Word made flesh? If God is more present in silence than in words, if our best words cannot aspire to more than pointing toward the God who is beyond them, then what are we to make of the Incarnate Word? Jesus could have come to us as the Incarnate Silence, after all, or as the Incarnate Mystery. That he was revealed to John as the Incarnate Word seems to assert the sayability of God in a whole new way. In Jesus the silent God found a voice. In Jesus the irreducible God took on a human body. And those of us who believe it assume responsibility for proclaiming it so that others might believe it too. Our relationship to the Word requires us to use words. Our vocation is not only to do what the Word told us to do but also to say what the Word told us to say, until the whole world is transformed by the news.

As I said earlier, this has had the effect of making Christianity an overly talkative religion, but the truth is that silence plays as central a role in Christian scripture as in Hebrew. In each of the gospels, the Word comes forth from silence. For John, it is the silence at the beginning of creation. For Luke, it is the silence of poor old Zechariah, struck dumb by the angel Gabriel for doubting that Elizabeth would bear a child. For Matthew, it is the awkward silence between Joseph and Mary when she tells him her prenuptial news, and for Mark it is the voice of one crying in the wilderness – the long-forgotten voice of prophecy puncturing the silence of the desert and of time.

Silence was the backdrop against which the Word began to be heard. While Jesus stood in the wings, John the Baptist prepared the way, using such ferocious language that many must have expected a fire-breathing messiah to drop from the sky. Instead it was Jesus who came among them, making so little noise that even John did not know who he was at first. Even when he spoke, Jesus created silence. Many of his sayings were so cryptic that no response was possible, while others were so offensive that replies were withheld. 'Love your enemies, do good to those who hate you, bless those who curse you, pray for those who abuse you' (Luke 6:27-28). Any questions?

Barbara Brown Taylor
When God Is Silent

Psalm 51

Ash Wednesday: Years A, B, C, verses 1-17
Fifth Sunday of Lent: Year B, verses 1-12 (Alt)
Proper 13/Ordinary Time 18: Year B, verses 1-12
Proper 19/Ordinary Time 24: Year C, verses 1-10

Say that this is my grief . . . and I must bear it. Look at it hard enough and say, 'How can I transform this liability into an asset?'

This psalm is one of the highest expressions of real religion ever reached in the Old Testament. It is the cry of a man who in the very depths of his heart recognises his own sin. Remember that it is the good man who most deeply feels his own sin. Paul spoke of himself as 'the chief of sinners'. The nearer a man approaches to God the more he realises his own unworthiness. The psalmist, as he compares life with what it ought to be, is humbled by a sense of his own sin. But it is in the offering that he must make to God that he rises to his greatest height. Inevitably the idea had crept into Jewish religion that sin could be atoned for by some kind of sacrifice, and that if a man offered the right sacrifice to God he could, as it were, make his peace with God. With that the psalmist completely agrees; but the sacrifice which he knows a man must offer is not an animal upon the altar, but the sacrifice of a broken and contrite heart.

William Barclay
Seven Fresh Wineskins

The quality of mercy is not strain'd;
it droppeth, as the gentle rain from heaven
upon the place beneath: it is twice blessed;
it blesseth him that gives, and him that takes.
'Tis mightiest in the mightiest; it becomes
the throned monarch better than his crown:
his sceptre shows the force of temporal power,
the attribute to awe and majesty,
wherein doth sit the dread and fear of kings;
but mercy is above his sceptred sway,
it is enthroned in the hearts of kings,
it is an attribute to God himself;

and earthly power doth then show likest God's
when mercy seasons justice.

William Shakespeare
The Merchant of Venice, IV. i. 179.

And Sunday after Sunday, week after week, people come to
God's church with broken hearts. They need a word of hope.
And the church has an answer – if it doesn't, it isn't a church.
The church must say in substance that brokenheartedness
is a fact of life. Don't try to escape when you come to that
experience. Don't try to repress it. Don't end up in cynicism.
Don't get mean when you come to that experience. . . . The
church must say to men and women that Good Friday . . . is
a fact of life. The church must say to people that failure is a
fact of life. Some people are only conditioned to success. They
are only conditioned to fulfilment. Then when the trials and
burdens of life unfold, they can't stand up with it. But the
church must tell men . . . that Good Friday's as much a fact
of life as Easter; failure is as much a fact of life as success;
disappointment is as much a fact of life as fulfilment. And
the church must tell men, 'Take your burden, . . . take your
grief and look at it, don't run from it.' Say, 'This is my grief . . .
and I must bear it.' Look at it hard enough and say, 'How can
I transform this liability into an asset?'

This is the power that God gives you. He doesn't say that
you're going to escape tension; he doesn't say that you're
going to escape disappointment; he doesn't say that you're
going to escape trials and tribulations. But what religion does
say is this: that if you have faith in God, that God has the
power . . . to give you a kind of inner equilibrium through
your pain. So let not your heart be troubled. . . . 'If ye believe
in God, ye believe also in me.' Another voice rings out, 'Come
unto me, all ye that labour . . . and are heavy laden.' As if to
say, 'Come unto me, all ye that are burdened down. Come
unto me, all ye that are frustrated. Come unto me, all ye with
clouds of anxiety floating in your mental skies. Come unto
me, all ye that are broken down. . . . Come unto me, all ye
that are heartbroken. Come unto me, all ye that are laden
with heavy loads, and I will give you rest.' And the rest that
God gives is the rest that passeth all understanding. . . . The
world doesn't understand that kind of rest, because it's a rest

that makes it possible for you to stand up amid outer storms, and yet you maintain inner calm. If the church is true to its guidelines, it heals the broken-hearted.

'A Knock at Midnight'
from *The Great Sermons of Martin Luther King, Jr.*

Psalm 52

Proper 11/Ordinary Time 16: Year C

Christian hope can only be so much beating of the air unless we are sustained by some vision which can set alight our minds, excite our imagination and nerve our faith.

Unlike most other psalms, Psalm 52 is neither prayer nor praise directed to God. Rather, verses 1-5 are addressed to a 'mighty one' – apparently a wicked, powerful person who intends to do violence to the psalmist and perhaps others of 'the righteous' (verse 6) or 'the faithful' (verse 9). Verse 6 is an affirmation about the righteous, who are then quoted in verse 7. Verse 8 is the psalmist's profession of faith. Only in verse 9 is God addressed directly. The uniqueness of Psalm 52 means that it 'resists form – critical analysis'; it is sometimes categorised as a prophetic exhortation or 'communal instruction' . . . the content of this exhortation or instruction focuses on the nature of true security, wealth, and power.

The alternatives for seeking security are clearly contrasted in verse 1. . . . Marvin Tate translates verse 1 as follows:

Why brag about evil, you hero!

– God's loyal love (*hesed*) does not cease.

As this translation and the subsequent verses suggest, security may be sought in self-assertion at the expense of others. This is what the 'mighty one' does; he has no qualms about lying, cheating, and stealing in order to get ahead (see the description of the perpetrators of evil in Amos 8:4-6, part of the Old Testament lesson for the day). In Tate's translation, 'hero' is used sarcastically; others suggest the derisive term 'big shot'. In any case, this person *loves* (verses 3, 4) 'evil' (verse 3; the word 'mischief' in verse 1 is the same Hebrew root) and is willing to use any means to get his or her own way, regardless of how destructive . . . or manipulative. . . . The 'mighty one' shows no concern for doing what is 'good' (verse 3; see also verse 9 and Psalms 34:15; 37:3, 27; Amos 5:14-15; and Micah 3:2) or speaking what is 'right'. . . . As James L. Mays puts it, 'The portrait is that of a person who turns human capacities and possession into the basis of his existence' . . . In short, the 'mighty one' embodies what is the essence of wickedness in the Psalms – autonomy – 'self-rule'. . .

The alternative to autonomy is dependence on God and God's *hesed* (verse 1; 'steadfast love,' 'loyal love'). Verse 1 already suggests that this alternative is the only true and enduring one, and verse 5 tells why (see Psalm 73:18-20). The affirmation that God 'will uproot' the wicked anticipates the image of the psalmist as a stable, fruitful tree in 52:8, which also contains the psalmist's explicit assertion that she or he has chosen the proper alternative – 'I trust in the steadfast love of God for ever and ever.' The psalmist knows the secret of life that has eluded the wicked: life depends ultimately upon God, not on ourselves and our possessions (see Luke 12:13-21, especially verse 15). . . .

The punishment of the wicked is that they cut themselves off from God, who is the source of life, and the reward of the righteous is that they are grounded in God and thus connected to life's source and destiny.

Verse 8 of Psalm 52 articulates the psalmist's connection to the source of life. Like a tree growing on the Temple grounds, the psalmist is rooted in God (see Psalms 1:3; 92:12-15; Jeremiah 17:5-8). In explicit contrast to the 'might one', the psalmist's trust is placed not in the self or in riches, but in God's *hesed*, which is for ever and ever (52:8; see verse 1; and note 'for ever' in verse 5). Consequently, while the existence of the wicked is characterised by greed (verses 2-4, 7), the life of the psalmist is characterised by gratitude to God (verse 9) – of God's 'name' or character. Thus, he or she promotes the 'good' that the wicked spurn (verses 3, 9). The NRSV's 'proclaim' is literally 'wait for', 'hope'. The psalmist is an example of those who, surrounded by opposition, live by faith and hope.

J. Clinton McCann, Jr
Texts for Preaching, Year C

As the last sentence of the above excerpt stresses the psalmist's faith and hope, I append some quotes on those themes. (R. D.)

Faith enables us to get free from:

The domination of place and time, for it gives the additional dimension of the spiritual and the eternal.

The domination of happenings, for we are not at the mercy of circumstances, but can draw upon the inexhaustible wisdom and grace of God.

The domination of the written word, for we do not identify it with the inerrant word of God, but test it by the incarnate word.

The domination of theology, for men's thoughts about God change, and our theories, however good, are seen to be imperfect.

The domination of puritanism, for we see that truth and love must be decisive about action.

The domination of conscience, for conscience constantly needs educating from our growing knowledge of God.

George Appleton
Journey for a Soul

Christian hope can only be so much beating of the air unless we are sustained by some vision which can set alight our minds, excite our imagination and nerve our faith. This is the Church for which I often weep and at which I sometimes rage and am often tempted to quit. But it is still the guardian of a gospel without which mankind would be robbed of hope.

Colin Morris
The Hammer of the Lord

'Thy kingdom come'

What is our hope concerning this world in which we are now living? Certainly Christ encourages us to have hope concerning it. We are to pray, 'Thy kingdom come on earth', and so to hope that God's rule may become apparent in the world everywhere.

Thus we hope to see races free from injustice to one another, for racial strife is a denial of the divine image in man. We hope to see nations so using the earth's resources and economic structures that all may have enough to eat, instead of some being affluent while others starve. We hope to see war, and the possibility of war, banished. We hope to see family life everywhere secure and stable, happy and unselfish, with sex fulfilling its true use in lifelong marriage. We hope to see chastity, honesty, and compassion prevail. We hope to see these things happen as part of a deep reconciliation between man and God through Jesus Christ. We hope to see people everywhere brought into fellowship with God through him. In all this we hold in one our hope about earth and our hope about heaven. A Christian can scarcely separate these hopes, as Jesus is the Lord of both earth and heaven.

Through the Year with Michael Ramsey
ed. Margaret Duggan

Psalm 54

Proper 20/Ordinary Time 25: Year B

Vengeance must be fully recognised as present, fully owned as my rage, and fully expressed with as much power and intensity as possible.

God is my helper

The detailed background of this personal lament is difficult to reconstruct. Apparently the psalmist's life is in danger from false accusation, and he is seeking God's vindication at the sanctuary (see 1 Kings 8:31-32). In any case he is seeking God's intervention on his behalf.

Appeal for vindication (54:1-2). The psalm begins with the appeal typical of laments. The parallelism between 'save' and 'vindicate' in verse 1 shows that the salvation for which the psalmist prays is vindication. The parallelism between 'name' and 'might' suggest that God's name is mighty to save.

The reason for the appeal (54:3). The reason for the appeal is that ruthless men are seeking the psalmist's life. These men 'do not set God before them' in terms of doing his will or fearing his judgements. They are practical atheists (see 10:4; 53:1).

Assurance and petition (54:4-5). Because God is his helper, the psalmist feels assured that God will vindicate him by causing their plotted evil to recoil upon his enemies, and in this confidence he petitions God to destroy them.

A vow to thank God (54:6-7). In response to God's deliverance of him the psalmist promises to make a freewill offering to God, accompanied by thanksgiving. A freewill offering was a kind of peace offering for which there was no binding legal requirement (Exodus 35:29; 36:3-5; Leviticus 7:16); it was a free expression of gratitude. Vengeance upon his enemies, which the psalmist heartily desires (verses 5, 7) at the hand of God, is not primarily a matter of personal animosity but would be understood by the psalmist as a manifestation of God's righteousness and faithfulness with the proverbial 'three score years and ten'.

A. B. Rhodes
Psalms

Dealing with one's enemies and vengeance are themes of this and many other psalms. So here follows a piece, one of the finest I have read, on vengeance, human and divine:

The most troublesome dimension of the psalms is the agenda of vengeance. It may also be the most theologically poignant, as we hope to show. The cry for retaliation at one's enemies at least surprises us. We do not expect to find such a note in 'religious' literature. It may offend us, and it does not fit very well in our usual notions of faith, piety, or spirituality. To some extent, we are prepared for it by our recognition . . . that the psalms reflect unabashed concreteness, candour, and passion. The psalms explore the full gamut of human experience from rage to hope. Indeed, it would be very strange if such a robust spirituality lacked such a dimension of vengeance, for we would conclude that just at the crucial point, robustness had turned to cowardice and propriety. The vitality of the psalms, if without a hunger for vengeance, would be a cop-out. But we need have no fear of that. There is no such failure of nerve, no backing down from this religion on the brink of stridency. Thus the expression of vengeance is not unnatural, unexpected, or inappropriate. But that in no way diminishes its problematic character.

The reality of vengeance. Let us begin with two acts of realism. First, *the yearning for vengeance is there in the psalms.* It is there, without embarrassment, apology, or censor. Whatever we say on the subject must be linked to that undeniable fact. We are not free to explain it away. If we are genuinely to pray the psalms, we must try to understand what is happening in such acts of piety. Certainly no expurgated, 'selective' version of the psalms will do. For that is only to push the problem away. Such 'selectivity' does not avoid the presence of the motif. Indeed, selective avoidance will cause us to miss the resources that we may find there.

The counterpart, a second act of realism, is that *the yearning for vengeance is here, among us and within us* and with power. It is not only *there* in the psalms, but it is *here* in the human heart and the human community. When we know ourselves as well as the psalter knows us, we recognise that we are creatures who wish for vengeance and retaliation. We wish in every way we can to be right and, if not right, at least stronger. Perhaps we do not engage in child abuse or spouse abuse, and we do not urge the death penalty (at least not all of us do). But in lesser ways, we assault verbally or we nurse affronts, waiting for their reversal and satisfaction. It could be that for some few, these passions are absent, or that, for more of us they are absent on occasion. But we must not be so romantic as to imagine we have outgrown the eagerness for retaliation. While developmental psychology may discern other more positive yearnings as an ideal, theological realism cannot afford such deception. The real theological problem, I submit, is not that vengeance is *there* in the psalms, but that it is *here* in our midst. And what is there *and* here only reflects how attuned the psalter is to what goes on among us. Thus, we may begin with a recognition of the acute correspondence between what is *written there* and what is *practised here*. The psalms do 'tell it like it is' with us.

. . . Psalm 109 surely engages in 'overkill' in its wishes and prayers against the 'wicked'. . . . Such imagination in which the speaker strains to be vivid and venomous and almost exhibitionist surely performs several functions:

a. It is no doubt *cathartic*. We need not flinch from the thera- peutic value of the psalms. In our heavily censored society, this is one place left in which it may all be spoken.

b. But it is more than cathartic. More than simply giving expression to what we have felt and known all along. In genuine rage, words do not simply follow feelings. They lead them. It is speech that lets us discover the power, depth, and intensity of the hurt. The psalms are acts of self- discovery that penetrate the façade of sweet graciousness.

c. The psalms serve to legitimate and affirm these most intense elements of rage. In such speech, we discover that our words (and feelings) do not destroy the enemy, that is, they are not as dangerous as we thought. Nor do our words bring judgement from heaven on us. The world (or God) is not as censorious as we feared. Such speech puts rage in perspective. Our feelings brought to speech are not as dangerous or as important as we imagined, as we wished, or as we feared. When they are unspoken, they loom too large, and we are condemned by them. When spoken, our intense thoughts and feelings are brought into a context in which they can be discerned differently. Notice that in Psalm 109, after the long recital of rage through verse 19, the intensity is spent. Then the speaker must return to the reality of heart and fear and helplessness in verses 22-25. The rage is a prelude to the real agenda of attitudes about oneself. . . .

Vengeance must be fully recognised as present, fully owned as my rage, and fully expressed with as much power and intensity as possible. . . .

This full rage and bitterness is yielded to God's wisdom and providential care.

Walter Brueggemann
Praying the Psalms

Psalm 62

Third Sunday of Epiphany/Ordinary Time 3: Year B, verses 5-12

At least, give God a chance.

A large part of the ability of this psalm to communicate with people in all ages lies in the manner in which it bespeaks both confidence in the power of God and a lack of confidence in the psalmist's own ability to persevere. The references to human frailty are obvious (verse 9), but it requires close attention to understand that the poet includes himself in the category of those who are *hebel* (breath). He must command his soul to be patient (verse 5), and his final words are stated in a mode not so much of affirmation, as of supplication (verse 12). Apart from God's strength, the psalmist cannot be sure of anything about himself except his own weakness.

It is therefore on the power of God that the writer focuses. Notice the string of epithets for God in verses 5-7: God is my hope; my rock; my salvation; my fortress; my deliverance; my honour; my mighty rock; my refuge.

This list is followed by other descriptive terms: a refuge (verse 8); power (verse 11); steadfast love (verse 12).

The superscription of the psalm contains the name of David, and, while there is nothing within the text of the poem to reflect directly upon David's life, the stories in the Old Testament of Israel's greatest king are illustrative of those meanings which the psalm intends to convey. One remembers David's fear before Saul (1 Samuel 21:10), yet his unwillingness to lay his hands on the Lord's anointed (24:6). Or again, David's fear for the life of his child, but his continued trust in God after the child's death (2 Samuel 12:15-23). There is a sense in which David is Everyman/Everywoman – or at least, every man and woman who is open to an encounter with God – exhibiting weakness and self-doubt on the one hand, but confidence in God on the other. Such is the life of the person of faith.

James D. Newsome
Texts for Preaching

142

I asked God for strength, that I might do greater things,
I was made weak, that I might learn humbly to obey . . .
I asked for health, that I might do greater things,
I was given infirmity, that I might do better things . . .
I asked for riches, that I might be happy,
I was given poverty, that I might be wise . . .
I asked for power, that I might have the praise of men,
I was given weakness, that I might feel the need of God . . .
I asked for all things, that I might enjoy life,
I was given life, that I might enjoy all things . . .
I got nothing that I asked for – but everything that I had
    hoped for,
Almost despite myself, my unspoken prayers were answered,
I am among all men, most richly blessed.

Unknown Confederate soldier. His words can be seen cast in bronze in the lobby of the Institute of Physical Medicine and Rehabilitation in New York City.

Hope and safety, security and strength were constantly being sought by the men I used to visit on a daily basis in the segregation units of the different prisons I served as chaplain.

Each 'seg' unit housed men who in one way and another had broken prison rules. They had appeared before the Governor (now called Head of Inmate Security) and had been sentenced to a period in the unit. One of my Statutory duties was to visit the 'seg' each day. Quite often there would be some violent inmates, some there for their own safety, some in for murder and therefore Category A prisoners and others who were known escapees. With the very violent inmate I had to have a two-man escort for safety reasons.

Of all the men I met in nine years service, two stand out. One because he threatened suicide and the other because of his bleak past, present and future.

I was in my office one day in a Devon prison when the telephone rang. 'Can you come quick to the "seg" unit, an inmate is going to "top" himself' (commit suicide). I rushed down, saw the duty officer, and was shown into the inmate's cell.

He was sitting with his head in his hands on a mattress on the floor. His story was a very sad one. His third child had just died after only a few weeks of life and the previous two children had also died very young. Apart from all this he had terrible guilt problems, but did not know how to approach God, frame a prayer, and ask for pardon for his past evil deeds. So I listened to his story, offered a prayer and left him feeling much better, promising me not to even consider suicide again.

The other inmate I first met in the 'seg' unit of a South Yorkshire prison. Some of his first words to me were, 'Chaplain, I can't sink any lower. I've just heard that my wife has left me, with the children. Now I have no home of my own, no job prospects on release, no friends on the 'out' who come to visit me. On top of all this, here I am in the 'seg', bottom of the pile.'

I listened to all this sitting on his bed and asked if he had any faith in God. 'Do you believe that there is a God and that he cares for you?' I asked. 'Well, when I was a kid I used to go to Sunday School, but I soon grew out of that, and I've never been near a church since.'

My response was to leave him with a few simple stepping stones back to God, such as telling God about his past and his present; asking his pardon for the past; asking for Divine help to sort out the mess he was in. 'At least, give God a chance,' were my parting words. 'I'll see you next week.'

On my return the following week, I was absolutely astonished at the transformation in the man. He looked 20 years younger, he was smiling and at peace. 'I didn't do everything you said, Chaplain, but God did pardon me, and I feel great. I've got purpose and hope back, thanks a lot.'

Each of these men, I believe, would have gladly taken the words of the psalmist in Psalm 62 for their own: 'In God alone there is rest for my soul, from him comes my safety; with him alone for my rock, my safety, my fortress, I can never fall.' (Psalm 62:1-2)

Ron Dale, 1999

Psalm 63

Third Sunday of Lent: Year C, verses 1-8

It is not given to all to have such faith; but even to hear of it is an inspiration, and an incentive to draw nearer to God.

'Thy steadfast love is better than life'

Deep longing for God and trust in his love are strikingly apparent in this prayer of one persecuted and afflicted.

Psalm 63:1; 'Early will I seek thee.' So the Greek version translated this verb, connecting it with the word for morning. Hence this psalm was widely used in the Christian Church as a morning hymn. Chrysostom says, 'The Fathers of the Church appointed it to be said every morning, as a spiritual song and a medicine to blot out our sins; to kindle in us a desire of God; to raise our souls, and inflame them with a mighty fire of devotion; to make us overflow with goodness and love, and send us with such preparation to approach and appear before God.' Although the verb probably means 'seek' simply, the words of Chrysostom well express the value of the psalm for the devotional life.

The exact setting of this lament is uncertain. Some suppose that the first verse indicates that the psalmist is an exile, but the words are probably metaphorical and reveal his feeling of desolation . . .

No one can miss the eagerness with which this psalmist looks for God. With all his being he thirsts for him and faints with longing. In the past he has experienced the Lord's power and glory in the temple (verse 2). It was not only the great prophet to whom the temple became resplendent with God's glory. This psalm shows that the ordinary Israelite could have the same sense of the divine majesty.

Verse 3 is the most precious gem in a psalm that is rich with treasures. Its setting in ancient Israel enhances its splendour. In an age when death meant the end of all that was of value and the passing into the gloom of Sheol, and among a people who saw God's richest blessing in a long and prosperous life, this psalm asserts that better even than life itself is the Lord's unwavering love. Here is security. Here is the sure foundation.

Hence he turns to glad thanksgiving and joyous praise. As throughout the New Testament, the thought of God's grace brings a man inevitably to a thanksgiving which not only drives out sadness but also quells all fears. The enemies and their threatenings are forgotten in the wonder of God's goodness. A feeling of security that is free from all anxiety is given by the conviction of God's nearness. 'It is not given to all to have such faith; but even to hear of it is an inspiration, and an incentive to draw nearer to God.' (Oesterley)

Cyril S. Rodd
Psalms 1-72

Trust in God

The spirit of God spoke to me and said: 'Go in the name of Jesus. I will go with you to help and support you in all you do. Trust me, you have never found me wanting. I will never ask you to do anything that is unacceptable to God.'

'I am your God and I delight in you, we shall never be parted. All the promises I have made to you will come true at the right time.' The Lord Jesus Christ who is always ready to help and never deserts those who truly love him, said, 'Do not be afraid, I will give you all you need.'

I know the Lord will help because he has never failed me wherever I have been. I have complete trust in him.

Margery Kempe
quoted in *The Joy of the Saints*

All manner of thing shall be well

One time, our good Lord said: 'All things shall be well.' And another time, he said: 'You shall see yourself that all manner of thing shall be well.' The soul understood several things from these sayings.

One was this: That it is his will that we should understand that not only does he take care of great and noble things but also of little and humble things, simple and small – both one and the other. And this is what he means when he says: 'All manner of thing shall be well.' For he wants us to understand that the smallest thing shall not be forgotten.

Something else I understood was this: That we see such evil deeds done, and such great harm caused by them, that it seems to us that it is impossible that any good deed should come out of them. And we look on them, sorrowing and mourning over them, so that we cannot find rest in the joyful sight of God as we ought to.

The trouble is this – that the range of our thinking is now so blinkered, so little and small, that we cannot see the high, wonderful wisdom and power and goodness of the blessed Trinity. And this is what he means when he says: 'You shall see for yourself that all manner of thing shall be well.' It was as if he said: 'Have faith, and have trust, and at the last day you shall see it all transformed into great joy.'

Julian of Norwich
quoted in *The Joy of the Saints*

Psalm 65

Thanksgiving: Year A
Proper 10/Ordinary Time 15: Year A, verses (1-8),
9-13
Proper 25/Ordinary Time 30: Year C

Power by itself might be a callous thing; love by itself might be a helpless thing. But God's love is backed by his power; and God's power is motivated by his love.

There are three thoughts in this psalm.

1. Verses 5-8 speak of God's greatness in the events of history. God bends circumstances to his will and shows his power in such a way that all men must stand in awe of him.

2. Verses 9-13 speak of the greatness of God in nature. The things by which man lives are the gifts of God; without the providence of God man would die, for the very processes of nature which give us food are in the hands of God.

3. Yet it is to this God who is supreme in history, this God whose greatness is seen in nature, that the prayers of men ascend. He welcomes his children to his presence.

God is love *and* power. Power by itself might be a callous thing; love by itself might be a helpless thing. But God's love is backed by his power; and God's power is motivated by his love.

For meditation: when I pray, do I remember the love and the power of God? I cannot ask too much from God, if my asking is in accordance with his will.

William Barclay
Seven Fresh Wineskins

Very few psalms for community thanksgiving are found in the psalter (see Psalms 67, 92, 107). A hymn may have served as the community's response to specific acts of divine providence, and thus no great need existed for writing special thanksgiving psalms. Psalm 65 is probably one of the exceptional psalms for communal thanksgiving.

All of the psalm is direct address to the Deity, although some scholars see a radical change of tone between verses 1-4 and verse 5 following. Some even argue for three psalms

(1-4, 5-8, 9-13). The composition appears, however, to be a unity, and the elements of sin, creation, and divine blessing of the crops/harvest noted in the text are not so unrelated.

Verses 1-4 focus on the human admission and divine forgiveness of sin. . . .

1. The occasion for the celebration and the praise of God is the fulfilment of vows. These may have been vows made to be carried out if certain conditions were met by God, such as providing a good crop year or forgiving sins, probably the latter. Moderns look judgementally on vows or deals with God, or at least we publicly express ourselves that way. Ancient Israel was unashamed of such arrangements.

2. A public, communal acknowledgement of sin is made. A basic feature of Israelite religion was a routine day of national repentance (Yom Kippur). Other days of repentance were held when deemed necessary. The minister who preaches on this psalm should imaginatively think about what such days of national repentance might do in contemporary culture, where admitting wrong and guilt is itself considered to be a national sin.

3. Worship in the temple is viewed as an exhilarating source of joy and blessedness. The goodness of the temple (verse 4c) probably refers to the sacrificial feasts eaten in the temple in conjunction with thanksgiving. (The covered-dish dinner has a long genealogy and a most sumptuous ancestry!)

In verses 5-8, the psalm shifts focus on the divine creation of the cosmos and the establishment of order in the world. Chaos is represented by the seas, the waves, the people (and the roaring and tumult). Over against these, God establishes, stills, and pacifies so that the regularity of nature in which the mornings and evenings follow each other provides successive shouts for joy. The verses in the psalm most reflective of the theme of thanksgiving as an agricultural festival are verses 9-13. The entire cycle of the harvest year is reflected in these verses. There is reference, first, to the autumn rains (called the early rains) that water the ground and make ploughing and sowing possible. In Palestine, the summer, from about mid-May until late September or early October, is completely rainless. During this period, the land dries up and vegetation dies. The early fall rains, from 'the river of God' in the heavenly world, soften the land and seeding follows. The winter rains make possible the growth of grain. Then in the late spring, harvest occurs. The harvest in verses 11-13 speaks of the bounty of the spring season; God's wagon drips fatness upon the land. Pastures, hills, meadows, and valleys give forth their crops and newborn animals, all considered the blessings of God.

John H. Hayes
Preaching Through the Christian Year: Year A

I commenced my ministry in the Bude Circuit of the Methodist Church in the early 1960s. We lived in a lovely Devon village and I had pastoral charge of five churches, three in Devon and two in Cornwall. It was there that I served my two-year probationary period before being ordained.

All the church members were farmers. Some farmed arable crops, but the majority had a dairy herd, with milk providing the most income. During my stay, I got to know farmers over a 300 square mile area and travelled about 12,000 miles a year in visiting farmers and their families. All of them loved the land, respected it, and enjoyed one of the highlights of the year, the harvest festival.

After nearly 40 years I am still in touch with some of those farming families who have never lost the link between the land and the Creator God who sustains and blesses everyone through its bounty.

But every harvest time reminds me of a Vincent van Gogh painting, a print of which hangs in my study. The picture shows a lone farmer, early in the morning, sowing his corn.

Behind him, appearing to sit on his head, is an enormous sun, just sitting on the horizon. To the farmer's left is a huge tree dominating earth and sky. In the distance is a tiny hamlet.

I remember reading somewhere that you will never see a sun like this, a tree like this, a farmer like this, or even land like this. And it's true. But what made me sit up and take more notice of the picture was the fact that the farmer has no facial features. No eyes, nose, ears, mouth. Why, I wondered, did Van Gogh not give him all these features? The only answer I can think of is that he represents the countless anonymous farmers who sow their seed and harvest it, for the benefit of us all.

The farmer himself is a wonderful study of concentrated movement as he carefully holds his corn-filled bag close to him with his left hand, and with his right, broadcasts the corn over the waiting ground.

The whole picture for me is a wonderful evocation of sowing and caring for the land, bringing to my mind the Psalmist's words: 'Thou visitest the earth and waterest it, thou greatly enrichest it; . . . thou providest their grain, for so thou hast prepared it.' (Psalm 65:9)

Ron Dale, 1999

Psalm 66

Sixth Sunday after Easter: Year A, verses 8-20
Proper 9/Ordinary Time 14: Year C, verses 1-9
Proper 23/Ordinary Time 28: Year C, verses 1-12

Such grateful testimony is often a means used by God to strengthen the faith of others.

The witness of gratitude

Psalm 66 is composed of two major parts: Israel's grateful witness to the nations (verses 1-12) and an individual's grateful witness to all who fear God (verses 13-20). The strophes of part one were probably sung by antiphonal choirs, and those of part two by an individual. The psalm was composed to be sung on the occasion when a particular man paid his vows in the Temple (see verses 13-15). The similarity in missionary thought between this psalm and Isaiah 40-66 suggests a postexilic date for the psalm.

Israel's witness to the nations (66:1-12). Israel's witness to the nations is so presented as to be a hymn of praise and thanksgiving to God. In the first strophe (verses 1-4) all the peoples of the earth are invited to praise God (compare 22:27; 98:4). In verses 3-4 the psalmist places a song on their lips. They are to proclaim that God's deeds are awesome, and that his enemies, out of fear, yield at least feigned obedience to him. Their announcement that 'all the earth worships thee' is more prophetic anticipation than literal fact (compare Isaiah 49:6).

In the second strophe (verses 5-7) the nations are invited to take cognisance of the mighty acts of God in the history of the Chosen People. . . . Two acts which stand out conspicuously are the crossing of the Red Sea (Exodus 14) and the crossing of the River Jordan (Joshua 3). In these and subsequent events God has shown that he keeps watch over the nation; therefore 'let not the rebellious exalt themselves'. Although the psalm was written centuries after the Exodus and the entrance into Canaan, the psalmist and his people could say, 'There did we rejoice in him.' They were present at the Exodus and entrance to Canaan as the Church of today was present at the crucifixion and resurrection of Jesus Christ.

In the third strophe (verses 8-12) the choir calls the nations to bless God for his preservation of Israel through many trials. This invitation rests upon the thought that because of Israel's survival she as God's missionary will bring God's saving light to the nations and she and they together will be God's people (see Isaiah 60:1-7, 61:9; 66:18-21). Israel's trials at God's hands are likened to the refining of silver (see Isaiah 48:10; Zechariah 13:9) and ensnaring in a net (see Lamentations 1:13; Job 19:6). God let men trample over his people with horses and chariots (compare Isaiah 51:23) and caused his people to go through fire and water (compare Isaiah 43:2).

Yet he has brought them to a new freedom. While many experiences of affliction are in the psalmist's mind, the Babylonian captivity is paramount.

The individual's witness to God-fearers (66:13-20). The hymn of the community has prepared the way for the psalmist to pay his vows and give his testimony. First, he pays his vows (verses 13-15). However, in addition to the votive offerings promised when he was in trouble, he offers burnt offerings of various kinds. The large number of sacrifices offered by this man indicates that he was a person of wealth and position.

The second strophe (verses 16-19) of this part of the psalm is testimony to what God has done for the psalmist. He is so grateful, he cannot contain himself. Such grateful testimony is often a means used by God to strengthen the faith of others. This individual worshipper knows that God would not have listened if his heart had been filled with hypocrisy (compare Luke 18:9-14).

A. B. Rhodes
Psalms

Psalm 66:16; 'Come and listen, all you who fear God, while I tell you what he has done for me.' The psalmist is now giving his own testimony, bearing his own witness, to the love and care of God.

There is of course a long tradition of this action in both the Old and the New Testaments as Israel looks back with gratitude for God's rescue from slavery in Egypt and His covenant, faithful love. Remembrance and Testimony to that love is often given to remind Israel of the rock from which he was hewn and also as a witness to the nations.

In the New Testament, Paul writes to the Galations, 'Then God, who had specially chosen me while I was still in my mother's womb, called me through his grace and chose to reveal his Son in me, so that I might preach the Good News about him to the pagans.' (Galatians 1:15)

In today's world, my own Church, (Methodist) asks all who desire to become local preachers and all who wish to be ordained, what their experience of God is. What makes them want to become preachers and ministers? What testimony do they have to the work and call of God?

I have sat in many a service and in many a synod listening, and so often being deeply moved by people from all walks of life telling 'how it was' for them. How God revealed himself, how he shaped and guided and helped them, and how he called each one to be a preacher and also a minister.

One man I heard told how it was just having a deep sense of wonder at the natural world. Through its beauty, God called. Quite often friends and relatives have pointed them to ministry. For myself, the call came one night. I was tucked up in bed and reading the Acts of the Apostles. Suddenly the risen Christ stood by my bed and used the words he spoke to Paul in the passage I was reading, to call me. 'And the Lord said to Paul one night in a vision, "Do not be afraid, but speak and do not be silent; for I am with you, and no man shall attack you to harm you; for I have many people in this city"' (Acts 18:9-10). Because of that experience I was later ordained. But not before committees, synods and the Methodist Conference had asked me to tell them, to give my testimony to my call, and say 'how it was' for me. Later on, I found amazing opportunities to bear by my own witness in many different settings; from the shop floor as an industrial chaplain to the studio of many BBC local radio stations and the World Service with, I was told, 50 million listeners. After such witness many people have found much encouragement and even been called by God to join the long chain of witness themselves.

Ron Dale, 1999

Psalm 67

Proper 15/Ordinary Time 20: Year A
Sixth Sunday of Easter: Year C

God the Governor of the nations

This is the true motive for evangelism – not the fear that men may die without Christ, but the grief that they continue to live without the happiness of knowing him.

In this psalm there is a fine merging of prayer and praise. Its dominant note is that of prayer. It is prayer, moreover, on the highest level. It asks for personal blessing, but its deepest passion is that all peoples may be blessed, and led to praise. If it was a harvest festival song, as the first part of verse 6 would indicate, then the local occasion is graciously submerged in a far wider outlook. The singer, even more remarkably than in the preceding psalm, recognises the true function of the holy nation. The word 'that' with which verse 2 opens, is of the utmost importance – that God's 'way may be known upon earth,' and his 'saving health among all nations,' is the ultimate purpose of his heart, and the mission of his people. (See also under Psalm 66 on the theme of testimony/witness.)

In order to do this the singer prays for blessing *on* and *through* them; *on* them, 'God be merciful unto us and bless us'; *through* them, 'and cause his face to shine upon us'. The central desire of the prayer is uttered at its centre (verses 3-5); and the method is again indicated at its close (verses 6-7). This is not asking in order to consume gifts upon personal lusts. It is rather a passion which is self-emptied and therefore pure. Such praying hastens the Kingdom.

G. Campbell Morgan
Notes on the Psalms

A refrain in verses 3 and 5 divides the psalm into three parts. The opening recalls the priestly blessing in Numbers 6:24-6. The grace of God and the joys of fellowship with him are sought, yet not as delights to be selfishly hoarded, but in order that the non-Jewish nations may see the Lord's salvation and live that good life which he both requires and offers. Thus God's gracious dealing with Israel will lead all men to give to him their worship.

Verse 4 expresses the thought of the Lord's just rule over

the whole world. 'Judge' is not 'condemn', but 'govern' and 'vindicate'. The word translated 'govern' is really 'lead', a word often used of the Lord's loving guidance of his people (see Exodus 13:17, 21; 15:13; Isaiah 57:18; 58:1), and only here applied to his caring for foreign nations (contrast Job 12:23).

Only at verse 6 do we discover that people have come to offer their thanksgiving for the harvest, and even then the psalm quickly turns to confident assurance of God's continuing blessing, or reverts to the earlier prayer. As the Israelite came to the temple with gratitude in his heart for the good gifts of the earth, he realised that God is infinitely more precious than his gifts (cf. Deuteronomy 26:11, where the harvest festival is the occasion for reciting the Israelite creed on the Exodus deliverance). So in the New Testament there is joyful thanksgiving on every hand, and no loss of faith in God as creator; yet when Paul thanks God for his 'gift beyond words' (2 Corinthians 9:15, NEB) it is, as always, Christ to whom he refers.

Throughout this psalm the narrow confines of the nation are burst asunder. It is the Lord, the God of Israel, who has given the harvest to his people, but the congregation looks for his righteous dominion over the whole world and to praises being offered by all men. The blessing Israel has received makes them a missionary people, and contains the hope that those who see his goodness will come to worship him. This is the true motive for evangelism – not the fear that men may die without Christ, but the grief that they continue to live without the happiness of knowing him.

Cyril S. Rodd
Psalms 1-72

The chosen people of God, Israel, was raised up by God so that all the nations of the earth might be blessed; in the words of the psalmist, 'that God's way may be known upon earth', and his 'saving health among all nations.' Often Israel failed in her mission to do this and the book of Jonah was written to underline this responsibility upon Israel to tell forth the pity, care and love of God for all. So here is an extract from a sermon by T. D. Meadley, former principal of Cliff College, a Methodist Training Centre: nobody who heard Tom Meadley preach on the Book of Jonah is likely to forget it. The title was 'The Sulky Prayer of a Successful Evangelist.' The story begins with the prophet being ordered by God to preach to the people of Nineveh which he was most unwilling to do. The sermon continues:

'Jonah has enough elementary wisdom to realise that he cannot defy God and merely loiter around as if nothing had happened. He is driven to escape as far as possible in the opposite direction. He takes a ticket to the ends of the known world. Tarshish, or Tarsessus, was on the extreme western tip of Spain, as remote from Nineveh as could be managed. Jonah vainly hopes to flee from the disapproving presence of God by leaving behind the place where the conflict was first provoked. Because he is a religious man, Jonah cannot bear the weight of a guilty conscience and therefore must go out of his way to establish his righteousness. He slams the fare on the counter to emphasise his honesty. (In the ancient world, passengers took the precaution of paying at the end of the journey, when the destination had been reached.)

'Why else should Holy Scripture waste valuable space in recording an elementary piece of honesty, "Jonah paid the fare," unless he ensured that due publicity was given to the behaviour? He is no anti-social criminal. He can look any dock-detective in the face. He boards the ship immediately, and descends to his cabin, not lingering to savour the vices of dockland.

'No human law court or conventional standard of morality could fault Jonah. He was engaged with perfect propriety on legitimate business. By any known observable criterion he was not a sinner. When later disaster threatened this ship, and suspicion fell on him as a probable cause, he took his medicine without murmur, over-ruling the compassionate hesitation of the crew, and enabling them to cast him to the waves. No one else shall suffer for his presumed misdeeds. To save his mates he willingly pays the price, even to the supreme sacrifice. He is the epitome of the Englishman's ideal of a good sport. (He would have made an admirable cricketer!) Nevertheless the whole point of the story, as far as it reflects on Jonah's character, is that he is a double-dyed damned sinner. The whole circumstance highlights the true nature of sin which can coincide with perfectly correct outward behaviour, namely that he was in the wrong inward and personal relationship with God. He was defying the personal call of God to a specific piece of service, on which the well-being of other people depended.'

Tom Meadley: Speaking for Himself
compiled by John Young

Psalm 68

Seventh Sunday of Easter: Year A, verses 1-10, 32-35

When God is awakened to action there will be a decisive sorting out, a decision made between those who are God's friends and those who are God's enemies.

The festival of the Ascension continues to exercise its influence in this set of readings. In this festival, the church plays on the imagery of 'going up.' In the liturgy, 'going up' refers to the ascent of the king to the throne; Jesus assumes the place of honour and power 'at the right hand' on the throne.

This psalm pleads for this 'going up' to power and authority: 'Let God rise up' (Psalm 68:1). Let God rouse God's self, let God assume and show power, let God be the powerful agent of change that God is capable of being. Everything can and will be changed when God is roused to power.

The fundamental petition (verses 1-3) is that the God who has been asleep should awaken to power (Psalm 121:4; Isaiah 51:9-11). That is, this rhetoric does not assume that God is constant in attentiveness and power, but that God moves in and out on God's proper business. Later in the psalm we shall see the reason for such a view of God. The psalm does not doubt that when God is awakened to action there will be a decisive sorting out, a decision made between those who are God's friends and those who are God's enemies (verses 1-2). God's power is not in doubt, but God's attentiveness must always be secured anew. The main reason to seek God's intrusive action is that God needs to act against those who oppose God's purpose. These opponents of God are variously named as God's 'enemies', as 'those who hate' God, and as 'the wicked'. They are not said to be the enemies of the one who prays, but the enemies of the God to whom the prayer is addressed. That is, the speaker suggests to God, those who are not my enemies, but yours. That which finally opposes God cannot continue to exist in God's presence.

. . . The righteous, antithetical to the wicked, are those who will benefit from God's arousal. They will welcome God's intrusion, because they regard themselves as properly aligned with God's intention.

The poet explicates the reason for the doxology of verse 4 (verses 5-6). The reason for praise is that this God characteristically does what enhances the righteous. Thus this God is the guardian, legitimator, and guarantor for the socially disenfranchised, widows and orphans. Moreover, this God is a custodian for the homeless, the ones without community, and an advocate for prisoners, who characteristically are the poor. Thus the righteous (verse 3) who celebrate (verse 4) are likely to be those without conventional social power, the widows, orphans, homeless, and imprisoned. These are the ones who need God to be aroused, who turn to God because they are otherwise helpless, and who anticipate a good life when God acts. Thus the petition of verses 1-2 and the entire urging that God should rise up makes most sense when the petition and urging are on the lips of the helpless and power-less. The reference in verse 6 to 'parched land' prepares us for the final section of the main part of our assigned reading (verses 7-10). Now, for the first time in the poem, God is addressed directly. In these verses, rain is part of the theophany that bespeaks God's terrible power and presence. In this historical recall, rain is simply one aspect of God's dramatic, cataclysmic coming to be present in Israel with sovereign power.

The significance of the image of rain changes, however, in verses 9-10. Now rain is not an element of theophany, but is simply God's gift to the land which lets the earth flourish; from theophany, the poem has moved to the reliability of creation, guaranteed by God's attentiveness.

The conclusion of these verses uses the term 'thy living ones' (Hebrew; NRSV and RSV, 'flock'). The verse indicates that the needy ones (i.e. afflicted, oppressed) now have found the rain-soaked land to be a place of goodness, a safe home. The reference to the needy (verse 10) recalls the needy in verses 5-6. The coming of rain is a rich gift to those who have no other resources for life.

Thus the psalm juxtaposes two very different motifs. First, Yahweh is the rain God who gives rain and causes life. With this image, we can understand how it is that God waxes and wanes and is not constant. God's absence is because the deathly gods of drought have their day of pre-eminence; this God of life returns when the rains come.

Second, rain becomes a way of speaking about caring social relations that let the needy share in the good life. Thus rain comes to mean all the showers of blessing, justice, right-eousness, equity, shalom. The two themes together, rain and care for the needy, that is, a motif of creation and a theme of covenant, converge in this theological affirmation. It is the rule of God over creation and through covenant that makes new life possible, because this God overrides the power of death.

. . . Israel joins all the earth in singing to and celebrating the God of creation and life, who has decisively defeated the power of death.

Walter Brueggemann
Texts for Preaching, Year A

A glade. The Ark is at the right, only the poop deck showing, with a ladder to the ground. *Noah* is taking measurements and singing a little song. He scratches his head and goes over the measurements again. Then he calls:

Noah: *(Softly)* Lord . . . *(Louder)* Lord . . . *(Very loud)* Lord! . . . Yes, Lord, it's me. Extremely sorry to bother you again, but . . . What's that? Yes, I know you've other things to think of, but after I've shoved off, won't it be a little late? . . . Oh, no, Lord, no, no. . . . No, Lord, please don't think that. . . . Oh, but naturally, of course, I trust you! You could tell me to set sail on a plank – a branch – on just a cabbage leaf. . . . Yes, you could even tell me to put out to sea with nothing but my loincloth, even without my loincloth – completely . . . Yes, yes, Lord, I beg your pardon. I know your time is precious. Well, this is all I wanted to ask you: should I make a rudder? I say, a rudder. . . . No, no, Lord. R for Robert; U for Una; D for . . . that's it, a rudder. Good . . . very good, I never thought of that. Of course, winds, currents, tides . . . What was that, Lord? Storms? Oh, and while you're there just one other little thing . . . Are you listening, Lord? *(To the audience)* Gone! . . . He's in a bad temper . . . Well, you can't blame him; he's so much to think of. All right; no rudder. *(He considers the Ark)* Tides, currents, winds. *(He imitates the winds)* Psch! . . Psch! . . . Storms. *(He imitates the tempests)* Vloum! Be da Bloum! Oh, that's going to be simply . . . magnificent! . . . No, no, Lord, I'm not afraid. I know that you'll be with me. I was only trying to imagine . . . Oh, Lord, while you're there I'd like just to ask . . . *(To the audience)* Che! Gone again. You see how careful you have to be. *(He laughs)* He was listening all the time. *(He goes to the Ark)* Storms! . . . I think I'll just put a few more nails in down here. *(He hammers and sings)*

. . . *(He admires his work)* And when I think that a year ago I couldn't hammer a nail without hitting my thumb. That's pretty good, if I do say so myself. *(He climbs aboard the Ark and stands there like a captain)* Larboard and starboard! . . . Cast off the hawsers! . . . Close the portholes! . . 'Ware shoals!

. . . Wait till the squall's over! . . . Now I'm ready, completely ready, absolutely ready! *(He cries to heaven)* I am ready! *(Then quietly)* Well, I should like to know how all this business is going to begin. . . . Magnificent weather – oppressively hot and no sign of a cloud. Well, that part of the programme is his look-out.

Andre Obey
Noah

Psalm 69

Proper 7/Ordinary Time 12: Year A, verses 7-10, (11-15), 16-18

Save me, O God! I have come into deep waters.

The voice that speaks in Psalm 69 is a voice of profound faith. Indeed, it is the voice of all our mothers and fathers in faith who have dared to believe and to speak. On this deadly Friday, we are bold to say that the voice which sounds here is the voice of Jesus, walking the last costly measure of obedience. And because it is the voice of the one who has suffered with us and for us, we say also that it is the voice of our common humanity, sore pressed, but not yet talked out of faith.

I pursue only one theme from the psalm. In this poem we notice that honest prayer is situated in the midst of deep threat:

I sink in deep mire, where there is no foothold; I have come into deep waters, and the flood sweeps over me. . . . rescue me from sinking in the mire; let me be delivered from my enemies and from the deep waters. Let not the flood sweep over me, or the deep swallow me up, or the pit close its mouth over me (verses 2, 14-15).

Twice the poet speaks of 'deep waters' that are rising and surging. The phrase refers to the primitive, elemental awareness that the dry land of creation is surrounded by the hostile, untamed waters of chaos. Those waters of chaos may subside, but then they come again, fierce and relentless, pounding at the edges of the dry land, laying siege to all our fragile arrangements and our little safe spots of earth, threatening to wash it all away.

The phrase 'deep waters' invites us to think large about Good Friday. Too much we have reduced the day to sin and forgiveness, to personal salvation 'through the blood.' The larger drama enacted is that the power of death is on the loose and it does its worst work on this day. That is why in some Gospel accounts, at the death of Jesus, there come earthquake and darkness and disorder. The chaos came for those dread hours because the king is dead, order has failed, and the raw elements of undomesticated chaos surge and laugh in ugly triumph.

We wait in the quiet and the dark to see if chaos will recede; we wait for three long hours. It is for us a time open for stocktaking and for noticing in honesty that the powers of chaos and death are indeed untamed, even among us. We

162

suspect that these powers take advantage of greed and hate and fear in order to do their work. But the power itself is deeper, at the muddy bottom of the river of life.

The prayer of faith arises exactly in the midst of chaos. The chaos comes as the economic order dysfunctions, and the index of unemployment and poverty and homelessness rises. The chaos comes when civility is replaced by terror, brutality, and harassment, and neighbours become victims and perpetrators of violence upon each other. The chaos comes as more and more poison is dumped into our brief earthly nest, poison that is profit driven. The land shrivels, the birds flee, and we do not yet connect greed with cancer. Life, public and broad, personal and intimate, is indeed in jeopardy, always so, but acutely so among us now, poignantly so on this Friday . . . in the deep waters.

What to do in our fearful helplessness as the waters rise? The voice of faith in this psalm brings the chaos into relation with the power of God. The chaos is so much more realistic and palpable than the power of God. The threat we can see, the power of God we can only speak about and trust in. But both times 'deep waters' are mentioned, it is in order that God should be addressed, brought to awareness, so that God must enter into the chaos and the chaos may be reshaped by the power of God. The psalmist prays: 'Save me, O God . . . I have come into deep waters . . . in your steadfast love rescue me from the deep waters (verses 1-2, 13-14).

Under threat, even on Friday, this psalm refuses to host the idea that chaos is limitless. The very act of the prayer is an affirmation that watery chaos has limits, boundaries, and edges, because the waters butt up against the power of God.

On this Friday of chaos, we are not watching simply the unbounded power of chaos savage the earth. We are rather watching chaos push to its extreme limit, doing its worst, most destructive work, and spending itself without finally prevailing. The psalm invites us to honesty about the threat. More than that, however, the psalm is buoyant in its conviction that all around the chaos, guarding its rise, monitoring its threat, is the counter power of life, only haunting and shadowing, not too soon evident, but abidingly there. This voice of faith acknowledges the chaos, but then submits it to the larger power of God. So Jesus in that supreme moment of threat, does not yield, but announces in evangelical triumph, 'It is finished.' It is decided! It is accomplished! It is completed in triumph!

So what to do in the midst of threat? Do what believing Jesus and trusting Jews and Christians have always done. Refuse the silence, reject despair, resist the devastating, debilitating assault of chaos, and speak a counterspeech. This psalm is not simply a passive, pious act of trust in God. It is rather a bold, abrasive speech which addresses God in the imperative, and which, in the utterance of the imperative, puts chaos on notice that we will not yield, will not succumb, will not permit the surging of the chaos to define the situation.

The response to the threat in this prayer is twofold, two items closely related, but clearly distinguishable. There is *the hovering, magisterial limit* of God that curbs the threat. And there is *the abrasive, insistent speech of faith* that evokes the limit of God. On this Friday, it is worth asking, as the waters of chaos rise before our very eyes: Do we wait in stunned, awed silence, counting on the power of God to curb? Biblical faith is never in favour of pious silence. It is rather for direct, assertive, insistent demand that refuses to sit silently while the waters rise. I can imagine this man Jesus and this people who have not lost their voice of faith, even on Friday, willing to speak shrilly against the flood, against the hate and the greed, against the poison and the fear and the indignity. For Israel believes that its faithful speech is the earnest harbinger of God's own majestic intrusion, that God comes into the deep waters at the behest of the faithful who watch in the night and who know that chaos is not normal and must not be docilely accepted.

Part of a sermon by Walter Brueggemann,
quoted in *The Threat of Life: Sermons on Pain, Power and Weakness*

Psalm 70

Wednesday in Holy Week: Years A, B, C
Proper 27/Ordinary Time 32: Year A, (Alt resp)

If out of love for our brother we are willing to sacrifice goods, honour and life, we must be prepared to do the same for our enemy.

This entire psalm is practically identical in form to Psalm 40:13-17. In Psalm 40, this material comprises part of a ritual text that was probably used by the king in worship before battle. What now appears as Psalm 70 is the lament or supplication portion that requests God's help in a coming crisis.

Psalm 70:1-3 provides a good example of what has been called the double wish of the lament psalms, because the request/wish to be saved is balanced by a request for the destruction of one's enemies or opponents. Frequently the calamity that is requested to befall one's enemy is very similar to the condition that the one praying faced. Thus numerous psalms reflect something of that attitude, so widely felt, namely, that those who plan evil should have a corresponding evil beset them. Christians often shy away in horror from the prayers in the psalms that request a destruction or a calamity to fall on one's enemies. Such sentiments seem contrary to the teaching and life of Jesus. We must, however, understand that the psalms sought to give full and appropriate outlets for people to express their true feelings and sentiments. It may be that only by verbalising such sentiments and expressions can they be overcome or transcended. Expressions of one's truest and deepest feelings may be necessary before one can release them and replace them with better feelings. In many ways, some of the psalms probably allowed persons to vent their anger and hostility to such a degree of animosity and with such a degree of revenge that the mere recital of such cursing wishes relieved the anxiety and pent-up emotions of the worshipper (e.g. Psalm 109).

The opening verse of Psalm 70, with its plea for God to hasten and deliver, is followed by two verses asking that the enemies be put to shame and turned back; that is, that their plans go awry, so they will end up being shamed. If the prayer was originally offered by the king, then the adversaries could be foreign powers or nations who were threatening hostile military action.

Verse 4 is an intercessory prayer, although the worshipper is included in the group being prayed for. The intercessor requests that all those who seek God and love his salvation rejoice and proclaim forever that God is great. This is obviously a prayer asking that the king and his subjects be victorious over the enemy or that they be spared a possible impending conflict. In the final verse, the worshipper reverts to an appeal on his or her own behalf. The fact that the one praying is described as poor and needy does not mean that the person was destitute and in poverty. Such expressions are metaphorical statements characterising the person in the most sharply drawn and the humblest terms in order to evoke God's aid.

The association of this psalm with Holy Week can be made in two ways: (1) like Jesus, the psalmist was challenged by enemies who sought his death and destruction; and (2) like Jesus, the psalmist prayed and made intercessory requests on behalf of others.

John H. Hayes
Preaching Through the Christian Year: Year B

Jesus, however, takes the law of God in his own hands and expounds its true meaning. The will of God, to which the law gives expression, is that men should defeat their enemies by loving them. In the New Testament our enemies are those who harbour hostility against us, not those against whom we cherish hostility, for Jesus refuses to reckon with such a possibility. The Christian must treat his enemy as his brother, and requite his hostility with love. His behaviour must be determined not by the way others treat him, but by the treatment he himself receives from Jesus; it has only one source, and that is the will of Jesus.

By our enemies Jesus means those who are quite intractable and utterly unresponsive to our love, who forgive us nothing when we forgive them all, who requite our love with hatred and our service with derision . . . Love asks nothing in return, but seeks those who need it. And who needs our love more than those who are consumed by hatred and are utterly devoid of love? Who in other words deserves our love more than our enemy? Where is love more glorified than where she dwells in the midst of her enemies?

Christian love draws no distinction between one enemy and another, except that the more bitter our enemy's hatred, the greater his need of love. Be his enmity political or religious, he has nothing to expect from a follower of Jesus but unqualified love. In such love there is no inner discord between private person and official capacity. In both we are disciples of Christ, or we are not Christians at all. Am I asked how this love is to behave? Jesus gives the answer: bless, do good, and pray for your enemies without reserve and without respect of persons.

'Love your enemies.' The preceding commandment had spoken only of the passive endurance of evil; here Jesus goes further and bids us not only to bear with evil and the evil person patiently, not only to refrain from treating him as he treats us, but actively to engage in heart-felt love towards him. We are to serve our enemy in all things without hypocrisy and with utter sincerity. No sacrifice which a lover would make for his beloved is too great for us to make for our enemy. If out of love for our brother we are willing to sacrifice goods, honour and life, we must be prepared to do the same for our enemy. We are not to imagine that this is to condone his evil; such a love proceeds from strength rather than weakness, from truth rather than fear, and therefore it cannot be guilty of the hatred of another. And who is to be the object of such a love, if not those whose hearts are stifled with hatred?

Dietrich Bonhoeffer
The Cost of Discipleship

Psalm 71

Tuesday in Holy Week: Years A, B, C, verses 1-14
Fourth Sunday of Epiphany/Ordinary Time 4: Year C,
   verses 1-6
Proper 16/Ordinary Time 21: Year C

There are not
enough shovels
on earth to bury
the truth.

God, the confidence of old age

This is pre-eminently a song of the aged, and like old age it is reminiscent. The singer passes from memory to hope, and from experience to praise. No very definite division is possible. Generally speaking, it may be noticed that the first part expresses need, and is principally a prayer; while the second half affirms confidence, and is principally praise.

The song opens with a prayer for deliverance (verses 1-8). This is not so much a cry out of present distress as a prayer that in the event of trouble he may be able to resort to God. The old man is discovered in that the first three verses are almost a direct quotation from a previous psalm (Psalm 31), perhaps one of his own. His experience of God from birth is his confidence that he will be heard now. This leads the song on in prayer that he may still be helped in age, for he has adversaries (verses 9-13). Here again are quotations from earlier psalms which the marginal references will aid the reader in discovering. The singer then rises to higher levels as he tells of his confidence in God, and asks that he may be helped to declare God to the succeeding generation. The psalm is a song of sunset, and it is full of beauty. There are storm clouds on the western sky. Some are spent, and some still threaten; but on all is a light which transfigures them.

G. Campbell Morgan
Notes on the Psalms

Richard Wurmbrand, a Rumanian Christian minister spent many years in prison, suffering for his faith. He has grown old in the faith, but as he says in this quote, 'I left prison still a Christian.' Psalm 71:3-4 reminded me of his amazing story; verse 4 says, 'My

God, rescue me from the hands of the wicked, from the clutches of rogue and tyrant.' In the prison Wurmbrand found God to be 'a sheltering rock', and was sustained through many hours of torture and brutality. Here is a small part of his story as he relates it:

In order to give a true account of my own particular experiences, as a man tortured, mocked and drugged in a solitary cell, I would have to invent words of my own; but then I could not communicate.

We did not live in the sphere of words there. St John says that on Patmos he saw. We can put into words what we saw only in the measure in which we could describe to a blind man Michelangelo's 'Pieta', or Leonardo's 'Mona Lisa'.

Moody said that a Christian on his knees sees more than a philosopher standing on tiptoe. If you want to know what hundreds of thousands of Christians have experienced . . . in Communist dungeons, don't stop at reading these sermons, but get down on your knees and ask God for the privilege of sharing the cross of the sufferers, of remembering them as though you were bound in chains with them.

But don't share only the outward physical suffering, the hunger, the tortures. Share what is far worse, the inner tempest, the doubts, the moments of despair. (Not possible today, but the principles apply to East Timor, Chechnya or any contemporary human suffering.)

These sermons are not what we usually understand by a sermon – the proclamation of God's truth – but an attempt to make others feel the storms of doubt, and sometimes even of rebellion against God, which assail a prisoner under such conditions. They assailed John the Baptist when he knew that Jesus was living not far from his prison yet never came to visit him. They forced Christ himself to ask God why he had forsaken him. Under normal circumstances, it would be blasphemy to suggest that the Heavenly Father could give up a righteous man. But Jesus was not preaching on the cross as priests do from their pulpits. He was experiencing suffering – the greatest mystery in the good and almighty God's creation – and was expressing what he felt at that moment when he cried, 'My God, my God, why hast thou forsaken me?'

There are not enough shovels on earth to bury the truth. And there are no pains enough to prevent truth and faith and love from triumphing at last, even when you pass through the worst temptations. I have doubted, I have had moments of despair, but these were all overcome. The sermons finish on a note of victory. I left prison still a Christian.

169

I started my first sermon as a young pastor with a story:

King David once summoned a jeweller and gave him the order: 'Make me a ring which will transform my mood from sorrow to joy or from joy to sorrow whenever I look on it. If you make it within a week, you will be royally rewarded. If not, you will be beheaded.' The jeweller left the palace a broken man. He knew that his life was lost. But in the palace courtyard little Solomon was playing. He noticed the sorrow on the man's face and asked him the reason. When the jeweller told him of the king's command, Solomon laughed and said, 'You must make a plain ring of tin, and engrave on it the words *Gam Ze Iavo* – this also will pass. That is all. If he looks at it when he is merry, my father will at once become serious, and when he is worried, a look at the ring will wipe the frown from his face.'

Gam Ze Iavo. So many terrible events have passed in my life. Now this has passed too. With Jesus the incarnation passed. Everything passes. It is as though nothing has happened to me today. My beloved God, let us walk again in companionship with one another. Amen.

Richard Wurmbrand
If Prison Walls Could Speak

Psalm 72

Second Sunday of Advent: Year A, verses 1-7, 18-19
The Epiphany: Years A, B, C, verses 1-7, 10-14

*Pray always for
all the learned,
the oblique, the
delicate. Let them
not be quite
forgotten at the
throne of God
when the simple
come into their
kingdom.*

A portion of this psalm was the responsorial psalm for the Second Sunday of Advent; today's verses are also the psalm selection for Epiphany during all three years of the lectionary cycle.

Epiphany, in the Western tradition, commemorates several themes: the visit of the Magi, the first manifestation of Jesus to the non-Jewish, Gentile world represented by the Magi, and the Church's missionary work in the modern world. Psalm 72 shares in this universal perspective and in seeing an inter-relationship of the Jewish people with the non-Jewish nations.

Psalm 72 was no doubt written as the community's inter-cessory prayer offered on behalf of the Davidic king at his coronation and/or the annual celebration of the king's rule. Perhaps no other text in the Old Testament gives such an elevated and yet humane portrayal of (or perhaps longing for) the ideal Davidic ruler. The monarch is depicted in this text as the embodiment of justice and compassion, as the inaugurator of a new era.

As an intercession, the psalm requests and petitions the Deity for many things, all mediated through the monarch. One of these, and thus the psalm's use on Epiphany Sunday, is the request for a universal rule, for a dominion that extends throughout the inhabited world (verses 8-11). A number of geographical expressions are employed to speak of this dominion: 'from sea to sea', 'from the River to the ends of the earth', 'Tarshish and of the isles', and 'Sheba and Seba'. The first two expressions are mythological in background and are used metaphorically to denote the entire world. The last two refer to the regions to the distant west of Palestine and to the distant lands of the east, respectively. The basis for such cosmic claims on behalf of the Judean monarch was the belief in God as creator. As creator of the world, God could make his earthly representative ruler of the world. Thus the doctrine of creation undergirded the extravagant claims of the Davidic monarch and gave birth to the hope of a universal rule for the Messiah.

Three actions by the nations are requested in the prayer, all expressing and demonstrating subordination to the Davidic ruler. Although all three are practically synonymous, one may detect a difference in the sources of the imagery. One (verse 9) is drawn from the area of warfare and denotes the surrender of a foe and the submission of an enemy. The one representation we possess of an Israelite king appears on the Black Obelisk of the Assyrian king Shalmaneser III (858-824 BC). On this inscription, the Israelite king Jehu (in about 841 BC) is shown kissing the ground (licking the dust) at Shalmaneser's feet. We know from the accompanying inscription that Jehu surrendered to the Assyrians. The second image (in verse 10) is that of paying tribute and bringing gifts to remain on peaceful terms. Throughout history, subordination to a superior state was always shown in the Middle East by the (generally annual) giving of gifts by the inferior. Finally, verse 11 draws on the practice of common protocol at the royal court. Bowing was the appropriate posture to greet the appearance of the king. Is it any wonder that the New Testament describes the veneration of the Magi with the story of their bringing gifts?

John H. Hayes
Preaching Through the Christian Year: Year A

Helena, the mother of Constantine, discovers the relics of the cross of Christ, and reflects on the three kings.

'Like me,' she said to them, 'you were late in coming. The shepherds were here long before; even the cattle. They had joined the chorus of angels before you were on your way. For you the primordial discipline of the heavens was relaxed and a new defiant light blazed amid the disconcerted stars.

'How laboriously you came, taking sights and calculating, where the shepherds had run barefoot! How odd you looked on the road, attended by what outlandish liveries, laden with such preposterous gifts!

'You came at length to the final stage of your pilgrimage and the great star stood above you. What did you do? You stopped to call on King Herod. Deadly exchange of compliments in which began that unended war of mobs and magistrates against the innocent!

'Yet you came, and were not turned away. You too found room before the manger. Your gifts were not needed, but they were accepted and put carefully by, for they were brought with love. In that new order of charity that had just come to life, there was room for you, too. You were not lower in the eyes of the holy family than the ox or the ass.

'You are my especial patrons,' said Helena, 'and patrons of all late-comers, of all who have a tedious journey to make to the truth, of all who are confused with knowledge and speculation, of all who through politeness make themselves partners in guilt, of all who stand in danger by reason of their talents.

'Dear cousins, pray for me,' said Helena, 'and for my poor overloaded son. May he, too, before the end find kneeling-space in the straw. Pray for the great, lest they perish utterly. And pray for Lactantius and Marcias and the young poets of Treves and for the souls of my wild, blind ancestors; for their sly foe Odysseus and for the great Longinus.

'For his sake who did not reject your curious gifts, pray always for all the learned, the oblique, the delicate. Let them not be quite forgotten at the throne of God when the simple come into their kingdom.'

Evelyn Waugh
Helena

Psalm 77

Proper 8/Ordinary Time 13: Year C, verses 1-2, 11-20

To brood upon sorrow is to be broken and disheartened, while to see God is to sing on the darkest day.

God, the healer of sorrows

This is a song of the healing of sorrow. It opens with the declaration of determination to cry to God, and then proceeds to explain the reason of this determination. Verse 10 is the pivot upon which the whole psalm turns, from a description of an experience of darkness and sorrow, to one of gladness and praise.

The first part tells the story of sorrow overwhelming the soul. The second gives a song which is the outcome of a vision which has robbed sorrow of its sting. In the first part, a great infirmity overshadows the sky, and there is no song. In the second, a great song pours itself out, and the sorrow is forgotten. The difference is that between a man brooding over trouble, and a man seeing high above it the enthroned God. In the first half, self is predominant. In the second, God is seen in his glory. A very simple method with the psalm makes this perfectly clear. In verses 1-9 there are 22 occurrences of the personal pronoun in the first person, and 11 reference to God by name, title and pronoun. In the second there are only three personal references and 24 mentions of God. The message of the psalm is that to brood upon sorrow is to be broken and disheartened, while to see God is to sing on the darkest day. Once we come to know that, our years are of his right hand, and there is light everywhere, and the song ascends.

G. Campbell Morgan
Notes on the Psalms

The very first verse of this psalm (I cry aloud to God, aloud to God, that he may hear me) reminds me powerfully of an incident that happened when I was at my first theological college.

The principal had invited me to become Chairman of the student body, and I had agreed; I had been doing the job for about three months when the memorable incident took place.

Before describing that though, I ought to say what my duties as Chairman were. The 'job description', given me verbally by the principal was:

To offer pastoral help to any student who needed it.

To maintain college discipline within the student body.

To report to the principal every morning to discuss any student problems.

To ensure that each student had a college job and did the necessary work each day.

To ensure 'lights out' at 11pm and lock all external doors, unlocking them each morning after ringing the rising bell.

It wasn't long before I added another job, that of making sure that the principal's wife had no worries when her husband was away on business. I used to pop up to the principal's flat, have a cup of tea and listen to any problems.

I was doing this one day when there erupted a cacophony of noise from one of the student's rooms. I shot off to find out what was going on. Quickly locating the sound and the room where it was emanating from, I barged in to find about 12 students having a prayer meeting. Their prayers were so loud that they could be heard in the local village, and complained about!

I simply shouted, 'Stop. If God is nearer than hands or feet – one of their favourite quotes – then why on earth are you shouting your prayers?' The students were so shocked at my intrusion that they began to whisper them. Never again did they 'cry aloud to God' during my period of office.

I can understand that some people may, in their distress, want to 'cry aloud to God' in prayer. My own experience though in more than 40 years, has been that no matter how tough the situation (my very first prayer was in North Africa at about 1am dreading being shot and asking God for help; even that prayer was a silent one) . . . no matter how tough the situation, God heard the 'whisper' of my prayer. Sometimes his response has been immediate, sometimes delayed, but always a response in love.

Ron Dale, 1999

Psalm 78

Proper 21/Ordinary Time 26: Year A, verses 1-4, 12-16
Proper 27/Ordinary Time 32: Year A, verses 1-7
Proper 13/Ordinary Time 18: Year B, verses 23-29
Holy Cross: Years A, B, C, verses 1-2, 34-38 (Alt)

Tell me that there's a better life than this.

This psalm is a recital of Israel's normative memory, much like that featured in Psalm 105, which recurs in the lectionary. In Psalm 78, however, the main point is to urge obedience to God's commands, and to warn of the disastrous consequences that follow from disobedience. Thus the sorry history of Israel is recited with a quite pronounced didactic purpose, binding the new generation to the commands of the Lord as the condition of well-being.

The psalm begins with the speaker taking the role of teacher, resolving to instruct the community, with particular reference to the younger generation (verses 1-4). The teacher summons Israel to listen, to be ready to be instructed (verse 1). The teacher promises to speak in 'parables' (or proverbs) and in old, well-established utterances ('dark sayings'). That is, the speaker indicates the genres to follow, which are intentionally pedagogical. The term rendered 'dark sayings' is unclear in its precise meaning. What is clear is that the instruction is intended to ground members of the community in the ancient conviction, that they are part of a coherent, responsible covenantal existence.

The accent is on the younger generation. This speaker knows that explicitly articulated instruction is necessary. Children do not inhale or receive by osmosis the full identity of this community, but depend on the intentional witness of adults. Thus the psalm aims at incorporating the young into the miracles and demands that constitute the identity of this particular community.

The specific substance of this instruction in 'sayings' is to testify to the wonders, miracles, and acts of great power that have been performed by the Lord for Israel. And, of course, those wonders and miracles are preserved and transmitted in the community by narrative. The teacher proposes to 'tell the old, old story', so that the telling may provoke a sense of peculiar belonging on the part of the listening, younger generation.

Now the teacher seems to change the subject (verses 5-7).

Where the earlier subject had been miracles, now the subject is testimonies ('decrees') and Torah commands. . . . Indeed, Israel is unthinkable without commands, and they must be taught and told. The purpose of this teaching and telling is 'so that':

1. The children should 'hope in God'. The hope offered in the Bible is not generic confidence or optimism, but is grounded in the specificity of a God who enacts wonders, decrees, and commands. The purpose of instruction is to *combat despair*, which makes the young an easy mark for other hopes that are, in fact, false.

2. The children shall remember the 'works of God', that is, be able to tell and trust the grounding, normative stories. These stories are not about Israel's achievements, but about God's overwhelming, inexplicable gifts to Israel. The purpose of instruction is to protect the young and to *combat amnesia*, whereby this defining memory is scuttled, either to embrace a single-dimensioned absolute future, or to opt for a memory that has no saving power and cannot keep its promises.

3. The children should 'keep his commandments', that is, live a life of responsible obedience and thereby turn enemies into neighbours and live in joyous, intimate communion with the Lord. The purpose of such learning of commandments is to *combat autonomy*, whereby the young come to think they are unconnected to anyone and are free to do whatever they please, thereby enacting a life of destructiveness to others and loneliness for self.

This reading of these verses notes a peculiar dialectic between learning *miracle narratives* and *covenantal commands*, or between *story* and *rule*. The reason for this transaction is that Israel regards both story and rule as Torah, the second derives from the first. Thus Psalm 78 reviews the previous stories, but in each case the narrative ends with a teaching about obedience.

This urgency of instruction is crucial in the life of the contemporary church. Much of the church, both adults and children, is illiterate about the defining tradition that gives the church its life. As a consequence, the church lives much of its life in modes of despair, amnesia and autonomy. It need not be so. A healthy, faithful alternative, however, requires the careful intentionality evidenced by this teacher on the part of caring adults. Only so will the next generation come to share the definitive passions of this community of faith.

Walter Brueggemann
Texts for Preaching, Year A

In the early 1990s I was a prison chaplain serving in a Category C prison and also in a Young Offenders' prison.

One day I took an internal telephone call and was asked to visit a young offender, newly in the prison.

I sat with him for a while, his head held in his hands, in a terrible despair. He looked at me and said, 'Chaplain, I'm fed up with crime. Tell me that there's a better life than this.' His words gave me a very moving opportunity to tell him that there was indeed a 'better' life and share with him the 'old, old story' of the Gospel of Christ.

The young inmate's condition is for me the perfect illustration of the previous quote from Walter Brueggemann, because the youngster was suffering deep despair, amnesia and autonomy.

He despaired of himself, his past and his present, with no hope for the future. His 'amnesia' was that he could not remember the Gospel stories from his Sunday School days, and therefore was cut off from the very Story that could tell him who he was, why he 'was', and where he was going. Namely, still a child of God, called to 'know and enjoy him forever', and on his way to a glorious future prepared for all who love God.

His rejection of the Christian faith had led him to believe in his own autonomy, that he could do what he liked, when he liked, and to whom he liked, leading him to a despairing isolation from family, friends and society.

I spent a long time in trying to spell out some of these things to him, and when I left he told me he was feeling a lot better. Whether he took on board the Gospel I don't know as I never saw him again. I hope he did, I pray he did, knowing for himself something of 'the glorious liberty of the children of God'.

Ron Dale, 1999

Psalm 79

Proper 20/Ordinary Time 25: Year C, verses 1-9

Don't let my prayer seem too little to you, God.

A lament over the destruction of Jerusalem

This communal lament is so similar to Psalm 74 that it must spring out of the same situation, probably the desecration of the temple and the fall of Jerusalem in 586 BC.

The destruction is vividly portrayed in verses 1-4. Foreign nations have seized the Lord's land, defiled his temple, made a ruin of his holy city, killed his worshippers and, with a further insult, left their bodies unburied as carrion. It is no wonder that the Jews who have survived utter an anguished cry – 'How long?' Believing that this disaster must be due to the Lord's anger at their wrong-doing, they plead that he will forget their sin and save them. Three grounds for his forgiveness are offered: his own nature – compassionate and always ready to deliver; their utter need and humiliation – they who are his own people; and the glory of his name – his own prestige among the heathen nations (verses 8-10, 11, 13).

Despair, perplexity, anguish of soul, consciousness of sin and an even more vivid consciousness of the cruelty of the enemy, lusting for plunder, murder and rape, intermingle. The wonder is that faith still survives and that the worshippers can still call themselves the flock of which the Lord himself is shepherd, and can still look forward to a time when they will once again be able to offer him glad thanksgiving.

Desires for vengeance find expression in verses 6 and 12. Here is a sub-Christian ethic. Yet it is hardly fitting for those who accept the nuclear deterrent to decry this bitter plaint from the chosen people whose city, temple, and religion were in ruins. For we now know that defence is no longer a possibility. The most that can be achieved is to inflict a terrible revenge. We have witnessed widespread destruction in cities like Hamburg, Dresden, Tokyo, Hiroshima, Nagasaki. Yet we are prepared to authorise this massive retaliation and bring death to innocent and guilty, to children and those yet unborn. Abraham refused to countenance this for Sodom.

Moreover it is unseemly for those who live in comfort and security to speak easily of loving our enemies. When those show forgiveness to the terrorists who killed their dearest, when those who have known the last safeguards of society broken down and have seen their loved-ones lying battered and lifeless in the gutters still believe in love – then we talk, in awed amazement, of the higher Christian way.

Cyril S. Rodd
Psalms 73-150

A cry for help from a character created by Dorothy Parker (1893-1967), the American satirist, famous for her humour.

Please, God, let him telephone me now. Dear God, let him call me now. I won't ask anything else of you, truly I won't. It isn't very much to ask. It would be so little to you, God, such a little, little thing. Only let him telephone me now. Please, God. Please, please, please. . . .

Ah, don't let my prayer seem too little to you, God. You sit up there, so white and old, with all the angels about you and the stars slipping by. And I come to you with a prayer about a telephone call. Ah, don't laugh, God. You see, you don't know how it feels. You're so safe, there on your throne, with the blue swirling under you. Nothing can touch you; no one can twist your heart in his hands. This is suffering, God, this is bad, bad suffering. Won't you help me? For your Son's sake, help me. You said you would do whatever was asked of you in his name. Oh, God, in the name of thine only beloved Son, Jesus Christ, our Lord, let him telephone me now.

Dorothy Parker
quoted in *For All Occasions*

Wrath, anger, indignation

God's attitude to sin is described in both Old Testament and New Testament in terms borrowed from the human passion of anger, indignation, and wrath. It is not to be thought of as an irrational, irresponsible action on the part of God, but rather as the manifestation, sometimes suddenly and immediately experienced, of that aversion to sin which is part of his character. It is especially called forth for presumptuous sin, and it shows itself in the severe punishment and even utter destruction of the offender.

180

It has been the custom to distinguish between the Old Testament as emphasising the divine wrath and the New Testament as emphasising the divine mercy and love, but such a sharp distinction is unwarranted. The Old Testament is the story of God's steady anger against sin in every form, whether within Israel or outside, coupled with his forbearance to execute the fierceness of his anger (Hosea 11:9), that is, to wipe out Israel entirely by allowing her to pay the proper penalty for her sin. The extreme example of both God's wrath and his forbearance is to be seen in Exodus 32:7-14, the story of the golden calf, especially since it was a saying of the Rabbis that in every sin there is something of the golden calf. God's wrath waxed hot against the people because of this crowning apostasy, but at the pleading of Moses, he 'repented of the evil which he said he would do' to them. In his wrath he remembered mercy (Habakkuk 3:2).

The New Testament shows everywhere the same twin attitude on the part of God, an intense anger against sin, and a great forbearance towards the sinner. It is by his grace that he is full of forbearance, for though he is strong and firm in his judgement against sin, it is not his will that any should perish, but rather that they should turn to him and live. Nevertheless, there does come at length the Day of Wrath, which is the day of God's final and irrevocable judgement against sin and all unrepentant sinners. This Day of Wrath is spoken of in the Gospels, in the Epistles, and in the Apocalypse; and the New Testament nowhere says that mercy has the last word. God's last word is of condemnation and destruction of sin and stubborn sinners on the one hand, and of full pardon and restoration to the divine favour to all who truly repent and have faith in him.

N. H. Snaith
quoted in *A Theological Word Book of the Bible*

Psalm 80

Fourth Sunday of Advent: Year A, verses 1-7, 17-19
Proper 22/Ordinary Time 27: Year A, verses 7-15
First Sunday of Advent: Year B , verses 1-7, 17-19
Fourth Sunday of Advent: Year C, verses 1-7 (Alt)
Proper 15/Ordinary Time 20: Year C, verses 1-2, 8-19

Restore us, O God, let your face shine, that we may be saved.

Restore us, O God

Psalm 80 is punctuated by a refrain that carries its theme: 'Restore us, O God (of hosts), let your face shine, that we may be saved!' (verses 3, 7, 19). The psalm is a corporate prayer appealing to God to resume the favour bestowed on Israel in the past, restoring all that had been lost because of his anger (verses 4, 12).

1. The opening petitions for God to hear (verse 1) and help (verse 2) are accompanied by vocatives invoking God as the shepherd-king of Israel who occupies a throne supported by cherubs and who appears in flashing theophany when his people-flock are threatened. All these appellations are related to the ark and its role in Israel's history and faith. The top of the ark was decorated with hybrid creatures associated with deity in the ancient Near East; these cherubs represented the base of the Lord's invisible throne, the place on earth of the royal presence of the one who reigns from heaven. The ark led Israel through the wilderness like a flock. It manifested the appearance of God when it was taken out with the armies of Israel (1 Samuel 4:4; 2 Samuel 6:2) and symbolised his presence when it rested in the temple (2 Kings 19:15; see Psalm 99:1). Shepherd is the title for God as king who leads, protects, and provides for his people. . . . God of hosts, the title used in the refrain and elsewhere, is the name particularly associated with the ark (verses 4, 7, 14, 19). It is to the way of God represented by this cluster of identifications that the prayer appeals, to the God who leads his people through the perils of history and saves them from its dangers.

   Verses 4-6 describe in succinct formulaic fashion the distress of the flock of the Lord. The Lord God of hosts has been angry for a long time with his people, even though they pray to him (verse 4; not 'angry with his people's prayers', as NRSV suggests). There is nothing wrong with the prayers; they just don't help. Mourning (verse 5) and humiliation (verse 6) continue to be the lot of the people of God.

2. The rest of the psalm develops the image of a vine; the congregation speaks of itself as a grapevine planted by the Lord.

3. Like the flock, the vine and vineyard represented a basic and familiar possession that was owned, cared for, and prized as a primary good of life. Here God is portrayed as the owner who secured a vine, planted it, and cleared space for its growth.

4. The psalm prays for the restoration of the vine from the very judgement upon the vineyard announced by Isaiah (compare verses 12-13 with Isaiah 5:5-6) that pose the theological question raised by the prayer. It contains no expression of penitence, no assessment by the congregation of its own past or present conduct. The prayer does acknowledge that the congregation's distress is the work of divine wrath; it does not complain that God's anger is unjust. The congregation does pledge its faithfulness to God (verse 18). Does the pledge imply an admission that they have not been faithful in the past? Yet these are only marginal notes in the psalm.

The prayer concentrates with a single focus on one thing and one thing alone – the divine Thou. It addresses the God identified in the invocations as the actor in the congregation's experience of salvation and suffering and seeks God's resumption of his earlier work as the means of restoration. The psalm is a witness that the congregation must in the long last and in its extremity look away from its own repentance to a kind of repentance in God. His turning away from wrath and returning to grace. The trust that God will in the end do so is based on nothing in the congregation. It is based on the self-understanding that the congregation is the work of God, there in existence, wholly and only as the act of God. Believing that, the congregation can hope that God will not abandon what he has begun. Paul spoke of that confidence to the infant church when he wrote, 'I am sure that he who began a good work in you will bring it to completion at the day of Jesus Christ' (Philippians 1:6). Sharing that confidence, the church sings a paraphrase of the psalm's refrain on its way through history. 'Revive us, revive us; restore to thy grace, and then we shall live in the light of thy face' (A. J. Gordon).

James L. Mays
Psalms

Psalm 81

Ninth Sunday of Epiphany: Year B, verses 1-10
Proper 4/Ordinary Time 9: Year B, verses 1-10
Proper 17/Ordinary Time 22: Year C,
*   verses 1, 10-16*

The worship of idols takes many forms, some direct and unmistakable, some far more deceptive and subtle.

Psalm 81 was a frequently used psalm in worship during the Second Temple period. Seven psalms were selected for singing in the temple during the course of a week. These were Psalm 24 (Sunday), 48 (Monday), 82 (Tuesday), 94 (Wednesday), 81 (Thursday), 93 (Friday), 92 (Saturday). Thus this psalm was used throughout the year. Its choice for such usage was probably based on the psalm's call for obedience.

Psalm 81 has frequently been interpreted as a prophetic liturgy used in worship to remind the people of the necessity to obey the law or even as part of a covenant renewal ceremony. In such an analysis, verses 1-3 call for the assembly to offer praise and worship to God; verses 4-5b provide the reason for worship; and verses 5c-16 contain the prophetic sermon spoken as a direct address of the Deity to the people, as was common in prophetic speech. . . .

Psalm 81 may be seen as part of the admonition to observe the law that formed a part of the great Autumn Feast.

The opening verses of this psalm call for various forms of praise, singing, shouting, and the playing of various musical instruments (see 2 Samuel 6:12-19 for some of the celebration that went on at festival times). . . .

The motivation for celebrating the festival is given in verses 4-5; namely, God commanded it and established it as a statute, ordinance and decree.

The divine oracle consists of two types of material: reviews of the past (verses 6-7, 10a, 11-12) and admonitions to obedience (verses 8-9, 10b, 13-16). The reviews of the past, on the one hand, stress the redemptive action of the Lord by emphasising the deliverance from Egypt and the testing in the wilderness. On the other hand, the reviews highlight the people's unfaithfulness to which God responded by giving them over to their stubborn hearts and allowing them to follow their own counsels (verse 12: a good sermon topic!). The admonitions call Israel to hear, to listen, to have no other gods (see Exodus 20:3; Deuteronomy 5:7), to be receptive to divine blessings – all with the promise that such responses will be rewarded abundantly.

John H. Hayes
Preaching Through the Christian Year: Year B

Verse 5b of Psalm 81; 'I can hear a voice I no longer recognise' (Jerusalem Bible) implies that Israel had forgotten who their God was, his name and his nature, and what he had done for them in the past. In the following verses God has to remind his people who he is and what he has done, and will do (cf. verse 10 and also verses 6-9). Amnesia on the part of Israel was very dangerous as it once led to the sin of the Golden Calf; worship offered to an idol because they had forgotten so early their deliverance from Egypt. The following passage spells out some of the dangers involved when we have the wrong pictures of God, his nature and his work:

Contemporary idolatries. The worship of idols takes many forms, some direct and unmistakable, some far more deceptive and subtle. In our own times we witness people, relationships, institutions, ideologies, movements and nations caught in the grip of contemporary ideologies. The contemporary idolatries that have captured our worship and servitude are familiar realities: money, possessions, power, race, class, sex, nation, status, success, work, violence, religion, ideology, causes and so on.

The militant power of the contemporary ideologies has captured the corporations and institutions of commerce, the state and branches of government, the private and public bureaucracies, the various professions, the schools and universities, media and entertainments, and the churches. The presence of these idols or gods is felt in our economic and political systems, our social and cultural patterns, crucially affecting the way we relate to one another. Idols perpetuate themselves by erecting self-justifying ideologies and informational systems with the ability to turn falsehood into seeming truth by the distortion of language itself. Biblically understood, idolatry originates in the human decision to seek life and salvation apart from the source of life in God. Idols are 'impostors of God', as William Stringfellow has described them. They may be things, ideas, persons or institutions exalted and worshipped as gods. Rather than these finite realities serving people, people come to serve and worship them as objects of ultimate concern that are allowed to substitute for God. Idolatry denies the place of God as the giver of life and the author of salvation, dehumanises people by making them pay homage to objects not deserving of worship, and denigrates the proper vocation of things meant to be servants of human life, not rulers over it.

Jim Wallis
Agenda for Biblical People

Psalm 82

Proper 10/Ordinary Time 15: Year C
Proper 15/Ordinary Time 20: Year C

Justice is one of the hardest things to achieve, as every parent, teacher and magistrate will agree.

More than half of this psalm is on the theme of God's justice and his demand for justice in human society (see verses 1-4, 8). Here is an excerpt from a sermon by John B. Taylor, Bishop of St Albans on the same theme.

The other day I had a furious parent on my doorstep. Her son had been accused of a particularly unpleasant act and was on the point of being expelled from his school. He protested his innocence and she claimed she knew her son well enough to know that he would never do such a thing, but then all mothers say that. I got on to the headmaster and heard the story from him. A group of boys were working in the school library one Friday afternoon and when they had left, the lady librarian found on her desk a piece of paper obviously intended for her. It contained a crude, hand-written poem in the foulest language, and she was going to resign unless the culprit was found and punished. The head had initiated an investigation and all the signs pointed to this particular boy. He had been one of the group, the handwriting was exactly like his and on a previous occasion he had been called to account for using obscene language. Although he denied responsibility, the headmaster was sure he was guilty and there was no alternative but to expel him. He could not let behaviour like this go unpunished. He had to make an example of the boy for the sake of the school. Mother was distraught. The boy stoutly pleaded innocence and demanded justice. The head was quite sure that justice was being done. But where was justice to be found? Everyone had a different view. What was justice to the head was claimed by the boy to be gross injustice; and what the mother thought was unprintable. It was Easter the boy was due to sit his A-levels in June, and this could wreck his whole career. What was I expected to do to secure justice for her, and was his story true? Or was the headmaster right?

The story had a happy ending. When the news of the expulsion got round the school, another boy confessed to the crime and clearly he was the guilty party. So he left, the boy and his mother received a fulsome apology, and justice was seen to be done.

Justice is one of the hardest things to achieve, as every parent, teacher and magistrate will agree. But everyone wants justice – for themselves and for other people. And there is nothing worse than being falsely accused of a crime you didn't commit – except being punished for it.

So I want to think about justice, not in one sermon but in many. For it has so many facets that it will take us a long time to come to terms with them all. And I want to begin with the Old Testament because that is where everything in the Bible begins; it contains the building blocks for Christian faith and morality.

God is the judge of the whole world. This says as much about the nature of the world and the people in it as it does about its creator. It carries the implications of consistency and accountability. The universe is not at the mercy of haphazard forces: there is a divine controller who calls its inhabitants to account. Indeed the word *shophet*, judge, defines the action of one who rules, who issues decrees, who makes decisions and to whom his creation will one day have to answer. He holds everything together. There is a pattern, an order in creation that emanates from him. He is supreme.

No human dictator therefore, however powerful, should be allowed to usurp God's authority, for he too will have to stand before the bar of God's judgement. A society that believes in God ensures that no individual can ever get away with having absolute and supreme authority. There is only room for one on the top rung of the ladder, and that is reserved for God. A godless society, on the other hand, is always prey to totalitarianism: the state, the party or the dictator takes the place of God and recognises no authority higher than itself. That is why it is essential for human freedom that God's rule be recognised. Without it, liberation turns into tyranny.

God's justice is tempered with mercy. If you go to the Central Criminal court at the Old Bailey you will see the figure of Justice dominating the skyline overhead. She stands with a drawn sword in one hand, a pair of scales in the other and she is blindfolded. The message is clear. The scales weigh up the rights and wrongs, the sword punishes, and there is no favouritism. That is justice, Roman style. But Hebrew justice was different. Because the judge had to settle disputes, and many of these were appeals for help from the underprivileged against the tyranny of more powerful neighbours, the judge of Old Testament times was often seen as the champion of the innocent with a special concern for the poor – 'the widow, the orphan and the stranger within your gates'. To them the judge was the defender of their rights, the protector against oppression, the one who could not be bribed.

188

So justice, Hebrew style, was 'He shall not judge by what his eyes see, or decide by what his ears hear; but with righteousness he shall judge the poor, and decide with equity for the meek of the earth' (Isaiah 11:3-4). Unmoved by signs of influence or sounds of power, the good judge gives the poor a fair hearing in every circumstance.

Shall not the judge of all the earth do right? Yes indeed, and we look forward to the day when all nations will acknowledge his justice and mercy, when he comes to judge the living and the dead.

John B. Taylor
Preaching on God's Justice

Psalm 84

Presentation: Years A, B, C (Alt)
Proper 16/Ordinary Time 21: Year B
Proper 25/Ordinary Time 30: Year C, verses 1-7

Each day, as they drew closer to the temple, their spirits would rise with happy anticipation; and instead of getting weaker with the journey, they would feel themselves actually growing stronger.

He feels envy

The subject of this chapter is envy. That's not usually a nice word because it is not usually a nice mood. In fact, it can be a very negative and destructive mood. When you envy another person you destroy your relationship with him, you wreck your own peace of mind and you set up a quarrel with God because you assume he has dealt unfairly with you. The Bible, especially the teachings of Jesus, issues strict warnings against the corrosive power of envy in the human soul. Paul listed 'envyings' as one of 'the works of the flesh' (Galatians 5:21 AV), and the medieval Church included it among the Seven Deadly Sins.

Yet there is also a positive, constructive side to envy. Surely it is possible to envy people, not with resentment in your heart but with admiration, because you long to share the qualities and opportunities that make them the sort of people they are. It cannot be sinful to regard a person who stands stalwart and serene in the face of tragedy and say, 'I envy his strength of character.' The man who wrote Psalm 84 displayed that right kind of envy. He envied other people their privilege of going to church. It was his reaction to their experience of God.

Listen to his passionate prayer: 'How amiable are thy tabernacles (How lovely are thy dwellings), O Lord of hosts! My soul longeth, yea, even fainteth for the courts of the Lord: my heart and my flesh crieth out for the living God.' That man wanted to go to church as desperately as a person dying of thirst wants a drink of water. We don't know who he was, though we do know that he lived in the land of the Bible several centuries before Christ. Some commentators believe that he must have been a devout Jew who went up to one of the great temple feasts every year but for some reason couldn't make it that year and felt deprived. Perhaps he looked at the sun high in the sky and thought of the fortunate people worshipping God at that very moment in the temple courts: 'Blessed are they that dwell in thy house: they will be still praising thee.' It is a rare person in the western world today who can identify himself with the writer of Psalm 84. We are more like the temple worshippers whom the psalmist envied. We can go to church and worship almost any time and anywhere we wish.

To begin with, he envies us *our security in God*. That comes across in his poetic reference to God's lesser creatures whose wings give them unlimited access to the temple courts: 'Yea, the sparrow hath found an house, and the swallow a nest for herself, where she may lay her young, even thine altars, O Lord of hosts, my King, and my God.' Not that the psalmist envied the birds. He envied a particular class of people who lived in the temple and made it their permanent home, the priests and choristers ever singing the praise of God. How privileged they were and still are.

The psalmist envied the temple worshippers *their strength in God*. That comes across from those verses where he says to God in prayer, 'Blessed is the man whose strength is in thee; in whose heart are the highways to Zion. . . . They go from strength to strength, every one of them in Zion appeareth before God.'

It has been suggested that the psalmist had in mind a second group of people who were related to the temple in a different way. He was thinking of the pilgrims travelling on foot from all parts of the country and converging on the Holy City. For those who came from a distance it would be a difficult and tiring journey, perhaps even dangerous if they had to cross waterless deserts and mountains that were infested by robbers and wild animals. Yet each day, as they drew closer to the temple, their spirits would rise with happy anticipation; and instead of getting weaker with the journey, they would feel themselves actually growing stronger.

On the human level they simply strengthened one another as people do in time of need. . . .

The psalmist envied the temple worshippers *their sufficiency in God*. That comes across from the familiar verse, 'For a day in thy courts is better than a thousand. I had rather be a doorkeeper in the house of my God, than to dwell in the tents of wickedness.' Commentators suggest that here the psalmist was thinking not only about the temple worshippers but about himself and his own relationship to the temple. Though he could not go the house of God, yet he continued to look toward the house of God. Though he couldn't always be in church, yet he could always be related to the church, and in that relationship he felt highly favoured. It has been speculated that he might have been a soldier on guard duty in the desert who wished that he could stand guard for one day at the gate of the temple. 'For a day in thy courts is better than a thousand.' Perhaps he saw in the distance the encampment of the enemy and murmured, 'I had rather be a doorkeeper in the house of my God, than to dwell in the tents of wickedness.'

Leonard Griffith
Reactions to God: Man's Response to God's Activity in the Psalms

Psalm 85

Proper 14/Ordinary Time 19: Year A, verses 1-2, 8-13
Second Sunday of Advent: Year B, verses 1-2, 8-13
Proper 10/Ordinary Time 15: Year B, verses 1-13
Proper 12/Ordinary Time 17: Year C

*Righteousness is
an intense desire
for harmony
springing out of
a great sensibility
to discord.*

The fortunes of Jacob

Psalm 85 is a prophetic liturgy in three parts: verses 1-3, 4-7,
8-13. Parts one and three were apparently rendered by individuals and part two by the congregation. The setting seems to
be the days of Haggai and Zechariah, shortly after the return
of a remnant of the Jews from Babylonian captivity.

Past mercies (85:1-3). 'Restore the fortunes' does not mean
the same thing in every context. Here it seems to refer to the
restoration of some of the Jews to their homeland in 538 BC
under Cyrus the Persian. This restoration was evidence that
God had forgiven their guilt and sin.

Present need (85:4-7). But the expectations aroused by the
Prophet of the Exile (Isaiah 40-66) have not been realised (see
Haggai 1:6-11; 2:15-19; Zechariah 1:12-17) and the people feel
that God's wrath still rests upon them. Therefore, they plead
for a restoration that will be a full salvation in every sense.

Future expectancy (85:8-13). The psalmist, whether he is
technically a prophet or not, receives a prophetic message
from God and delivers it prophetically. God will grant his
well-being ('peace') and salvation to those who revere him,
and the Temple will be rebuilt that God's 'glory' or revealed
presence may dwell in the land (see 63:2; Ezekiel 43:4;
Zechariah 2:1-5; compare Exodus 40:34-35; 2 Chronicles 7:1-3).
The Temple of Zerubbabel was completed in 516 BC, but the
ultimate revelation of God's glory in the midst of his people
was to be made in the Incarnation of the Son of God (John
1:14; 2 Corinthians 4:6).

Verses 10-13 are similar in thought and language to Isaiah
40-66. God's Covenant, love, faithfulness, righteousness, and
peace will bless his people, who in turn will reflect the character of their Saviour. Material blessings will accompany
spiritual growth (compare Matthew 6:33).

A. B. Rhodes
Psalms

As an undergraduate I remember going to the University mission in 1963. It was led by Trevor Huddleston – then Bishop of Masasi in Tanganyika. The main addresses were given in the Examination Schools. They were well attended. Many of us arrived in good time hoping to get a seat near the front. We were chatting excitedly amongst ourselves, waiting for the Bishop to arrive. I was curious to see him, having been deeply moved by his book, *Naught for our Comfort* – about apartheid in Sophiatown, South Africa.

There was a sudden silence. We all turned round and looked at the entrance. Yes, the Bishop had indeed arrived. All eyes were fixed on him. In complete silence he walked slowly up the hall, not hurrying. I studied his demeanour carefully. First impressions are important. Here was some-one I immediately took to be righteous. 'Righteousness' was somehow written into his features. This observation was later confirmed by what he said and the kind of life he lived. Four hours a day in prayer and worship were impressive. That this devotional life was balanced by thought and action completely won me over. I concluded he was a man in a 'right' relationship with God, and in a right relationship with people, hence for me a living example of 'righteousness'.

William Sykes
Visions of Love

Righteousness is a word that has been much misunderstood, because it means so much, and is hard to define. In common with words like Christianity, Socialism, Liberty, it is so difficult to define; it requires too much trouble, so that it has been left out and despised like words that need much pondering over. It goes to the root of our nature, strikes below the reason, is deeper than hunger and thirst, stronger than fear of death. Those are blessed who love righteousness most. Only those souls can grow to fullness, who will drive on to completion of development, to the final completion of human nature for which we are made. Righteousness is an intense desire for harmony springing out of a great sensibility to discord. So righteousness and peace have kissed each other. (For this last sentence compare Psalm 85:10b – Ron Dale)

G. A. Studdert Kennedy
The New Creation in Christ

Psalm 86

Proper 7/Ordinary Time 12: Year A, verses 1-10,
  16-17
Proper 11/ Ordinary Time 16: Year A, verses 11-17

To say, 'Be it unto me according to thy word' is to accept God's signified will and to set about doing it in faith.

The Lord, the mighty helper of the needy

This psalm is peculiar in many ways. Its first peculiarity is that the name of God which dominates is Adonahy, or Lord, which indicates absolute Lordship, and by the use of which the singer shows his sense of submission and loyalty. The name Jehovah is used four times, thus revealing the singer's sense of God as Helper; and the name God five times, thus revealing his consciousness of the Divine might. The supreme sense however, is that of the Divine authority. The next matter of special note is that while the psalm is a beautiful and consecutive song, it is largely composed of quotations from other psalms, thus revealing the singer's familiarity with them. The references in the Revised Version will enable the reader to trace these quotations.

Finally, the psalm is unique in its method of urging a petition upon the ground of some known fact. This is clearly seen if the use of the word 'for' is noticed (verses 1-5, 7, 10, 13). In the first four verses the facts are those which indicate his attitude toward God. In the last four the facts are those revealing God's attitude toward him. The revelation for us is that of true approach to God in times of need. This must be based upon our relation of absolute submission to him. It must be expressed in harmony with spiritual desires as expressed by the fellowship of the faithful. It must be urged in consecration and courage.

G. Campbell Morgan
Notes on the Psalms

I want to pick up the themes of submission and loyalty to God mentioned in the previous reading. I have been strongly influenced by an experience I had in the 1960s when my loyalty and my submission to God's will were sorely tempted. I was in my second appointment as an ordained minister, serving in an old Lancashire cotton town. I loved the honest, ordinary folk of the town, but I soon saw that church life was in decline. So how was I to minister in this situation? What could I do to reverse that decline? Was it not a hopeless scenario? What could anyone do to stem the drift away from church life? On top of all this I was wondering how I was going to manage financially as I was not well paid then.

One night a wealthy businessman gave me a lift to and from an important church meeting. Prior to dropping me off after the meeting, we sat in the darkened car with rain drumming powerfully on the roof. My friend suddenly said to me, 'Ron, you're wasting your time in the church. I have a far better job on offer and you will make ten times what you currently get paid.' He was very insistent and wanted a quick decision. So I pondered his very generous offer. In the end though, I said that whilst I appreciated his concern and offer, I could not possibly accept as I had a very strong call from the risen Christ to do his work as a minister. So no matter how hard the task, I believed he wanted me to be faithful to him and the call he had given me. So I said no. My friend thought for a moment, and his parting words to me were, 'You are a damned fool.' With those words ringing in my ears I walked home through the rain. Subsequently I really enjoyed a number of marvellous opportunities for ministry within the town. It proved a tough, but enjoyable ministry.

Ron Dale, 1999

She (Mary, the Mother of Jesus) has a unique place in the Christian understanding of holiness. She carries a marvellous statement of holiness as a trust in and communion with God, learned and maintained (like her son's later obedience) through the things one suffers, a belonging to God worked out through the needs and decisions of every day. And this belonging to God is a matter of saying, 'Be it unto me according to thy word' and sustaining all the action that follows from such desire, such commitment.

The action is of two kinds, relative to the double nature of God's will. God's will is, on the one hand, all that *is* at any given moment, in the sense that he permits the existence of the whole state of affairs in which the believer finds himself. It is God's permissive will for every believer at any given moment that he should be alive in that world in those conditions. To say 'Be it unto me according to thy word' means, with a dropping of rancour and an assumption of open-armed readiness, to accept the conditions, because it is the will of God, who cannot be other than loving, that one should in fact *be* just now in those circumstances. God's will is, on the other hand, what he wants us to *do* in this moment: the action or endurance or enjoyment he calls us to offer him in these circumstances. To say 'Be it unto me according to thy word' is to accept God's signified will and to set about doing it in faith.

J. Neville Ward
Friday Afternoon

Psalm 89

Proper 8/Ordinary Time 13: Year A, verses 1-4, 15-18
Fourth Sunday of Advent: Year B, verses 1-4, 19-26
(Alt)
Proper 11/Ordinary Time 16: Year B, verses 20-37

*Like the sun,
the Church's
passion is meant
to generate both
heat and light.*

This psalm offers the fullest exposition in the Old Testament of the divine covenant with David and the promises this covenant involved (see verses 19-37).

Psalm 89 is in reality a lament that speaks of the divine promises to David after they have all been called into question. The conclusion of the psalm, verses 38-51, bemoans the humiliation of the Davidic ruler who is the object of divine wrath, whose covenant is renounced, whose strongholds are in ruin, and for whom all the promises of God seem to have failed. The description of the king's condition simply piles up one disappointing condition upon another. The psalm ends with a complaint about the loss of God's love and faithfulness and a prayer for God to note how the king bears in his bosom the insults of the nations roundabout and how the enemies mock the footsteps of the anointed (the Messiah).

If one takes this material as reflective of some actual historical situation, then the king must have suffered a severe humiliation in battle. In fact, the psalm sounds as if it is a description of the consequences that resulted from the destruction of Jerusalem by the Babylonians.

But this week's psalm lection does not focus on the humiliation aspects of the psalm; it focuses on the positive. Verses 1-4 both remind and praise God for divine faithfulness and steadfast love, which are always the basis for confidence. Note that God is reminded that steadfast love is for ever and his faithfulness as sure as the heaven. (Although the minister may not wish to highlight the point, these are exactly the divine qualities called into question in verse 49. Perhaps few psalms so stress the twofold quality of the Deity – the divine care and the divine forsakenness – as does this psalm). God is made to recall that he swore to David that his descendants would rule for ever and his throne endure for generations. The ancient Hebrews were not bashful when it came to reminding God of the divine commitments and to reiterating the promises on which they banked their hopes. (One should remember that when this psalm was read or used in public worship, the person who spoke the first four verses with their calm serenity and secure promises was aware of the trauma yet to be expressed before the psalter scroll was rolled together and neatly tied and tucked away again.)

Verses 19-24 focus on portions of God's eternal promises to David and recall the words in God's vision in which David was chosen and exalted among his people (see 2 Samuel 7). Several factors about David and God's relationship to him are stressed, and it must be recalled that the David spoken of here is more the idealised David of messianic quality than the David of history. First, David was found by God (see 1 Samuel 16:1-4). Here the emphasis is placed on the divine initiative. The true servant is the one whom God separates out, not the one who grasps at equality or the one who strives for superiority. He who would claim to be the messiah should always be questioned. Second, as the anointed, David is set apart, set aloof from the rest, where he, like the New Testament Messiah, must know what it means to be one 'apart'. Third, David is promised that victory over his enemies and dominance over his foes are part of the assurance granted, for it is God who stands behind him and strikes down his opponents and foes. The interpreter must remember here that ancient Israelite life was always threatened and that survival could never be taken for granted. Although this emphasis on being constantly threatened might sound a bit paranoid, even Jesus is said to have struggled with Satan in the wilderness. Finally, the psalmist quotes God as promising that faithfulness and love for David are certain and that in God's strength David's horn will be exalted – that is, his status will be secure.

The psalm, like Advent, calls on people to rely on God's promises even when those promises seem to lie shattered at the feet of those who pray, but who pray for the coming redemption in spite of the realities within which they live.

John H. Hayes
Preaching Through the Christian Year: Year B

Psalm 89:36-37 says, 'I see his throne like the sun, enduring for ever like the moon, that faithful witness in the sky.' It reminded me of a very different approach by Dr Colin Morris:

In another simile, the Church is described as 'fair as the moon'. There is a terrifying stillness about the moon, a passivity well illustrated by those miraculous television shots of astronauts bouncing like ungainly clowns across its god-forsaken terrain. . . .

Yet that barren cinder glows with a strange luminosity when the rays of the sun strike it. The moon is not a primary power-source, a generator; it is a reflector, beaming to earth light issuing from a source outside itself. So the moon-image pinpoints a mode of the Church's life which may seem to some unfashionable if not downright reactionary – the necessary passivity of the Church, her gracious ministry of reflectiveness. We need this insight to counter one of our besetting sins, hyperactivity – the neurotic urge to be seen doing something. We seem to have come full circle. Once we took refuge in piety to avoid the claims of action; now we are in danger of taking refuge in action from the claims of spirituality. What we lack is the will to *be*. The Church's problem is one of identity rather than function. Because we do not know who we are, we do not know what to do. We have anaesthetised by frenetic activity that quiet brooding joy and silent anguish which were marks of Christ's ministry of *acceptance*.

As the moon symbolises one mode of the Church's life, *reflectiveness*, so the sun represents its complement – *passion*. It shows the strength of the Gospel that this clash of opposing qualities has rarely torn the Church apart. Instead, under one banner have marched (though they occasionally got out of step!) those who *know* and those who *burn* – mystic and militant, scholar and evangelist, priest and crusader . . . merging cold and heat without producing tepidity; emblazoning on one banner black and white without merging both into pallid grey; joining hot-blooded Latin and reserved Northerner; ebullient African and mystic Asian without denaturing any of them. So moon and sun may represent violently opposed modes of being without either negating the other. Both are held together in one galaxy which transcends and effortlessly contains them. Like the sun, the Church's passion is meant to generate both heat and light.

Colin Morris
The Hammer of the Lord

Psalm 90

Proper 25/Ordinary Time 30: Year A, verses 1-6, 13-17

Proper 28/Ordinary Time 33: Year A, verses 1-8, (9-11), 12

Proper 23/Ordinary Time 28: Year B, verses 12-17

I find it deeply satisfying to know that God is Lord of the future, one who assures me that there is a future for me also.

This psalm thinks of three things.

1. The greatness of the eternal God. To God a thousand years are but as a watch in the night; before God the generations of men rise and pass away.

2. The brevity of the life of man. At its longest man's life is but a moment. And many of us make our short and trouble-beset life far worse than it might be by our rebellion against God.

3. The psalmist is certain that man's brief life can only attain to any kind of worth and peace when it is lived in obedience to and in communion with God. Man's dignity lies in the fact that he is a child of God.

This psalm is not an utterance of dark pessimism. It is a summons to lose man's little life in the fullness of the life of God.

A prayer:
O God, help me to rest my restlessness in your peace;
to rest my weakness in your strength;
to rest my little life in the vastness of your eternities.

William Barclay
Seven Fresh Wineskins

Jehovah the eternal refuge of man

The main purpose of this psalm is revealed in the prayer with which it concludes (verses 13-17). This prayer is prefaced by a meditation on the frailty of man (verses 3-12), in the light of the eternity of God (verses 1-2). By this backward method of analysis we gain a conception of the general scheme of the psalm which now enables us to take the three movements in their orderly sequence.

The eternity of God is described in three stages. First, as measured by the history of his people, he has ever been their dwelling-place. Second, as measured by creation, he was before all. Finally, whether the mind travels backward or forward to the vanishing point, he is still God. In this light man is seen in the frailty of his being. To God, a thousand years are comparatively nothing, and in every millennium men appear and pass in a sequence as orderly as that of the grass, but in a life as transitory. This frailty is the more feeble because man is a sinner; and therefore out of harmony with God. Yet this very eternity of God is the hope of man in his frailty and sin, and the heart is lifted to Jehovah in a prayer that the mornings, the days, the years of brief life may all be set in true relation to him. Satisfaction, gladness, success in work must all come from the right relation of man in his frailty to the eternal Lord.

G. Campbell Morgan
Notes on the Psalms

When I think about the concept of time I sometimes get haunted by my transient existence. Time seems to fly by, very rarely pass slowly.

There have of course been occasions when time has dragged, for example waiting for the end of my twelve-hour shift in the Army in North Africa. I would do a tour around the ammunition dump thinking it would pass a good half-hour, only to find when looking at my watch that only six or seven minutes had actually elapsed. A twelve-hour shift seemed endless. Sometimes waiting for a special event like my birthday or Christmas also seemed to make time drag its feet.

However, some years ago I was taught an interesting way of looking at time by an Anglican nun. I was attending my local cathedral Quiet Day. All the cathedral staff were present along with myself and some Free Church colleagues. The nun leading the day was a lovely, deeply spiritual person. During one of her three talks she spoke about time and problems people sometimes had when thinking about its swift/ slow passage. One helpful way of looking at time according to the nun was to imagine standing in a river. You had then two basic choices. Either you looked down the river, or up it. If you looked down river you saw the water flowing away from you, a bit like time running away and rapidly passing. If this was done, then one's life also appeared to be flowing away on the river of time.

However, if you looked up the river, you saw the water coming towards you and this symbolised your future coming to meet you. That meant of course that it was fine if you were looking forward to *good* times, things and experiences; but maybe with a sense of dread if they happened to be *bad* things.

I discovered also that in Biblical thinking there are two main words used for time. One is *Chronos* meaning chronological time, time by the hour, and the other is *Kairos*, a time of opportunity and fulfilment, a time when things are ripe for the plucking. Maybe also, God's hour, the time when he decides what shall be. A decision that human beings have no influence over.

I find it deeply satisfying to know that God is Lord of the future, one who assures me that there is a future for me also, a future in his hands and offered in love to all who will receive it.

Ron Dale, 1999

Psalm 91

Proper 24 (29): Year B, verses 9-16
First Sunday of Lent: Year C, verses 1-2, 9-16
Proper 21 (26): Year C, verses 1-6, 14-16

Real trust does not seek to test God or to prove his faithfulness.

My refuge and my fortress

'If you desire,' writes Athanasius to Marcellinus, 'to establish yourself and others in your devotion, to know what confidence is to be reposed in God, and what makes the mind fearless, you will praise God by reciting the ninetieth (ninety-first) Psalm.' That experience and commendation of Psalm 91 is repeated again and again in the history of its use and interpretation. It is a classic on the sure providence of God as the citadel of faith. The hymn 'Sing Praise to God, Who Reigns Above' echoes its confidence in God and is a good companion to the study of it.

1. The literary structure of the psalm has two major parts, distinguished by the style of direct address to an individual 'you' (verses 1-13) and by that of a declaration in the divine first person (verses 14-16). The theme and those to whom the psalm is addressed are identified at the beginning: those who trust themselves to the protection of the Lord (verses 1-2). A description of the Lord's protection from many dangers follows (verses 3-13). The declaration lets hearers and readers of the psalm know that God confirms the trust of those who are committed to him (verses 14-16). The psalm seems to be the work of a teacher who seeks to nurture the trust of the faithful by encouraging each of them to take the Lord as their refuge from all the troubles of life.

2. 'Refuge' used as a metaphor for God's care and protection is a pervasive theme in the psalter. It is frequently employed in prayers and confessions of confidence in God as a noun (e.g. 14:6; 46:1; 61:3) and as a verb ('take refuge', e.g. 2:11; 5:11; 11:1). In general secular use, the verb means to seek protected space (Judges 9:15) from threatening dangers. Verb and noun belong to the psalmist's vocabulary of trust in God (note the parallel in verse 2). They are primarily items in a word field used to speak of the Lord as protector of those who hold to him: fortress, stronghold, dwelling place, shelter. The idiom 'shadow/shade of the wings of

204

the Lord' belongs to the vocabulary (see verse 4; 17:8; 36:7; 57:1; 63:7). The life of the faithful in Israel was set in an environment of threatening dangers. This vocabulary and its frequency in the psalms brings out the important role of trust in coping with the anxieties that beset their life.

3. The dangers listed in verses 3-13 do not seem to reflect any particular historical or social setting. They are, rather, a catena of the more drastic anxieties to which individual life in Israel was subject. They are named – some with idiomatic hyperbole (e.g. 'snare of the fowler', 'dash your foot against a stone'), some in general terms (e.g. 'evil', scourge'), and some directly (pestilence, lion and adder). The pairs of diurnal and nocturnal dangers (verses 5-6) may be demons of types known from ancient Near Eastern sources. In these other cultures, procedures that used charms and magic and ceremonies of exorcism were employed to counter supernatural dangers. In Israel, as this psalm shows, trust in the Lord and only that became the one religious resource on which the faithful depended. One of the potential dangers feared by the pious in Israel was 'the punishment of the wicked'. Using exaggerated numbers, verses 7-8 promise that, should such a punishment strike thousands, the faithful will only see it happen but not be harmed by it. The entire list is composed as a poetic survey that is a spiritual antidote to the range of anxieties that could afflict the lives of Israelites. Though its items are strange to other and later times, it still does its work of anchoring the soul in the midst of anxieties with different names.

4. The psalm itself poses a danger. Because its assurance of security is so comprehensive and confident, it is especially subject to the misuse that is a possibility for all religious claims, that of turning faith into superstition. In Judaism and Christianity, bits of the texts have been worn in amulets that were believed to be a kind of magical protection for those who wore them. The promise that the ministering angels would guard the way of the pious (verse 11) was one of a bases of belief that God assigns individual believers a personal angel to watch over them, and the angel easily became the focus of concern and piety. In an infamous use of Scripture, Satan employed verses 11-12 in his attempt to corrupt Jesus (Matthew 4:5-7; Luke 4:10-11). The psalm must always be read and understood in the light of that encounter. Satan placed Jesus on the pinnacle of the temple and challenged him to jump off to test

God's promise that the angels would bear him up. The temptation was to take the promises of God into the control of his own will and act. That would have shifted the power of the promise from the fee sovereignty of God to individual wilfulness. Jesus saw that as a way to test God, not as the way of trust. Real trust does not seek to test God or to prove his faithfulness.

James L. Mays
Psalms

In the face of suffering

How does the Christian conquer the temptation of suffering? Here, the end of the book of Job is a great help to us. In the face of suffering Job has protested his innocence to the last, and has brushed aside the counsels to repentance from his friends who try to trace his misfortune back to a particular, perhaps hidden sin of Job. In addition, Job has spoken high-sounding words about his own righteousness. After the appearance of God Job declares: 'Therefore I abhor myself, and repent in dust and ashes' (Job 42:3, 6). But the wrath of God is not now turned against Job, but against his friends: 'for ye have not spoken of me the thing that is right, as my servant Job hath' (Job 42:7). Job gets justice before God and yet confesses his guilt before God. That is the solution of the problem. Job's suffering has its foundation not in his guilt but in his righteousness. Job is tempted because of his piety. So Job is right to protest against suffering coming upon him as if he were guilty. Yet this right comes to an end for Job when he no longer faces human beings but faces God. Face to face with God, even the good, innocent Job knows himself to be guilty.

Dietrich Bonhoeffer
Temptation

Psalm 92

Proper 6/Ordinary Time 11: Year B, verses 1-4, 12-15
Eighth Sunday of Epiphany/Ordinary Time 8:
  Year C, verses 1-4, 12-15

A lot of religion
has become unreal,
unreal because
unrelated to
human activity.

Psalm 92 is the only psalm designated 'for the Sabbath Day'. Exactly why it was singled out is unclear. Perhaps it is because the references to God's 'work'/'works' in verses 4-5 can be understood as a reference to creation, and the Sabbath was also associated with creation (see Genesis 2:1-3; Exodus 20:8-11). Or perhaps it is because the Sabbath was to be a day totally devoted to praising God (verses 1-2), a day on which the people of God were to gather for worship (verse 13). Or perhaps it is because the name 'Yahweh' occurs seven times.

Psalm 92 is usually categorised as an individual song of thanksgiving. In verse 1-4, the psalmist at least implicitly invites others to share in thanksgiving for his or her having been 'made . . . glad' (verse 4). Verses 10-11 sound like a description of the psalmist's deliverance, in which case they too would be characteristic of a thanksgiving song. But it is unclear whether the verbs in verses 10-11 should be translated in the past tense (NRSV) or the future tense. In other words, has the psalmist already been exalted and the enemies defeated, or are these events still in the future? This uncertainty highlights another major aspect of Psalm 92, that is, it is concerned with the life and future of the righteous (verses 12-15) and the wicked (verses 7, 9, 11), as were Psalms 1 and 37 (Sixth and Seventh Sundays After Epiphany). Because verse 7 recognises that the wicked do flourish temporarily, and because it is likely that the verbs in verses 10-11 should be translated in the future tense (as in verse 9), it is best to approach Psalm 92 not so much as a song that celebrates a particular deliverance, but rather as a psalm that affirms the ultimate triumph of God's sovereignty and the deliverance of God's people.

While the wicked may and indeed do flourish *for now*, they 'shall perish' (verse 9; see Psalms 1:6; 37:20). This assurance, as in Psalms 1 and 37, is founded on the conviction that is highlighted in Psalm 92:8, the exact centre of the psalm: Yahweh is 'on high for ever'. In other words, God rules the world (see 'on high' in Psalm 93:4; Psalm 93:1 specifically affirms that God reigns, as do Psalms 95-99). Verse 8 of Psalm 92 is sandwiched between two verses that focus on the wicked, or the 'evildoers' (verses 7, 9). In terms of the structure of the psalm and in terms of the reality of the psalmist's world, the affirmation of God's rule is made in the very midst of evil. The perspective is eschatological. The good news is that *even now*, in the midst of evil, praise and joy are possible (verses 1-4) and the righteous 'flourish' (verses 12-13) and are fruitful (verse 14) in an enduring way that declares that God is upright, loving, and faithful (verses 2, 15; 'declare' in verse 2 and 'showing' in verse 15 translate the same Hebrew verb).

The theme of declaring makes Psalm 92 especially appropriate for Epiphany. What is to be declared gets at the very heart of God's character – 'steadfast love' and 'faithfulness' (see for example Exodus 34:6-7; Psalms 98:3; 138:2). The declaration is to be made throughout every day (see 'morning' and 'night' in 92:2) and throughout a lifetime (see 'old age' in verse 14). It involves both liturgical activity (verse 3) and style of life (verses 12-14). By their worship and their work, the righteous declare that their lives and futures belong not to themselves but to God. This affirmation is particularly effective at this point in the psalter. Psalm 90 opened Book IV of the psalter with a portrayal of human transience (verses 3-12) accompanied by a plea for God's favour (90:13-17). It is as if Psalm 92, especially verses 1-4, affirms that the plea of Psalm 90 has been answered: the psalmist has been made glad (92:4; see Psalm 90:14-15), 'sing(s) for joy' (92:4; see 'that we may rejoice' in Psalm 90:14), and celebrates God's 'steadfast love in the morning' (92:2; see Psalm 90:14). God's 'work' has been made manifest to the psalmist (92:4; see Psalm 92:16). Confronted with general human transience (Psalm 90) and at least the temporary prosperity of the wicked (92:7 – the language here is reminiscent of that applied to all humanity in 90:5-6), the psalmist declares the reality of divine protection (see 'rock' in 92:15 and faithfulness in verse 2).

Verse 12 specifically recalls verse 7. Whereas the wicked 'flourish' only briefly, 'like grass', the righteous 'flourish' (verses 12-13) like fruitful, stately trees that are 'planted' in God's garden (see Psalm 1:3; Jeremiah 17:7-8). With God as both foundation and source of nourishment, the righteous are able to take root, grow, and be fruitful (see Luke 6:43-49). As the similar text in Jeremiah 17 suggests, the real difference between the righteous and the wicked is that the righteous trust God and the wicked trust themselves (see esp. Jeremiah 17:5, 7). Psalm 92 affirms that trusting ourselves alone is illusory and ultimately destructive (verses 7, 9). It is thus a sobering warning to a generation like ours that generally 'cannot understand this' (verse 6). As much as any generation before us in the history of the world, we are inclined to trust our own intelligence, strength and technology more than we trust God, one another, or anything else. A renewed sense of the greatness of God's works and the productivity of God's design for the world is urgently needed (see verse 5).

Thus like Psalms 1 and 37, the eschatological affirmation of God's rule calls for a decision. The decision to find our security in God rather than self suggests another possible dimension to Psalm 92 as a Sabbath song. The Heidelberg Catechism states that the Fourth Commandment requires 'that I cease from my evil works all the days of my life, allow the Lord to work in me through his Spirit, and thus begin in this life the eternal Sabbath' (question 103). Psalm 92 affirms that in recognising and yielding ourselves to God's rule (verse 8), we experience even now the measure of life and peace – 'the eternal Sabbath' – that God intends and will accomplish for the world and its creatures (Isaiah 55:10-13).

J. Clinton McCann, Jr.
Texts for Preaching

Picking up the thought in the above piece about our trust in our-selves and our technology, rather than trust in God, I discovered the following passage many years ago when working as an industrial chaplain in Lancashire. The incident relates to a village campaign (in China) to educate the commune in the manufacture and use of ball-bearings – a very considerable advance, of course, over the wooden wheel and square axle:

Tengshi-hi of the Hupeh Province had burned incense before his metal idol all his life. There came into the village The Golden Dragon Agricultural Co-operative (with its campaign in the use of tools and ball-bearings). Tengshi decided to contribute his idol to the scrap campaign. And as he moved out this ancestral knick-knack he said: 'O God, be not angry with me; I burned incense before you many years, but nothing was changed, and the fields were still ploughed by oxen; but mechanisation has now come, and I respectfully request you to change yourself' – presumably into ball-bearings! We may be amused by the sudden transition from a lofty theme of Providence . . . to ball-bearings, but in fact the same process has taken place in the West. Our reliance on technology is readily discernible, once we stand back and look around us, but the shift of belief, of human assumption, can also be evidenced in fascinating social documentation. . . . A lot of religion has become unreal, unreal because unrelated to human activity. On a massive scale great numbers have simply thrown it overboard.

E. R. Wickham
Encounter with Modern Society

Psalm 93

Ascension Day: Year B (Alt)
Proper 29/Ordinary Time 34: Year B

With Jesus . . .
what was to be
his triumph was
what others
would consider
his defeat.

Meditating on God

I see in the writer of this psalm a man who simply meditates on God. He is content to ask for nothing. Unlike many other psalmists, he complains about nothing. Intercession is not his concern. Whatever he does at other times when he comes into God's presence, now he wants only to meditate on God, and especially on his greatness. He devotes himself to this alone, sometimes addressing God (verses 2, 5), sometimes allowing us to share his thoughts with him.

How can he conceive of the majesty of God, how describe his greatness? Human language is of little use, but he has no other means of expressing what is on his mind. He calls on two pictures to help him: the picture of the king, and the picture of the sea.

The king (Psalm 93:1). It is difficult for us who live in the modern world to conceive of what kingship conveyed in old days. Perhaps our grandparents or great-grandparents found that easier than we do. They knew what Queen Victoria meant – that little woman who reigned over those large parts of the world which were painted red in their school atlases, having immense authority over vast millions of her subjects. Today, across the world, the idea of kingship has been tarnished by the atrocities of many who have occupied the thrones of their countries. And the junction of kingship and democracy has been – and is – a tricky one. But speak the word 'king' to a person living at the time of our psalmist, and he would see in the person of David enough marks of power, dignity and care to make him pray for a Messiah with similar marks. Kingship and nobility went hand in hand.

The sea (Psalm 93:3). Jews did not like the sea. The great Mediterranean spoke of the danger of the unknown. Those few who set sail on it in their frail ships knew all too well of its treachery and its menace. The writer of the book of Revelation assures his readers that, in the new heaven and the new earth of his vision, 'there was no longer any sea' (Revelation 21:1).

And yet, our psalmist had stood and watched the crashing breakers as the tide came in. Frightening for landlubbers like himself. But there was power in those waves, and purity

211

in the waters that seemed to consume earth's rubbish and uncleanness. *Power and purity* – he must grant them that. With awe, he saw in the waves the marks of their Maker. 'Mightier than the sound of great waters, mightier than the breakers of the sea, mightier on high is the Lord' (verse 4).

Further, this God is not only a God of ineffable majesty. He is a God concerned with law and order in his creation and among his creatures. He has made his mind and will known by the 'decrees' which he has given (verse 5). Of this the sheer beauty of God's 'house', the temple (verse 5), gives at least some hint.

'Throughout the ages': it is a fitting note on which to end the psalm. In the light of God's eternity and human transience, we can only bow in wonder.

Donald Coggan
Psalms 73-150: The People's Bible Commentary

Caesar entered Rome with his chariot drawn by six tawny lions; Pompey used elephants to pull his, while other Roman emperors came riding golden chariots led by six or eight magnificent stallions. Kaiser Wilhelm II had hoped to have the streets of Jerusalem widened so that he might enter in a gilded carriage; the best that could be done was to heighten the Jaffa Gate so that he could come in on horseback to the dedication of the Lutheran Church of the Redeemer.

Hitler wanted to parade triumphantly into Paris after its fall, but his adjutants discouraged him from doing so. However, his General von Bock, chief of Army Group B, reached the city before his troops, and took the salute of the first combat troops. Arches and columns, plaques and memorials have long heralded the historical entry of great conquerors and resplendent kings. With Jesus, it was a donkey, a little fanfare, but hardly a triumph. What was to be his triumph was what others would consider his defeat.

Anon.

Psalm 95

Third Sunday of Lent: Year A
Proper 29/Ordinary Time 34: Year A, verses 1-7a

An uplifting thought is that all the vast power of God is moved by his love.

This psalm is an invitation to worship God.

The psalmist calls upon men to worship God for two reasons.

1. He is the creator and sustainer of all things. The earth, the hills, the sea and the dry land are the work of his hands. He is supreme in power.

2. But this God of might, majesty and power is not only creator of the world and of all men; he is the shepherd whose sheep we are.

So here again the psalmist thinks of the power of God and the love of God. We must bow ourselves before the power of God, but we can rest ourselves in the love of God. An uplifting thought is that all the vast power of God is moved by his love.

William Barclay
Seven Fresh Wineskins

Jehovah the King; a warning

We pause here to note a connection between a group of psalms, namely 93-100. These eight constitute the songs of the King, arranged in conformity with the needs of the people. The first (93) affirms his enthronement and government. The next (94) expresses the hope of his people even in the midst of circumstances of trial. Then follow six, dealing with the fact of his Kingship in varied ways.

The present one declares his supremacy, and utters a note of warning against that which must inevitably hinder his people from realising the rest of his reign. Calling first for praise to the King, the singer celebrates his supremacy. He is above all other authority, and is the God of all nature. He is, moreover, the God of his people; and therefore they should worship in submission and reverence before him (verses 1-7a). Then the warning note follows, reminding them of the sins of their fathers which, as to their cause, consisted in failure of faith, which expressed itself in refusal to bow in submission to his will. That sin excluded them from rest, and the children are warned to profit from the ancient story. Such a King demands loyalty, and it must be more than that of a song; it must express itself in submission to his government.

G. Campbell Morgan
Notes on the Psalms

Because Psalm 95 calls on God's ancient people for loyalty to him as their King and God, as well as joyful worship and thanksgiving, I include this story from the early ministry of Leslie Weatherhead, an outstanding Methodist Minister of the mid-twentieth century. The setting is India where Leslie Weatherhead was serving as a missionary.

He (Weatherhead) was sensitive to the fact that for those Indians who were persuaded to change from their native religion to the Christian faith there was often a considerable price to be paid. One law student came to him and asked to be baptised secretly. Weatherhead explained that this was not possible, since baptism was an open confession of faith in Christ. He asked the young man the reason for the request, and was told that if he was baptised during a public service, his father would cut off his allowance and he would not be able to complete his degree, which meant that his whole future career would be finished. Weatherhead was deeply sympathetic, conscious that his own faith had never cost him that much, but felt that he had to insist that baptism must be an open confession of faith or it was nothing. The student accepted the condition and was duly baptised during a public service crowded with his fellow students. Then everything happened as he had expected. His father cut off his allowance and he had to leave the university. Instead of becoming a barrister he became a clerk to a fishery concern. Giving an account of this incident in a sermon preached many years later, in 1945, on 'Has a Country at War the Right to Export the Gospel of Peace?', Weatherhead described how, when he came to leave India, the young man was at the station in Madras to see him off. Weatherhead told him how sorry he was that his conversion had meant such a sacrifice for him. 'I cannot describe to you folk here today the thrill in his voice and the light in his eyes, when he gripped my hand and said, "But it is worth it."'

John Travell
Doctor of Souls

Psalm 96

Christmas Day 1: Years A, B, C
Proper 24/Ordinary Time 29: Year A, verses 1-9
    (10-13)
Ninth Sunday of Epiphany: Years A, C, verses 1-9
Proper 4/Ordinary Time 9: Year C

The psalmist's God is both Creator and Judge. This God is our God for ever.

The Gospel for the second addressee

If we take Psalm 96:10, 'Say among the nations, "Yahweh is king"', as our beginning point concerning the 'second addressee', that is, the world out beyond Israel, then we consider the Oracles Against the Nations as the place where Israel did indeed 'say among the nations' concerning Yahweh. The Oracles Against the Nations constitute in the several prophets statements that are, on the face of it, addressed directly to the nations concerning the rule of Yahweh. The Oracles are, to be sure, an odd corpus in Old Testament literature and have been largely ignored in interpretive conversations concerning the 'publics' of biblical address.

We may first of all ask to whom these Oracles were addressed, given their ostensible address to the nations. It is easiest, and most commonly concluded, that the Oracles were intended for the ears of Israel, to give salvific assurance to Israel. These Oracles characteristically threaten the nations with judgement from Yahweh, and judgement upon the nations amounts to liberation for Israel whom the nations have oppressed. In this light, the Oracles function as a counter-theme to the prophetic judgements against Israel. If, however, we take the formal address of the Oracles seriously, we cannot regard them as simply assurances to Israel, but may consider them as genuine addresses to the nations beyond Israel. Paul Raabe has suggested that the Oracle is given in Israel but intended to be overheard by the nations.

First, the message concerns Yahweh's sovereignty, splendour, and purpose, which must be honoured. The first issue does not concern the destiny of the nations but *the glorification of Yahweh*. That glorification, of course, takes place as the nations cease to mock and trivialise Yahweh and adhere to Yahweh. I may suggest two aspects of this honouring of Yahweh now 'become king'. One aspect is *the naming of Yahweh*, as though the nations must all become intentionally and explicitly Yahwistic. While there is some hint of this in the Oracles, it is surely not a major accent. More important is *the doing of Yahweh*, that is, the *praxis* appropriate to Yahweh's character and rule. This praxis means to forgo arrogance, autonomy, and brutality, and to be responsive to Yahweh's sovereignty and therefore to Yahweh's intention for *mercy and compassion*, not only toward Israel but toward other nations. The Yahwistic insistence is that the policies and practices of foreign nations should reflect the valuing of humanity, or as Israel regularly codes humanity, 'widows, orphans, and sojourners'. The gospel of Yahweh's kingship has direct and immediate insistences for socio-economic, political, and military policy for every centre of power, all of which are under the aegis of Yahweh.

Walter Brueggemann
Cadences of Home; Preaching Among Exiles

Summons to worship

This psalm is a summons to worship, as indeed Psalm 95 is also: 'Let us bow down in worship, let us kneel before the Lord who made us, for he is our God' (Psalm 95:6, 7). It is a summons to adoration. William Temple defined worship as 'the submission of all our nature to God . . . and all of this (is) gathered up in adoration, the most selfless emotion of which our nature is capable and therefore the chief remedy for that self-centredness which is our original sin and the source of all actual sin' (readings in St John's Gospel). Adoration is an admission of God's greatness and our littleness. It is at the very heart of prayer.

Jesus is recorded as rebuffing the devil's invitation to him to fall down and worship him with a quotation from Deuteronomy 6:13: 'You shall do homage to the lord your God and worship him alone.' (Matthew 4:10)

Posture in worship does matter. We have noted the psalmist's 'Let us kneel' (95:6). Paul 'kneels in prayer to the Father' (Ephesians 3:14). The heavenly creatures surrounding God's throne in the Seer's book of Revelation 'prostrate themselves in worship' (4:10 and 5:14). There is less kneeling in public worship then there used to be. Is that a thing too trivial to mention here? I think not. To stand to attention while praying, or to kneel to express the reverence due to

God is at once an antidote to sloppiness and a tribute to the almightiness of God. 'Obeisance', my dictionary reminds me, 'is an attitude of deference or homage'. The opening verses of this psalm breathe *worship*: 'Day by day proclaim his victory'.

Lifting up holy hands

These miracles of creation which are our bodies can be the means by which we acknowledge the 'otherness' of God. We lift up holy hands; we kneel to pray. Our bodies have a language of their own in worship, playing their part in a paean of praise which echoes the language of nature itself – heavens, sea, fields, trees of the forest all praising their Creator's name (verses 11, 12). There is holy attire, too, which can glorify God (verse 9). This 'holy attire' (not the 'beauty of holiness' of older versions!) consists of the vestments which the priests of the Lord put on when they led the temple worship. No detail in public worship or in private devotion is too small to demand our attention and our obedience – 'Majesty and splendour attend him, might and beauty are in his sanctuary' (verse 6). The psalmist's God is both Creator (verse 5) and Judge (verse 13). This God is our God for ever.

Donald Coggan
Psalms 73-150: The People's Bible Commentary

Psalm 97

Christmas Day 2: Years A, B, C
Seventh Sunday of Easter 7: Year C

Batter my heart,
three person'd
God; for, you as
yet but knock,
breathe, shine and
seek to mend.

Like Psalm 96, this text focuses on the kingship and reign of God and of the consequences of God's coming in judgement.

The psalm opens with a statement that 'the Lord reigns', 'is king', or 'has become king', and that the whole earth and the coastlands (the island to the west) should rejoice and be glad. Such an announcement assumes the existence of a new state of being, a new reality that can only be greeted or announced but not humanly brought into being or created.

The qualities or effects of God's reign are described in verses 2-5, using the metaphorical language of a thunderstorm (see also Psalm 29). With some simplification, the reign and presence of God as king may be said to reflect the following conditions (using the NJPSV): *mystification* ('Dense clouds are around him, righteousness and justice are the base of his throne'), *purgation* ('Fire is his vanguard, burning his foes on every side'), *illumination* ('His lightnings light up the world; the earth is convulsed at the sight'), *transformation* ('Mountains melt like wax at the Lord's presence, at the presence of the Lord of all the earth') and *proclamation* ('The heavens proclaim his righteousness and all the peoples see his glory').

Two human responses are noted (in verses 7-8). Shame and dismay overtake the idol-worshippers, who are exposed as practising futility in their worship (because even the other gods must bow to the Lord; verse 7c). Shame is the consequence of being discovered as something other than what we have claimed to be. On the other hand, Zion and the daughters (i.e. towns) of Judah can rejoice in God's judgements (verse 8). Here the idea of rejoicing in judgement is based on the fact that judgement, which vindicates by revealing the truth, is salvation. The people proclaim their readiness to be judged with confidence in the outcome.

The final section of the psalm (verses 10-12) concentrates on God's preservation of those who belong to the people of God. They have nothing to fear. Note the three actions of God emphasised: the Lord loves, preserves, and delivers. The opening line of verse 10 has no hesitancy in declaring that God loves those who hate evil. Ancient Israel had no qualms about affirming hatred if it was hatred of that which

God did not condone. The righteous and the upright in heart in verse 11 are probably synonymously used terms. The righteous were those declared in the right in judgement. Because in biblical thought the heart was the centre of the will and the intellect, being upright in heart was being consistent in thought and action. (The heart's association with the intellect has been preserved when we say, 'Memorise things by heart.') Though the psalm closes with a call to rejoice – that is, a call to let human emotions be given free reign – it also closes with a call to worship and give thanks to God.

John H. Hayes
Preaching Through the Christian Year: Year A

I once heard Colin Morris preach a superb sermon on what he called 'The Four "M"s of God: his mystery, mercy, majesty and magnetism'. Afterwards I borrowed the outline and preached a sermon on it, acknowledging to Colin what I had done. Here is a part of that old sermon on the theme of the mystery of God, evoked for me in the previous quotation concerning God's reign (see Psalm 7:2; 'Cloud and darkness surround him'). Here also, I must confess the wonderful inspiration I received from 'Day of Trinity' by Lansing Lamont, the best account of the making of the first atomic bomb I have ever come across.

I wonder what sort of thoughts, what sort of response the word Trinity evokes in you? Perhaps visions of searing cathedrals, hymns and anthems and organ music; in fact all the legend, ritual and mystery of the Christian Church.

For a group of scientists in the desert of New Mexico, early in 1945 however, the word Trinity stood for mystery and suspense in a very different sphere, for Trinity was the name given to the world's very first atomic bomb site, and was given by its director, Dr Robert Oppenheimer, who was inspired by some of John Donne's poetry:

Batter my heart, three person'd God; for, you
as yet but knock, breathe, shine and seek to mend.

Trinity – because it spoke of mystery, of awe, of the unknown as well as the known. Yet the cathedral for the very first atomic bomb was not made by human hands – for its spires were a range of mountain peaks; its nave, the pink desert floor; its only hymn, the sweeping sigh of the night wind and the crackle of thunder in the distant mountains. In those early years there was an aura of mystery hanging over the testing ground, for scientists were preparing to do something that had never been done before in the whole history of the human race; detonate an atomic bomb. There was so much that was a mystery and unknown; would the bomb explode at all? If it did, what would be the force of it? Scientists even gambled on how powerful the explosion would be; some said it would be equal to 2,000 tons of TNT, others said 20,000 tons; nobody knew. It was a terrible and awesome mystery.

As I read the account of all this in Lansing Lamont's *Day of Trinity*, I was fascinated to realise that the men involved could only think and describe the event in words that were biblical. For they were all conscious that what they were doing could not be compared with anything else on earth, the mystery and the unknown power could only be thought of in terms of the majesty of God; the mystery, power and glory of his being . . .

When that first atomic bomb exploded, the temperature at its centre was four times that at the centre of the sun and more than 10,000 times as hot as the sun's actual surface. The blast was first like a bell in shape, then a ball, then a mushroom that slowly changed to a huge question mark, one I believe that is still hovering over us as to the mystery of the power released and its usage.

Ron Dale

Psalm 98

Christmas Day 3: Years A, B, C
Easter Vigil: Years A, B, C
Sixth Sunday of Easter: Year B
Proper 27/Ordinary Time 32: Year C
Proper 28/Ordinary Time 33: Year C
Holy Cross: Years A, B, C, verses 1-5 (Alt)

I was in prison –
and you: forgot
I existed.

'O sing unto the Lord a new song'

This tremendous hymn of praise to the Lord, the creator of all things, who has saved his people and is about to bring in his universal kingdom of righteousness, may well mark the climax of this part of the festival.

A double call to praise contains a double description of the wonders which evoke this worship of the Lord. In verses 1-3 his salvation of his chosen people is proclaimed. He has remained faithful to his covenant promise and has openly vindicated them in the sight of the hostile nations. There follows the hope for the future (verses 4-9). The Lord is about to secure that justice throughout the world which the powers of darkness have tried to pervert.

Salvation, loyalty to the covenant, victory over the waters of chaos, the Lord's imminent sovereignty over the whole world in righteousness – the themes have become familiar from the other psalms in this group (96 is specially close to this one). But here all is taken up into a glorious song of adoration. Such worship is the only response man can rightly offer as he hears of God's salvation.

Cyril S. Rodd
Psalms 73-150

If the main themes of Psalm 98 are those of God's kingship, his uni-
versal judgement and rule as he comes to save, then all of those
themes find their ultimate fulfilment in the coming of Jesus at
Bethlehem; in his life and work; in his death, resurrection and

ascension. He comes as a helpless child, but the day is coming when every knee shall bow to him as Lord of the nations. That theme is well illustrated in Matthew 25:31-46, a parable of Jesus on the final judgement. It begins, 'But when the son of Man comes in his splendour with all his angels with him, then he will take his seat on his glorious throne. All the nations will be assembled before him and he will separate men from each other like a shepherd separating sheep from goats' . . . Those who have fed the hungry, given drink to the thirsty, made the lonely welcome, clothed the naked, visited the sick and those in prison . . . all of these will inherit the Kingdom. But what of those who did not practice all these 'good works'? Here is one of Colin Morris' broadcast talks given on BBC Radio 4, entitled 'I was Hungry and . . .'

Here is a well-known saying of Jesus in the words of the Bible. How would we deal with it in real life?

Lord, when was it we saw you hungry, thirsty, a stranger, naked, in prison, or ill and did nothing for you?

I WAS HUNGRY – AND YOU:
Told me the Lord helps those who helps themselves.
Complained about the price of veal. What's veal?
Sighed, 'No fatty foods! You'll never get a coronary' – as though I have the least interest in what my death certificate reads.
Said it had to do with world food prices beyond your control
    – in which case, how come you aren't hungry too?
Kindly gave me a free copy of the Bible. Do I eat it boiled,
    roasted or fried?
Just never noticed.

I WAS THIRSTY – AND YOU:
Lectured me on the evils of drink.
Poisoned my water supply with effluent from your factory.
Recommended Vaseline for my cracked lips.
Moved into my country to drill for oil instead of water.
Just never noticed.

I WAS A STRANGER – AND YOU:
Assured me you'd let that room before discovering I was black
    – you just forgot to remove the vacancy notice from your
    window.
Shook me warmly by the hand after worship and never asked
    my name.
Said I was welcome to pray in your church but not sleep in it.
    I wonder why you looked so embarrassed?
Just never noticed.

I WAS NAKED – AND YOU:
Envied me my lovely tan.
Blushed and slammed the door – nice to have the luxury of
    privacy!
Charged me with indecent exposure.
Suggested I emigrate to a warmer climate.
Laughed at my spindly legs.
Never noticed? Oh, you noticed all right, and asked me to go
    away in case your children noticed too.

I WAS IN PRISON – AND YOU:
Forgot I existed.
Apologised that it would be months before my case was heard
    because the judges are terribly overworked.
Put me in a cell with two old hands who really taught me the
    tricks of the trade.
Released me, apologising profusely that you daren't risk
    giving me that job in your firm but you were sure I'd
    understand, etc., etc. I understand all right – that's why
    I'm picking your pocket.

I WAS ILL – AND YOU:
Told me to pull myself together and think happy thoughts –
    after all, that plus a trip round the world worked wonders
    for you.
Worked nurses into the ground for a mere pittance.
Said there was no known cure for my disease and then spent
    more millions on armaments.
Just never noticed.

Now I am no longer hungry, thirsty, a stranger, naked, in
prison or ill. I *am* no longer. Somehow I could never get
across to you. Now I've got a cross. It reads RIP. Indeed I do
Rest in Peace. Do you?

Colin Morris
Get Through Till Nightfall

Psalm 99

Proper 24/Ordinary Time 29: Year A
Last Sunday of Epiphany, Transfiguration:
  Years A, C

We cannot establish contact outside ourselves except through him, through his word, and through our following of him. To think otherwise is to deceive ourselves.

Holiness

This is another enthronement psalm (see Psalms 47, 97, etc.). In commenting upon Psalm 98 [in *Psalms 73-150: The People's Bible Commentary*], we noticed the danger of repetitiveness in worship. Repetition, however, is a very different matter. To be 'repetitive' is to repeat something pointlessly, to no purpose. Repetition is to repeat something deliberately, with a clear and defined purpose. For instance, the repetition of a word or phrase in a poem or psalm can be a powerful means of fastening a concept in the mind. Psalm 99 illustrates this well. Three strong hammer-blows should ensure that the nail is in place. 'Holy is he' (verse 3). 'Holy is he' (verse 5). Then, with a slight elaboration of the refrain, 'Holy is the Lord our God' (verse 9). The holiness of God is the main theme of this psalm.

When young Isaiah's hero-king (Uzziah) died in disgrace, the prophet had a vision of another King greater than any other earthly monarch. He heard the seraphim calling to one another, 'Holy, holy, holy is the Lord of Hosts: the whole earth is full of his glory' (Isaiah 6:3); seraphim are thought of as heavenly beings in attendance on God, as earthly rulers were attended by a courtly retinue.

Soliloquy and exhortation

The psalm hovers strangely between a kind of soliloquy with God and an exhortation to those for whom the psalmist is writing. In soliloquy with God, he uses such phrases as 'your great and terrible name' (verse 3), 'you have established equity . . .' (verse 4), 'you answered . . . forgave . . . called them to account' (verse 8); in exhortation to worshippers he calls us to 'exalt the Lord our God and bow down' (verses 5 and 9). The writer finds encouragement in the justice of God (verse 4), and in the fact that God answers prayer (verse 8). He illustrates this last point by giving three instances from Israel's history of men who interceded with God and whose

Israel's history of men who interceded with God and whose prayers were heard (verses 6-8). He had in mind the moving story of Moses when the Israelites had sinned – 'If you will forgive them, forgive; but if not, blot out my name . . . from your book' (Exodus 32:20-35). He had in mind Aaron, who under somewhat similar circumstances, made expiation for the people, 'standing between the dead and the living, and the plague was stopped' (Numbers 16:46-50). He had in mind Samuel who 'prayed aloud to the Lord on behalf of Israel, and the Lord answered his prayer' (1 Samuel 7:8-9). He turns from history to the God of history – 'You answered them; you . . . forgave' (verse 8).

We need more women and men who will read the history of their people, and who will read their daily newspaper, thoughtfully and prayerfully, in a spirit of soliloquy with God, recognising that history is, in a real sense, 'His story' – that he is indeed the God of history. Such people will engage with him in a spirit of faith, praying for mercy, praying for justice and equity, meditating on the holiness of God.

Donald Coggan
Psalms 73-150: The People's Bible Commentary

Picking up the theme of mediating and interceding with God on behalf of his people, indeed all people, here are the thoughts of Dietrich Bonhoeffer:

By calling us he (Christ) has cut us off from all immediacy with the things of this world. He wants to be the centre, through him alone all things shall come to pass. He stands between us and God, and for that very reason he stands between us and all other men and things. *He is the mediator,* not only between God and man, but between man and man, between man and reality. Since the whole world was created through him and unto him (John 1:3; 1 Corinthians 8:6; Hebrews 1:2), he is the sole Mediator in the world. Since his coming man has no immediate relationship of his own any more to anything, neither to God not to the world; Christ wants to be the mediator. Of course, there are plenty of gods who offer men direct access, and the world naturally uses every means in its power to retain its direct hold on men, but that is the very reason why it is bitterly opposed to Christ, the Mediator. . . .

The call of Jesus teaches us that our relation to the world has been built on an illusion. All the time we thought we had a direct relation with men and things. This is what had hindered us from faith and obedience. Now we learn that in the most intimate relationships of life, in our kinship with father and mother, brothers and sisters, in married love, and in our duty to the community, direct relationships are impossible. Since the coming of Christ, his followers have no more immediate realities of their own, not in their family relationships nor in the ties with their nation nor in the relationships formed in the process of living. Between father and son, husband and wife, the individual and the nation, stands Christ the Mediator, whether they are able to recognise him or not. We cannot establish direct contact outside ourselves except through him, through his word, and through our following of him. To think otherwise is to deceive ourselves.

Dietrich Bonhoeffer
The Cost of Discipleship

Because Psalm 99 is also used at Transfiguration, here is a piece on the need for transfiguration, seeing God and walking with him in everyday life:

Beach Thomas tells us that, at one time, the first Lord North-cliffe was threatened with complete blindness, and that that horror of gross darkness had drawn very near. And yet, after six weeks of anxious and repeated re-examination by the puzzled specialists, they came to the conclusion, which proved right, that in themselves the eyes were not only sound, but abnormally quick and keen, able as they flashed past in a car, to read, in full, notices in quite small print pasted on shop windows. But the eyes were the eyes of a hunter, or a gamekeeper, or the like, designed for use in a far-stretching country of wide spaces and remote horizons. And, compelled to change their natural focus, and concentrate day after day on the rapid scanning of many reams of newspaper print, the tired and outraged optic nerves at last flatly rebelled. And, so I understand, things righted themselves, and kept right, when to the breathless activities of that bustling city office . . . there was added a country life, with ample gardens . . . and long views that have no end at all, but melt into the distances – all which, far from straining, rested eyes made for them. . . .

We, too, were fashioned for life on a great scale, and in a land of far distances, for the unseen and eternal, for the big spiritual realities, for fellowship with God. But the seen and the temporal is so fussy and noisy, so blatant and self-assertive, so aggressively there, that it catches our attention, entangles and holds our minds. And, since we have shut ourselves into a world far narrower than that for which we are meant and fitted, our eyes, unnaturally focused on these little matters, are growing blind. . . . Our fathers had a sixth sense which we are losing – a feeling of God's presence, a capacity for seeing him, and walking with him. And this not only in the cool of the day, but in the rush and heat and dust of common life.

A. J. Gossip
In the Secret Place of the Most High

Psalm 100

Proper 6/Ordinary Time 11: Year A
Christ the King/Proper 29/Ordinary Time 34: Year A
Thanksgiving: Year C

Imagine a man about to be executed talking of joy, happiness, gladness. Either he has gone mad or he has a secret of joy that his enemies cannot touch.

He feels joyful

Convictions is a book by the Archbishop of Canterbury which contains a collection of addresses and sermons given at various times during his distinguished career. In the first one, called 'Retrospect and Prospect', he takes a look at the present state of the Church, gives thanks for some encouraging signs of life and expresses hopes for the future. One hope is the recovery of joy. He says, 'My hope is that the Church in the next few years will recapture its joy. Should I be misunderstood if I said that in recent years we have had something of a surfeit of ecclesiastical breast-beating? Of course, the Church has plenty to repent of, so let us repent, and do it thoroughly. But let us not go to the world as if we had nothing to be thankful for. God has worked gloriously through his Church again and again, and is doing so today.'

Donald Coggan
Convictions

The Archbishop is right. A joyless Church is a contradiction in terms. Of all people on earth Christians should be the most joyful, yet of all people on earth Christians are sometimes the most doleful. At least, that's what often comes across on Sunday mornings, and it not only surprises strangers but saddens them.

Such was the experience of a remarkable Christian woman, Gert Behanna, who in her later years became a popular author and lecturer. She had been a New York socialite who by middle-age had made a total wreck of her life, then found Jesus Christ and was healed in body and soul. She wrote a magazine article saying that she had never been to church before her conversion but she went there eagerly, looking forward to meeting the lucky people who had known Jesus for years. She expected them to be ecstatic in their joy and she felt sure they would warm her heart with enthusiasm and love. Instead, she was chilled by their gloom and sheer unfriendliness. She thought that it might be an isolated experience, so she made the rounds of several churches. In every congregation she found the same long-faced, listless people and felt bewildered. She asked, 'How could they come into God's presence Sunday after Sunday without breathing in the joy that danced in the very air?'

How indeed? Especially when they take upon their lips the most joyous words ever written: 'Make a joyful noise unto the lord, all ye lands. Serve the lord with gladness; come before his presence with singing . . .' Such is Psalm 100, commonly called the Jubilate. In its Old Testament form or its metrical version composed by William Kethe, the sixteenth-century Scotsman and friend of John Knox, it is the psalm most frequently used in synagogue services and in Christian worship throughout the world. There is scarcely a week, scarcely a day when God is not praised with the familiar words, 'Make a joyful noise unto the Lord, all ye lands . . .' A cheerful voice! Why not a cheerful heart? The psalmist's words of joy? Why not his spirit of joy?

The answer is that we have to share the secret of his joy. The psalm itself makes clear that it was not a contrived mood, not a bubbling emotion and frothy sentiment that he manu-factured in the presence of God. The joy of the author of Psalm 100 grew out of his creed. Actually it was his response to his own deep convictions about God. He tells what those convictions are, he celebrates them; and if we could celebrate them we might possess the secret of his joy.

. . . Imagine a man about to be executed talking of joy, happiness, gladness. Either he has gone mad or he has a secret of joy that his enemies cannot touch. Of course, Jesus did have a secret. 'Believe in God,' he told the disciples. Believe that there *is* a God, that he is sovereign, that he cares for us and will stay with us for ever.

That was the secret of joy for one of the most beloved and popular entertainers of our time. In the middle of the summer before he died he sent a Christmas card to his friends. He knew that he was dying and would not be around to greet them at Christmas. It was a plain blue folding card. On the front was printed his name, *Duke Ellington*, and above and below he had written by hand, 'Merrie Christmas . . . Happy New Year . . . Love'. Inside were the following lines which he evidently composed:

I don't light a lamp to see the Sun
Don't need proof of God,
Because I know there ain't
a-gonna be but *one*.

The silliest thing ever read,
Was that somebody said,
   'God is dead.'
The mere mention of the first word,
Automatically eliminates
The second and the third.

Something 'bout believing that's greater than pleasure,
Something 'bout believing that's more than treasure,
Something 'bout believing that's beyond measure,
God Almighty.

Leonard Griffith
Reactions To God: Man's Response to God's Activity in the Psalms

Psalm 103

Proper 19/Ordinary Time 24: Year A, verses (1-7),
8-13
Eighth Sunday of Epiphany /Ordinary Time 8:
Year B, verses 1-13, 22
Proper 16/Ordinary Time 21: Year C, verses 1-8

The experience of life not only reveals the measure and strength of our beliefs, it creates our beliefs.

God surpasses

One scarcely expects the Dean of an English cathedral to have a bias against Church music, but such was the case with Dean Inge of St Paul's Cathedral in London. In his published *Diary* he implies that the surest way to drive religion out of the great prayers, creeds and passages of Scripture is to set them to music and put them at the mercy of a choir. Perhaps we can sympathise with the 'gloomy Dean', especially with regard to some of the psalm-settings, ancient and modern. There is a lugubrious Russian setting to Psalm 103 which even the most limited choirs used to sing with depressing frequency. It drags along in a minor key like a funeral dirge over the death of God. That was how it seemed to me until I once heard it sung by an American Negro male choir. These men redeemed this piece of music for me, they brought it to life, they sang it not slowly and mournfully but with rapid joy and exultation as a great outburst of praise to the living God.

That is certainly the mood of Psalm 103, a mood set by its familiar opening verse:

> 'Bless the Lord, O my soul: and all that is within me, bless his holy name.'

Praise is not self-generating; it does not spring as a root out of dry ground. We feel no impulse to praise, no reason to give thanks for anything in this life as long as we are getting only what we deserve. Why thank your employer for your weekly pay envelope if you have earned its contents? Why should a child thank his parents for food, clothing, shelter and education? I heard of an adolescent who gave a mature answer to one of his teachers when she told him that he ought to be more grateful to his parents. He said, 'I didn't ask to be born. My parents brought me into the world for their own enjoyment. They are only doing for me what I deserve. Why should I thank them?' In a sense we can take the same attitude to God. So God created us, but we didn't ask to be created. So God provides for us, but isn't that the natural obligation of a responsible father? Why give thanks to God when he is doing for us only what we deserve? Let God do more for us than we deserve, and we shall have reason to thank him.

Well then, read Psalm 103, because that's what it is all about. A single theme runs through this mighty anthem of praise – the theme of God's grace. 'Grace' is one of those religious words which has been worn thin with over-use like an old coin, so that now we hand it around freely, scarcely recognising its true value. When a hospital patient confessed that she was having a hard time hanging on to her religious faith, I tried to comfort her by saying that in these days, when faith comes hard to all of us, the one certainty to which I still cling is my experience of the grace of God. 'What is grace?' she asked; and for the moment I registered surprise that she, a Christian woman, should ask such a question. I tried to explain that grace means something extra in life, like the flowers and letters and get-well cards she had received from kind friends; it was a gracious thing for them to do. The grace of God means God's extra, the way he deals with us beyond our deserving, the good things he gives us, not because he has to give them but because he wants to give them. That is what makes him God. In his goodness to men he goes further than we are willing to go, he does for us what no other person would ever do, he is *a God who surpasses* all our human limitations. He showed himself to be that kind of God in the experience of the Hebrew psalmist; and if there is a single admonition that can be inferred from Psalm 103, it is this: *Don't underestimate God!* . . .

> 'Bless the Lord, O my soul, and forget not all his benefits: Who forgiveth all thine iniquities; who healeth all thy diseases; Who redeemeth thy life from destruction; who crowneth thee with loving kindness and tender mercies; Who satisfieth thy mouth with good things; so that thy youth is renewed like the eagle's . . .'

> This is the God in whom Jesus taught men to believe, the gracious God whose kindness surpasses all our human limitations. To such a God we can confidently pray. Jesus prayed, with such an obvious sense of reality and power that his disciples begged him, 'Lord, teach us to pray', so he taught them and taught the whole human race the most perfect of all prayers which begins, 'Our Father which art in heaven . . .'

Leonard Griffith
God in Man's Experience: the Activity of God in the Psalms

The experience of life not only reveals the measure and strength of our beliefs, it creates our beliefs. A man for many years may repeat the words, 'Bless the Lord, O my soul, and forget not all his benefits', and imagine he knows the meaning of gratitude and the sacrifice of praise. So he may in some degree. But one day in the middle years there flashes upon him, in the light that life supplies, the true mercies under which he has lived through the years – the undeserved patience of his wife, the health and love of his children, the sweetness and strength of friendships, the courage and hope that have never quite forsaken him as he strove and shouldered burdens and faced the dark hours; the times when his feet nearly slipped when he stumbled, yet did not fall – and then, like dawn over the eastern hills, he beholds the unfailing mercies of God over all in all, and with deep-throated praise he cries, 'Bless the Lord, O my soul, and all that is within me bless his holy Name,' and the word 'benefits' becomes crowded with particular providences shining through the years.

A. E. Whitham
The Discipline and Culture of the Spiritual Life

Psalm 104

Pentecost: Years A, B, C, verses 24-34, 35b
Proper 24/Ordinary Time 29: Year B, verses 1-9,
  24, 35c

God, of your
goodness, give me
yourself, for you
are enough for me.

The gift of life

Enjoy this psalm! Before you examine it in any detail, read it through at a run. If you own a video of one of David Attenborough's nature films, play it as a commentary on this psalm. And if you want a good read which fills out this psalm, you could try Ecclesiasticus 42:15-43:33 in the Apocrypha. This psalm is an invitation to us to stop and look:

What is this life if, full of care,
We have no time to stand and stare? (W. H. Davies)

I shall never forget the leisurely moments I spent in a car looking straight into the eyes of a lion in Africa, and the feeling of a certain oneness with him in the gift of the life that flowed through each of us.

Grand procession

Our poet ranges widely. Under his guidance, heaven and earth, winds and flames, seas and rivers, beasts and birds, grass and grain, wine and oil pass before us in grand procession. He is enjoying himself, and he is sure that God enjoys himself as creator and caretaker of it all (verse 31). A probable translation of verse 26 is: 'Sea-monsters swim therein, Leviathan which you formed for yourself as a plaything.' In this, the psalmist is at one with the writer of the first of the Genesis creation stories; after the record of God's creative acts comes the refrain 'and God saw that it was *good*'. (One can imagine a carpenter who has made a beautiful table standing back, rubbing his hands, and saying: 'That's *good*!')

If, as we are suggesting, it is right to think of God as enjoying his creation and delighting in it, should we not be hearing more about God's enjoyment of and delight in that particular part of it which is humankind? 'God created human beings in his own image . . . and God saw all that he had made, and it was very good' (Genesis 1:27, 31). Granted, that idyllic picture is of humankind before the 'Fall'. But God does not love us because we are good. He loves us for what we are and what we can become. The father's arms were around the returning prodigal son not because he was good – he doubtless still smelt of the pig sty! – but because he was the son of his father's begetting, with the promise of a future of limitless possibilities. Julian of Norwich wrote, 'He loves us and enjoys us, and he wills that we love him and enjoy him, and firmly trust him; and all shall be well.' And again: 'He delights in us for ever, as we shall in him, by his grace.'

The implications of this emphasis on God's attitude to his creation are clear: the physical world is sacred and must be treated with reverence. It was a West African who wrote:

Enjoy the world gently,
Enjoy the world gently,
For if the earth is spoiled
It cannot be repaired.
Enjoy the world gently.

What is true of the physical world is true of human beings. However depraved they are, they are to be loved as children of the Most High.

Donald Coggan
Psalms 73-150: The People's Bible Commentary

He keeps all that is made

He showed me a little thing, the size of a hazelnut, in the palm of my hand, and it was as round as a ball. I looked at it with my mind's eye and I thought, 'What can this be?' And answer came, 'It is all that is made.' I marvelled that it could last, for I thought it might have crumbled to nothing, it was so small. And the answer came into mind, 'It lasts and ever shall because God loves it.' And all things have being through the love of God.

In this little thing I saw three truths. The first is that God made it. The second is that God loves it. The third is that God looks after it.

What is he indeed that is Maker and Lover and Keeper? I

cannot find words to tell. For until I am one with him I can never have true rest or peace. I can never know it until I am held so close to him that there is nothing in between.

For he is endless and has made us for his own self only, and has restored us by his blessed Passion, and keeps us in his blessed love. And he does all this through his goodness.

God, of your goodness, give me yourself, for you are enough for me.

Julian of Norwich
quoted in *The Joy of the Saints*

Psalm 105

*Proper 12/Ordinary Time 17: Year A, verses 1-11,
45b (Alt)*

*Proper 14/Ordinary Time 19: Year A, verses 1-6,
16-22, 45b*

*Proper 17/Ordinary Time 22: Year A, verses 1-6,
23-26, 37-45c*

*Proper 20/Ordinary Time 25: Year A, verses 1-6,
37-45*

*Who knows for
what we live and
struggle and die . . .
this, the purpose
of our lives,
the end of all
our struggles,
is beyond all
human wisdom.*

God of the Covenant

Psalm 105 belongs among the hymns in which God is
praised as the Lord of history. It is closely related to Psalms
78 and 106 in content, but, unlike these psalms, it contains no
mention of Israel's sins. The purpose of the psalm is to praise
the Lord as the God of the Covenant in a ceremony of
Covenant renewal. The psalmist makes use of much of the
material in Genesis 12-50 and Exodus 1-17. Verses 1-15 are
quoted by the chronicler in 1 Chronicles 16 together with psalm
96 and three verses from psalm 106, as representative of the
thanksgiving sung on the occasion of David's transferring
the Ark to Zion.

Summons to grateful praise (105:1-6). The People of God are
summoned to proclaim God's marvellous deeds to the nations
(compare 9:11) and to praise him with joy and gratitude as
they remember his marvellous work on their behalf (see
Deuteronomy 7:18; 8:2) and his 'judgements' (see Exodus 6:6;
7:4; 12:12). The designation of the worshipping community as
'offspring of Abraham his servant, sons of Jacob, his chosen
ones' (verse 6) lays stress upon election to privilege (see verse
43), service and obedience (see verse 45). . . .

The famine in Canaan in the time of Jacob (Genesis 41:54)
is considered as an act of God (compare 2 Kings 8:1; Haggai
1:11). The expression 'staff of bread' (see Leviticus 26:26;
Ezekiel 4:16) carries the same meaning as our present-day
reference to bread as 'the staff of life.' Joseph was sent ahead
to Egypt as a slave and tested by the word of promise, which
had come through dreams in his youth (see Genesis 37:5-11),
until the promise was fulfilled by his exaltation at the hand
of Pharaoh (Genesis 41).

The purpose of God's blessing (105:43-45). God delivered his Chosen People with joyous singing (see Exodus 15) and gave them the lands of the peoples living in Canaan, to the end that they should obey his laws (compare 78:7; Deuteronomy 4:1, 40; 26:17-18). Privilege enjoins a corresponding responsibility (see Amos 3:2; Luke 12:48).

A. B. Rhodes
Psalms

Psalm 105:17-22 harks back to Joseph and his saving work for his family, the Egyptians and others in rescuing them from famine. So a meditation on Joseph and his life:

'Who indeed knows the secret of the earthly pilgrimage? Who knows for what we live and struggle and die, who knows what keeps us living and struggling while all things break about us . . . this, the purpose of our lives, the end of all our struggles, is beyond all human wisdom.' So are the thoughts of Stephen Kumalo in Alan Paton's *Cry the Beloved Country*. It was only Stephen's deep faith in God that sustained him and helped him to believe that life did make sense and that God was involved and would bring good out of evil; and this he does in the end in a surprising and beautiful way.

But the classic story in the Old Testament that superbly illustrates the providence of God is the story of Joseph.

He was only 17 when the story opens. His father doted on him arousing jealousy in his 11 brothers. They also began to hate him when he disclosed his dreams to them. How at harvest time all his brothers' sheaves bowed down to his; and later, of how the sun, moon and eleven stars bowed to him. In a fury, the brothers plot to kill Joseph, but sell him as a slave instead. He is employed by Potiphar, captain of Pharaoh's guard in Egypt where, 'because God was with him', Joseph prospered and was put in charge of all Potiphar's household. Unfortunately, Potiphar's wife desires Joseph but he refuses her and ends up in prison on trumped-up charges.

Later on in the prison Pharaoh's butler and baker have dreams that baffle them, but Joseph interprets correctly. Into the story now comes another key phrase from the lips of Joseph, 'Do not interpretations belong to God?' So that, when Pharaoh has his disturbing dreams that nobody can interpret, Joseph is sent for. He correctly interprets and as a reward is placed second only to Pharaoh in governing Egypt through seven years of plenty, followed by seven years of famine.

You can see from the story that God did not will all the evils that came to Joseph any more than he wills the baffling evils of our time: war, hunger, and racial hatred among others. He did not will the treacherous behaviour of Joseph's brothers, but he used the tragedy creatively, even making the wrath of men to serve him. But this divine alchemy bringing good out of evil often depends upon, as with Joseph, our willing co-operation. Joseph refused the way of bitterness and retaliation; instead he kept his spirit alert and sensitive to God, and so was able to turn his sufferings to glorious gain and lead captivity captive. Ultimately it was not the brothers' hatred, but God who brought Joseph to Egypt, and moreover, to preserve life.

Look into the New Testament and you see the same kind of thing in the story of Jesus. Born in a stable, not a palace or hospital, or a house, but a stable and laid in a manger among the animals. If you had been there and seen the startling poverty, smelt the stench, experienced the cold and seen maybe the wistful look on Mary's face in desiring a better start and home, you may have thought, 'Surely there is no God, there can't be, or he would never allow this to happen.'

But see later on how Jesus lived, and how he died. 'Why should such a beautiful life come to such a terrible end? Surely there is no God, there can't be or he would never have allowed this to happen.' Only in the resurrection story are we made to realise that God was involved in all the sufferings of his only Son. Not allowing evil to conquer, but bearing it and making the wickedness of men to praise him.

Let me refer again to *Cry the Beloved Country*. There you have the story of a heartbroken black minister, Stephen Kumalo. Why was he heartbroken? Because his only son had drifted into bad company; into crime; into reform school; into murder; the murder of a white man; but not just any white man, but one who had stood up for human rights, one who had given his whole life in dedicated service to fight apartheid, one who wrote, lectured and acted to get a fairer social order in South Africa. Stephen Kumalo's son had killed *this* man, his own and his people's best friend.

Why was Stephen Kumalo heartbroken? Because of the troubles of his sister and brother, because of his ramshackle church, because his own people were drifting away into the big cities. But he reckoned without the providence of God. For the white father of the murdered boy read his son's writing and was so impressed that he decided to do all in his power to help black people. So, he planned and built a new reservoir; gave away milk to needy children; and had plans drawn up for a new church for Stephen Kumalo. Therefore out of a stark tragedy which broke the heart of a black minister and his white neighbour came a new sympathy, a new hope, a new life for the black people of a remote South African valley; and all of this would never have happened had not a son, an only son, died a painful death.

So for us, a Son, an only son, has lived and died. His death was tragic, stark, black, terrifying; but *God was in it*, reconciling us all to himself and bringing new life to us all.

Ron Dale, 1999

Psalm 106

*Proper 23/Ordinary Time 28: Year A, verses 1-6,
19-23*

*Should we not
give some thought
to what indeed
happens when
holiness comes
into collision
with human sin
and folly?*

Faithless people

The writer cared deeply for the nation of which he was a
member, and longed for its spiritual welfare. Like the writer
of Psalm 105, he looked back over its history. But whereas
the writer of that psalm stresses the faithfulness of the God
who had entered into a covenant relationship with his people,
the writer of this psalm stresses the faithlessness of a people
who, time and time again, failed to live up to their part of the
agreement.

The language used to describe the offence caused to God
by the people's sin – his purpose to destroy the people (verse
23), to strike them down (verse 26), his anger (verses 29, 32,
40), his loathing of them (verse 40), and so on – distresses us
even though it is softened by references to his pity (verse 44),
his boundless love (verse 45), his compassion (verse 46). The
psalmist is trying to find language to convey God's detestation
of national sin, the breach of covenant by which a nation turns
from godliness to paganism, and the inexorable consequences
of such conduct-dispersion among the nations (verse 27),
plague (verse 29), defeat (verses 41, 42). Before we jettison
such a picture of an angry God, should we not give some
thought to what indeed happens when holiness comes into
collision with human sin and folly?

Disease

It does not take a great deal of imagination to see the modern
counterpart of what is described in verse 15. In the affluent
West particularly, there is a society 'given what they asked'. Its
members have voted for money in abundance, for a salacious
press, for corrupt leadership, for noise, for dissipation – and
they have got it in full measure. But is it meeting their deepest
needs? It has been followed by 'a wasting sickness', a *disease*
at their vitals. We are breeding a race unable to think, fed on
misleading soundbites, unable to endure silence, restless and

not content to stand and stare, unable to ponder, still less to pray. A wasting disease is on the rampage. Forsaking the true God, we have fashioned for ourselves a pantheon of false gods. One by one they will topple and fall, and leave us stripped and naked. Then, and perhaps *only* then, God will in his 'boundless love', 'relent' and rouse compassion for them in the hearts of their captors. He will 'call to mind his covenant' and deliver his people.

Donald Coggan
Psalms 73-150: The People's Bible Commentary

Psalm 106:19-23 tells of Israel's idolatry in making the Golden Calf; of God's anger and threat to destroy his people and of Moses standing in the breach before God to turn away his wrath. A classic story of the power of intercession. So here is a lovely story on the same theme from Mount Athos:

In 1938 a man died on Mount Athos. He was a very simple man, a peasant from Russia who came to Mount Athos when he was in his twenties and stayed for about fifty years . . . For a long time he was in charge of the workshops of the monastery. The workshops of the monastery were manned by young Russian peasants who used to come for one year, for two years, in order to make some money, really farthing added to farthing, in order to go back to their villages with a few pounds perhaps, at the utmost, to be able to start a family by marrying, by building a hut, and by buying enough to start their crops.

One day other monks, who were in charge of other workshops, said, 'Father Silouan, how is it that the people who work in your workshops work so well while you never supervise them, while we spend our time looking after them and they try continuously to cheat us in their work?' Father Silouan said 'I don't know. I can only tell you what I do about it. When I come in the morning, I never come without having prayed for these people and I come with my heart filled with compassion and with love for them, and when I walk into the workshop I have tears in my soul for love of them. And then I give them the task they have to perform in the day and as long as they will work I will pray for them, so I go into my cell and I begin to pray about each of them individually. I take my stand before god and I say, 'O Lord,

243

remember Nicholas. He is young, he is just 20, he has left in his village his wife, who is even younger than he, and their first child. Can you imagine the misery there is that he has had to leave them because they could not survive on his work at home? Protect them in his absence. Shield them against every evil. Give him courage to struggle through this year and go back to the joy of meeting, with enough money, but also enough courage, to face the difficulties.' And he said, 'In the beginning I prayed with tears of compassion for Nicholas, for his young wife, for the little child, but as I was praying the sense of the divine presence began to grow on me and at a certain moment it grew so powerful that I lost sight of Nicholas, of his wife, his child, his needs, their village, and I could be aware only of God, and I was drawn by the sense of the divine presence deeper and deeper, until of a sudden, at the heart of this presence, I met the divine love holding Nicholas, his wife, and his child, and now it was with the love of God that I began to pray for them again, but again I was drawn into the deep and in the depths of this I again found the divine love. And so,' he said, 'I spend my days, praying for each of them in turn, one after the other, and when the day is over I go, I say a few words to them, we pray together and they go to their rest. And I go back to fulfil my monastic office.'

Anthony Bloom
School for Prayer

When I look back over my years as a Methodist circuit minister, the inspiration and drive to help the homeless has been given by those poignant words of Jesus in Matthew's Gospel, 'foxes have earths, birds in the sky have nests, but the Son of Man has nowhere that he can call his own.' (Matthew 8:20)

Whilst serving in Birmingham I had two very different jobs in caring for the homeless. In the first, I was part of an ecumenical team that went out most evenings on what was called 'the soup run'. This meant tracking down those who were homeless and sleeping rough in different parts of the Second City, sitting among them and sharing hot soup and a roll and much banter and conversation. I always found that the experience deeply touched me, especially as I listened to some of the stories men had to tell. Some of them came from very good social backgrounds and were well educated. Often it had been a broken marriage or a lost job that had led to the downward spiral. So in that context, soup, bread roll and chat was not much. But I comforted myself by remembering the words of Jesus, 'Inasmuch as you did unto the least of these, my brethren, you did it unto me.'

The easier part for me at least, was serving on the main committee that supervised all work amongst the homeless in Birmingham and occasionally running the 'Delousing Centre'; a very strange experience indeed!

My other work was to assist a very wealthy businessman buy up cheap houses, renovate them, and then install a group of about six homeless ex-prisoners. To provide work as well, we started up a painting and decorating company with our own special transport.

Each home had one person designated to do all the catering, with the other residents doing some of the other chores.

At times it was like walking on egg-shells because some of the men were recovering alcoholics who at times relapsed into drink and went on a 'bender'. This always led to violence and a lot of peace-making from those of us involved in the operation.

One resident used to relapse fairly often and used to get very angry. I could have cheerfully kicked him out, but my colleague would say very quietly, 'As long as he needs a home, he has one, no matter what he does to deserve otherwise.' I certainly learned new meanings to the oft-used words, 'grace' and 'love'. I believe that the writer of Psalm 106 knew something of the deeper meanings of those two words as he meditated on the works of his Lord.

Ron Dale, 1999

Psalm 107

Proper 26/Ordinary Time 31: Year A, verses 1-7, 33-37
Fourth Sunday of Lent: Year B, verses 1-3, 17-22
Proper 7/Ordinary Time 12: Year B, verses 1-3, 23-32
Proper 13/Ordinary Time 18: Year C, verses 1-9, 43

Make no important decisions when any kind of storm is trying to blow you away.

Jehovah the redeemer

We now begin the fifth and last book of the psalter. In this book the music is richest and fullest. It begins in this psalm on the fundamental notes, and rises through major and minor, by the way of the songs of ascents, to the final measures of perfect praise contained in the doxology.

The first 32 verses contain a wonderful story of redemption, using that word in its sense of deliverance from positions and circumstances of peril. In a prologue the theme of the songs is stated. A people redeemed and gathered by Jehovah is called upon to declare the fact.

Then follow four strophes in which the redemption is illustrated in four ways. Each of these ends with the same appeal for praise, varied by description suitable to the previous illustration. The first illustration is that of homelessness. The second is that of bondage. The third is that of affliction. The last is that of a storm. The homeless, Jehovah led to a city of habitation; the enslaved, he led into liberty; the afflicted, he healed; the storm-tossed, he led to calm and a haven. All through, the connection between sorrow and sin is clearly seen. The method of Jehovah is described as that of dealing with sin in order to bring the healing of sorrow. Such deliverances demand worship, and the song is a psalm of praise interspersed with sighings after more perfect praise.

G. Campbell Morgan
Notes on the Psalms

The psalm lection for today mentions in verse 23 those who 'went down to the sea in ships, doing business on the great waters' and what happened on 'the great waters'. Their experience was of a terrible storm that made the sailors 'reel and stagger like drunken men, and they were at their wit's end'.

Now, whilst the storm was very real to the sailors, and, to be caught in one at sea can prove a terrifying experience, the storm can also stand symbolically for those storms of life that afflict everybody at times.

Emotional storms due to angry words with family or friends; spiritual storms that come suddenly upon us and we feel afraid like the early disciples on Galilee; the storms caused by bereavement, the loss of a dear member of one's family or a close friend and especially a child; the economic storm that results from losing one's job and all the readjustments needed; the storm that comes with personal illness and the threat of death.

As a working minister I shared in very many stormy times with people from all social backgrounds. I remember on one occasion trying to persuade two young people to keep together within the marriage bond. My advice was – and I very rarely gave advice – 'be like the camel when the Ghibli blows'. When the hot desert wind churns up sand everywhere, the camel kneels down, closes his eyes, and stays put until the storm is over. So make no important decisions when any kind of storm is trying to blow you away.

The author of Psalm 107 says of God that, 'He made the storm be still'; so, for those involved in the storm, 'Let them thank the Lord for his steadfast love, for his wonderful works to the sons of men!' (Psalm 107: 29a; 31)

Ron Dale, 1999

Psalm 110

Ascension: Year C

Sit at my right hand

In using the Apostle's Creed to declare its faith, the Church says over and over again, 'I believe in Jesus Christ . . . who sits at the right hand of God.' In this declaration a spatial metaphor is used to speak about the identity and role of Jesus in relation to God. The statement is the nearest approximation the Church has to an answer to the question of where Jesus is now. The place of this phrase in the confessions is based on the repeated citation of Psalm 110:1 in the New Testament: Matthew 22:44; Mark 14:62; 16:19; Luke 22:69; Acts 2:34-35; 7:55; Romans 8:34; Ephesians 1:20; Colossians 3:1; Hebrews 1:13; 8:1; 10:12; 1 Peter 3:22.

The psalm, then, served as a text for the installation of a king in office. In the culture in which it was used, the office was far more than a position; it was a status in the very order of things that endowed a person with identity and powers. The person was endowed with the identity of the office. The esoteric and sometimes violent things said in the psalm are traditional cultic speech and express the ways kingship was understood in Judah. It is an Israelite adaptation of what was said to kings in the nations round about in the conduct of inaugural rituals. The divine sayings in verses 1 and 4 are the crucial words by which God through the prophet bestows office. Whoever sat at the right hand of a king on formal occasions was next to him in rank and identified as the official empowered to represent the king and carry out his policy.

Psalm 110 has come to be used widely in the liturgy on the day of our Lord's ascension. It puts that celebration, and every confession of faith in the ascension and session of our Lord, in the perspective of the old Testament witness to the office that Jesus occupies. The poetic and prophetic vision of the psalm lets us see the enthronement of Jesus at the right hand of God as the great theological reality of the Christological present. The crucified and risen Jesus has been 'installed' as the one for whom and through whom God is working out his purpose in the world.

The psalm holds the enthronement of Jesus in relation to the question of political power in the world. It insists that the office of Jesus concerns nations and rulers. The office of regent of God has been filled and fulfilled by a person who was not a ruler and had no national constituency. In the Old Testament the messianic king had his first context in the Lord's use of Israel's national history as a declaration of his sovereignty. In Jesus the messianic office completes the prophetic and apocalyptic direction and is consummated in the context of cosmic and universal history. But that is not an abdication of any claim on the nations and rulers of this world. Instead, it is an assertion that every nation and ruler is subject to the royal judgement of Messiah Jesus. His ways and values are final. No claims to 'divine right' or any semblance of it by rulers, dictators, presidents, and so forth, are valid. The goal of world history is not to be found in the destiny of any people or nation, nor is the governance of any leader the way to it. Indeed, all the nations who think and dream of autonomous dominance and destiny are in that way enemies of the coming kingdom of God and its Messiah, including the one in which we happen to live. The psalm is a repeated invitation to think that way about the question of power in the world.

The psalm is also a declaration to the Church about its relation to the Jesus whose session at the right hand of God it confesses. Jesus is King! the meaning of that symbolic word makes absolute claims on the obedience of the community and its members. His instructions and commands are not subject to approval and revision. They are, rather, provisions for us to acknowledge the coming kingdom of God in living. The psalm, with its focus on the relation between Messiah and nations, puts special emphasis on the command of Jesus to the Church to make disciples of the nations (Matthew 28: 20). That mission is the action assigned to the Church in relation to these 'enemies' of the Christ. Faithfulness to that assignment is the way the Church shows it believes its confession and knows that all power in heaven and earth is given to Jesus. The meaning of the symbol 'King' also makes an absolute claim on our trust. Because it is Jesus who is divine King of the universe, we may take hope. After all, the King is the eternal priest. God turns no other face to his people than the visage of mercy and grace and love known through the person Jesus. That person in all the particularity known through the Gospels is at God's right hand.

James L. Mays
Psalms

Ascension: the absent and the present Christ

Happily for the preacher and mercifully for the congregation, there are always at least two ways of looking at any text. The texts for Ascension Day and its Sunday are vivid examples of this option. The vividness of the events described in the Acts of the Apostles does not necessarily make any clearer our understanding of them, and yet there is an implicit choice available to us in the text (Acts 1:11). You may choose between the 'upward' and the 'downward' visions of the Acts of the Apostles, and your choice, I suspect, depends upon your sociology and astronomy fully as much as it depends upon your theology and your Christology.

In the upward vision of the text there is that wonderful motion and movement toward the skies, a second Easter with its triumph over natural order and its promise of great things to come in that other bright and brilliant place. Christ returns to that heavenly splendour from which he has come in the form of a human being, to the heavenly throne and the glories of the divine court to be seated at the right hand of God the Father Almighty, from whence he shall come to judge both the quick and the dead. That is what the creed says, and that is the flavour of the music we sing at Easter: 'The head that once was crowned with thorns is crowned with glory now', 'Soar we now where Christ has led, following our exalted head', and that greatest of all Christian hymns, 'Christ the Lord is risen today'.

The imagination of poets, painters, and preachers has been exhausted in thinking about heaven, what it is like and the glories that await those who enter there where God reigns and Christ is his Viceroy. The direction is clearly 'up, up, and away'. The cold, dreary earth with its petty reason and its silly pride are 'lost in wonder, love, and praise'. The Ascension reminds us of that wonderfully enigmatic passage in the Revelation of Saint John, '. . . and lo, in heaven an open door . . .' A glimpse of heaven, a hint of the future, a sense of promise. Despite the clutter of American and Soviet tin cans floating about in the heavens, despite the scientific conquests of the moon and outer space, the idea of the skies still fascinates, and the notion of heaven still demands notice and interest.

Peter J. Gomes
Sermons: Biblical Wisdom for Daily Living

Psalm 111

Fourth Sunday of Epiphany/Ordinary Time 4: Year B
Proper 15/Ordinary Time 20: Year B
Proper 23/Ordinary Time 28: Year C

Those who have seen and understood God's love delight in joyful thanksgiving.

The graciousness of the Lord

This is a hymn of praise written by an individual with conscious art, but intended to be sung during the temple worship, possibly at one of the great annual festivals (see verse 1). The alphabet structure prevents any close development of the thought. Instead, many illustrations are given of the Lord's loving care of his people.

The Lord is above all else the covenant God. His character was revealed in the Exodus salvation to which the writer seems to be alluding in verses 4-6 and 9. The covenant is thus grounded upon the Lord's love for Israel. It is no bargain between equals – he *'commands'* his covenant, imposing upon Israel what is in reality a gracious offer, for when his people are in need he remembers his covenant obligations to help them. It is with the thought of the covenant in mind that the Lord's *'righteousness'* (verse 3) must be understood. It is no bare justice, but the deliverance and vindication to which his love hastens. The covenant contains *'precepts'*, however, which govern Israel's life – though not as a severe demand, but rather as the Gift of God for the rich development of Israel's national well-being (cf. verses 7-8). And all this is as enduring as the Lord himself. The psalmist emphasises that the Lord's righteousness and fidelity to the covenant, his laws and the very covenant itself are established *'for ever'* (see verses 3, 5, 7-8, 9). The Lord's nature is love, as has been displayed so plainly in Israel's history. Yet he is also *God*, holy and to be feared. . . .

Those who have seen and understood God's love delight in joyful thanksgiving. The psalmist can do no other than join in the worship of the whole congregation, and he is confident that the everlasting graciousness of God will be matched by everlasting praise (verses 1 and 10).

Cyril S. Rodd
Psalms 73-150

The fear of the Lord is the beginning of wisdom (Psalm 111:10)

I am about to say a good word for fear. Fear is a fine thing, a very fine thing; and the world would be a poorer place without it. Fear was one of our firmest but gentlest nurses. 'No fears, no grace!' said James in the second part of *The Pilgrim's Progress*, and Mr Greatheart seemed of pretty much the same opinion. They were discussing poor Mr Fearing. 'Mr Fearing,' said Greatheart, 'was one that played upon the bass. Some say that the bass is the ground of music. The first string that the musician touches is the bass, when he intends to put all in tune. God also plays this string first, when he sets the soul in tune for himself. Only here was the imperfection of Mr Fearing: he could play upon no other music but this, till towards his latter end.' Here, then, we have the principle stated. You must tune from the bass, for the bass is the basis of music. But you must rise from the bass, as a building must rise from its foundations, or the music will be a moan and a monotone. The fear of the Lord is the beginning of wisdom; but the wisdom that gets no farther is like music that rumbles and reverberates in one everlasting bass. . . .

Of course, the value is not stable or permanent. Nobody said that fear was wisdom. What the wise man said was that fear was the *beginning* of wisdom. The sooner that the beginning is developed and brought to a climax, the better it will be. But meanwhile a beginning is something. It is a step in the right direction. It is the learning of the alphabet.

F. W. Boreham
'Mushrooms on the Moor'
quoted in *Daily Readings from F. W. Boreham*

Psalm 112

Fifth Sunday of Epiphany/Proper 1/Ordinary Time 5:
Year A, verses 1-9, (10)
Proper 17/Ordinary Time 22: Year C

Man lives not
to glorify and
promote himself
but to bring glory
and honour to God.

The man who fears the Lord

Identical acrostic structure, similarity of vocabulary, and a common emphasis on the fear of the Lord (111:10-112:1) indicate that Psalms 111 and 112 were written by the same poet.

'Praise the Lord' stands outside the acrostic structure in both psalms. However, Psalm 111 is a hymn and Psalm 112 is wisdom poetry, in which the psalmist seeks to instruct others in the desirability of living a God-fearing life.

The happiness of the God-fearer (112:1). The psalm begins with the wise man's pronouncement of a beatitude upon the man who so reveres the Lord that he keeps his commandments with joy (compare 1:1-2; 40:8; 119:35, 97). The psalmist seems to have carried over the thought of the fear of the Lord from the last verse of the preceding psalm.

A description of the God-fearer (112:2-9). In these verses the beatitude of verse 1 is developed. The God-fearer will have a powerful and influential posterity. He himself is prosperous and so uses his prosperity in benevolent deeds that he continually enjoys the rewards of such righteousness (see Ezekiel 18:20), since it is patterned on the righteousness of God (111:3). The light of prosperity and joy (see 97:11; Isaiah 58:10) follows the darkness of trouble and sorrow in the lives of the upright. The subject in the clause of verse 4b is uncertain. As the clause stands, it means that God is the source of such light because he is gracious, merciful, and righteous. But if the God-fearer is the subject, his character reflects the character of God as set forth in Psalm 111:4b.

The God-fearer is generous and lends (compare 37:21, 26), and conducts his affairs so as to injure no one. Borrowing took place usually in the case of critical need, and a lender was forbidden to profit out of his brother's misfortune by charging interest (see 15:5; Deuteronomy 23:19-20). Generous living issues in stability (compare 15:5) and in the gratitude of those who will not let the name of their benefactor be forgotten (verse 6; compare 111:4a). On account of the security of faith the righteous man is undisturbed by evil reports. He is confident that God will administer justice to his adversaries.

Verse 9ab is parallel to verse 3 and is quoted by Paul in 2 Corinthians 9:9 to encourage Christian liberality.

The antagonist of the God-fearer (112:10). The wicked man is infuriated at the happiness of the righteous man, but his purpose will not be fulfilled (compare Proverbs 10:24). Obviously the psalmist has presented only the general principle of reward and punishment. Nevertheless, there is need for an optimism that does not overlook any of God's blessings, material or spiritual.

A. B. Rhodes
Psalms

Psalm 112:4a says, 'For the upright he shines like a lamp in the dark.' Hence some comments on Matthew 5:14-15 describing those who follow Christ as the 'light of the world'.

True disciples are also the light of the world. Without forgetting the necessity of inner integrity, they must give a witness to the world by word and especially by life; they must visibly attest God's life-changing power and outgoing goodness: A city situated on the top of a hill or mountainous ridge is inescapably visible. The good life of the disciples must be equally visible and attractive. Returning to the light illustration, the lamp is used to make the same point. Men do not hide it under a basket or tub (holding about a peck), but put it on a lampstand, where it gives maximum light to all in the house (the illustration implies a one-room house). Jesus' meaning is clear. The light (not of verbal witness but here) of good works must shine out so that men see it and thereby are led, not to praise the one who does the good deeds, but to praise the Father in heaven whom it is the disciple's single and constant purpose to honour and serve. 'Father in heaven', a favourite phrase in Matthew, refers to God not as remote, inaccessible, and indifferent towards men, but as exalted, majestic, rightfully man's Lord, and so entitled to all honour and obedience. Man lives not to glorify and promote himself but to bring glory and honour to God.

Floyd V. Filson
The Gospel According To St Matthew

Verse 9 of Psalm 112 mentions giving to the poor, so some thoughts concerning them.

In one way and another, all my working ministry I have had to deal with poverty in one form or another. For some years I worked in Birmingham amongst the homeless and those recently discharged from prison and, somehow, whenever my dog-collar has been seen certain men of the road, homeless and unemployed, have approached me, for the poor somehow believe that money is the answer to everything, but of course it is not.

Here are a few snapshots of experiences that I have had in the past:

One dark winter night I was called out to see a man who some church people had taken into their home as he had begged for help. When I first met him I came straight to the point. 'If it's money you want, tell me now, and I will help you.' He said that money was not the problem. His biggest problem was fear of a gang who were out to get him. For three long hours he told his story that made no real sense. So in exasperation I said, 'Look, I don't really believe a word. How much money do you want?' His quick response was '£3'; so I gave him it and left in anger. I went on to meet people I should have seen hours earlier and they heard the story with some amusement. I said I'd been conned. The response I got from one man was, 'Well, that's your job, isn't it?' 'Certainly not,' was my reply.

A slightly inebriated poor man stood inside a church door in Lancashire, saw me enter, and immediately asked for money. I said gently that I felt that he'd had enough to drink and anything I gave him would also be spent on it. He followed me into a crowded street shouting, 'You Protestant bastard,' arousing puzzled and amused looks from passers-by.

I once saw a 'blind man' begging in Jerusalem at about midday. He suddenly looked at his watch, took a quick look round, and shot off in a car.

Once on holiday in Majorca, in a lovely, crowded shipping area, I saw what appeared to be a pile of old black cloth. As I stopped to look, a gnarled and withered hand appeared begging for money. I gave nothing, but to this day my conscience burns because I felt that here was someone I could have helped.

In our society a fair amount of help that can be obtained from various social services, but is it enough? I do not know the answer to that one. As I write, the government has just appointed a supremo to clear the streets of London of people sleeping rough, and as I understand, even soup-runs and shelters are not the answer. The genuinely needy I try always to help personally, but I still hate it when people try to 'con' me.

Ron Dale, 1999

Psalm 113

Visitation: Years A, B, C
Proper 20/Ordinary Time 25: Year C

The Lord is not an unconcerned transcendent Deity but the caretaker of the dispossessed and the unpossessing.

Three general considerations about this psalm should be noted initially:

1. It, along with Psalms 114-118, was employed in temple services (at the time of the slaughter of the lambs) and in home celebrations (as part of the meal ritual) during the Passover festival; thus the imagery of the psalm came to be associated with the events of the Exodus, which was commemorated in the Passover ritual.

2. The psalm has many similarities to the Song of Hannah in 1 Samuel 2:10, with which it may profitably be compared; the similarity of both of these to Mary's Magnificat in Luke 1:46-55 has led to their connection with Visitation.

3. The psalm shares in a common biblical motif, which might be called the 'reversal of fate' or the 'from rags to riches' sentiment.

The genre and structure of the psalm are clear. It is a hymn used to express and instil faith and particular beliefs by and in the congregation. The initial verses (1-4) are a summons to praise God, temporally and in all time and for ever (verse 2), and geographically in all places and everywhere (verse 3). Verses 5-9 provide the motivations, the reasons why God should be praised. These are presented in the form of a question (verses 5-6) and an answer (verses 7-9). The psalm develops a dialectic in the Divine and thus speaks about God in contrasting ways. In the question (verses 5-6), God is highly exalted; God sits above looking far down upon earth and even far down upon the heavens. If such a transcendent God must squint to see the earth, then surely the course of events and the status of individual persons must be beyond divine purview. The answer given to 'Who is like the Lord?' comes, however, as unexpected in its content. The Lord is the one who reverses the fate of the unfortunate, who transforms the status of those whom society judges as failures. The Lord is not an unconcerned transcendent Deity but the caretaker of the dispossessed and the unpossessing. The heavenly Lord is involved in earthly human existence.

Verses 7-8 concern the reversal of status of the male. The poor and the needy would have been those condemned by fate and fortune to marginal participation in the life of the community. These would have been forced to live in poverty at the peripheries of society. Perhaps they had gotten in that condition by the accident of birth, misfortune, poor harvests, illness, or debt. The dust and the ash heap refer to the city garbage dump, where the dispossessed and the unpossessing as well as the sick and leprous (see Lamentations 4:5; Job 2:8; Leviticus 13:45-46) made their domicile, grubbed for survival, begged for a handout, and got food and clothing from family and friends if they had any. Such places of last resort are similar to modern old folk's homes and public shelters as well as dump hovels where the world's refugees congregate. A male living in such conditions in ancient times would have been without social standing and without self-respect and confidence. So much for verse 7, the 'before' in the psalmic commercial.

The 'after' we find in verse 8. The ones suffering deprivation and ostracism are made to sit with the nobles/princes, that is, with the rich and powerful. To 'sit with' implies acceptance by others and self-assurance by the new participant. (Remember the difference between standing integration and sitting integration in the South. 'Sit-ins' marked a new state in the civil rights movement because to 'sit with' is to share.) For the ideal of one who sits with the nobles, see Job 29:1-25.

The transformation of the unfortunate female is noted in verse 9. The mother was not really 'at home' in the extended family of her husband; that is, she had no real security or sense of fully belonging and participating until she and her children created their own space and place in the family. The wife, always brought into the husband's family, was an outsider to her in-laws until children transformed her into an insider and made her 'at home'. It must have been lonely in such a situation for the barren wife – so much so, that barrenness could be understood as a disgrace if not a curse from God (see Genesis 16:2; 20:18; 1 Samuel 1:5; Luke 1:25). Many of the matriarchs of Israel, however, were barren (Sarah, Rachel, Hannah) for a long time before they produced a child viewed as the result of divine intervention.

John H. Hayes
Preaching Through the Christian Year: Year A

Rediscovery of transcendence

It is true that the American sociologist of religion Peter Berger, who created a sensation some years ago with his book

A Rumour of Angels, has no illusions about the survival of religion as a mass phenomenon: 'It is a fairly reasonable prognosis that in a 'surprise-free' world the global trend of secularisation will continue. An impressive rediscovery of the supernatural, in the dimensions of a mass phenomenon, is not in the books. At the same time, significant enclaves of supernaturalism within the secularised culture will also continue. . . . Berger invites the theologians to 'seek out what might be called signals of transcendence within the empirically given human situation. And I would further suggest that there are prototypical human gestures that may constitute such signals.' At the same time, for Berger, these 'prototypical human gestures' are 'certain reiterated acts and experiences that appear to express essential aspects of man's being, of the human animal as such'.

Berger, then, finds 'signs of transcendence' – for instance – in man's propensity for order. Faith in order, he thinks, is 'closely related to man's fundamental trust in reality'.

. . . Man's propensity for order is grounded in a faith or trust that, ultimately, reality is 'in order', 'all right', 'as it should be'. Needless to say, there is no empirical method by which this faith can be tested. To assert it is itself an act of faith. And 'the most fundamental of ordering gestures, that by which a mother reassures her anxious child', is for Berger a sign of transcendence: The content of this communication will invariably be the same – 'Don't be afraid – everything is in order, everything is all right.' The child's 'trust in reality is recovered, and in this trust he will return to sleep.'

Even in play, man transcends his reality, his ordinary life, the mechanical uniformity of society, when he partly nullifies the familiar setting in space and time and its limits, setting up a world of meaning of his own with its own rules. Berger sees these ciphers of transcendence also in the argument from hope, . . . in the argument from damnation, that is, in man's longing for a justice transcending earthly justice, . . . or in the 'argument from humour', which can rise above man's most wretched reality, seen as not definitive.

Seen in this way, the rediscovery of transcendence means 'a regaining of openness in our perception of reality . . . The principal moral benefit of religion is that it permits a confrontation with the age in which one lives in a perspective that transcends the age and thus puts it in proportion.

(My comment on transcendence is that it must be firmly held with immanence, and incarnational theology. For if we strongly emphasise transcendence, God becomes remote, 'up there' and unrelated to our

life. Conversely, if we overstress the Babe of Bethlehem, we become sentimentally mawkish, and God is diminished. Ron Dale)

Main quote by Hans Kung
Does God Exist?

Psalm 114

Easter Vigil: Years A, B, C
Easter Evening: Years A, B, C
Proper 19/Ordinary Time 24: Year A (Alt)

When God emptied the tomb, he revealed himself to be Lord over nature also.

'When Israel went forth from Egypt'

In the three-year Lectionary, there is a listing of several texts that might be used for the first celebration of Easter at the Vigil before the dawn of Easter day. This psalm is last in the list and is paired with the resurrection accounts in all three Synoptic Gospels. As such, that is an inspired choice, for no Old Testament reading could better set forth the awe and joy associated with the resurrection of Christ, and few Old Testament readings could better join Old Testament and New as the account of the one saving history.

When God set his love upon his people (cf. Deuteronomy 7:7) and manifested his power over the empire of Egypt by delivering Israel, not only his lordship over empires was revealed, but also his lordship over all of nature (verses 3-4). The Red Sea saw him and fled before him, its waters rolled back to allow Israel to pass through on dry land (Exodus 14:22). The Jordan knew its Lord and ceased in its flow (Joshua 3:14-17; 4:23-24). Mount Sinai quaked when God descended upon it (Exodus 19:18), and the hills skipped like rams in a pasture before his presence (cf. Psalm 29:6).

Indeed, God in his relation with Israel showed himself Lord of all – God of gods (cf. Exodus 12:12), Lord over nature, Ruler of all peoples. And so verse 7 of our psalm calls on the entire earth to tremble before the might and glory of the omnipotent One of Jacob (cf. Psalm 96:9; 99:1, etc.). The Lord is awesome in his power and majesty.

Yet it is precisely this awesome, mighty Ruler of all who condescends to be with his people and who bends to give them aid in their extremities (verse 8). When they wander through the dry and desolate desert and have no water to drink, the Lord provides them water from a rock that they may live (Exodus 17:6; cf. Numbers 20:11). The mighty Lord of all is also the Saviour of his people.

Is there a better description of our God who raises Jesus Christ from the dead? Certainly he is showing himself Lord over empires when the women discover that empty tomb on Easter morn. Jesus died at the hands of the Roman Empire's executioners. He had been sentenced to death by the Roman Prefect, Pontius Pilate, the fifth governor of the province of Judea, who was concerned for his own position and reputation. But God raised his Son and showed that his will triumphed over even Rome's.

When God emptied the tomb, he revealed himself to be Lord over nature also. It is not natural for human beings to rise from the dead. The laws of the natural world consign all things and persons to die; everything hastens to its end. But the God who created nature's order and who sets its laws in motion is not bound by our observations of what is natural, nor is he determined by the limits of what he himself has created. He is Sovereign over nature's ways, and he is the Lord of life and death, bringing forth a resurrection when such seemed impossible. It is no wonder that the women at the tomb were afraid and awestruck when they heard, 'He is not here; for he has risen.' (Matthew 28:6)

In fact, there is a note in the accounts of the resurrection that link it closely with our psalm. As the women approach the tomb of Jesus on Easter morning, they wonder how they will roll away the stone that seals the tomb so that they may anoint Jesus' dead body. In Mark and Luke, the women find the stone already rolled aside and the angel(s) tell them that Christ has risen. But in Matthew's account we read, 'And behold, there was a great earthquake; for an angel of the Lord descended from heaven and came and rolled back the stone . . .' (Matthew 28:2). 'The mountains skipped like rams, the hills like lambs.' God shook the earth at the resurrection of his Son as he shook it also at the sea and at Sinai.

It is appropriate, therefore, to sound the imperative of Psalm 114 on Easter Eve. 'Tremble, O earth, at the presence of the *Lord*, at the presence of the God of Jacob.' Or as Psalm 99 puts it, 'The *Lord* reigns; let the people tremble' (verse 1). God reigns over all history and nature at the resurrection of our Lord. Human powers and human beings could not defeat him. All of our sins gathered together to pound the nails through his hands on that cross, and we in our pride thought that we had done with God for ever. But God's Son forgave us our sin and was raised triumphant over it, for ever the victor over earth's death and all its evil. And now nothing in heaven or on earth can deter him until he is acknowledged as Lord of all by every bowed knee and confessing tongue.

The miracle, though, the awesome miracle beyond Christ's resurrection from the dead, is that this God, this Lord of all, has chosen us along with Israel to be his own possession and to be with us all our lives. Seeing our thirst in the wilderness of our days, our longing for guidance and meaning and good, he has stooped to give us drink from the living water of his Spirit (cf. John 4:10-15). And that water gives us a 'spring of water welling up to eternal life' (John 4:14). Because Christ lives, we too can live – abundantly, joyfully, eternally – if we live in him through trust in his working in us.

Elizabeth Achtemeier
Preaching Hard Texts of the Old Testament

Psalm 116

Third Sunday of Easter: Year A, verses 1-4, 12-19
Proper 6/Ordinary Time 11: Year A, verses 1-2, 12-19
Holy Thursday: Years A, B, C, verses 1-2, 12-19
Proper 19/Ordinary Time 24: Year B, verses 1-9

The pathway of life is as slippery for the Christian as for any man.

Some grave peril had surrounded the psalmist and threatened his very life. Probably it was some serious illness. On his recovery, he lifts up his heart and voice in glad thanksgiving to God.

Verse 8 speaks of the threefold deliverance that God can work for those who put their trust in him.

1. You have delivered my soul from death. Like other mortal men the Christian must die; but for him death is an adventure rather than a terror. It is, as someone calls it, 'a gate on the skyline', leading not into unknown darkness but into the glory of the presence of God.

2. You have delivered my eyes from tears. The Christian is not immune from sorrow; but his sorrow turns to trustful acceptance when he remembers that 'a father's hand will never cause his child a needless tear'.

3. You have delivered my feet from falling. The pathway of life is as slippery for the Christian as for any man; the temptations he has to face are the temptations which are common to all. But he has within him grace which can keep him clean and which enables him to keep his garments unspotted from the world.

William Barclay
Seven Fresh Wineskins

Jehovah the deliverer from death

This is the fourth song of the Hallel (see note on page 265)[1]. In it the note of triumph over death, with which the last one closed, is elaborated.

The singer had evidently been in some grave peril in which he had practically despaired of life. From the peril he has been delivered by Jehovah, and now sings his praise. It has two movements. The first tells of his love, and declares its reason and its issue (verses 1-9). The second tells of his resulting faith, breaks forth into new exultation, and affirms his determination to praise (verses 10-19).

His love is the outcome of Jehovah's love manifested on his behalf when in the very bonds of death he cried to him. The issue is that he will walk before Jehovah. His faith thus confirmed, he breaks into new song, and dedicates himself afresh to the high service of thanksgiving.

Whatever the local circumstances which gave rise to this song, it is evident that all its rich meaning was fulfilled, when in the midst of that little company of perplexed souls, the shadows of the One Death already on him, Jesus sang this song of prophetic triumph over the sharpness of the hour of passion to which he was passing. He has made it over to all his own as their triumph song over death.

G. Campbell Morgan
Notes on the Psalms

1. In Judaism, Psalms 113-118 are known as the Hallel, Hymn of Praise, or the Egyptian Hallel (see 114:1); and are sung at the Feasts of Passover, Weeks, Tabernacles, and Dedication (Hanukkah). At Passover, Psalms 113-114 are sung before the meal and Psalms 115-118 after it. The hymn sung by Jesus and his Apostles after the Last Supper (Matthew 26:30; Mark 14:26) was probably Psalms 115-118; it is also possible that Psalms 113-114 were sung before the supper. (From *Psalms*, A. B. Rhodes)

'For you have delivered my soul from death', is the fourth verse of Psalm 116, and 'Praise the Lord', the last verse; and these twin themes are at the heart of the psalm. Here then a reading on each theme.

Flowers of resurrection

Latin American Christians of our century have added to the fourteen traditional stations of the cross, which came from Spain, a fifteenth, which they call the resurrection. In Canto Grande the many cardboard crosses are taken back down from the wooden cross and replaced by white carnations as signs of the resurrection. The cross of hunger is replaced by the flower of sharing which takes place in the *comedores populares,* the kitchens for the poor, where mothers come together to prepare in common economical and nutritious meals for their children. The cross of injustice is replaced by the justice that the people demand on their protest marches, so that the officials will finally meet their obligations towards the families by providing water, light, health care, and schools. The cross of disease becomes the flower of health, for which voluntary health workers speak up by carrying out education and organising campaigns for hygiene. The cross of poverty becomes the flower of water, reflected in the water project: all residents of the communities have agreed to communal work Sunday after Sunday to construct a drinking water tank for Motupe and Montenegro.

The cross of death is replaced by the flower of life. In this symbolic action the cross of dark wood appears whiter and whiter, covered by the flowers of resurrection. Then the people also kiss this new cross.

Dorothee Soelle
Celebrating Resistance: The Way of the Cross in Latin America

Brought to the Father

When a sinner is brought to Christ, he is brought to the Father. Jesus gave himself for us, 'that he might bring us to God'. Oh! what a sight breaks in upon the soul – the infinite, eternal, unchangeable God! I know that some of you have been brought to see this sight. Oh! praise him, then, for what he is. Praise him for his pure, loving holiness, that cannot bear any sin in his sight. Cry, like the angels, 'Holy, holy,

holy, Lord God Almighty.' Praise him for his infinite wisdom – that he knows the end from the beginning. In him are hid all the treasures of wisdom and knowledge. Praise him for his power – that all matter, all mind, is in his hand. The heart of the king, the heart of saint and sinner, are all in his hand. Hallelujah! for the Lord God omnipotent reigneth. Praise him for his love; for God is love. Some of you have been at sea. When far out of sight of land, you have stood high on the vessel's prow, and looked round and round – one vast circle of ocean without any bound. Oh! So it is to stand in Christ justified, and to behold the love of God – a vast ocean all around you, without a bottom and without a shore. Oh! Praise him for what he is. Heaven will be all praise. If you cannot praise God, you never will be there.

Robert Murray McCheyne
'Thanksgiving Obtains the Spirit' (1839)
from *The Lion Meditation Collection*

Psalm 118

Palm/Passion Sunday: Years A, B, C,
*   verses 1-2, 19-29*
Easter: Years A, B, C, verses 1-2, 14-24
Second Sunday of Easter: Year C, verses 14-29 (Alt)

The righteous are not self-congratulatory. Rather, they are exuberantly grateful.

Palm Sunday is a juncture at which two conflicting emotions collide. On the one hand, there is the festal jubilation over the entry of the king into his royal city, a procession of majesty that dwarfs all other such ceremonial entrances, as this King dwarfs all other kings. This note of celebration is struck, in the gospel account, by the shouts of the crowd. 'Hosanna! Blessed is the one who comes in the name of the Lord! Blessed is the coming kingdom of our ancestor David!' (Mark 11:9-10)

On the other hand, however, there is a strong sense of foreboding, which tempers the joy of the moment. All perceptive persons who come to the Palm Sunday festival (including modern worshippers) are aware that the exaltation of the King, which is shortly to occur, and of which the Palm Sunday entrance is the prelude, will be deeply scarred by pain and death.

This amalgam of sensations, anticipation, thanksgiving, supplication – is evidenced in the psalm lection, where the various emotions are juxtaposed so strikingly that one must raise questions about the psalm's logical coherence. After the initial formulaic thanksgiving (verses 1-2), the psalmist's song of gratitude over having been saved by the Lord's power (verse 21) is soon matched by his petition to the Lord for action (verse 25). The psalmist speaks now to the gatekeepers (verse 19), then to the Lord (verse 21), and ultimately to the people (verse 29). Yet through the whole there is a constant motif: we, the people, have arrived to celebrate God's wonderful presence. Fling open the gates that we may enter!

Thus, of the two principal moods of Palm Sunday, Psalm 118:1-2; 19-29 is clearly weighted in favour of joyous celebration. Yet even here the shadow of the cross cannot be blotted out entirely. The stone that the Lord has chosen as the 'chief cornerstone' has been rejected by others, and all who have read the story through to its conclusion know that these evil forces still lurk nearby in their attempt to make this rejection permanent.

In its entirety, Psalm 118 is a psalm of thanksgiving sung

by one who has been to the edge of the abyss and who has been delivered by God (see especially verses 10-14). But only in the verses that form this day's lection do we encounter the theme of pilgrimage to the Holy Place. In its original setting, this was most likely Jerusalem at a time of special significance – the autumn festival, perhaps – the 'day that the Lord has made' (verse 24). In that setting, the 'gate of the Lord' (verse 20) is the gate of the city or of the Temple. 'The one who comes in the name of the Lord' (verse 26) is the pious pilgrim.

In its Palm Sunday application, however, much of this meaning is transformed. The procession is not that of a devout band of worshippers, but of a king and his court. (Some scholars insist that . . . this psalm celebrated the re-enthrone-ment of the Davidic monarch . . .) The 'blessed . . . one' is no representative pilgrim, but the King of kings. The 'day that the Lord has made' (verse 24) is not an annually repeated occasion, but a once-and-for-all moment leading up to the humiliation and exaltation of this Messiah-king.

Striking in its singularity in this text is verse 22, which juts quite unexpectedly above the surrounding context. Nothing has been said to this point in the entire psalm about a building stone, nor is the matter broached again. The thought appears as an exclamation mark in the middle of a sentence: 'The stone that the builders rejected has become the chief cornerstone.'

And the question naturally arises: to what or to whom is the psalmist referring? To declare that this is some pre-existing proverb which has been incorporated into the psalm may be quite true, for the lines do have a certain axiomatic ring to them. But what flow of logic within the mind of the psalmist called forth their use, and of what building has this rejected stone become the chief corner? . . . The writers of the New Testament could think of no one to whom these lines applied more appropriately than the about-to-be-rejected Jesus, who becomes the adored and reigning risen Christ (Mark 12:10 and elsewhere). 'This is the Lord's doing; it is marvellous in our eyes'. (Psalm 118:23)

Indeed, it is the power of God in the events of Christ's passion and resurrection that Christians celebrate when we use this text as a Palm Sunday lection. The power of God is at the text's heart and core. For that which occurred at Calvary and the open tomb shattered all human expectations, even those – especially those – of the men and women who were eye-witnesses of the events. More than logic or 'nature' were on display here. The One who entered the city as a ridiculous-looking, donkey-riding King destroyed the bonds of sin and death. He did so by the strength of a loving and redeeming God.

Thus the climax of the lection, which in verse 1 appears to be an overly familiar refrain (compare Psalms 107:1; 136), here becomes a surge of thanksgiving from hearts that have been touched by a God whose saving love extends to the grave and beyond.

'O give thanks to the Lord, for he is good, for his steadfast love endures for ever.' (Psalm 118: 29)

James D. Newsome
Texts for Preaching

The voice of the psalm is one of grateful righteousness (Psalm 118:15-20). The 'righteous' are not necessarily the good or the obedient or the pious. The text speaks of the 'tents of the righteous', where the rescued live (verse 15), the 'gates of righteousness' through which the obedient enter to worship (verse 19), and the entry of the righteous, the willingness of the Lord's rescued to come to worship (verse 20). This community consists of those who have known God's massive action on their behalf and who live their lives in glad response to that action. While there is a moral dimension to righteousness, this psalm concerns those who are glad benefactors of God's powerful love. They are righteous because of what they have received from God.

The righteous are not self-congratulatory. Rather, they are exuberantly grateful. They shift all the attention away from themselves to the rescuing power of God. Thus the grateful rescued sing three times, 'The right hand of God' (verse 15-16), an allusion to God's powerful, continuing purpose and presence. The Church knows at Easter, as this psalm knows, that Easter would not have happened, and new life would not have been given, except by God's powerful intrusion. . . .

The reading ends in boundless gratitude (verses 21-24). God has answered. God has heard the need. God has rushed to intervene. God has changed death to life. God has over-powered Friday for the sake of Sunday. The rejected one, left for dead, is the valued one (verse 22). What a day (verse 24)! The day of rescue is a day for joy. What a day – Easter Day – life day – beginning day. It is a special day. . . . This is the day of God's power for life . . . our day of singing and gratitude. On this day, God's people are at a beginning, not an ending.

Walter Brueggemann
Texts for Preaching, Year A

Psalm 119

Sixth Sunday of Epiphany/Proper 2/
   Ordinary Time 6: Year A, verses 1-8
Seventh Sunday of Epiphany/Proper 3/
   Ordinary Time 7: Year A, verses 33-40
Proper 10/Ordinary Time 15: Year A, verses 104-112
Proper 12/Ordinary Time 17: Year A, verses 129-136
Proper 18/Ordinary Time 23: Year A, verses 33-40
Proper 26/Ordinary Time 31: Year B
Fifth Sunday of Lent: Year B, verses 9-16 (Alt)
Proper 24/Ordinary Time 29: Year C, verses 97-104
Proper 26/Ordinary Time 31: Year C, verses 137-144

When a man is sure of God . . . he finds delight and pleasure in living by God's laws.

John Ruskin, writing of those portions of the Bible which he had been made to memorise in boyhood, says, 'That which cost me most to learn, and which was to my child's view, chiefly repulsive – the 119th Psalm – has now become of all the most precious to me.' This is the longest of the Psalms (176 verses in all) and it should be savoured slowly and at intervals rather than at one sitting, else the reader will suffer a case of mental indigestion. Fortunately the intervals are well-defined. The psalm is set in the form of an acrostic. There are 22 stanzas corresponding to the 22 letters in the Hebrew alphabet. Each stanza has eight lines, and each line begins with the same Hebrew letter. In the English equivalent it would mean that each of the eight lines of the first stanza begins with the letter A, each line in the second begins with B, and so on throughout the alphabet.

But we musn't be bored or even too fascinated by this artificial arrangement. The psalmist was not an old-fashioned preacher using a homiletical gimmick which eclipsed the content of his message. He was a great poet possessed by a great truth and he employed the best literary device in order to impress that truth upon his readers. It was not just an academic truth either, but the constitutive principle of his life, the basic philosophy that drew the divergent trends of his personality together and made him a complete human being. A single theme runs through this longest of the psalms. That theme is God's Law, variously expressed as God's statutes, precepts, commandments, testimonies, word, ways and judgements. The psalmist has brought God into his experience, and God has given him, among other blessings, a Law that unifies his little life around a single philosophy and gives it meaning and purpose.

The psalmist [tells us] that there is pleasure in keeping God's Law.

> Blessed are the undefiled in the way, who walk in the law of the Lord. Blessed are they that keep his testimonies, and that seek him with the whole heart.

The rest of the psalm is a prayer and, as such, it tells us more about the author than we could learn if he spoke directly to us. This Hebrew poet has found God's Law to be such a never-failing source of delight and happiness and joy in his life that he proclaims his gladness not to man but to God. He thanks God out of a full heart:

> O how I love thy law! It is my meditation all the day . . . thy law is my delight . . . Thy testimonies are wonderful . . . Thy statutes have been my songs in the house of my pilgrimage . . . I have rejoiced in the way of thy testimonies, as much as in all riches . . . The law of thy mouth is better unto me than thousands of gold and silver . . . The righteousness of thy testimonies is everlasting: give me understanding, and I shall live . . .

There are some people who might raise an eyebrow at this man's enthusiasm for God's Law. 'An odd sort of character,' they say. 'Probably a fanatical legalist. What normal person actually takes pleasure in keeping laws?' Most of us believe that laws are necessary and good for the well-being of society and we observe them because we have to, not always because we want to. Ever since we were children at school, governed by the rules of the classroom, we have regarded laws as the compulsive and restrictive element in life which it was fun to throw off from time to time. Ever since Adam and Eve men and women have rebelled against the laws of God, believing that there was greater pleasure in freedom from those laws than in being bound by them. Our generation has reacted quite vehemently against God's laws, a reaction sanctified by modern moralists and by some theologians who claim that there is no such thing as a fixed code of human behaviour laid down by a Supranatural God and applicable to every situation. Some would go further and say that there is no such thing as a Supranatural God. How does this double denial affect a man in his search for the pleasure and happiness that will give meaning to his life?

Canadians recall the furore in the press and Parliament

caused by a popular television programme in the autumn of 1966. It consisted partly of a film, produced in Britain, which showed a young man and a woman, on more than friendly terms, occupying the same bed and discussing in a desultory manner whether they wanted to get married. An unseen interviewer then spoke to each of them separately and asked some shockingly intimate questions about their rather promiscuous sex life. The programme raised a chorus of protests from indignant taxpayers who resented this publicly-financed garbage being dumped into their living rooms. Strangely enough, there were no protests against another feature of the same programme which showed a live interview with an Episcopalian Bishop whose ventilation of his own doubts and floundering efforts to answer questions indicated that he is well on his way to rejecting the Bible idea of God. Can it be that most viewers failed to see the connection between these two features in the programme? When a man is sure of God, a Creator, Sovereign God who governs the world according to his laws, and when a man loves that God he finds delight and pleasure in living by God's laws. When a man rejects the God of Mount Sinai he turns to other delights and pleasures, even those that exploit, pervert and destroy human personality.

One of the big lies being circulated in our day is the spurious claim that the religion of Jesus contains no rules. A school child has only to read the New Testament in order to find out that Jesus stated explicitly that he came not to abrogate the laws of God but to make those same laws more positive, more spiritual and more demanding. What are the Beatitudes if not the laws of the Kingdom of God? Jesus enunciated them not to take pleasure out of life but to put pleasure into it. Each one begins with the word 'Blessed', the key-word of Psalm 119; and their whole point is precisely that in living by these divinely-given rules of humility, meekness, purity and righteousness, a man will find a unifying philosophy of life that brings him the highest happiness and makes him a complete person.

In God's Law the psalmist found also a *moral purpose* that gave meaning to his life. Indeed, he impresses me as the one man in the Old Testament who truly incarnates the beatitude of Jesus: 'Blessed are they which do hunger and thirst after righteousness.' He has one consuming ambition, an insatiable appetite to understand and obey and fulfil the Law of God for his life. How fervently he prays:

> Teach me, O Lord, the way of thy statutes; and I shall keep it unto the end. Give me understanding, and I shall

keep thy law; yea, I shall observe it with my whole heart. Make me to go in the path of thy commandments; for therein I do delight. Incline my heart unto thy testimonies, and not to covetousness . . . O that my ways were directed to keep thy statutes . . . Behold, I have longed after thy precepts: quicken me in thy righteousness . . .

Some men have found that enduring purpose in the Law of God. Once it was my privilege to spend half an hour in the home of Karl Barth, chatting informally with the great theologian. He was 72 years of age at the time, and I innocently asked if he planned to bring out any more volumes of his monumental *Dogmatics*. He laughed with youthful vigour and replied, 'Of course! And when I complete the doctrinal works I shall go on to Christian ethics.' Barth spoke in a larger sense than he realised. Christian ethics are always ahead of us, even at the age of 72, and not only as an academic study but as the enduring purpose of God for our lives. No man ever reaches a point where he can cease to pray, 'Give me understanding, and I shall keep thy law; yea, I shall observe it with my whole heart.' The one purpose that will unify a man's life and give it meaning to the very end – and, we believe, beyond that end – is the creation of moral character.

The Law of God gave the psalmist *comfort in his affliction*. He tells God that, but for his delight in the Law, he would have perished in his affliction. Even in trouble and anguish he still found pleasure in trying to live by God's commandments. Indeed, he says that it was good for him to be afflicted so that he might learn God's statutes. The psalmist does not specify the nature of his affliction, but we gather that it was brought on by powerful enemies who framed him, tried to trap him and lay in wait to kill him. Even princes spoke against him and persecuted him without a cause. The most descriptive passage in the psalm begins at verse 81 where the author tells God that his soul faints, his eyes fail, he has become like a bottle in the smoke; the proud have digged pits for him, wrongfully persecuted him and almost destroyed him; but he hopes in God's word, he does not forget God's statutes nor forsake God's precepts.

God's Law gave the psalmist *a source of hope*. A single phrase keeps recurring in his long, sustained prayer, the phrase, *'according to thy word'*. Everything he asks from God – strength, comfort, salvation, mercy – he asks according to God's word. Whenever it refers to God's word the psalmist's prayer reaches sublime heights of assurance and hope.

Thou hast dealt well with thy servant, O Lord, according

to thy word . . . Remember thy word unto thy servant, upon which thou hast caused me to hope . . . Thy word is true from the beginning: and every one of thy righteous judgements endureth for ever . . . For ever, O Lord, thy word is settled in heaven . . . Thy word is a lamp unto my feet, and a light unto my path . . .

It recalls another phrase, frequently used in our common speech and intended to tell us a great deal about a person – 'His word is as good as his bond.' Applied to a friend, it means that we can trust what he says; we can rely upon his word as though it were a legal guarantee and stake our lives upon the truth of it. Applied to God, it means that God's Law is backed up by God's Word. The life which God commands us to live and work for here upon earth contains its own promise and guarantee that this life is right, eternally right, and that in the end it will be the only life that prevails and gives meaning to the individual and society.

A television show, produced a few years ago, exercised a tremendous impact on public imagination. Its moral power lay in the play within the play. Lounging in a New York bar, a half-drunk intellectual virtually acted out before the other customers a drama which he had written. The scene takes place in the United Nations Building on the eve of World War Three. The great powers have declared war and have set midnight as the zero hour when they will press the ominous buttons that let loose the flames of hell upon earth. Meanwhile, they have agreed to a four-hour truce to allow the world's most able men to assemble for the purpose of testing a computer. According to the inventor this machine, if supplied with man's highest wisdom, can provide the answer that will prevent the human race from stumbling over the edge of chaos. The computer stands in the centre of the council chamber. One by one they come forward – statesmen, educators, militarists, philosophers, poets, economists, journalists, scientists – each pouring into this cold automaton the distilled wisdom of the ages according to his branch of knowledge. But nothing happens. The entire world trembles over Death's chasm, and nothing happens until one minute before midnight. Then, suddenly, the computer shudders and its lights flicker. From its mouth comes a slip of paper which the inventor takes in his and reads before the hushed assembly. This is the answer, the supreme wisdom which alone can save civilisation from violent suicide: 'Thou shalt have no other gods before me . . . Thou shalt not make unto thee any graven image . . . Thou shalt not steal . . . Thou shalt not kill . . . Thou shalt not covet . . .'

How can we be sure that this is in fact the highest wisdom,

on which we can depend and in which we can hope for the world's salvation and for our own? We can be sure because, like the Old Testament psalmist, we have hope in God's Word, and because the Word of God, in the sense of God's eternal guarantee, has been fulfilled in the New Testament. The Fourth Gospel begins, 'In the beginning was the Word, and the Word was with God, and the Word was God.' In this Word 'was life, and the life was the light of men. The light shines in the darkness, and the darkness has not overcome it' (RSV). That's what the Gospel story is all about. It tells us that this eternal Word of God 'became flesh, and dwelt among us, full of grace and truth'. Jesus is the Word of God, the Law of God, the life of God made visible in history, and the darkness has not overcome it. Here on earth he lived that life with clear and lofty grandeur and carried it unhurt through death. His was the one complete life this world has ever known: it combined all the unifying qualities of pleasure, moral purpose, comfort and hope. He gives this complete life to us as we identify ourselves with him in faith and obedience, for he came that we 'may have life, and have it abundantly'.

Leonard Griffith
God in Man's Experience: the Activity of God in the Psalms

Psalm 121

Second Sunday of Lent: Year A
Proper 24/Ordinary Time 29: Year C

Our religion must be for everyday use.

This is called the Pilgrim's psalm: its subject is how God helps, protects, delivers and blesses those who travel along the road of life, trusting in him.

The picture it sets before us may have been suggested by the actual Pilgrim Way that led up to Jerusalem. All of them are pictures of life as we know it.

I ask you to look at these with me, and you will discover, I am sure, that ultimately they are drawn from the deep religious experience of the psalmist.

The first picture is of the Road itself – with its ups and downs, its rough and smooth places made by the tread of feet; by armies on the march, by camels and donkeys in convoy; a road thick with dust or slippery mud on the level, and on the slopes, rough with flints and outcropping rocks. Yes: it is a road in the east right enough. But it is also the road we all have to travel, with infinite possibilities in the daily routine of being tripped and upset by little things.

When the psalmist writes, 'He will not suffer thy foot to be moved', he is thinking of how we must continually 'watch our step', look where we are going, plant our feet squarely down, and, with the help of God, do our utmost to keep our balance. How cross-gained, ill-tempered and annoyed by little things the best of us can become.

Our religion must be for everyday use, and only as we use it so, and daily rely on God to help us, shall we be able to keep right on to the end of the road, however rough or smooth the path may be.

The second picture is of a landscape sizzling under the midday sun.

We do not have heat in northern latitudes to compare with the heat of eastern lands. To experience the power of the sun as the psalmist knows it, we have to live where men take to underground rooms about nine o'clock in the morning: where doors and windows are shut and shuttered from dawn to dusk, and the temperature rises to 130 degrees in the shade.

That is the kind of sun the psalmist knew, and it can only represent life in its hardest-to-bear dealings with us – 'life's crushing load'. Most of us no doubt, have experienced or will experience such at some time or other. What does or what ought our trust in God do for us then? This is what the psalmist found it did for him:

'The sun shall not smite thee by day. The Lord is thy shade on thy right hand.' For the great trials of living – the really big risks of the road, he says, there is nothing like the shelter and the shade of trust in God.

There is a third picture in the psalm – the picture of a camp at night, with a full moon looking down on it. We see the outline of a sentry at his post. Presumably he is alert at his post, though the camp is sunk in sleep. Even if he is, what sentry, however alert, can keep robbers out, who are the very colour of the ground along which they crawl, and who, in their movements are as silent as the night itself?

British soldiers in the East, with rifles strapped to their bodies, have been known to awake in the morning, their rifles gone, and that under the very noses of the sentries. In the same way people like you and me have sometimes awakened to the discovery that virtue and peace have been taken from us, looted from our possession by those robbers – the lust of the eye, the lust of the flesh and the pride of life.

Is their any sentry who will watch over us and guard us in our unguarded moments, who will rouse us at the approach of temptation before the worst has happened? The psalmist says there is: 'He that keepeth thee will not slumber. Behold, he that keepeth Israel shall neither slumber nor sleep.' To commit ourselves nightly into his care and keeping is a necessary precaution in view of the subtlety of the evil that besets us. How unprotected are those who trust to their own watchfulness and do not know the peace of God standing sentry over their hearts!

We have not done with the significance of the picture when we have said that.

When the sun goes down the heat of the ground rises and is dissipated in the cloudless and illimitable sky, and the air grows suddenly chill. With the moon riding high in the heavens men shiver in their tents. However good a tent, a blanket is better!

How men can bear the mystery and vastness of the universe and their own insignificance in the scheme of things without faith in God I do not know. At best, life is a lonely experience, and there are losses and disappointments that make it hard to feel the glow of interest in life and love for our fellow-men. It is a great comfort at such times to warm the heart with the promises and the company of Christ. Only so we can preserve our courage and our faith. 'Behold, he that keepeth Israel

WINDOWS ON THE PSALMS

shall neither slumber nor sleep. The Lord is thy keeper. The Lord is thy shade upon thy right hand. The sun shall not smite thee by day nor the moon by night.

The psalmist has a fourth and last picture of the road we must all travel.

It may be a little strange to us, unless we have been in the East and seen the old caravanserais at intervals by the road-side – great khans or inns for the relief of travellers.

In that inn people spend a night or a day, seldom more, unless inclement weather compels a longer stay. It is usually a case of 'here today and gone tomorrow'. Entrances and exits, exits and entrances, and, in-between, all kinds of contacts with all kinds of travellers. Isn't that a picture of life? We cannot always choose our company, we cannot live our lives in isolation from our fellows. All sorts of influences play upon us in our working and in our leisure hours. We meet those who help us morally and spiritually and we meet those whose outlook and whose conduct are hostile to the ideals we seek to be loyal to. How are we to keep our souls clean and unspotted from the world?

To achieve that there is nothing like a simple trust in the reality of God, in his holiness and love. If that had not been the psalmist's testimony he would not have ended his 121st psalm as he did: 'The Lord shall preserve thee from all evil; he shall preserve thy soul. The Lord shall preserve thy going out and thy coming in from this time forth and even for evermore.'

Sermon by Ernest D. Jarvis
published in *My Way of Preaching*

Psalm 122

First Sunday of Advent: Year A

Poverty or a high standard of living is irrelevant to religion except insofar as the failure of the rich to help the poor reveals a lack of love, and destitution can crush the spirit.

A pilgrim prays for Jerusalem

This pilgrim song may have been chanted at the close of one of the great festivals in Jerusalem, as the pilgrims were preparing to return to their homes. The psalmist recalls his eager expectation as he sets out in company with others to come up to the holy city. He speaks of the greatness of Jerusalem as the centre of the religious life of the nation, and prays for its welfare.

The first two verses express the joy of worship (cf. 42 and 84). The psalmist's words sound strangely in an age when churches are poorly attended and criticisms of the services are often heard. Medieval or Victorian buildings, and an archaic liturgy in which the meanings of many of the words have changed, tend to make religion appear remote from modern life, although the experiments which are being made in forms of worship show that church leaders are aware of the problems and are seeking to bring a new vitality and relevance. There are many, moreover, who see little connection between personal belief and corporate worship. Few of us would dare to claim that we have the eager desire for God which the psalmist shows. Our world, with its emphasis on individual choice in religion and morality and the sharp cleavage between secular and sacred, is very different from that of ancient Israel, and we may be tempted to say that devotion was much easier for the psalmist. Yet the gladness which he shows as he joins with others to go on pilgrimage to the temple must be ours if we are to claim to be believers at all.

Jerusalem was more to the people of Israel than simply the political capital of the country. It meant all that Rome means to the Roman Catholic, and more, for it was the city that God himself had chosen to be his earthly dwelling place. It was the foremost sanctuary in the land. Here alone, after the reforms of Josiah, could sacrifice be offered. Here the Lord's justice was dispensed by king and priest. . . . The psalmist speaks of the unity of the nation at worship. This is where true unity is to be found. The final section (verses 6-9) is a call to pray for the welfare of Jerusalem. . . . The motives for the psalmist's prayer should be noticed – for the sake of his brethren and of the temple. To the Christian, prosperity is no valid end in itself. Poverty or a high standard of living is irrelevant to religion except insofar as the failure of the rich to help the poor reveals a lack of love, and destitution (and material comfort!) can crush the spirit. The true end is personal relationships with men and with God.

Cyril S. Rodd
Psalms 73-150

Psalm 122:1-2, 6-9

This is another of the psalms which are called 'Songs of Degrees'. It has three thoughts:

1. There was the joy of the present moment as the sacred city came in sight. Is there always joy in our hearts as we enter the house of God?

2. There was the memory of the past. The history of David and his city passed through the pilgrim's mind. When we worship, something of the history of the Christian church and the memory of revered men and women who have worshipped in our own church in former years must be in our minds.

3. There was a prayer for the future. 'Peace' in Hebrew was not just the absence of trouble; it included everything that was for the good of man, body and soul. So the pilgrim prayed for the good of the Church in the days to come. When we enter God's house let us pray that we may be strengthened to play our part in the task of the Church which lies ahead.

William Barclay
Seven Fresh Wineskins

Peace

Generally the biblical sense of 'peace' is determined by the positive conception of the Hebrew word *shalom* . . .

Shalom is a comprehensive word, covering the manifold relationships of daily life, and expressing the ideal state of life in Israel. Its fundamental meaning is 'totality' (the adjective *shalem* is translated 'whole'), 'well-being', 'harmony', with stress on material prosperity untouched by violence or misfortune. Peace is 'the untrammelled, free growth of the soul (i.e. person) . . . harmonious community; the soul can only expand in conjunction with other souls . . . harmony, agreement, psychic community; . . . every form of happiness and free expansion, but the kernel of it is the community with others, the foundation of life'. This well-being is manifested in every kind of good for man's bodily health (Psalm 38:3; Ecclesiasticus 38:7), strengthening and security (Daniel 10:19; Judges 6:23), a long life of happiness ending in natural death (Genesis 15:15), prosperity and abundance (Lamentations 3:17; Psalm 37:11; Zechariah 8:12; Job 5:19-26; Leviticus 26:6ff. Cf. 'Is it well with?' RV margin, 'is there peace to?') . . .

Peace is the normal and proper condition of men in relationship with one another, enjoyed most intimately in the family (Genesis 13:8), and extended to others by a covenant (1 Samuel 20:42) which determines relationships and is so 'a covenant of peace'. To greet with peace, send away in peace, is to confer a benefit and to admit to mutual confidence and inviolability (Genesis 42:23; Judges19:20); hence the question, 'Is it peace?' (1 Samuel 16:4f). Enjoyed in Israel as a single and harmonious community (2 Samuel 17:3; Exodus 18:23; Psalm 125:5), to which others may be admitted if subservient (Deuteronomy 20:10-12), but not if they threaten to corrupt Israel (Deuteronomy 23:6; Ezra 9:12). The good as opposed to the evil (Proverbs 12:20; Psalm 28:3), the fruit of righteousness (Psalm 37:37) denied to the wicked (Isaiah 48:22). The source of peace in all its forms is Jehovah, the God of peace (Judges 6:24; Isaiah 45:7), who overcomes the forces of disharmony in the heavens (Job 25:2), who blesses Israel (Leviticus 26:6; Psalm 29:11; 85:3-12), the House of David (1 Kings 2:33), the priesthood (Malachi 2:5), the faithful Israelite (Psalm 4:8) with peace.

A Theological Word Book of the Bible
article by Alan Richardson

Psalm 123

Proper 28/Ordinary Time 33: Year A
Proper 9/Ordinary Time 14: Year B

*I am devoted to
my master and my
wife and children;
I do not wish to
go free.*

A personal psalm

What a charming little psalm this is! There is something personal about it – 'I lift up my eyes to you' (verse 1). And there is also a group here – '*Our* eyes are turned to the Lord' (verse 2); 'Show *us* your favour, Lord' (verse 3). The psalmist speaks for a suffering community, he does not specify who were making trouble, but his people are insulted and held up to contempt (verse 4).

It is the metaphors of verse 2 which have aroused my interest – the picture of a slave with his eyes following his master's hand, a slave-girl with her eyes following her mistress's hand. It is a picture of close attention; the eyes are fixed, ready to obey the slightest indication or direction.

Understanding and affection

Of course everything depends on the character of the master/mistress. If they are brutal, then the attitude of the slave is one of fear, even of terror: that hand might hold a lash! The word slave conjures up for us a picture of harsh domination. But it was not always thus when slavery was part and parcel of the fabric of society. In a big household there would be a wide range of activities, and the work of some slaves would be honourable and responsible. In Exodus 21, there are laws laid down for the right treatment of slaves. For example, when a Hebrew buys a slave, his period of service must not exceed six years; after that he goes free. But Exodus 21:4-6 envisages a situation where the slave's conditions have been such that he has no desire for freedom: 'I am devoted to my master and my wife and children; I do not wish to go free.' The eyes of such a slave have no fear in them when they are fixed on their master's hand. The slave looks for any indication of his master's will, so that he may carry out his directions without hesitation or delay. There is an interaction between master and slave based on a relation not of coercion but of mutual understanding and affection.

Paul delights to speak of himself as the slave of Jesus Christ. That kind of slavery spelt freedom for him. His eyes were fixed on his Lord for the slightest indication of his will. Life for this slave meant glad obedience to his Master. And Jesus himself, of course, gladly took on 'the form of a slave' (Philippians 2:7), seeking to serve, rather than to be served (see Matthew 20:28).

There are two verses of poetry that have meant much to me during my ministry as a bishop in the Church of God. They were written by Charles Hamilton Sorley, who, at the age of 20, was killed in the First World War in 1915. They were sung, at my request, when I took up my work at Bradford (1956), York (1961) and Canterbury (1975). Set to music by Charles Wood, they have moved me greatly, and still do. I share with you two verses for your meditation.

Meditation
This sanctuary of my soul
unwitting, I keep white and whole,
unlatched and lit, if thou should'st care
to enter and tarry there.

With parted lips and outstretched hands
and listening ears thy servant stands.
Call thou early, call thou late,
To thy great service dedicate.

Donald Coggan
Psalms 73-150: The People's Bible Commentary

Looking to the Lord

This psalm is a free composition of mixed type, though it is primarily a lament of the community. The first verse is in the first person singular and may have been sung by a priest. The remainder of the psalm is in the first person plural and was probably sung by the congregation. This combination of persons also gives the psalm the form of a liturgy.

Eyes of hope (123:1-2). The priest or other representative of the people looks to God as the King of the universe, enthroned in heaven, and therefore able to grant his people's request. As slaves turn to their masters and mistresses for everything good, so God's people look to him for grace in time of need (compare Isaiah 30:18).

A plea for grace (123:3-4). 'Have mercy upon us' is better translated, 'Be gracious unto us'. The enemies of God's people are 'at ease' in their privileged position and therefore scornful and proud (cf. Job 12:5; Amos 6:1; Zechariah 1:15). Some identify these enemies as the Samaritans and the other neighbours of the Jews in the time of Nehemiah. Others identify them as the people among whom the Jews of the Dispersion were living. It is significant that the psalmist heaps no imprecation upon them.

A. B. Rhodes
Psalms

Psalm 124

Proper 16/Ordinary Time 21: Year A
Proper 21/Ordinary Time 26: Year B

Is there any man who has not had some great deliverance in his life?

This is characteristically the psalm of deliverance. Scholars have suggested that it may be connected with the time when the Jews came back to Jerusalem and began to rebuild the shattered walls of the city. Then indeed their enemies did rise against them and try to hinder God's work (cf. Nehemiah 4:7-23).

Is there any man who has not had some great deliverance in his life? It may be that God has preserved us in some time of danger; it may be that in sickness God led us back from the gates of death; or when we were nearly making shipwreck of life by falling to some grave temptation that God held us back. Even if nothing as memorable as that has happened to us, at least we have been brought through all the chances and changes of life to this present hour. Like the psalmist we can say, our help is in the name of the Lord.

William Barclay
Seven Fresh Wineskins

God intervenes

There was a director of a camp for underprivileged boys who very seldom broke up a fist-fight. He might punish the assailants afterwards but he usually allowed them to fight it out. He hated bullying and tried to teach his lads the rules of fair play but, if two campers did come to blows, he rarely interfered. He believed that every boy must learn to fight his own battles and not look for help when he was getting the worst of it. Once in a while this wise camp director made an exception. On one occasion a group of bullies began terrorising the whole camp. During the day they would send word to some smaller lad that they intended coming to his tent that night to beat him up and they gloated at the thought of his fearful reaction. One little fellow, after getting the grim warning, trembled in terror half the night but he might as well have gone to sleep because his attackers never arrived. In fact, he never saw them again. When the camp director heard of the juvenile 'protection racket' he stepped in promptly and sent the offenders home.

Is that a true picture of God in man's experience? Can we think of him as a Divine Camp Director, watching over his unruly brood, who steps in and takes sides when the strong rise up to exploit the weak? We are at once repelled and attracted by the idea. The thought of God taking sides conjures up all the wars in history when men have prayed for the annihilation of their enemies because they believed that God was fighting on their side. It recalls a modern play in which a middle-class businessman surveys his prosperity and piously declares, 'I have never doubted that God was on my side.' This seems a crude theology, and we pride ourselves on having outgrown it. We consider it more enlightened and mature to think of God not as an external factor who brings us help from outside our situation but as an internal factor always at work within our situation. We are about ready to dispense with the idea of a God who takes sides.

Yet that would be a pity, because it means that we miss one of the great truths of the Bible – not an academic truth, either, but a fact of human experience. Psalm 124 closes with a verse often used by Christian congregations as a Call to Worship: 'Our help is in the name of the Lord, who made heaven and earth.'

The picture of God that emerges from Psalm 124 is a picture of a God who intervenes, a God who takes sides with the weak when the strong rise up to destroy them. It is a picture drawn from human experience and it does not stand alone, because the record of God's dealings with his people in the Old Testament shows him consistently to be that kind of God. Again and again he intervenes at the eleventh hour to save his people from certain disaster. Out of Egypt come a million slaves, pursued by the armies of Pharaoh, their escape cut off by the forbidding waters of the Red Sea. They are trapped. Suddenly and unexpectedly a strong east wind drives back the shallow waters and drops after the Israelites have crossed in safety. On the heights of Mount Tabor a tiny Hebrew garrison looks helplessly at Sisera's great attacking army in the valley below. What chance have they against those gleaming chariots? Suddenly clouds fill the sky, and a torrential rain turns the valley into a bog, immobilising the chariots, demoralising the invader and giving Israel such a victory that it could be said, 'The stars in their courses fought against Sisera.' Within the walls of Jerusalem the terrified citizens await the crushing blow from Sennacherib, the Assyrian dictator, who boasts that he has them shut up like a bird in a cage. The blow never falls. At dawn they see no sign of the besieging army and, when they venture near the Assyrian camp, they find it wiped out by a sudden deadly disease. This is the activity of God in the Old Testament, a God who takes sides with the weak and intervenes when the strong rise up to destroy them.

The Bible sees no conflict between the idea of an immanent God who works within our human situation and the idea of a transcendent God who intervenes from outside. That conflict has been created by modern theology. The Bible sees God as both immanent and transcendent. The God beside and within us is also the God above and beyond us, the high and lofty One *who inhabiteth eternity*, the Creator and Controller of the universe. Because God is sovereign, because he rules the world which he created, he does preserve the right to and the power to intervene in its affairs and to shape them according to his purposes and preferences. We can truthfully share the conviction of the psalmist who said, 'Our help is in the name of the Lord, who made heaven and earth.'

Leonard Griffith
God in Man's Experience: the Activity of God in the Psalms

Psalm 125

Proper 18/Ordinary Time 23: Year B

The vision of God is the spring of moral fruitfulness.

This psalm is one of a larger group, the 'songs of ascents' (Psalms 120-134), which ostensibly concern a pilgrimage up to the Temple in Jerusalem. This psalm begins, then, with 'Mount Zion' on its mind. It is immediately clear, however, that reference to Mount Zion is only part of a rhetorical strategy in the psalm, and not a real concern of the poem. Rather, the psalm urges an equitable practice of justice in public affairs, an accent that resonates with the readings in Proverbs and James.

Psalm 125:1-2 are cast as sapiential sayings, which make an appeal to the stability and safety of the city of Jerusalem, which is, by common consent, impregnable and always safe from attack (see 2 Samuel 5:6). The psalm, however, refers to Mount Zion only to make a comparison. The point of the comparison is the stability and safety of those who trust (*bth*). Trust in God generates stability and precludes any 'tottering'. Those who stay close to the Lord are completely safe and immune to threat.

Verses 3-5b of Psalm 125 turn from assurances to moral affirmations. . . . The assertion is that 'the land allotted to the righteous' will not be ill-governed or ill-managed, in rapacious, covetous ways. The phrasing . . . may be taken in two quite different ways. On the one hand, if the verse is related to Israel's tradition of land conquest, then its concern is general and public. The allotted land is the land of promise, and the 'sceptre' may refer to the rule of the king. On the other hand, the saying may be related to the wisdom tradition, as in our readings in Proverbs. In that reading, the 'land allotted' refers not to a large theological promise, but simply to the land arrangements in a local, settled agricultural economy. Then the comment on governance may simply mean that the land is honoured through just practices, and is not abused or exploited. In either reading, verse 3 suggests an interrelation between patterns of social power and the ways in which the land is cared for, honoured, and kept productive. Both persons' land will be honoured, or both together will be abused.

The indicative statement of verse 3 is followed in verse 4 by a prayer, the only petition of the psalm. 'Those who do good' in this verse are the 'righteous' who do no wrong in verse 3. The ones who do good are the pious, devout keepers of Torah who obey the commands and create a healthy environment of social stability. These upright are to receive 'good' from God, that is, a blessing that will make the land fertile. This petition assumes a tight moral calculus without *good* (as in Psalm 1).

While the grammatical formulations of verse 4 (petition) and verse 5 (assertion) are difficult, most likely they are intended to perform the same rhetorical function. They serve to guarantee that Israel does indeed live in a morally coherent, morally reliable world. The psalm, like Torah piety in general and Psalm 1 in particular, operates in a tight theory of 'deeds-consequences'. Good neighbour practice makes for a secure position in the land.

The theory of moral coherence voiced in verses 3-5b may sound to us like arrogant self-satisfaction, as those who prosper in the land congratulate themselves on their virtue. The same theory, however, can also be taken as a keen discernment that the capacity of the land to produce (as a gift from God) is indeed dependent upon healthy, just, social relations. That is, one cannot abuse neighbour and expect good to come in one's environment. If we take that reading of the verse, then we can detect that verses 1 and 2 about *security*, are indeed dependent on verses 3-5a, concerning *right living*.

We should also note, however, that this psalm has a narrow and conventional view of 'good' in contrast to the readings in Proverbs and James. Here good is done for the 'good-doers'. In the other readings, it is urged and required that good must be done, especially to the true poor and needy, regardless of their moral qualification. The tension between those two urgings continues to be present among us and unresolved, even now.

The last phrase of the psalm (verse 5c) seems added on in order to claim the whole psalm for a specifically Jerusalem theology. That is, the links to 'Israel' provide a clue for how the psalms are to be read canonically. But even if the line is an addendum, the line connects in two important ways with the preceding. On the one hand, the theme of *shalom* looks back to Jeru*shalom* in verses 1-2. The city of Jerusalem is, in the Bible, the focal habitat of God's gift of well-being, where Israel will be secure in its identity. That is the whole point of pilgrimage to Jerusalem, to go to one's safe home. On the other hand, *shalom* is the outcome of the good-doing, urged in verses 3-5a. This last line of yearning for peace derives appropriately from what has gone before. It makes specific the hope, promise, and petition of the psalm. It knows the place where God's *good-doing* and Israel's *good-doing* converge.

Walter Brueggemann
Texts for Preaching, Year B

The spring of moral fruitfulness

Christianity, when it is true to its own genius, is able to believe in humanity recklessly, despite all that saddens and discourages, because it has seen the vision of God, the eternal source of all worth and wonder – lifting us up to become sons and daughters of God. That is the spring of all creative effort, sureness of touch and mastery in life. On the whole and in the long run those men and women have been most effective in changing and remodelling the present world, who have realised that goodness, in whatever form, is not in the end something that we produce, but something that claims us and is imparted to us by the eternal and unchanging goodness. The vision of God is the spring of moral fruitfulness. The source of all creative conviction is the vision of one who is 'faithful and true', unchanged in underived perfection.

F. R. Barry
The Relevance of Christianity

Psalm 126

Third Sunday of Advent: Year B (Alt)
Proper 25/Ordinary Time 30: Year B
Thanksgiving: Year B
Fifth Sunday of Lent: Year C

*Deprivation
in the present,
the temporary
suspension of
gratification,
can be seen as
the means to
fuller realisation
in the future.*

This psalm has been selected as a companion reading to Isaiah 61:1-4, 8-11 because of its assumed connection with the return from exile, which parallels the Isaiah statements about the coming events of redemption. The association of the psalm with the Exile appears to be a secondary development, however. The psalm was probably written for use in the fall [autumn] festival, which fell just before the fall rains and the fall planting. The theme of the psalm – the reversal of fortune – fits nicely, however, with the Isaiah text.

The first half of the psalm (verses 1-3) looks back to the past, probably to the preceding year's festival time, whereas the last half (verses 4-6) looks forward with intercession to the future.

The opening verse is translated in various ways. An alternative to the NRSV is the translation, 'When the Lord determined the destiny [or set the fate] for Zion'. Such a determination was probably considered part of the annual fall festival, which marked the end of the old year and the beginning of the new. It was believed that during the festival, God decreed what would happen during the coming year and thus set the destiny for the future. Remnants of a similar perspective can be seen in our beliefs about beginning anew with resolutions and a clean slate on New Year's Day. The past restoration or determination of fortunes is recalled in the psalm as a glorious time. The expectations of the future on that previous occasion made the people seem as if they were dreaming; that is, the expectations were uninhibited by the normal limitations of reality. Laughter and joy were the characteristics of the experience. God had done or decreed great things, things to be recognised even by the nations, the Gentiles (see Psalm 98:1-3, which also belongs to the fall festival context).

The prayer of petition and appeal in verses 4-6 requests a good future in the coming time that would reverse the status of the present. (Just as our New Year's resolutions and expectations exceed the realities of the year, so it was in ancient Israel.) The dry wadi beds, the dusty gullies of the Negev desert, are used to symbolise the present, and the way in which these could be transformed into watercourses with growing vegetation by the coming rainy season symbolise the hoped-for future. Such imagery may have been a proverbial picture indicative of a sudden and drastic change.

Mythological and primitive concepts underlie the references to sowing with weeping; reaping with joy. The association of tears with sowing is based on several factors: tears symbolise rainfall; sowing involves death, for the seed must 'die' to appear as new grain growth; planting is a gamble and a risk; and the scattering of seeds resembles the shedding of tears. Such customs as weeping when sowing are found in many cultures around the world. Significant also is the idea of performing one type of action in the present so as to achieve the opposite at a later time. Deprivation in the present, the temporary suspension of gratification, can be seen as the means to fuller realisation in the future. Weep now and shout for joy later.

John H. Hayes
Preaching Through the Christian Year: Year B

One man who certainly 'sowed in tears' before reaping a transformed life was Henri Charriere, author of *Papillon* and *Banco*. Henri had been sent to Devil's Island in punishment for a crime he did not commit. With the help of friends he escapes, floating to freedom on a home-made raft and landing in Venezuela. At one stage he has an interview with Irenée de Bruyne, Bishop of Curaçao. The Bishop says: 'Reflect my son, if you had not been forced to undergo this calvary you would never have been able to raise yourself so close to divine truth. . . .The people, the system, the workings of this horrible machine that has ground you down, and the fundamentally evil beings who in their different ways have tormented and harmed you, have in fact done you the greatest service they possibly could. They have brought a new person into being inside you, better than the first, and it is to them that you owe it that you now possess a sense of honour, kindness and charity, as well as the will-power needed to conquer all these difficulties and become a finer man.'

Henri Charriere
Papillon

Psalm 127

Proper 27/Ordinary Time 32: Year B

He imparts his gifts to us while we are asleep!

'God giveth to his beloved in sleep.' (Psalm 127:2; RV)

A newspaper headline read, 'Learn while you sleep.' Reuter reported from Paris (18 January, 1957) that a psychologist, Jaques Genevay, had invented a 'robot teacher' which he claimed reduces the mental effort of learning by eighty per cent. This machine is designed to repeat anything to be learned at intervals throughout the night while the learner is asleep. The words of our text come immediately to mind.

We are all familiar with those beautiful words of promise to the sleepless and the bereaved, so frequently and reverently inscribed on tombstones, 'For so he giveth his beloved sleep'. There is no reason why we should lose such a lovely phrase, but there is also no reason why we should not profit by the equally lovely yet more accurate translation, preserved for us in the margin of the Revised Version, 'He giveth to his beloved *in* sleep'. The emphasis is not so much on the gift *of* sleep, as on a gift *in* sleep, during sleep.

The first hearers of this precious promise were in dire need of just such a word. They lived in a besieged city. Incessant watchfulness was the order of the day and night. The diminishing band of survivors had to sustain long hours of exhausting concentration. They were almost too tired to sleep. The consequent weariness dulled their spiritual awareness. The slightest thought of God was crowded out of their minds.

It is to people in this distraught state that the psalmist addresses himself in the name of God. 'Except the Lord build the house, they labour in vain that build it: except the Lord keep the city, the watchmen waketh but in vain. It is vain that ye rise up early, and so late take rest, and eat the bread of toil; for so he giveth to his beloved in sleep.' Recall, cries the psalmist, the limits of your strength and the power of God. When you have done everything you can, you are still in the hands of a Higher Power. Your greatest enemy is within your gates! Your excessive wakefulness is bad for efficiency. Remember that he who keeps Israel neither slumbers nor sleeps. He is awake and working while we sleep. He imparts his gifts to us while we are asleep! You can learn while you sleep!

The Word of God reminds us that many of the best gifts of life come to us when we are prone, relaxed, inert. Do you remember how John Bunyan opens his masterpiece

The Pilgrim's Progress? 'As I walked through the wilderness of this world, I lighted on a certain place where was a den, and laid me down in that place to sleep; and as I slept I dreamed a dream . . .' The den was Bedford gaol. His wife and children he might never see again. Especially he was anxious for his little blind daughter, but he laid him down in that den to sleep, and God gave to his beloved John Bunyan in sleep one of the profoundest guide-books to the spiritual journey ever penned.

The most obvious gift of sleep is refreshment; its main function is a recharging of the exhausted batteries. Poetry and common sense unite in tribute to the restorative power of sleep. The murderer Macbeth pleads for sleep,

'. . . that knits up the ravell'd sleave of care,
The death of each day's life, sore labour's bath,
Balm of hurt minds . . .' (II. ii. 37-9.)

Coleridge selects the exact word to describe the relief of the weary pleader for an interval of unconsciousness:

'To Mary Queen the praise be given;
She sent the gentle sleep from heaven,
That *slid* into my soul.'

Common sense often advises, 'You need a good night's rest; you'll feel better in the morning; you'll see things differently tomorrow!' One of the greatest crises during the inter-war years was in 1931, when the economic blizzard hit this country, and the recently installed Labour Government received its first major setback. The Prime Minister, Ramsay MacDonald, came to the palace one evening and said to King George V, 'It is all over with me. My party will not follow me. All that I have tried to do has failed. There is nothing for your majesty to do except send for Mr Baldwin and ask him to try to form a government.' The King replied, 'I don't want to do that. I want you to stay as trustee for the poor. You are over-wrought now. Go home and go to bed. Come here tomorrow morning, and I will have Baldwin and Herbert Samuel to meet you. We will see if we can arrange for a National Government, to include you all three.' Archbishop Lang, commenting on this story, said, 'That "Go to bed!" saved the country!'

T. D. Meadley
Part of an unpublished sermon

295

Psalm 128

Proper 12/Ordinary Time 17: Year A

*Treasure is
knowing that
one belongs not
to self, or to work,
or vocation, or
ambition, but
that one belongs
to God.*

Reverence, the basis of a happy home

The affinities between this and the preceding psalm are evident. Both are wisdom psalms, and in both the home is a major theme. The combination of wisdom teaching and a strong love for Zion places the date in the postexilic period.

The happiness of the reverent man (128:1-2). That man is happy with internal and external blessings whose reverence for God issues in right conduct. This psalmist would agree with the author of Psalm 111 that 'The fear of the Lord is the beginning of wisdom' (verse 10; cf. Proverbs 9:10). One of the external aspects of happiness is to be able to eat the fruit of one's labour (see Isaiah 65:21-22), for in the history of the ancient people of God war, oppression, drought, blight and insects have often caused the farmer to go hungry. It is not the psalmist's purpose to deal with exceptions to his general pronouncement of happiness.

The fruitfulness of his wife (128:3-4). Another aspect of happiness is a fruitful wife within one's house. 'Within your house' means 'in the inner parts of your house'. Which are reserved for the women. As the reverent man's sons gather about the table, they appear to him as young olive shoots which have grown up around the parent tree. The olive tree is an evergreen and therefore a symbol of continuing vitality (cf. 52:8; Jeremiah 11:16). Again the psalmist does not deal with exceptions to his general principle. All of us know godly couples who are childless.

The prosperity of his people (128:5-6). These verses are cast in the form of a priestly benediction. God is thought of as sending forth his blessing from Zion because it is his earthly dwelling (cf. 14:7; 20:2; 134:3). But the blessing is not confined to a long life and numerous descendants; it includes also 'the prosperity of Jerusalem'. As the centre of Jewish life, Jerusalem is the mother of all God's people (Psalm 87) and therefore their representative and symbol. In other words, the godly man is a member of the Church, and his happiness is incomplete apart from the well-being of God's larger family (cf. Hebrews 11:40). Appropriately, then, the psalm is concluded with the words, 'Peace be upon Israel' (cf. 125:5).

A. B. Rhodes
Psalms

Psalm 128 speaks of the happiness of those who 'fear' the Lord. Here is a piece that says more or less the same thing, but from a very different perspective: (for 'treasure' read happiness).

The one who is rich toward God, Jesus says, is the one who recognises here and now that treasure is not in what one has or even in what one leaves or gives away, or even in what one does. Those are not riches. Treasure is in who one is, and ultimately that treasure is defined in terms of the relationship one has with God. Treasure is knowing that one belongs not to self, or to work, or vocation, or ambition, but that one belongs to God. You don't belong to your talent or to your skill or identity in the world. Treasure is in knowing that you are loved, and that knowledge of self and relationship and purpose is what treasure is all about. Treasure means rich in relationship to God, that which the world cannot give and which therefore the world and all of its adversities and all of its trials and tribulations cannot take away. The one who would then be truly rich is the one who cultivates that treasure, that knowledge, and who does so with all of the effort that other people use to cultivate earthly but perishable goods. So that when you leave 'everything', as we all most certainly will leave everything, you can take *it* with you, for *it* is the only thing you ever truly had, and that is the love of God.

Peter J. Gomes
Sermons: Biblical Wisdom for Daily Living

Psalm 130

Fifth Sunday of Lent 5: Year A
Proper 5/Ordinary Time 10: Year B
Proper 8/Ordinary Time 13: Year B
Proper 14/Ordinary Time 19: Year B

Any person with any conscience at all will be more troubled about the wrong they have done and the good they have failed to do than about anything else in the world.

'*Out of the depths I have cried unto thee, O Lord . . .*' The person who wrote those words has plenty of company. He was in the depths, and the depths of life are a well-populated place. Most people have been there at one time or another, and the chances are that they will be there again. Crushing disappointment can plunge a person into the depths. So can tragic bereavement or physical pain. In the case of the psalmist it was the shame of moral failure, the burden of unforgiven sin. He cried out to God from the depths of guilt.

The truth is that any person with any conscience at all will be more troubled about the wrong they have done and the good they have failed to do than about anything else in the world. In fact, their guilt, unless they deal with it, may make them quite wretched and may lie beneath the surface of their mind like a splinter beneath the surface of the skin.

How does a person deal with the sense of guilt? The answer is that they cannot deal with it themselves. They cannot forgive their own moral failures any more than a doctor can remove his own appendix. The forgiveness, the healing, the cure must come from beyond themselves.

One of the most celebrated examples in our time is Charles Colson, the United States Government lawyer, who was arrested and sentenced for his complicity in the Watergate scandal. He went through a religious experience which he describes in his book, *Born Again*. At the heart of it was a crisis of guilt which some of the other conspirators, to their own loss, did not experience. They protested their innocence and insisted that they were unjustly accused. Colson, however, from the depths of guilt turned to God, as the psalmist did, and the guilt became for him a part of the most healing experience he had ever known.

The most positive result of the psalmist's guilt is that it put him in a mood to receive God's forgiveness, a mood of waiting and hope and expectation:

I wait for the Lord, my soul doth wait, and in his word I

do hope. My soul waiteth for the Lord more than they that watch for the morning . . .

The picture is that of watchmen on guard at the walls of the city, looking impatiently for the first signs of dawn, knowing that, though it comes slowly, it will surely come. The psalmist sees himself as a watchman who believes that God's forgiveness will come, and who waits, perhaps impatiently, for God actually to forgive him.

A person has to make that move from theology to experience if he hopes to rise out of the depths of guilt. So it happened to Martin Luther. 'Oh, my sin, my sin!' he sobbed in anguish. One day an old monk came to his cell and tried to comfort him. He told the tortured and sorrowing Luther to repeat over and over again the article of the Apostles' Creed, 'I believe in the forgiveness of sins'. Luther did so and found some solace in the mere repetition of the words. 'Ah,' said the old monk, 'you must believe not only in the forgiveness of David's sin and Peter's sin. It is God's command that we believe that our sins are forgiven us. The testimony of the Holy Ghost in thy heart is this, 'Thy sins are forgiven thee'.

It is not generally known that Psalm 130 influenced John Wesley's religious experience. Most people know that it happened one evening at a little Moravian chapel in London while he listened to a reading of Luther's Preface to Paul's Roman Epistle and felt his heart strangely warmed. When we read in Wesley's Journal the account of that day, May 24, 1738, we discover that he earlier worshipped at St Paul's Cathedral where the anthem was, 'Out of the deep I have called unto thee, O Lord'. To Wesley that was a picture of his own soul. He had been in the depths for a long time. Like the psalmist he believed that there is forgiveness with God and like the psalmist he waited desperately for God to forgive him. That happened a few hours later when he said, 'I felt that God had forgiven my sins, even mine . . .'

Leonard Griffith
Reactions to God: Man's Response to God's Activity in the Psalms

The face at the window

'My soul waiteth for the Lord more than they that watch for the morning' (Psalm 130:6). The image is one of exquisite tenderness and pathos. The night is long and dreary, and the tired

watchers press their faces every now and then against the window-pane, eager to discover beyond the rugged ranges some grey glimmer of the coming dawn.

There is a striking story of Professor Huxley. One Sunday the great scientist was staying in a little country town. 'I suppose,' said Huxley to another who was there, 'you are going to church.' 'Yes,' he replied. 'What if, instead, you stayed at home and talked to me of your religion?' 'No,' was the reply, 'for I am not clever enough to refute your arguments.' 'But what if you simply told me of your own experience – what religion has done for you?' So the other man did not go to church that morning. He stayed at home and told Huxley the story of all that Christ had been to him. And presently there were tears in the eyes of the great agnostic as he said, 'I would give my right hand if I could believe that!' Huxley's face was at the window . . .

'The Luggage of Life'
quoted in *Daily Readings from F. W. Boreham*

Psalm 131

Eighth Sunday of Epiphany/Ordinary Time 8: Year A

There really is no wealth in life, no knowledge, no success, nothing that gives a deep and lasting sense of fulfilment unless it comes as a gift from God.

Modern man moves at a hectic pace; he lives at a feverish pitch. His nerves are in a constant state of stress and tension, and he can find no rest, no peace. He tries to soothe his excited nerves with alcohol, sleeping drugs, tranquilliser pills, physiotherapy and weekends in the country – anything to stop his hands from trembling, anything to help him relax. Some of us know from first-hand experience that the great problem of our lives these days is how to achieve a sense of inner calm.

The experience of a Hebrew psalmist comes close to our need. One Old Testament scholar called the writer of Psalm 131 a 'hot-blooded man'. He seems to have been an excited man, perhaps the ancient type of the modern go-getter who with usual conceit reaches for the stars. Like his modern counterpart he had travelled every day from morning till night in high gear, his pride, envy and pretentiousness giving him no rest, no peace. But something had happened to him, something that changed the whole picture and altered his mood completely. Like a squalling baby, soothed at his mother's breast, he had ceased his convulsive crying and found a deep sense of inner contentment and calm.

What had, in fact, happened to the psalmist? His words tell their own story:

> I do not occupy myself with things too great and too marvellous for me. But I have calmed and quieted my soul. (RSV)

Somewhere in a moment of clear insight this man had come to terms with himself. He had proclaimed an armistice in the civil war between his ambitions and his limitations. He had resigned from the rat race. He had decided to stop reaching for the stars. It took courage to make that decision and even greater courage to confess it openly, but the effect seems to have been a spiritual rebirth like starting life all over again.

This is not an easy decision to make, especially in a competitive society that worships the cult of success. How did the psalmist do it? Simply give up the struggle because of the fatigue and disillusionment of middle-age? Simply quit trying like a distance runner who slows to a walk because he knows that he cannot win anyway? Psalm 131 may be brief, only three verses in all, but as a spiritual autobiography it leaves nothing to the imagination. 'Hope in the Lord,' writes the psalmist. This man had brought God into his experience and, in doing so, discovered a great truth – that there really is no wealth in life, no knowledge, no success, nothing that gives a man a deep and lasting sense of fulfilment unless it comes as a gift from God. The awakening to this truth can have a profoundly calming effect on a man's soul.

We can see at least four possibilities for the writer of Psalm 131. He may have been a *careerist*, ambitious in a worldly, materialistic sense. If he were alive today he would be the sort who wants to get ahead and make the most of his opportunities and climb to the top of the ladder professionally and socially. Perhaps he was, in fact, a merchant or landowner, blessed with a natural ambition to work hard and make money and generally succeed.

There is nothing vulgar about that. Society owes its progress to men and women who rise above the level of mediocrity and pursue their careers, driven by the honest ambition to succeed. We should still be writing letters with quill pens, still travelling by horse and buggy, still dying of diphtheria, unless someone at some time had been ambitious enough to invent typewriters, jet aeroplanes and vaccine. Yet we must reckon with the danger that a man's ambition can be a destroying passion; it can run away with him and make him a nervous wreck.

It is possible also that writer of Psalm 131 was *a theologian*, deeply engaged in the study of the science of God and searching for the truth about ultimate things. Here again he teaches us the importance if coming to terms with our limitations.

His opening words, 'O Lord, my heart is not lifted up, my eyes are not raised too high,' find an echo in the New Testament. You hear it in a parable of Jesus – 'And the publican, standing afar off, would not lift up so much as his eyes unto heaven.' It is a posture of humility, an acknowledgement of the infinite distance between man and God, a confession that the Being of God is a Being clothed in mystery; and you don't tie mystery up in neat bundles of understanding. Must we understand a mystery, however, in order to appropriate it? A small boy asked an old sailor, 'what is the wind?' After a long pause the sailor answered, 'I don't know. I can't tell you. But I know how to hoist a sail.' Endless questions about the winds of God baffle even the most profound theologians. You will go spiritually berserk trying to answer them all. But the wind of God is real. Believe in it, hoist your sail to it and you may find serenity and peace.

The Hebrew poet may have been a moral and social idealist. That would have been in keeping with his character. Many of Israel's prophets and psalmists felt themselves to be divinely called to denounce national evils and elevate the moral tone of Jewish society. In this respect our psalmist may have occupied himself with great and marvellous things and in this respect he may have been forced to came to terms with his own limitations. Perhaps he faced the truth that many an idealist needs to face – that reaching for the stars can be a noble form of escapism, a concern with the impossible as an excuse for evading the possible.

So, perhaps the psalmist took stock of his own situation. Perhaps he analysed it realistically. He could not eradicate social corruption, but what could he do? He could try to conduct his own affairs with integrity. He could not expurgate the nation's lust but he could keep his own heart pure. He could not eliminate juvenile delinquency but he could discipline his own children. He could not put an end to wars but he could make peace within his own relationships. He could not be a saint but he could be a good man. He could not clutch the stars but he could settle for something less than the stars. He could not solve the world's problems but he could try to tackle the immediate, practical problems at hand and leave the larger issues to God.

This Hebrew poet, whose words suggests that he might have been a careerist, a theologian or an idealist, could also have been *a sufferer* – in which case he has more to teach us about coming to terms with our limitations. Like the unhappy Job, he may have been hit by a personal disaster or, like the Jews in exile whom Job represents, he may have been crushed by the weight of national calamity. From his psalm we infer that he had not accepted his suffering passively but that, like Job, he had lifted an angry face to heaven, shaken his fist at God and demanded to know the reason why.

Most of us, when we suffer, and the pain of body or mind becomes too intense, begin to whimper as the psalmist did. Excitedly we cry out, 'Why did this happen to me? What have I done to deserve it? Why doesn't God do something to stop it?' The psalmist admits that he whimpered, but then he tells us that, like a child soothed at its mother's breast, he stopped whimpering. He did so because he stopped reaching for the stars – which means, probably, that he gave up trying to understand what mortal man can never understand. He came to realise that some of life's experiences will never make sense to the human mind but that, if we learn to accept them and to trust in the wisdom and providence of God, we may at least manage our own lives with composure.

Leonard Griffith
God in Man's Experience: the Activity of God in the Psalms

Psalm 132

Christ the King/Proper 29/Ordinary Time 34: Year B, verses 1-12, (13-18)

This is my resting place for ever and ever.

This psalm, one of the 'royal psalms', concerns the role of David in moving the Ark of the Lord into the city of Jerusalem. The narrative of 2 Samuel 6 suggests that this was a historical event, wrought by David with much pious pageantry. It is equally plausible, however, that the movement of the Ark was a regular, repeated event in Israel's liturgical calendar. The retrieval of the Ark is a dramatic way of establishing and asserting the 'real presence' of God in the shrine of Jerusalem.

A second derivative reality also operates in the movement of the Ark. Because the king is caretaker, custodian, and champion of the Ark in the shrine, the Ark is inevitably linked to the dynasty of David, and serves willy-nilly to help legitimate that dynasty.

Psalm 132:1-5 asserts the remarkable piety of David. According to this text, David pledged his utter devotion to the Lord, such devotion that David made it a primary pledge of his monarchy that he would remain unsatisfied until the Lord's Ark was adequately housed. It may be that this sentiment refers to David's statement in 2 Samuel 7:2, but that resolve on David's part is not to be assessed historically, but as a liturgical enactment of the resolve of the dynasty. The statement helps to show that the dynasty was passionately concerned for the Lord. Whether authentic or not, such piety is no doubt politically useful.

Verses 6 and 7 of Psalm 132 purport to add a historical note, but the locus of the Ark here may be only liturgical (see 1 Samuel 7:1-2; 2 Samuel 6:1-15). The Ark as 'dwelling place' and 'footstool' is taken to be the throne on which the invisible God sits. The Ark is indeed a vehicle for 'real presence'.

Now the God who sits on the Ark is addressed directly (Psalm 132:8-10) – see Numbers 10:35-36 for a like pointed address to the Ark. The God of the Ark is addressed, seeking authorisation for the recognition of priests who will be legitimated to supervise the shrine. Thus the reiteration of the oath of David serves to legitimate the priesthood, which is in fact a tool of the king. (See the Epistle reading concerning another priestly authorisation.) The address to the Ark and the request for a priest, however, are for 'David's sake'

(Psalm 132:10). Thus it is recognised that priestly authorisation was a gesture useful for the king.

The Davidic agenda in Psalm 132, hinted at in verses 1-5 and verses 8-10, now becomes explicit in verses 11 and 12. In verse 2, David has made an oath to the Lord, now the Lord makes a corresponding oath to David. This oath appears to be an alternative rendering of the great promise of 2 Samuel 7:11-16, also reiterated in Psalm 89:28-37. Only here, the promise is made conditional, as it is not in 2 Samuel 7:11-16: 'If your sons keep my covenant . . .' One can see by comparing this version of the promise to the other renditions that there are powerful political interests at work in establishing a right version of the promise. By making the monarchy conditional on Torah obedience, this version completely undermines the monarchic claims of a guaranteed (ontological?) future, and subordinates the king to the Torah. In the end then, the king has no special, privileged promise from God, but is like every other Israelite, subject to the Torah requirements and vulnerable to Torah sanctions of blessing and curse. Thus monarchy is thereby emptied of its theological pretension and seen to be only a provisional political arrangement.

Having considerably minimised the claims of the monarchy, Psalm 132 now proceeds to make its primary positive point in verses 13-18, that the Lord has indeed chosen Zion as a normative habitat. It is conventional to lump together the Temple claim and the royal claim; in practice they no doubt reinforce each other. Here, however, at least in theory, monarchy is diminished in theological significance, and Temple (= Ark) is elevated in importance.

Beginning at verse 14, the remainder of the psalm is a decree in the mouth of God, who sits on the Ark. The Lord affirms that Zion is a chosen, enduring place of presence. Zion, where the Ark and the Lord dwell, will be a place of special blessing and prosperity. Note well, precise reference is made to bread for the poor (verse 15). Zion will be a place of faithful, effective, joyous priests (verse 16). Thus a full liturgical apparatus is founded and authorised. In the end the Davidic claim cannot be nullified, and it is here reasserted (verses 17-18).

This is an odd text, and one is left unsure of its intention. Paired as it is with other readings, we may note some pertinent accent points:

1. Full, real presence in worship is affirmed.

2. That full, real presence requires an authorised priesthood, on which see the Epistle reading.

3. The Temple presence is oddly in tension with political interests and ambitions. Those political ambitions are acknowledged, toned down, and then finally affirmed. One can see the Gospel reading as an overlay of this tension, for the kingship is always 'of this world/not of this world'. Whereas the presence is assured, the political apparatus attached to it is more precarious. Even in such a self-conscious text, it is recognised that religious reality does not easily match up with political legitimacy. Finally, after *presence* it is *Torah* obedience that makes political authority viable.

Walter Brueggemann
Texts for Preaching, Year B

Psalm 133

Proper 15/Ordinary Time 20: Year A
Second Sunday of Easter: Year B
Proper 7/Ordinary Time 12: Year B, (Alt)

At the point of unity . . . the Lord bestows his blessing.

Community of worship

What community did the writer have in mind when he wrote this psalm? It is one of the 'songs of the ascents'. Possibly he was surprised and delighted at the unity which he noted in those who came up to the festival in Jerusalem (verse 1). They had come from different countries. They had widely differing backgrounds. But they were one in their desire to worship the God of Israel. In this they were a band of brothers. It was refreshing as if the dew of snow-capped Heron in the north were falling on the parched areas in the south (verse 3).

From the beginning of the Christian movement, oil has been widely used. Mark records that when Jesus sent out the Twelve on their journey, they 'anointed many sick people with oil and cured them' (Mark 6:13). James bids anyone who is ill to 'send for the elders of the church to pray over him and anoint him with oil in the name of the Lord . . .' (James 5:14.) Oil symbolised Christ's presence to heal, and has been part of the rites of baptism, confirmation and ordination in many branches of the Church (as well as in the coronation of sovereigns). It speaks of warmth and comfort and health and is increasingly used in informal services of healing today.

Unity for mission

The World Council of Churches recently celebrated the fiftieth year of its inception. Much has happened in the sphere of Church unity during that half-century. If at times progress has been slow at the level of agreement arising out of official consultations, immense progress has been made at the grassroot levels of parish and diocese. There, ordinary worshippers have got to know one another, to pray together, to evangelise together. Brothers and sisters in Christ have discovered a unity which has surprised them. We may expect further progress at that level, while we continue to pray for courageous thinking and leadership from the 'officials' of the churches. At the point of unity, 'there the Lord bestows his blessing' (verse 3).

A quotation

St Aelred was a twelfth-century abbot of Rievaulx in Yorkshire. Sensitive, gentle, holy, he drew around him men of similar character to his own, and did much to humanise the Cistercian order. He wrote:

The day before yesterday I was walking around the cloister of the monastery, the brethren were sitting around forming as it were a most loving crown. In the multitude I found no one whom I did not love and by whom I felt sure I was not loved. I was filled with such joy that it surpassed all the delights of the world. I felt my spirit transfused into all and the affection of all to have passed into me, so that I could say with the prophet: 'Behold how good and pleasant it is for brothers to dwell together in unity.'

Donald Coggan
Psalms 73-150: The People's Bible Commentary

How good it is for brothers to live together

This short wisdom psalm is by no means easy to interpret. Besides the difficulties of detail which are noted below, the general background and intention of the psalmist are uncertain.

1. Some think that it is concerned simply with family life, the references to Aaron and Zion being introduced to adapt it for cultic use. The old Israelite ideal was for all of the sons to live together at home and care for the family estate (cf. Deuteronomy 25:5, and the sense of regret at the separation of Abraham and Lot, Genesis 13, and Jacob and Esau, Genesis 27:41-45; 36:7). It is suggested that this psalm comes from the time when the old social order was breaking down.

2. Others think of the brothers as fellow Israelites, and suggest that the psalm comes from such a period as when Nehemiah

was endeavouring to build up the population of Jerusalem (Nehemiah 11).

3. A third view links the psalm with the coming together of the men of Israel at one of the festivals. In worshipping the Lord the nation finds its unity and receives his rich blessing . . .

The oddity of the second verse makes it difficult to sing this psalm today. Yet the theme is of permanent significance, whether we refer it to the family, secular society, or the religious community. 'In unity' is not actually expressed in the original, although the writer must have been thinking of harmony and concord. Such corporate fellowship is 'good' and 'pleasant', yet the psalmist is very certain that the blessing is not inherent in it but comes down from the Lord himself. The Christian will recall such passages as 1 John 3:10, 14.

Cyril S. Rodd
Psalms 73-150

Psalm 136

Easter Vigil: Years A, B, C, verses 1-9, 23-26

God works

In his remarkable book, *Come Out The Wilderness*, Bruce Kendrick tells of a pastor who went to see an old man who lived by himself in a tenement in New York's East Harlem. The old man met him on the sidewalk, and together they made their way through the stale stench of the mouldering building to the small single room at the top that was his home. The ceiling sagged, and the dark, brown paper hung in shreds from the dirty walls. They both sat on the bed which took up three-quarters of the space. Finally the old man brought out his Bible that fell open at the psalms, many of which he had learned by heart because he was nearly blind. His favourites were heavily thumbed, the pages were yellow and worn, and when the pastor looked at them he saw that they had one thing in common – they were all psalms of praise; not psalms of comfort for a man who lived in this grim, grey slum but psalms of thanksgiving to God.

It would be impossible to use the psalms as an aid for worship and *not* give thanks to God. Every mood known to the human heart can be found in the Hebrew Psalter, but from first to last the prevailing mood is one of thanksgiving. Someone has written, 'All the way through the Book of Psalms you feel that you are walking on a smouldering volcano of praise, liable to burst out at any moment into a great flame of gratitude to God.' The men who wrote the psalms praised God endlessly, but not for material benefits – freedom, security, comfort, prestige and prosperity. They had none of these things, none of the temporal blessings for which men usually give thanks to God. The psalmists praised God for eternal blessings which are independent of time and circumstance. They praised God for himself, for what he was and what he had done.

Chiefly the psalmists gave thanks for what have been called the mighty works of God. They looked out on the marvellous world, they looked into their own lives, they looked back over history and they saw many wonderful things which to them allowed of no explanation apart from the activity of God. They had never seen God himself but they could point to signs of his presence and power. The God of their experience was *a God who works*, a God who had done great things, and for these they gave him glory and praise.

A solo voice cannot do justice to the Hallelujah Chorus. It takes a full choir, a choir of choirs, to sing the great hymns of thanksgiving to God. To get the full impact of this mood in the Hebrew Psalter we need to listen to a choir of psalmists chanting their praises in thrilling harmony and setting forth in a mighty chorus the greatness, the glory and the majesty of God. For its sheer simplicity, however, and because it was written for use in the temple worship, we single out Psalm 136, one of the less familiar songs of praise. The opening verses sound like the summons of a trumpet:

O give thanks unto the Lord; for he is good:
for his mercy endureth for ever.
O give thanks unto the God of gods:
for his mercy endureth for ever.
O give thanks to the Lord of lords:
for his mercy endureth for ever.

Having called us to worship, the psalmist then enumerates the mighty works of God which prove him a God worthy of our worship, because he is truly God and because he has done what God alone can do.

The psalmist calls us to praise God for his mighty work in *Creation*.

O give thanks . . .
To him who alone doeth great wonders . . .
To him that by wisdom made the heavens . . .
that stretched out the earth above the waters . . .
that made the great lights . . .
The sun to rule by day . . .
The moon and stars to rule by night:
for his mercy endureth for ever.

This Hebrew poet has obviously steeped his mind in the thought of the first chapter of Genesis, that wonderful poetic description of God's great scheme of creation which starts with star-dust and moves upward, step by step, to the grace and glory of human personality.

We do not have to be reminded that there are difficulties in the way of this belief. We know that the writers of the Old Testament lived in a pre-scientific age when men explained a great many things, including Creation itself, in terms of the Supernatural. Now we are not so sure that there ever was an act of Creation. When somebody asked Bertrand Russell how he would explain the universe, he replied that the universe doesn't need an explanation. The universe is just there – that's all. His viewpoint finds support from some astronomers who look through the telescope at the farthest galaxies, millions of light years away, and pronounce their verdict that, so far as they can see, the universe never had a precise beginning, nor will it have a precise ending. There is also the fact that in many areas the role of the Supernatural has been taken over by man himself who is now beginning to perform what might always have been called the mighty works of God. A modern psalmist might well chant phrases of man 'who alone doeth great wonders . . . who makes great lights . . . who causes the rain to fall . . . who wipes out disease and who one day may discover in a test tube the secret of creating human life.'

There is an amusing scene in the Broadway play, *Inherit the Wind* by Jerome Lawrence and Robert E. Lee which dramatises the notorious Scopes trial in Dayton, Tennessee. It concerned a public school teacher summoned to court for questioning in his classroom the literal interpretation of the Creation story in Genesis. At one point in the dialogue the defending attorney, who impersonates Clarence Darrow, produces a rock which he claims to be millions of years old. His opponent, who impersonates William Jennings Bryan, protests that the rock cannot be more than six thousand years old, because Bishop Usher proved conclusively that Creation itself occurred only in the year 4004 BC – to be precise, on 23 October in the year 4004 BC at 9am. Whereupon Darrow throws the court into gales of laughter by asking sarcastically, 'Was that Eastern Standard Time? It wasn't daylight saving time, was it? Because the Lord didn't make the sun until the fourth day!'

This kind of argument is sound and correct until it confuses causes with techniques and leads to false conclusions. Clever people assume that, if they can somehow explain things scientifically, they thereby dispose of God and prove the Bible writers wrong. They ignore the fact that the writers of the Old Testament were not interested in scientific explanations. How could they be? They knew nothing about science. They wrote in poems and myths, and why not? Poetry and mythology have always enjoyed equal status with science as vehicles of the truth. The truth that laid hold on the psalmists and which they tried to express was that the universe could not have existed eternally. It must have had a beginning and it must have had a Creator. To them the whole scheme of Creation seemed too marvellous and logical to have happened accidentally. Behind it must be a Divine Intelligence, a Creative Mind. It must be the mighty work of God.

Leonard Griffith
God in Man's Experience: The Activity of God in the Psalms

Psalm 137

Proper 22/Ordinary Time 27: Year C, (Alt)

Our zeal for God's glory cannot cause us to sink into hatred, not even for our enemies. Leave the enemies to God.

By the waters of Babylon

If we ask what principally is expressed in Psalm 137, it is not bitterness over suffering at the hands of the Babylonians, nor is it anguish over the destruction of Judah's capital city. Rather, it is religious zeal for the honour of God.

Jerusalem was not important to Israel because it was a beautiful city or the centre of Israel's Davidic monarchy or the hub of Israel's commercial and cultural life. Jerusalem was important because on its hill of Zion stood the temple of Solomon. And in that temple, in its Holy of Holies, rested the Ark of the Covenant that formed the base of the throne of God. God dwelt in the midst of his people, invisibly enthroned above the cherubim's wings that overspread the ark from each end (1 Samuel 4:4; 1 Kings 8:1-21).

Moreover, because God dwelt in the temple in the midst of his people, the Songs of Zion celebrated God's defence of Jerusalem. 'God is in the midst of her,' reads Psalm 46:5, 'she shall not be moved.' 'Within [Jerusalem's] citadel, God has shown himself a sure defence (Psalm 48:3). Jerusalem is 'the city of our God, which God establishes for ever' (Psalm 48:8).

But in this Psalm, Jerusalem is nothing but rubble, the psalms of Zion were sung merely as entertainment for foreigners, the Ark of the Covenant has been lost, and God's defence of Israel has amounted to nothing. In short, God has been dishonoured as one who has not saved his people. 'Where is your God?' the Babylonians jeer (Psalm 79:10; cf. Lamentations 2:15). 'Why hasn't he defended Jerusalem?' 'Doesn't he have the power?' 'Your psalm said Jerusalem would never be moved.' 'We moved it, didn't we? Ha, ha, ha!' Those are the taunts and scorn that eat at the psalmist's soul. God is on trial in this psalm, and he seems to have been defeated. That cannot help but remind us of the jeering that took place at the foot of Jesus' cross.

> And those who passed by derided him, wagging their heads, and saying, 'Aha! You who would destroy the temple and build it in three days, save yourself, and come down from the cross! (Mark 15:29-30)

For the disciples of Jesus, God was on trial there too as he was for the exiles in Babylonia.

Contrary to the disciples, who were sure that Jesus' death was the end of their hopes for God's redemption of Israel (cf. Luke 24:31), our psalmist retains the belief that despite the sufferings of the exile and despite Jerusalem's ruined condition, God is still the Lord in charge of events. Verses 5-7 are really an affirmation of the psalmist's continuing faith in the Lord. God is still present in the midst of his people, and so Jerusalem is still the psalmist's highest joy. And God can still act as Lord over the nations, remembering the treachery of the Edomites at the time of the fall of Jerusalem and judging them for their deeds.

We should note that the call for vengeance upon Edom is directed to God in verse 7. The psalmist is not taking matters into his own hands. Rather, he is turning over all retribution to the Lord. We find such prayers very frequently in the psalter.

We find the same prayer on the lips of the prophet Jeremiah when his neighbours and friends try to kill him: 'O Lord of hosts, who judgest righteously, who triest the heart and the mind, let me see thy vengeance upon them, for to thee I have committed my cause.' (Jeremiah 11:20)

Paul wrote to the church at Rome, 'Beloved, never avenge yourselves, but leave it to the wrath of God; for it is written, "Vengeance is mine, I will repay, says the Lord"' (Romans 12:19; cf. Hebrews 10:30). These psalmists and Jeremiah and Paul too leave any and all retribution up to God, to do what he will. They therefore prevent building up in themselves that hatred and spirit of revenge that eats at the hearts and souls of so many people and that finally ruins those people's own lives. Indeed, Paul counsels that by leaving all to God, we may heap burning coals upon an enemy's head – that is, coals of repentance that lead to peace.

Given the fact that the psalmist, in verse 7 of our passage, turns retribution over to the Lord, it is difficult to believe that the words of verses 8-9 come from his lips. Rather, I believe they are responses of others to the psalmist's words in verses 4-7, and they speak an entirely different message. These speakers themselves want revenge for what the Babylonians did to them in the destruction of Jerusalem and the exile, and they utter bloodthirsty curses on that nation. There is no trust in God's requital in such expressions. Hatred towards Babylonia is spit out from hating hearts. It is also doubtful that such hatred stems from a concern for God's honour and glory. The psalmist of verses 4-7 was concerned above all that God, the Lord in Zion, be honoured as Ruler over all. These speakers in verses 8-9 are concerned only for themselves and their own hurt.

315

Maybe that tells us something about hatred – that it never honours God or is concerned with his lordship. It is centred solely in human hearts that are concerned only for themselves. And perhaps that is the reason that our Lord, dying on his cross while the mob below his feet jeers and scorns him, responds not in hatred for his executioners and mockers but with words of forgiveness, 'Father, forgive them, for they know not what they do' (Luke 23:34). That prayer acknowledges that God is still in charge of everything that is happening, and it glorifies and honours God for the loving and forgiving Lord that he is. It is good to be concerned for the reputation of God, as our psalmists of verses 1-7 were deeply concerned. And we enlarge God's reputation throughout the world by telling all nations what God has done. But our zeal for God's glory cannot cause us to sink into hatred, not even for our enemies or for those whom we think are God's enemies. Leave the enemies to God. Trust that he is in fact the Lord. For by so doing we will glory God's holy name.

Elizabeth Achtemeier
Preaching Hard Texts of the Old Testament

Psalm 138

Proper 16/Ordinary Time 21: Year A
Proper 5/Ordinary Time 10: Year B
Fifth Sunday of Epiphany/Proper 1/
    Ordinary Time 5: Year C
Proper 12/Ordinary Time 17: Year C

Trouble and enemies are the givens in life; grace and preservation to endure and overcome them are the sustaining gifts.

This psalm may be subdivided into three parts. Verses 1-3 thank and praise God; verses 4-6 extol the grace and glory of God and their impact on the rulers of the world; and verses 7-8 express trust in God.

The general tone of the psalm clearly identifies it as a thanksgiving. It differs, however, from most thanksgiving psalms in two ways:

1. There is no description of the trouble or the distress from which the person was rescued (see verse 3, which refers to an appeal to God at an earlier time of distress).

2. The psalm is addressed directly to the Deity throughout (verse 8a is possibly an exception), whereas most thanksgivings are addressed to a human audience.

The person offering thanks in the original usage of this psalm was probably the king. This is suggested by the references to the kings of the earth in verses 4 who hear the words of the Lord's mouth, perhaps words spoken by the Judean king. Also, the king was especially the one at God's right hand (verse 7; see Psalm 110:1).

Several elements in the psalm call for elucidation:

1. The reference to 'before the gods' (verse 1) could mean one of several things. Ancient translations read 'before the angels', 'before kings', or 'before judges'. If the reference is to pagan gods, then the worshipper could be saying no more than, 'I sing your praise in an alien culture.' If the reference is to heavenly beings (see Psalm 29:1; 82:1), then the phrase could denote worship before the heavenly council of God.

2. To bow down toward the temple does not imply that the worshipper is in some foreign land or away from Jerusalem. This could be a reference to worship or activity at the temple gate, near the main altar, or in the temple courtyard.

3. The lowly may not refer to a class – the poor, the down-trodden, or others in similar conditions – but could be a

self-designation, even of a king – the lowly over against the Divine.

4. The verb translated 'perceives' in verse 6b may mean, on the basis of an Arabic parallel, 'to humble'. Thus 'the haughty he humbles from afar'.

The statement of trust in verses 7-8 gives expression to a serene confidence – almost. Verse 8c still resorts to petition even after the statement of assurance. Note that the psalm does not assume that life will be free of distress and problems but only that God will preserve one through them all. Trouble and enemies are the givens in life; grace and preservation to endure and overcome them are the sustaining gifts.

John H. Hayes
Preaching Through the Christian Year: Year A

Verses 4-5 of Psalm 138 say that 'All kings on earth give thanks to you, for they have heard your promises; they celebrate the Lord's actions, 'great is the glory of the Lord!'

This reminds me of the three kings who brought their gifts to the infant Jesus. For they represent all the nations of the world bringing their treasure to the Infant King. But more than that as you realise in reading their story. Because the first thing they did on coming into the presence of Jesus was to fall on their knees and worship him.

Dorothy L. Sayers in her play, *The Man Born to be King*, (Victor Gollancz Ltd, 1943) tells of the kings coming to Jesus and also their response to him which I found most interesting:

Wife   Come in, my lords, come in. Please mind your heads. I fear 'tis but a poor, lowly place.

Caspar   No place is too lowly to kneel in. There is more holiness here than in King Herod's Temple.

Melchior   More beauty here than in King Herod's palace.

Balthazar   More charity here than in King Herod's heart.

Caspar   O lady, clear as the sun, fair as the moon, the nations of the earth salute your son, the Man born to be King. Hail, Jesus, King of the Jews!

Melchior   Hail, Jesus, King of the World!

Balthazar   Hail, Jesus, King of Heaven!

Ron Dale, 2000

Psalm 139

Proper 11/Ordinary Time 16: Year A, verses 1-12, 23-24
Second Sunday of Epiphany/Ordinary Time 2: Year B, verses 1-6, 13-18
Proper 4/Ordinary Time 9: Year B, verses 1-6, 13-18
Proper 18/Ordinary Time 23: Year C, verses 1-6, 13-18

He could no more get away from God than he could get away from himself. The God whom he wanted to escape was the ground and depth of his own being.

Psalm 139:7 says, 'Where could I go to escape your spirit? Where could I flee from your presence?' The answer, according to the psalmist, is nowhere; because God is omnipresent. He is everywhere, and that in the psalmist's thought is comforting and beneficial. But not so at first for Francis Thompson who tried desperately to flee from God and recorded so powerfully in his poem, 'The Hound of Heaven':

I fled him, down the nights and down the days;
I fled him, down the arches of the years;
I fled him, down the labyrinthine ways
Of my own mind; and in the midst of tears
I hid from him, and under running laughter.
Up vistaed hopes, I sped;
And shot, precipitated,
Adown Titanic glooms and chasmed fears,
From those strong Feet that followed, followed after.
But with unhurrying chase,
And unperturbéd pace,
Deliberate speed, majestic instancy,
They beat – and a Voice beat
More instant than the Feet –
'All things betray thee, who betrayest me.'

I pleaded, outlaw-wise,
By many a hearted casement, curtained red,
Trellised with intertwining charities
(For, though I knew his love who followed,
Yet I was sore adread
Lest, having him, I must have naught beside);
But, if one little casement parted wide,
The gust of his approach would clash it to.

Fear wist not to evade as Love wist to pursue.
Across the margent of the world I fled,
And troubled the gold gateways of the stars,
Smiting for shelter on their clangéd bars;
Fretted to dulcet jars
And silvern chatter the pale ports o' the moon,
I said to dawn, Be sudden; to eve, Be soon;
With thy young skyey blossoms heap me over
From this tremendous Lover! . . .
Still with unhurrying chase,
And unperturbéd pace,
Deliberate speed, majestic instancy,
Came on the following Feet,
And a Voice above their beat –
'Naught shelters thee, who wilt not shelter me.'

Nigh and nigh draws the chase,
With unperturbéd pace,
Deliberate speed, majestic instancy;
And past those noiséd Feet
A Voice comes yet more fleet –
'Lo, naught contents thee, who content'st not me.'

Now of that long pursuit
Comes on at hand the bruit;
That Voice is round me like a bursting sea;
'And is thy earth so marred,
shattered in shard on shard?
Lo, all things fly thee, for thou fliest me!
Strange, piteous, futile thing,
Wherefore should any set thee love apart?
Seeing none but I makes much of naught' (He said),
'And human love needs human meriting:
How hast thou merited –
Of all man's clotted clay the dingiest clot?
Alack, thou knowest not
How little worthy of any love thou art!
Whom wilt thou find to love ignoble thee,
Save me, save only me?

All which I took from thee I did but take,
Not for thy harms,
But just that thou might'st seek it in my arms.
All which thy child's mistake
Fancies as lost, I have stored for thee at home:
Rise, clasp my hand, and come!'

Halts by me that footfall:
Is my gloom, after all,
Shade of his hand, outstretched caressingly?
'Ah, fondest, blindest, weakest,
I am he whom thou seekest!
Thou dravest love from thee, who dravest me.'

Francis Thompson
'The Hound of Heaven'

God pursues: 'A man who has never tried to flee God has never experienced the God who is really God.' So writes Paul Tillich in his influential book, *The Shaking of the Foundations.* Tillich goes on to say, 'There is no reason to flee from a god who is the perfect picture of everything that is good in man . . . a god who is nothing more than a benevolent father, a father who guarantees our immortality and final happiness.' But a *just* God, suggests Tillich, a God who knows everything about us, even the things that we ourselves have not the courage to face – we actually hate that God and sometimes wish he were dead. Tillich reminds us that Martin Luther was terribly shocked when he recognised within himself a hatred for the all-knowing God and a desire to escape him. Luther knew, however, that he could no more get away from God than he could get away from himself. The God whom he wanted to escape was the Ground and Depth of his own being.

Leonard Griffith
God in Man's Experience: the Activity of God in the Psalms

Psalm 143

Easter Vigil: Years A, B, C

*In the situation
of complete
helplessness the
soul prepares
for its prayer.*

No man is righteous

This is the last of the seven penitential Psalms (6, 32, 38, 51, 102, 130, 143). The psalmist acknowledges that his suffering at the hands of enemies is the consequence of his own sin, and seeks God's forgiveness and deliverance. His dependence on many other psalms indicates a postexilic date.

Invocation (143:1-2). First, the psalmist invokes God's attention to his prayer. The second sentence in verse 1 should be translated, 'In thy faithfulness answer me with thy salvation.' The word 'faithfulness' shows that the psalmist appeals to God in relation to the Covenant. The word 'righteousness' often has the meaning of 'salvation'. 'deliverance', or 'vindication' (see 51:14; 98:2; 103:6; Isaiah 40-55). Here the psalmist is seeking deliverance from sin and enemies. Implicitly he confesses that he cannot stand guiltless before God; in that sense 'no man living is righteous' before God (compare Job 4:17; 9:2; 15:14, 25:4). Paul seems to quote these words freely in Romans 3:20 and Galatians 2:16.

Complaint (143:3-4). The leader of the psalmist's enemies has 'pursued' him, 'crushed' his life, and made him 'sit in darkness like those long dead'. The exact nature of their persecution is uncertain. The psalmist may be in the darkness of a prison or at the point of death through the wicked plots of his enemies. He is desolate and appalled at such cruelty, for it goes beyond anything he has deserved as a recompense for his sin.

Backward look (143:5-6). He recalls God's mighty acts on behalf of his people in times past as a basis of hope that he will deliver him now. As the parched soil thirsts for the refreshing rain, so he longs for a fresh manifestation of God's blessing.

Petition (143:7-12). Here the psalmist makes more specific the appeal begun in the invocation. He does not want to die prematurely ('go down to the Pit'). Therefore he prays, 'Let me hear in the morning of thy steadfast love.' Although it is possible to take 'in the morning' as a figure for 'soon', it should probably be understood literally. The psalmist has been falsely accused and he anticipates some kind of revelation from God that will vindicate him 'in the morning'. He seeks

God's instruction as well as his deliverance, and requests that his Spirit leads him in a way free from his present obstacles (that is, 'on a level path'). As God's servant he bases his final appeal for help on God's name (that is, his revealed character), righteousness and steadfast love. From the psalmist's point of view the destruction of his enemies is a necessary manifestation of his own deliverance.

A. B. Rhodes
Psalms

Jehovah, the confidence of the desolate

So far as the human situation is concerned, it is a cry of despair, and a terrible one indeed. The life is smitten, the spirit is overwhelmed, and the whole complaint ends with a statement, 'My heart within me is desolate'. That final word 'desolate' has in it the sob of an unillumined sea. Yet the psalm opens with an earnest cry to Jehovah, and after the declaration of need, is to the end a determined act of faith.

In the situation of complete helplessness the soul prepares for its prayer, and the words which indicate the method of preparation are interesting. 'I remember . . . I meditate . . . I muse.' The issue of this is immediately declared, 'I spread forth my hands unto thee.' The earnestness of the soul is manifested in the urgent petitions which follow: 'Make haste . . . hide not thy face . . . cause me to hear . . . cause me to know . . . deliver me . . . teach me . . . quicken me.' Personal consecration in this endeavour to lay hold upon the infinite resource is manifested in the affirmations. 'In thee do I trust . . . I lift my soul unto thee . . . I flee unto thee to hide me', and finally, 'I am thy servant'. Through all the urgency and the earnestness there is also manifest an unshaken confidence. 'Thou art my God' is the central word around which all the others gather.

G. Campbell Morgan
Notes on the Psalms

Psalm 145

Proper 9/Ordinary Time 14: Year A, verses 8-14
Proper 13/Ordinary Time 18: Year A, verses 8-9,
*   14-21*
Proper 20/Ordinary Time 25: Year A, verses 1-8
Proper 12/Ordinary Time 17: Year B, verses 10-18
Proper 27/Ordinary Time 32 Year C, verses 1-5,
*   17-21 (Alt)*

My littleness matters little. My faithfulness in evangelism matters much.

For a spring morning

There is scarcely a cloud in the sky of this psalm. No mention is made of the sinister side of life; no bringing of a charge against God because he seems to be doing nothing about human wickedness; no rage against tyrants; no complaints. Well, there is a cloud in verse 20b ('the wicked he will utterly destroy'), but it is only the size of a man's hand. The psalmist and the poet, Robert Browning, would seem to agree: 'God's in his heaven – all's right with the world!' It is the psalm for a spring morning or for those rare moments when, say, at the end of a Bach cantata, one comes to earth again and whispers, 'If that be so, there must be goodness at the heart of the universe'. It's the psalm for a new day when the celebrant says, 'This is the day the Lord has made,' and the congregation shouts back, 'We will rejoice and be glad in it.'

Look at the verbs [in the AV] – extol, bless (verse 1), praise (verse 2), praise, declare (verse 4), declare (verse 6), utter, sing (verse 7). Look at the description of God in his majesty – his compassion (verse 8), his might (verse 12), his faithfulness (verse 14), his nearness (verse 18), his care (verses 19-20). Make your own list; this one is incomplete. But even as it stands, it gives the lie to the notion that the God of the Hebrew Scriptures is a stern, wrathful and remote figure.

Evangelistic task

'One generation will commend your works to the next and set forth your mighty deeds' (verse 4). This pinpoints the evangelistic task of the Church as one age leads on to another. 'We have a gospel to proclaim', to 'commend' to the upcoming generation, to pass on in its entirety, to interpret in terms that can be understood, to relate to new knowledge. The Church which is not alert to this task will perish in its tracks. One of the litmus tests of the vitality of the Church in any generation is its obedience to the divine commission: 'Go . . . to all nations and make them my disciples.' (Matthew 28:19)

This verse (4) pinpoints also the liturgical task of the Church – the primary place of worship in its life and thought – 'to set forth his most worthy praise', as the 1662 Prayer Book puts it. Generation after generation, all over the world, in great cathedrals and under African trees, in humble kitchens and by the side of hospital sickbeds, the divine work goes on. I see worship as a vast river, a universal stream, into which each generation, each local church, each worshipping individual, makes its own contribution. Or, if you prefer a different picture, I see it as an eternal orchestra, making its praise heard in heaven. Into this ongoing music, I chip in. If, by reason, let us say, of extreme sickness, I am unable to pray or join in public worship, the music goes on and I need not worry. Or if my contribution is a bit flat or out of tune, it is subsumed into the music of the Church where Church triumphant and Church militant unite before the throne. My littleness matters little. My faithfulness in evangelism and worship matters much.

Donald Coggan
Psalms 73-150: The People's Bible Commentary

'On the glorious majesty of thine honour, and on thy wondrous works I will meditate.' (Psalm 145:5)

In a memorable passage toward the end of *The Decline and Fall of the Roman Empire,* Gibbon describes the triumph of the most majestic masterpieces of Roman architecture. Huns, Goths and Vandals had done their worst. The city had been sacked again and again; the hand of the iconoclast had been pitiless. Everything destructible had been ruthlessly destroyed; yet some things remained – and those things were the big things. The fretwork and the fancy work, the delicate carvings and the dainty ornamentations had fallen before the brutality of the Vandals; but the towering columns and colossal arches defied alike the teeth of time and the malice of the barbarian. The big things stand. It is ever so.

Every preacher knows that it is the great themes that hold the field . . . The preacher of small subjects is doomed. A minister was closing his ministry, and a venerable member of his congregation, in bidding his pastor a tearful 'goodbye', remarked, 'Well, sir, I am sorry to see you go. I never had but one objection to you: your preaching was always *too horizontal!*'

'I almost envy some of these good people who can stand in the middle of one of their prayers and touch all four sides,' said a woman. 'They know what they want, and are satisfied when they get it; but I want the moon and the stars and the sun thrown in!' The preacher must take note. The pulpit is the place for magnificent verities. It is the home of immensities, infinities, eternities. 'We must preach more upon the great texts of the Scriptures,' said Jowett. 'We must preach on those tremendous passages whose vastness almost terrifies us as we approach them.'

Taken from *Daily Readings from F. W. Boreham*

Psalm 146

Third Sunday of Advent: Year A, verses 5-10
Proper 18/Ordinary Time 23: Year B
Proper 27/Ordinary Time 32: Year B
Proper 26/Ordinary Time 31: Year B
Proper 15/Ordinary Time 10: Year C
Proper 21/Ordinary Time 26: Year C

Trust is a natural and necessary response to life; without which we could not survive.

He feels trust

Put not your trust in princes, nor in the son of man, in whom there is no help. His breath goeth forth, he returneth to his earth; in that very day his thoughts perish.

Trust people but not too much – that is the theme of Psalm 146. On the surface it seems like a cynical theme and not too realistic. We have to trust people. All good community life depends upon it. We exercise trust every time we step on a pedestrian crossing, every time we board an aeroplane or eat in a restaurant or get a prescription filled at a drug store. We trust the surgeon who takes our life in his hands, the teacher who moulds our children's minds, the politician who takes our tax money and governs our country. Business depends on trust; where it is present we can buy and sell without fear. Family life can be happy only when husbands and wives, parents and children can have confidence in one another. International treaties and the achievement of world peace depend on mutual trust. We really have no other choice. Trust is a natural and necessary response to life; without it we could not survive.

The writer of Psalm 146 does not dispute that. He knows that we have to trust people but at the same time he insists that we ought not to trust them too much. There is a limit beyond which trust becomes unreasonable expectation and lays upon people a burden which they are not able to bear. It's like driving across a bridge. For years the bridge stands strong, carrying a normal load of traffic, but vehicles multiply and get bigger, and one day under a high wind too many bunch together on the bridge, and it collapses. The bridge itself is not defective; it simply wasn't designed to carry such a heavy load. Such is the human spirit which breaks under too heavy a load of trust. That is why the psalmist says, in effect, trust people but not too much.

It is important to emphasise that he is not being cynical. Nothing in Psalm 146 indicates that the author had a low view of his fellow-men. If he doesn't trust people, it's not because they are deficient in character but because they are human, frail and fallible, they collapse like the bridge. Eventually they grow old and die and can therefore guarantee no permanency to their plans and purposes. 'In that very day' their thoughts perish.

The psalmist may have suffered a similar experience. In a personal crisis he may have counted on the support of a loyal friend who had stood by him all through his life, but, when he went for help, he found that his friend, whom he hadn't seen for a while, had become old and senile and incapable of helping him. It is the experience of a faithful employee whose boss puts his hand on his shoulder and says, 'As long as I am alive you've got a job with this company.' The employee might well ask, 'How long do you expect to stay alive?' One day the boss suffers a fatal heart attack, there is a reshuffling of the power structure, and the axe falls. 'His breath goeth forth, he returneth to his earth; in that very day his thoughts perish.'

Or the psalmist may have been thinking of some national crisis. His situation may have been like that of the prophet Isaiah who grew up during the long and prosperous reign of King Uzziah, probably the greatest king in Palestine since Solomon. The people's admiration invested him with all the qualities of ideal monarchy. He represented security to them. They trusted him and thought he would live for ever. To their dismay, however, he contracted leprosy, and his leprosy was seen as the judgement of God upon a sin in which the whole nation was involved. It must have been shattering for the young Isaiah to realise that, although Uzziah had been a good king, he was mortal and fallible and the people had been mistaken to place in him such absolute trust. If Psalm 146 had been written at that time, Isaiah could well have quoted it.

We are looking at the ultimate failure of humanism. The humanist believes that man, having mastered his physical environment, should be able, without any help from outside, to solve his basically moral problems and make this earth a paradise. Yet the weakness of that argument is that moral accomplishments are not always carried over from one generation to another. A single generation can dissipate, exhaust or destroy the moral legacy of centuries. We have seen that happen in more than one country during our lifetime. To be sure, idealists can lift the human race to high levels but they can guarantee no permanency in their plans and purposes. 'In that very day his thoughts perish.' That does turn people into cynics, as it turned H. G. Wells into a cynic. In his early years he rejoiced in the godlike capacities of man but in his last book, *Mind at the End of its Tether*, he wrote:

> The human story has already come to an end . . . and homo sapiens in his present form is played out. The stars in their courses have turned against him, and he has to give place to some other animal better adapted to face the fate that closes in more swiftly upon mankind . . . Our universe is not merely bankrupt; there remains no dividend at all; it is not simply liquidated; it is going clean out of existence.

There is no such despair in Psalm 146. Its author is not saying that we mustn't expect anything of our fellow-men but rather that we must not expect too much of them. To give them absolute trust is to ask the impossible and therefore to experience a crisis of confidence. Civilised life demands that we trust one another; but we shall find a broken reed if we lean on our neighbours as we can lean only upon God. *That* is the positive thrust of Psalm 146. The author wants not to discourage faith in people but to encourage faith in God. After counselling us not to put our trust in earthly rulers he says, 'Happy is he that hath the God of Jacob for his help, whose hope is in the Lord his God.' In that affirmation he responds to his own experience of the grace and goodness of God. He believes that while there is a limit to trust in man, there is no limit to trust in God. We can trust God implicitly, absolutely and eternally.

Leonard Griffith
Reactions to God: Man's Response to God's Activity in the Psalms

Psalm 147

Second Sunday of Christmas: Years A, B, C,
verses 12-20 (Alt)
Fifth Sunday of Epiphany/Proper 1/
Ordinary Time 5: Year B, verses 1-11, 20c

When a man sees the greatness of God he bows down and worships.

The God of nature and the God of Israel

This psalm consists of three sections, each of which is in the form of a complete hymn of praise (verses 1-6, 7-11, 12-20). The Lord is worshipped as the God of Israel who has restored Jerusalem after the exile, and as the mighty creator who controls the stars and the forces of nature and provides for man and beast. . . . The intermingling and repetition of ideas in this psalm convey powerfully the thought that the Lord's greatness cannot be limited to any one activity, but that it must be seen in all its varied manifestations.

1. He is the Lord of nature. His numbering and naming of the stars not only indicates that he is ruler of the universe, but probably includes the assertion that he is supreme over the heathen gods and over the fates of men, for astrology and astral cults were widespread in the ancient world (verse 4; cf. Isaiah 40:26).

2. His power over natural forces is directed to the welfare of all his earthly creatures (verses 8-9, 16-18; cf. 104:27-28; Job 38:41). Jesus pointed to this providence as a proof of God's goodness and loving care (Matthew 6:25-34; Luke 12:22-32).

3. He is the Lord of morality who upholds justice, lifting up the down-trodden, crushing evil-doers, and caring for those who turn to him in reverence and trust (verses 6 and 11).

4. By his 'word' he controls nature (verses 15 and 18). This same *word* instructs men in the moral way (verse 19). In the Old Testament the word of God is active in creation, the giving of the Law, and the message of the prophets (cf. 33:6; Genesis 1; Exodus 20:1; Deuteronomy 5:22; Isaiah 40:8; Jeremiah 1:4, 9; Amos 3:1). In the New Testament the word of God redeems and judges men (Hebrews 4:12; 1 Peter 1:23), and John boldly asserts that in Jesus the 'Word became flesh.' (John 1:14)

5. He is Israel's God whose salvation has been seen in the rebuilding of Jerusalem and the gathering of Jews scattered in exile. Security and abundant prosperity for the restored community are his blessings (verses 2-3, 13-14).

6. The psalm ends with a strong affirmation of the election faith. In the life of no other nation has God worked as he has in Israel's history. To no other nation did he reveal his Law. But this is not teaching, it is adoration. When man sees the greatness of God, he bows down and worships. In his praise is his creed.

Cyril S. Rodd
Psalms 73-150

God acts

There is a delightful story about a man who went to an old friend to ask for a loan of money without collateral and at no interest. The friend assumed at once that deadpan expression and evasive eye that we mortals use when discussing finances. He replied that he frankly did not feel their present friendship close enough to justify such a claim on it. That jolted the supplicant. 'John,' he exclaimed, 'how can you say that to me? We were boys together. I coached you for examinations. I saved you from drowning once. I helped you get started in business. I persuaded my cousin to marry your sister.' 'Oh,' replied John with an inclusive wave of his hand, 'I remembered all that. What bothers me is – what have you done for me lately?'

That question bothers a lot of people about God. What has God done for us lately? What is he doing for us right now? We remember that God has done some great things in the past. With the psalmists of the Old Testament we praise him for his mighty works in Creation, Providence and Redemption. But these are God's finished works; they were finished long before we were born. We want to know what God has done for us lately and what, if anything, he is doing for us right now.

Psalm 147 is one of the greatest statements in the Bible of the activity of God. It opens with a call to thanksgiving: 'Praise ye the Lord: for it is good to sing praises unto our God; for it is pleasant; and praise is comely.' Every verse begins with a verb, 26 of them in all, each setting forth some phase of God's activity. We are told that God *heareth, telleth, lifteth, maketh, goeth, delighteth, sendeth, causeth*, etc. These verbs are all in the present tense, as compared to those psalms which praise God for his mighty works in the past and are therefore set in the past tense. Psalm 147 shows him as a God who has not only done great things but who does great things. He does them for Israel, but the point is that he does them. He is *a God who acts*. A study of this psalm may help us to answer the question, What has God done for us lately and what, if anything, is he doing for us right now?

Leonard Griffith
God in Man's Experience: the Activity of God in the Psalms

Psalm 148

First Sunday of Christmas: Years A, B, C
Fifth Sunday of Easter: Year C

Not even the land of the dead is beyond the reign of the risen Christ.

Psalm 148 has been copied in the song of praise of the three men in the burning fiery furnace (added in the Septuagint to Daniel 3).[1] In form it is an extended hymnic introduction, which we may think of as sung by the priest (choir) at a cultic ceremony, which according to verse 14 was based on the establishment of salvation for the Israelite cult community. The revelation of the divine 'name' . . . and its majesty and of the presence of God in the midst of his people are the theme of the song of praise which the whole world is called upon to sing. The glorification of the Creator and Preserver of the world fulfils the ultimate depth of meaning which unites the inanimate created things and the living creatures in a mutual relationship; to praise the sole majesty of God is the final goal which unites the whole universe in a communion of God's service. This tremendous vision of God and of the world has found expression in the magnificent architectural structure of the psalm, starting with the heavens (verses 1-6), the call to praise God descends to the earth (verses 7-10), then turns to mankind (verses 11-12) and ends (verses 13, 14) with the community of God's people, in whose midst the divine salvation which is the cause and the theme of the hymn became visible and actual. The hymn follows as it were, the course of the epiphany which God and the revelation of his salvation take as he comes down from heaven to appear before his people.

(Psalm 148:1-6) The song of praise sung by the heavens opens in the heights; the grand symphony which the world created by God sings to the praise of its Maker. The celestial hosts, angels and principalities, sun, moon and shining stars, even the celestial ocean; in short, all the things which have been called into existence by God's command and are maintained by his decrees are messengers of God called to proclaim his creative power and glory (cf. Psalm 19:1).

(Psalm 148:7-10) This is the service which the celestial world owes to its divine Lord. The *vox caelestis* is joined by the voices of the earthly choirs: land and sea (the mention of

1. Included in the Apocrypha (verses 28-68) as 'The Song of the Three Holy Children' (the Benedicite).

333

the dragons in this context is striking and shows that the creation story with its tradition of the combat of the gods against the powers of chaos forms the background of the psalm), the natural elements which traditionally precede the theophany as God's attendants (cf. The Sinai theophany and especially 1 Kings 19:11ff.), fire, hail, snow and 'smoke', and the wind that executes the divine command, mountains and plants and all kinds of animals (cf. Genesis 1:1) are engaged in the same service, that of glorifying their Maker.

(Psalm 148:11-14) In the third section where the call to sing the praise of God forms the conclusion, the psalmist turns to mankind, in particular to the rulers of the world of nations (verse 11) and to the whole cult community, comprising all ages (verse 12). Verses 13 and 14 contain both the justification for and the theme of the song of praise; to the cult community are revealed both the name of God and his exclusive supremacy and majesty over heaven and earth; his nearness and presence convey to the people of God both assurance of salvation and new vitality (this is the meaning of the image of the 'exalting of the horn'; cf. Psalms 89:17; 132:17). That belief in salvation is the culmination of the whole psalm and is of crucial importance to the whole world. For it points at the same time beyond itself to the consummation of salvation which the angel host proclaimed from heaven to all the world at the first Christmas as the Good News of the birth of a Saviour.

Artur Weiser
The Psalms

All creation's praise

'And I heard every created creature which was in heaven, and upon earth, and beneath the earth, and all things in them, saying: Blessing and honour and glory and dominion for ever and ever to him who sits upon the throne and to the Lamb.'

Now the chorus of praise goes so far that it cannot go farther, for it reaches throughout the whole of the universe and the whole of creation. There is one vast song of praise to the Lamb . . .

The creatures which are in heaven add their praise. Who are they? More than one answer has been given and each is lovely in its own way. It has been suggested that the reference is to the birds of the air; the very singing of the birds is a song of praise. It has been suggested that the reference is to the sun, the moon and the stars; the heavenly bodies in their shining are praising God. It has been suggested that the phrase gathers up every possible being in heaven – the living creatures, the elders, the myriads of angels and every other heavenly being.

The creatures which are beneath the earth add their praise. That can only mean the dead who are in Hades, and here is something totally new. In the Old Testament the idea is that the dead are separated altogether from God and human kind and live a shadowy existence. 'In death there is no remembrance of thee; in Sheol who can give thee praise?' (Psalm 6:5) . . .

Here is a vision which sweeps all this away. Not even the land of the dead is beyond the reign of the risen Christ. Even from beyond death the chorus of praise rises to him.

William Barclay
The Revelation of John, Volume 1

Psalm 149

Proper 18/Ordinary Time 23: Year A
All Saints: Year C

In this way the heart rejoices without words and the boundless expanse of rapture is not circumscribed by syllables.

From the fifth century and up to the present day this psalm has constantly been interpreted as referring to Maccabean times, though the composition itself does not go beyond very general allusions which fit into every age. During the Thirty Years War the psalm was used as a battle-cry on behalf of the Roman Catholic princes and was also misused by Thomas Munzer to sanction his lust for vengeance. We cannot even be certain that the psalm was composed for a victory celebration. All that we can infer from it is that it is a hymn sung to celebrate the kingship of the Lord (verse 2) during the worship of the community of the 'godly ones' (verse 1), who, dancing the festal dance to the accompaniment of musical instruments, praise the 'name' of God their Maker (verse 3), rejoice in the salvation granted to the people of God, and discern in the execution of the judgement on the Gentiles and their rulers the task which according to the written tradition (verse 9) God has allotted to them. All these features can equally well be accounted for by the festival cult of the pre-exilic period . . .

(Psalm 149:1-3) Likes Psalms 33:3 and 96:1, the psalm opens with a call to the festival congregation resting (verse 5) in the grounds of the Temple at Jerusalem (verse 2) to sing the praise of God, who as their Maker and King has revealed his 'name' and has once more entered upon his reign at his feast (hence a 'new song').

(Psalm 149:4-6) In verse 4 the reasons for this call are given: God's gracious good pleasure rests upon the members of the cult community and this fact inspires them with awe and humility, so that the worshippers are here called 'the humble'. But the members of the festal congregation are at the same time lifted up by the salvation whereby God glorifies himself in them so that they reflect that 'glory' back to the divine Giver in their song of praise. This is the proper duty of the cult community celebrating the feast and the true meaning of their worship, of which verses 5 and 6 are an inspired description.

(Psalm 149:7-9) The opposite aspect of salvation is the judgement on the ungodly Gentiles; this, too, serves the glorification of God's rule and had its traditional place in the cultic

ceremony. . . . The fact that it is described as the 'judgement' on them, that is 'written', allows us to presume here an allusion to a tradition fixed in writing, perhaps the destruction of the pagan nations of Canaan, the accomplishment of which had continually been made the religious duty of the people of Israel (cf. Deuteronomy 7:1ff; 20:13) and which was described in the earlier historical tradition (e.g. in the Book of Joshua). In listening to those ancient traditions the members of the Israelite community of the Lord have obviously experienced the manifestation of the terrible severity of the divine power as an actual present event, just as vivid as the miraculous help which they themselves were able to receive from God; and the concluding statement that by means of the execution of the judgement on the pagan nations the glory of the people of God is also made manifest is to be understood exclusively on the assumption that it is the glory of God which is the real subject throughout.

Artur Weiser
The Psalms

Singing to the Lord

(The theme of praise to God given by all creation, kings and rulers, young men and women, is taken up in this comment on the New Testament.)

Sing to him a new canticle. Have done with the old; you now know the new canticle. The new man, the New Testament, the new canticle. The new canticle does not belong to the old man; none but the new man can learn it, the man who, having once belonged to the Old, is born again by grace and henceforth belongs to the New Testament, which is the kingdom of heaven. Our whole longing yearns after it, singing the new canticle. Let our life, not our tongue, chant this new song. *Sing to him a new canticle. Sing well unto him.* Each one will ask how to sing to God. Sing to him but do not sing out of tune. He does not like his ears wounded. Sing well, brother. Suppose some fine musician is among your audience and you are told: 'Sing to please him.' You feel terrified to sing, being untrained in the art of music, for you may grate upon the artist, because the expert will censure the flaws which pass unnoticed by the unqualified. Well then, who can offer to sing well before a God who is such a judge of the singer, such a critic of every part, such a keen listener? When will you bring the art of singing to such a pitch as not to jar in the slightest upon such perfect hearing? Lo and behold, he sets the tune for you himself, so to say; do not look for words, as if you could put into words the things that please God. Sing *in jubilation*: singing well to God means, in fact, just this: singing in jubilation. What does singing in jubilation signify? It is to realise that words cannot communicate the song of the heart. Just so singers in the harvest, or the vineyard, or at some other arduous toil express their rapture to begin with in songs set to words; then as if bursting with a joy so full that they cannot give vent to it in set syllables, they drop actual words and break into the free melody of pure jubilation. The *jubilus* is a melody which conveys that the heart is in travail over something it cannot bring forth in words. And to whom does that jubilation rightly ascend, if not to God the ineffable? Truly is he ineffable whom you cannot tell forth in speech; and if you cannot tell him forth in speech, yet ought not to remain silent, what else can you do but jubilate? In this way the heart rejoices without words and the boundless expanse of rapture is not circumscribed by syllables. *Sing well unto him in jubilation.*

St Augustine on the Psalms
[Augustine of Hippo]

Psalm 150

Second Sunday of Easter: Year C

All peoples, all creatures, all realms of Nature must add their voices if his name is to be worthily magnified.

The content as well as the structure of the psalm seems to depend on the liturgical form. The psalm is a hymnic exposition of 'Praise the Lord'. Its sentences say *who* is praised (verse 1), *why* he is praised (verse 2), *how* he is to be praised (verses 3-5), and finally, *who* is to praise him. The One praised is God ('el), whose sanctuary is above the vault of the heavens. Title and location identify the Lord as the supreme sovereign who rules over all (cf. 29:10; 96:6; Ezekiel 10:1). The Lord is to be praised as the one who reigns. He is to be praised for his mighty deeds that manifest his immeasurable greatness, his works of creation and salvation. Verse 2 summarises in a poetic line what is said in all of Psalms 145 and 147. The Lord is to be praised in music. The list in verses 3-5 seems intended to include all the instruments that could be used in the performance of worship (cf. 98:5-6). Tambourine and dance are there! This emphasis on music in the final psalm reminds us of all the introductory notations concerned with musical performance and the fact that even prayers adopted as psalms were set to music. It is a witness to the power of music, its amazing potential for evoking beauty and feeling and for carrying vision beyond the range of words into the realm of imagination. That we sing the praise of God is no accidental custom. Music performed, sung, enacted is so much a dimension of praise that words of praise without music need to be musical in rhythm and elegance if they are to serve as praise. The very poetry of the psalms is musical in quality and has been easily set to music of every age and culture. The name of the Lord set to music or voiced in language that is musical – that is praise.

The final line calls upon everything that has breath to praise the Lord. In the Old Testament vocabulary, 'breath' (neshama) more than any other term designates the vitality of the physical life of the human being that comes from God. The term is not a common one and is used in a significant pattern of contexts. The original human being received the breath of life from God (Genesis 2:7). All human beings have life by God's gift of breath that brings vitality and reason (Job 32:8; 33:4; Isaiah 42:5). If God should withdraw his breath, all would return to the dust (Job 34:14-15). The breath of life is, in the long last, the human being's only possession, and in this the human being is dependent upon the Lord (Isaiah 2:22). No other use of breath could be more right and true to life than praise of the Lord. No other sound could better speak the gratitude of life than praise of the Lord. So the psalm concludes with a vocative addressed to all of humanity calling for a simultaneity of praise with life. The final call echoes the promise that 'all flesh will bless his holy name for ever and ever' at the end of Psalm 145; the promise and the call form a significant inclusion around the fivefold 'Hallelujah' that concludes the psalter.

As the final psalm in the psalter, Psalm 150 tells us something about the book. It brings to a resounding climax the increasing dominance by hymns of praise that sets in with the hymns to the Lord's reign in the 1990s. . . . The book that began with a commendation of Torah of the Lord as the way of life ends here with an invitation to praise of the Lord as the use of life. The correspondence between the repeated verb 'praise' (hillel) and the title of the book in Hebrew, *Praises* (tehillim), argues that those who gave the book its name understood the book itself to contain the praises of the Lord, offered to all that have breath. The book is the language by which life can say its dependence and obligation and gratitude to the Lord. Hallelujah.

James L. Mays
Psalms

Jubilation

Again and again in those psalms which are classed by Gunkel as hymns we are struck by the note of exhilaration, almost of hilarity. Sacred joy ripples through their lines and must have pealed through the voices of the singers. Gunkel himself thus describes it: 'These hymns reveal very impressively how strong was the enthusiasm for Israel's God. No language could adequately express the feelings of the people as they gathered for his worship. Again and again we come upon the exhortation that not only the rejoicing Jews should thus sing praises to the Lord, but that all peoples, all creatures, all realms of Nature must add their voices if his name is to be worthily magnified. The hymn of the seraph in Isaiah 6:3 was sung with such power that the pillars of the heavenly palace were shaken – *that* is how the Lord should be praised.'

Indicative of this exuberant spirit are the Hallelujah psalms towards the end of the psalter. These are so called because they begin or end with 'Hallelujah'. It must however be pointed out that in our English versions the word is sometimes hidden, because the translators have occasionally been content to give as their rendering, 'Praise ye the Lord'. That indeed is the literal meaning of the Hebrew word, but it sounds rather pedestrian in comparison with the more explosive term 'Hallelujah'.

Dr J. A. Selbie, judging from the meaning of the root from which the word is derived, considers that in 'Hallelujah' the idea of making a noise appears to be prominent. If so, the psalmists were not in the least ashamed to call for a full blast in joyful praise.

In Psalm 150 every instrument in the band is commissioned to swell the volume of praise – the trumpet or ram's horn, harp and lyre, timbrel or hand-drum, stringed instruments, flute, clanging cymbals and high sounding cymbals. Stringed instruments, wind instruments, percussion instruments – all were to be employed, and then the writer of that psalm, as if not content with the orchestra which he has invoked, urges finally: 'Let everything that has breath praise the Lord: Hallelujah.' So he closes his psalm and the psalter.

W. E. Farndale
The Psalms in New Light

Index of Sundays and Special Feasts

Year A

First Sunday of Advent   *Psalm 122*

Second Sunday of Advent   *Psalm 72:1-7, 18-19*

Third Sunday of Advent   *Psalm 146:5-10*

Fourth Sunday of Advent   *Psalm 80:1-7, 17-19*

Christmas Day 1   *Psalm 96*

Christmas Day 2   *Psalm 97*

Christmas Day 3   *Psalm 98*

First Sunday of Christmas   *Psalm 148*

Second Sunday of Christmas   *Psalm 147:12-20*

The Epiphany   *Psalm 72:1-7, 10-14*

First Sunday of Epiphany/The Baptism of the Lord
Ordinary Time 1   *Psalm 29*

Second Sunday of Epiphany/Ordinary Time 2   *Psalm 40:1-11*

Third Sunday of Epiphany/Ordinary Time 3   *Psalm 27*

Fourth Sunday of Epiphany/Ordinary Time 4   *Psalm 15*

Fifth Sunday of Epiphany/Proper 1/Ordinary Time 5
Psalm 112:1-9, (10)

Sixth Sunday of Epiphany/Proper 2/Ordinary Time 6
Psalm 1; 119:1-8

Seventh Sunday of Epiphany/Proper 3/Ordinary Time 7
Psalm 119:33-40

Eighth Sunday of Epiphany/Second Sunday before Lent
Ordinary Time 8   *Psalm 131*

Ninth Sunday of Epiphany (see also Proper 4)

Last Sunday of Epiphany/Sunday next before Lent/
Transfiguration Sunday   *Psalm 2; Psalm 99*

First Sunday of Lent   *Psalm 32*

Second Sunday of Lent   *Psalm 121*

Third Sunday of Lent   *Psalm 95*

Fourth Sunday of Lent   *Psalm 23*

Fifth Sunday in Lent   *Psalm 130*

Palm/Passion Sunday   *Psalm 31:9-16; Psalm 118:1-2, 19-29*

Easter Day   *Psalm 118:1-2, 14-24*

Second Sunday of Easter   *Psalm 16*

Third Sunday of Easter   *Psalm 116:1-4, 12-19*

Fourth Sunday of Easter   *Psalm 23*

Fifth Sunday of Easter   *Psalm 31:1-5, 15-16*

Sixth Sunday of Easter   *Psalm 66:8-20*

Seventh Sunday of Easter   *Psalm 68:1-10, 32-35*

Pentecost   *Psalm 104:24-34, 35b*

Trinity Sunday   *Psalm 8*

Proper 4/Ordinary Time 9   *Psalm 31:1-5, 19-24; Psalm 46*

Proper 5/Ordinary Time 10   *Psalm 33:1-12; Psalm 50:7-15*

Proper 6/Ordinary Time 11   *Psalm 100; Psalm 116:1-2, 12-19*

Proper 7/Ordinary Time 12   *Psalm 69:7-10, (11-15), 16-18; Psalm 86:1-10, 16-17*

Proper 8/Ordinary Time 13   *Psalm 13; Psalm 16; Psalm 89:1-4, 15-18*

Proper 9/Ordinary Time 14   *Psalm 45:10-17; Psalm 145:8-14*

Proper 10/Ordinary Time 15   *Psalm 65:(1-8), 9-13; Psalm 119:104-112*

Proper 11/Ordinary Time 16   *Psalm 86:11-17; Psalm 139:1-12, 23-24*

Proper 12/Ordinary Time 17   *Psalm 105:1-11, 45b; Psalm 119:129-136; Psalm 128*

Proper 13/Ordinary Time 18   *Psalm 16; Psalm 17:1-7, 15; Psalm 145:8-9, 14-21*

Proper 14/Ordinary Time 19   *Psalm 85:1-2, 8-13; Psalm 105:1-6, 16-22, 45b;*

Proper 15/Ordinary Time 20   *Psalm 67; Psalm133*

Proper 16/Ordinary Time 21   *Psalm 124; Psalm 138*

Proper 17/Ordinary Time 22   *Psalm 26:1-8; Psalm 105:1-6, 23-26, 37-45c*

Proper 18/Ordinary Time 23   *Psalm 119:33-40; Psalm 149*

Proper 19/Ordinary Time 24   *Psalm 103:1-7, 8-13; Psalm 114*

Proper 20/Ordinary Time 25   *Psalm 105:1-6, 37-45;*
   Psalm 145:1-8

Proper 21/Ordinary Time 26   *Psalm 25:1-9; Psalm 78:1-4, 12-16*

Proper 22/Ordinary Time 27   *Psalm 19; Psalm 80:7-15*

Proper 23/Ordinary Time 28   *Psalm 23; Psalm 106:1-6, 19-23*

Proper 24/Ordinary Time 29   *Psalm 96:1-9, (10-13); Psalm 99*

Proper 25/Ordinary Time 30   *Psalm 1; Psalm 90:1-6, 13-17*

Proper 26/Ordinary Time 31/Fourth Sunday before Advent
   Psalm 42; Psalm 43; Psalm 107:1-7, 33-37

All Saints' Day   *Psalm 34:1-10, 22*

Proper 27/Ordinary Time 32/Third Sunday before Advent
   Psalm 70; Psalm 78:1-7

Proper 28/Ordinary Time 33/Second Sunday before Advent
   Psalm 90:1-8, (9-11), 12; Psalm 123

Proper 29/Christ the King/Ordinary Time 34   *Psalm 95:1-7a,*
   Psalm 100

Year B

First Sunday of Advent   *Psalm 80:1-7, 17-19*

Second Sunday of Advent   *Psalm 85:1-2, 8-13*

Third Sunday of Advent   *Psalm 126*

Fourth Sunday of Advent   *Psalm 89:1-4, 19-26*

Christmas Day 1   *Psalm 96*

Christmas Day 2   *Psalm 97*

Christmas Day 3   *Psalm 98*

First Sunday of Christmas   *Psalm 148*

Second Sunday of Christmas   *Psalm 147:12-20*

The Epiphany   *Psalm 72:1-7, 10-14*

First Sunday of Epiphany/The Baptism of the Lord
   Ordinary Time 1   *Psalm 29*

Second Sunday of Epiphany/Ordinary Time 2
   Psalm 139:1-6, 13-18

Third Sunday of Epiphany/Ordinary Time 3   *Psalm 62:5-12*

Fourth Sunday of Epiphany/Ordinary Time 4   *Psalm 111*

Fifth Sunday of Epiphany/Proper 1/Ordinary Time 5
Psalm 147:1-11, 20c

Sixth Sunday of Epiphany/Proper 2/Ordinary Time 6
Psalm 30

Seventh Sunday of Epiphany/Proper 3/Ordinary Time 7
Psalm 41

Eighth Sunday of Epiphany/Second Sunday before Lent
Ordinary Time 8   *Psalm 103:1-13, 22*

Ninth Sunday of Epiphany (see also Proper 4)
Psalm 81:1-10

Last Sunday of Epiphany/Sunday next before Lent/
Transfiguration Sunday   *Psalm 50:1-6*

First Sunday of Lent   *Psalm 25:1-10*

Second Sunday of Lent   *Psalm 22:23-31*

Third Sunday of Lent   *Psalm 19*

Fourth Sunday of Lent   *Psalm 107:1-3, 17-22*

Fifth Sunday of Lent   *Psalm 51:1-12; Psalm 119:9-16*

Palm/Passion Sunday   *Psalm 31:9-16; Psalm 118:1-2, 19-29*

Easter Day   *Psalm 118:1-2, 14-24*

Second Sunday of Easter   *Psalm 133*

Third Sunday of Easter   *Psalm 4*

Fourth Sunday of Easter   *Psalm 23*

Fifth Sunday of Easter   *Psalm 23:25-31*

Sixth Sunday of Easter   *Psalm 98*

Seventh Sunday of Easter   *Psalm 1*

Pentecost   *Psalm 104:24-34, 35b*

Trinity Sunday   *Psalm 29*

Proper 4/Ordinary Time 9   *Psalm 81:1-10;
Psalm 139:1-6, 13-18*

Proper 5/Ordinary Time 10   *Psalm 130; Psalm 138*

Proper 6/Ordinary Time 11   *Psalm 20; Psalm 92:1-4, 12-15*

Proper 7/Ordinary Time 12   *Psalm 8; Psalm 9:9-20;
Psalm 107:1-3, 23-32; Psalm 133*

Proper 8/Ordinary Time 13   *Psalm 30; Psalm 130*

Proper 9/Ordinary Time 14   *Psalm 48; Psalm 123*

Proper 10/Ordinary Time 15   *Psalm 24; Psalm 85:1-13*

Proper 11/Ordinary Time 16   *Psalm 23; Psalm 89:20-37*

Proper 12/Ordinary Time 17   *Psalm 14; Psalm 145:10-18*

Proper 13/Ordinary Time 18   *Psalm 51:1-12; Psalm 78:23-29*

Proper 14/Ordinary Time 19   *Psalm 34:1-8; Psalm 130*

Proper 15/Ordinary Time 20   *Psalm 34:9-14; Psalm 111*

Proper 16/Ordinary Time 21   *Psalm 34:15-22; Psalm 84*

Proper 17/Ordinary Time 22   *Psalm 15; Psalm 45:1-2, 6-9*

Proper 18/Ordinary Time 23   *Psalm 125; Psalm 146*

Proper 19/Ordinary Time 24   *Psalm 19; Psalm 116:1-9*

Proper 20/Ordinary Time 25   *Psalm 1; Psalm 54*

Proper 21/Ordinary Time 26   *Psalm 19; Psalm 124*

Proper 22/Ordinary Time 27   *Psalm 8; Psalm 26*

Proper 23/Ordinary Time 28   *Psalm 22:1-15; Psalm 90:12-17*

Proper 24/Ordinary Time 29   *Psalm 91:9-16; Psalm 104:1-9, 24, 35c*

Proper 25/Ordinary Time 30   *Psalm 34:1-8, 19-22; Psalm 126*

Proper 26/Ordinary Time 31/Fourth Sunday before Advent   *Psalm 119; Psalm 146*

All Saints' Day   *Psalm 24, Psalm 34:1-10, 22*

Proper 27/Ordinary Time 32/Third Sunday before Advent   *Psalm 127; Psalm 146*

Proper 28/Ordinary Time 33/Second Sunday before Advent   *Psalm 16*

Proper 29/Christ the King/Ordinary Time 34   *Psalm 93; Psalm 132:1-12, (13-18)*

Year C

First Sunday of Advent   *Psalm 25:1-10*

Fourth Sunday of Advent   *Psalm 80:1-7, Psalm 89:1-4, 19-26*

Christmas Day 1   *Psalm 96*

Christmas Day – 2   *Psalm 97*

Christmas Day 3   *Psalm 98*

First Sunday of Christmas   *Psalm 148*

Second Sunday of Christmas   *Psalm 147:12-20*

The Epiphany   *Psalm 72:1-7, 10-14*

First Sunday of Epiphany/The Baptism of the Lord
 Ordinary Time 1   *Psalm 29*

Second Sunday of Epiphany/Ordinary Time 2
 Psalm 36:5-10

Third Sunday of Epiphany/Ordinary Time 3
 Psalm 19; Psalm 63:1-8

Fourth Sunday of Epiphany/Ordinary Time 41
 Psalm 71:1-6

Fifth Sunday of Epiphany/Proper 1/Ordinary Time 5
 Psalm 138

Seventh Sunday of Epiphany/Proper 3/Ordinary Time 7
 Psalm 37:1-11, 39-40

Eighth Sunday of Epiphany/Second Sunday before Lent/
 Ordinary Time 8   *Psalm 92:1-4, 12-15*

Ninth Sunday of Epiphany (see also Proper 4)   *Psalm 96:1-9*

Last Sunday of Epiphany/Sunday next before Lent
 Transfiguration Sunday   *Psalm 99*

First Sunday of Lent   *Psalm 91:1-2, 9-16*

Second Sunday of Lent   *Psalm 27*

Third Sunday of Lent   *Psalm 63:1-8*

Fourth Sunday of Lent   *Psalm 32*

Fifth Sunday of Lent   *Psalm 126*

Palm/Passion Sunday   *Psalm 31:9-16; Psalm 118:1-2, 19-29*

Easter Day   *Psalm 118:1-2, 14-24*

Second Sunday of Easter   *Psalm 118:14-29; Psalm 150*

Third Sunday of Easter   *Psalm 30*

Fourth Sunday of Easter   *Psalm 23*

Fifth Sunday of Easter   *Psalm 148*

Sixth Sunday of Easter   *Psalm 67*

Seventh Sunday of Easter   *Psalm 97*

Pentecost   *Psalm 104:24-34, 35b*

Trinity Sunday   *Psalm 8*

Proper 4/Ordinary Time 9   *Psalm 96:1-9*

Proper 5/Ordinary Time 10   *Psalm 30; Psalm 146*

Proper 6/Ordinary Time 11   *Psalm 5:1-8; Psalm 32*

Proper 7/Ordinary Time 12   *Psalm 14; Psalm 22:19-28;*
   Psalm 42; Psalm 43

Proper 8/Ordinary Time 13   *Psalm 16; Psalm 77:1-2, 11-20*

Proper 9/Ordinary Time 14   *Psalm 30; Psalm 66:1-9*

Proper 10/Ordinary Time 15   *Psalm 25:1-10; Psalm 82*

Proper 11/Ordinary Time 16   *Psalm 15; Psalm 52*

Proper 12/Ordinary Time 17   *Psalm 85; Psalm 138*

Proper 13/Ordinary Time 18   *Psalm 49:1-12;*
   Psalm 107:1-9, 43

Proper 14/Ordinary Time 19   *Psalm 33:12-22;*
   Psalm 50:1-8, 22-23

Proper 15/Ordinary Time 20   *Psalm 80:1-2, 8-19; Psalm 82;*

Proper 16/Ordinary Time 21   *Psalm 71; Psalm 103:1-8*

Proper 17/Ordinary Time 22   *Psalm 81:1, 10-16; Psalm 112*

Proper 18/Ordinary Time 23   *Psalm 1; Psalm 139:1-6, 13-18*

Proper 19/Ordinary Time 24   *Psalm 51:1-10*

Proper 20/Ordinary Time 25   *Psalm 79:1-9; Psalm 113*

Proper 21/Ordinary Time 26   *Psalm 91:1-6, 14-16; Psalm 146*

Proper 22/Ordinary Time 27   *Psalm 37:1-9; Psalm 137*

Proper 23/Ordinary Time 28   *Psalm 66:1-12; Psalm 111*

Proper 24/Ordinary Time 29   *Psalm 119:97-104; Psalm 121*

Proper 25/Ordinary Time 30   *Psalm 65; Psalm 84:1-7*

Proper 26/Ordinary Time 31/Fourth Sunday before Advent
   Psalm 32:1-7; Psalm 119:137-144

All Saints' Day   *Psalm 149*

Proper 27/Ordinary Time 32/Third Sunday before Advent
   Psalm 17:1-9; Psalm 98; Psalm 145:1-5, 17-21

Proper 28/Ordinary Time 33/Second Sunday before Advent
   Psalm 98

Proper 29/Christ the King/Ordinary time 34   *Psalm 46*

Special Feasts, Years A, B and C

Holy Name   *Psalm 8*

New Year   *Psalm 8*

Baptism of the Lord   *Psalm 29*

Ash Wednesday   *Psalm 51:1-17*

Monday in Holy Week   *Psalm 36:5-11*

Tuesday in Holy Week   *Psalm 71:1-14*

Wednesday in Holy Week   *Psalm 70*

Holy Thursday *Psalm 116:1-2, 12-19*

Good Friday   *Psalm 22*

Holy Saturday   *Psalm 31:1-4, 15-16*

Easter Vigil   *Psalm 16; Psalm 19; Psalm 42 and 43; Psalm 46;
Psalm 98; Psalm 114; Psalm 136:1-9, 23-26; Psalm 143*

Easter Evening   *Psalm 114*

Ascension   *Years A, B, C: Psalm 47; Year B: Psalm 93;
Year C: Psalm 110*

Annunciation   *Psalm 40:5-10; Psalm 45*

Visitation   *Psalm 113*

Presentation   *Psalm 24:7-10; Psalm 84*

Holy Cross   *Psalm 78:1-2, 34-38; Psalm 98:1-5*

Thanksgiving   *Year A: Psalm 65; Year B: Psalm 126;
Year C: Psalm 100*

Index of Authors and Translators

Achtemeier, Elizabeth	261, 314
Appleton, George	136
Augustine of Hippo	337
Barclay, William	132, 148, 201, 213, 264, 280, 281, 286, 334
Barry, F. R.	291
Bloom, Anthony	243
Bonhoeffer, Dietrich	166, 206, 226
Boreham, F. W.	252, 299, 325
Brueggemann, Walter	29, 43, 63, 94, 139, 158, 162, 176, 216, 270, 289, 305
Buechner, Frederick	16
Bunyan, John	74
Campbell Morgan, G.	155, 168, 174, 195, 201, 213, 246, 264, 323
Charriere, Henri	293
Coggan, Donald	211, 218, 225, 229, 235, 242, 283, 308, 324
Dale, Ron	35, 47, 49, 58, 80, 97, 106, 109, 143, 150, 153, 174, 178, 195, 202, 220, 244, 246, 255, 318
Davies, W. H.	235
Dru, Alexander	70
Farndale, W. E.	340
Filson, Floyd V.	254
Fynn	51
Gomes, Peter J.	126, 250, 297
Gossip, A. J.	227
Griffith, Leonard	25, 45, 54, 75, 89, 102, 110, 124, 190, 229, 232, 271, 286, 298, 301, 311, 321, 327, 331
Guinness, Michele	61, 83
Hayes, John H.	41, 60, 78, 85, 129, 148. 165, 171, 184, 98, 219, 257, 292, 317
Hendry, G. S.	34
Hopkins, Gerard Manley	56
Hort, F. J. A.	100

Jarvis, Ernest D.	277
Julian of Norwich	146, 236
Kempe, Margery	146
Kierkegaard, Søren	70
King, Edward	84
King, Martin Luther	12, 39, 133
Kossoff, David	68
Kung, Hans	258
Mays, James L.	11, 18, 51, 57, 72, 105, 120, 122, 182, 204, 248, 339
McCann, J. Clinton	21, 135, 207, 229
McCheyne, Robert Murray	2, 66
Meadley, T. D.	66, 156, 294
Morris, Colin	14, 137, 199, 222
Muggeridge, Malcolm	56
Newsome, James D.	69, 96, 117, 142, 268
Obey, Andre	49, 160
Parker, Dorothy	180
Ramsay, Malcolm	137
Rauschenbusch, Walter	42
Rhodes, A. B.	82, 93, 99, 108, 123, 139, 152, 193, 238, 253, 265, 284, 296, 323
Richardson, Alan	38, 281
Rodd, Cyril S.	104, 113, 125, 145, 155, 179, 222, 251, 280, 309, 330
Shakespeare, William	132
Snaith, N. H.	22, 180
Soelle, Dorothee	265
Spurgeon, Charles Haddon	19
Stewart, James S.	114
Stachan, R. H.	78
Studdert Kennedy, G.A.	194
Sykes, William	194
Taylor, Barbara Brown	130
Taylor, John B.	187
Thompson, Francis	319
Travell, John	214

Wallis, Jim	185
Ward, J. Neville	196
Waugh, Evelyn	172
Weiser, Artur	333, 336
Wickham, E. R.	209
Witham, A. E.	234
Wurmbrand, Richard	31, 86, 168

Acknowledgements

The Publishers wish to thank all those who have given their permission to reproduce copyright material in this publication. The readings listed below are all in copyright and the addresses of the copyright owners are given at the end of this section.

Psalm 1

Whenever you set out to build . . . (Martin Luther King, Jr), taken from *The Great Sermons of Martin Luther King, Jr*, published by Hodder & Stoughton. Used by permission of Laurence Pollinger Ltd.

Psalm 1 teaches that life is a journey . . . (James L. Mays), taken from *Psalms*, published by Westminster John Knox Press, 1994.

Psalm 2

Power – that's the word for our day . . . (Colin Morris), taken from *What the Papers Didn't Say and Other Broadcast Talks*, published by Epworth Press, 1971.

In his wonderfully imaginative book . . . (Frederick Buechner), taken from *Telling the Truth: The Gospel as Tragedy, Comedy & Fairy Tale*, published by HarperCollins, 1977.

Psalm 4

Psalm 4 is an individual prayer . . . (James L. Mays), taken from *Psalms*, published by Westminster John Knox Press, 1994.

Psalm 5

This is a biblical word . . . (N. H. Snaith), taken from *A Theological Word Book of the Bible*, published by SCM Press, 1956.

The book of Psalms begins by . . . (J. Clinton McCann, Jr), taken from *Texts for Preaching, Year C*, published by Westminster John Knox Press, 1994.

Psalm 8

When I consider thy heavens . . . (Leonard Griffith), taken from *Reactions to God: Man's Response to God's Activity in the Psalms*, published by Hodder & Stoughton, 1979.

Psalm 9

When experiencing a time . . . (Richard Wurmbrand), taken from *If Prison Walls Could Speak*, published by Hodder & Stoughton, 1972. Used by permission of William Neill-Hall Ltd.

These verses assume a triangle . . . (Walter Brueggemann), taken from *Texts for Preaching*, published by Westminster John Knox Press, 1995.

Psalm 13

These words are employed . . . (G. S. Hendry), taken from *A Theological Word Book of the Bible*, ed. Alan Richardson, published by SCM Press, 1956.

Let's take a look at some of . . . (Ron Dale) © Ron Dale.

Psalm 14

Continuing the theme . . . (Martin Luther King, Jr), taken from *The Great Sermons of Martin Luther King, Jr*, published by Hodder & Stoughton. Used by permission of Laurence Pollinger Ltd.

In the Old Testament . . . (ed. Alan Richardson), taken from *A Theological Word Book of the Bible*, published by SCM Press, 1956.

Psalm 15

Psalm 15 was originally used as . . . (John H. Hayes), taken from *Preaching Through the Christian Year: Year A*, published by Trinity Press International, 1992.

Perhaps the really remarkable . . . (Walter Brueggemann), taken from *Texts for Preaching: Year A*, published by Westminster John Knox Press, 1995.

Psalm 16

The sixteenth Psalm is one of those . . . (Leonard Griffith), taken from *God in Man's Experience: the Activity of God in the Psalms*, published by Hodder & Stoughton, 1968.

If ever I was asked about the . . . (Ron Dale) © Ron Dale.

Psalm 17

Mum and Anna shared many likes . . . (Fynn), taken from *Mr God, this is Anna*, published by HarperCollins Publishers, 1974.

My theology tutor . . . (Andre Obey), taken from *Noah*, published by Heinemann Publishers. Used by permission of Heinemann Educational Publishers.

Psalm 17 is a prayer . . . (James L. Mays), taken from *Psalms*, published by Westminster John Knox Press, 1994.

Dr. William Sangster the great . . . (Ron Dale) © Ron Dale.

Psalm 19

About three years ago . . . (Ron Dale) © Ron Dale

A motorist, driving along a city . . . (Leonard Griffith), taken from *Reactions to God: Man's Response to God's Activity in the Psalms*, published by Hodder & Stoughton, 1979.

Psalm 20

The practice of praying for rulers . . . (James L. Mayes), taken from *Psalms*, published by Westminster John Knox Press, 1994.

There once lived a monk . . . (Ron Dale) © Ron Dale.

Psalm 22

Whenever I have led a group . . . (Michele Guinness), taken from *Child of the Covenant*, published by Hodder & Stoughton, 1985.

Like Psalm 51, this psalm has . . . (John H. Hayes), taken from *Preaching Through the Christian Year: Year A*, published by Trinity Press International, 1992.

Psalm 23

As you know, this psalm begins . . . (Walter Brueggemann), taken from *The Threat of Life: Sermons on Pain, Power and Weakness*, published by Augsburg Fortress, 1996.

Psalm 24

A too exclusive preoccupation . . . (T. D. Meadley), taken from *Top Level Talks: The Christian Summit Meeting*, published by Epworth Press, 1969.

A man, very hungry, was caught . . . (David Kossoff), taken from *A Small Town Is a World*, published by Robson Books, 1979.

Psalm 25

Heartache and alienation . . . (James D. Newsome), taken from *Texts for Preaching*, published by Westminster John Knox Press, 1995.

Psalm 26

Vindicate me, Lord . . . (James L. Mays), taken from *Psalms*, published by Westminster John Knox Press, 1994.

Psalm 27

A picture in a popular magazine . . . (Leonard Griffith), taken from *God in Man's Experience: the Activity of God in the Psalms*, published by Hodder & Stoughton, 1970.

Psalm 29

Because 'the voice of the Lord' is . . . (R. H. Stachan) taken from *The Fourth Gospel*, published by SCM Press, 1960.

The open heavens, the voice of God . . . (John H. Hayes), taken from *Preaching Through the Christian Year: Year A*, published by Trinity Press International, 1992.

With the advent of propaganda . . . (Ron Dale) © Ron Dale.

Psalm 30

Mother's own marriage . . . (Michele Guinness), taken from *Child of the Covenant*, published by Hodder & Stoughton, 1985.

Here we have one of the best . . . (A. B. Rhodes), taken from *Psalms*, published by SCM Press, 1960.

I will thank him . . . (Edward King) © Control.

Psalm 31

How terrible is a God who strips . . . (Richard Wurmbrand), taken from *If Prison Walls Could Speak*, published by Hodder & Stoughton, 1972. Used by permission of William Neill-Hall Ltd.

This psalm is a lament . . . (John H. Hayes), taken from *Preaching Through the Christian Year: Year A*, published by Trinity Press International, 1992.

Psalm 32

Blessed is he whose transgression . . . (Leonard Griffith), taken from *Reactions to God: Man's Response to God's Activity in the Psalms*, published by Hodder & Stoughton, 1979.

Psalm 33

Let us begin with a presupposition . . . (Walter Brueggemann), taken from *Praying the Psalms*, published by St Mary's Press.

Psalm 33 is a hymn which brings . . . (A. B. Rhodes), taken from *Psalms*, published by SCM Press, 1960.

Psalm 34

This song of thanksgiving . . . (James D. Newsome), taken from *Texts for Preaching*, published by Westminster John Knox Press, 1995.

O taste and see that the Lord is . . . (Ron Dale) © Ron Dale.

Psalm 36

The character of the righteous God . . . (A. B. Rhodes), taken from *Psalms*, published by SCM Press, 1960.

All our spirits . . . (F. J. A. Hort) © Control.

Psalm 37

This wisdom poem of quiet . . . (Cyril S. Rodd), taken from *Psalms 1-72* (Epworth Preacher's Commentaries), published by The Epworth Press.

This question still vexes . . . (Leonard Griffith), taken from *God in Man's Experience: the Activity of God in the Psalms*, published by Hodder & Stoughton, 1970.

Psalm 40

It is important to note . . . (James L. Mays), taken from *Psalms*, published by Westminster John Knox Press, 1994.

I have told the glad news . . . (Ron Dale) © Ron Dale.

Psalm 41

The happiness of the righteous . . . (A. B. Rhodes), taken from *Psalms*, published by SCM Press, 1960.

Shortly after the train crash . . . (Ron Dale) © Ron Dale.

Psalms 42 and 43

One of the most distinguished . . . (Leonard Griffith), taken from *Reactions to God: Man's Response to God's Activity in the Psalms*, published by Hodder & Stoughton, 1979.

Psalm 45

This is a song . . . (Cyril S. Rodd), taken from *Psalms 1-72* (Epworth Preacher's Commentaries), published by The Epworth Press.

Balaam stood there looking down . . . (James S. Stewart), taken from *King For Ever*, published by Hodder & Stoughton, 1974.

Psalm 46

Faust, in the old story . . . (James S. Stewart), taken from *A Faith to Proclaim*, published by Hodder & Stoughton, 1953.

This much-loved psalm . . . (James D. Newsome), taken from *Texts for Preaching*, published by Westminster John Knox Press, 1995.

Psalm 47

The Lord's rule . . . (James L. Mays), taken from *Psalms*, published by Westminster John Knox Press, 1994.

Psalm 47 is a hymn that praises . . . (James L. Mays) taken from *Psalms*, published by Westminster John Knox Press, 1994.

Psalm 48

The prevailing mood . . . (Leonard Griffith), taken from *Reactions to God: Man's Response to God's Activity in the Psalms*, published by Hodder & Stoughton, 1979.

This is one of the songs of Zion . . . (A. B. Rhodes), taken from *Psalms*, published by SCM Press, 1960.

Psalm 49

In a sermon called . . . (Peter J. Gomes), taken from *Sermons: Biblical Wisdom for Daily Living* by Peter J. Gomes, published by Harper-Collins Publishers Inc., 1998.

A wisdom psalm . . . (Cyril S. Rodd), taken from *Psalms 1-72* (Epworth Preacher's Commentaries), published by The Epworth Press.

Psalm 50

Our God comes . . . (Barbara Brown Taylor), taken from *When God Is Silent*, published by Cowley Publications, 1998.

The opening verses of this psalm . . . (John H. Hayes), taken from *Preaching Through the Christian Year: Year A*, published by Trinity Press International, 1992.

Psalm 51

This psalm is one of the highest . . . (William Barclay), taken from *Seven Fresh Wineskins*, published by Labarum Publications Ltd, 1985. Used by permission of Mr Ronnie Barclay.

And Sunday after Sunday . . . (Martin Luther King, Jr), taken from *The Great Sermons of Martin Luther King, Jr*, published by Hodder & Stoughton Ltd. Used by permission of Laurence Pollinger Ltd.

Psalm 52

Christian hope can only be . . . (Colin Morris), taken from *The Hammer of the Lord*, published by The Epworth Press, 1973.

What is our hope . . . (Michael Ramsey), taken from *Through the Year with Michael Ramsey*, published by Hodder & Stoughton, 1975. Used by permission of William Neill-Hall Ltd.

Unlike most other psalms . . . (J. Clinton McCann, Jr), taken from *Texts for Preaching: Year C*, published by Westminster John Knox Press, 1995.

Faith enables us . . . (George Appleton), taken from *Journey for a Soul*, published by HarperCollins.

Psalm 54

Dealing with one's enemies . . . (Walter Brueggemann), taken from *Praying the Psalms*, published by St Mary's Press.

The detailed background . . . (A. B. Rhodes), taken from *Psalms*, published by SCM Press, 1960.

Psalm 62

A large part of the ability of . . . (James D. Newsome), taken from *Texts for Preaching*, published by Westminster John Knox Press, 1995.

Hope and safety . . . (Ron Dale) © Ron Dale.

I asked God for strength . . . (Unknown Soldier) © Control.

Psalm 63

Deep longing for God . . . (Cyril S. Rodd), taken from *Psalms 1-72* (Epworth Preacher's Commentaries), published by The Epworth Press.

Psalm 65

There are three thoughts . . . (William Barclay), taken from *Seven Fresh Wineskins*, published by Labarum Publications Ltd, 1985. Used by permission of Mr Ronnie Barclay.

Very few psalms for community . . . (John H. Hayes), taken from *Preaching Through the Christian Year: Year A*, published by Trinity Press International, 1992.

I commenced my ministry . . . (Ron Dale) © Ron Dale.

Psalm 66

Psalm 66 is composed of two . . . (A. B. Rhodes), taken from *Psalms*, published by SCM Press, 1960.

Come and listen, all you who fear . . . (Ron Dale) © Ron Dale.

Psalm 67

The chosen people of God . . . (Tom Meadley), taken from *Speaking for Himself*, compiled by John Young, published by Cliff College, 1999.

A refrain in verse 3 and 5 divides . . . (Cyril S. Rodd), taken from *Psalms 1-72* (Epworth Preacher's Commentaries), published by The Epworth Press.

In this psalm there is a fine . . . (G. Campbell Morgan), taken from *Notes on the Psalms*, 1946. © Control.

Psalm 68

The ark is at the right . . . (Andre Obey), taken from *Noah*, published by Heinemann Publishers. Used by permission of Heinemann Educational Publishers.

The festival of the Ascension . . . (Walter Brueggemann), taken from *Texts for Preaching*, published by Westminster John Knox Press, 1995.

Psalm 69

The voice that speaks . . . (Walter Brueggemann), taken from *The Threat of Life*, published by Augsburg Fortress, 1996.

Psalm 70

Jesus, however, takes the law . . . (Dietrich Bonhoeffer), taken from *The Cost of Discipleship*, published by SCM Press, 1959.

This entire psalm is practically . . . (John H. Hayes), taken from *Preaching Through the Christian Year: Year B*, published by Trinity Press International, 1993.

Psalm 71

In order to give a true account . . . (Richard Wurmbrand), taken from *If Prison Walls Could Speak*, published by Hodder & Stoughton, 1972. Used by permission of William Neill-Hall Ltd.

This is pre-eminently a song . . . (G. Campbell Morgan), taken from *Notes on the Psalms*, 1946. © Control.

Psalm 72

A portion of this psalm . . . (John H. Hayes), taken from *Preaching Through the Christian Year: Year A*, published by Trinity Press International, 1992.

Helena, the mother of Constantine . . . (Evelyn Waugh), taken from *Helena*. Used by permission of Peters Fraser & Dunlop on behalf of the Evelyn Waugh Trust.

Psalm 77

This is a song of the healing . . . (G. Campbell Morgan) taken from *Notes on the Psalms*, 1946. © Control.

The very first verse of this psalm . . . (Ron Dale) © Ron Dale.

Psalm 78

This psalm is a recital ... (Walter Brueggemann), taken from *Texts for Preaching*, published by Westminster John Knox Press, 1995.

In the early 1990s ... (Ron Dale) © Ron Dale.

Psalm 79

This communal lament ... (Cyril S. Rodd), taken from *Psalms 73-150* (Epworth Preacher's Commentaries), published by The Epworth Press.

God's attitude to sin ... (N. H. Snaith), taken from *A Theological Word Book of the Bible*, published by SCM Press, 1956.

Please, God, let him telephone me ... (extract from a character created by Dorothy Parker), used by permission of the National Association for the Advancement of Coloured People.

Psalm 80

Psalm 80 is punctuated ... (James L. Mays), taken from *Psalms*, published by Westminster John Knox Press, 1994.

Psalm 81

Verse 5b of Psalm 81 ... (Jim Wallis) © Control.

Psalm 81 was a frequently used ... (John H. Hayes), taken from *Preaching Through the Christian Year: Year B*, published by Trinity Press International, 1993.

Psalm 82

The other day ... (John B. Taylor), taken from *Preaching on God's Justice*. Used by permission of Continuum International Publishing Group Ltd.

Psalm 84

The subject of this chapter is envy ... (Leonard Griffith), taken from *Reactions to God: Man's Response to God's Activity in the Psalms*, published by Hodder & Stoughton, 1979.

Psalm 85

As an undergraduate ... (William Sykes), taken from *Visions of Love*, published by The Bible Reading Fellowship, 1992. Used by permission of the author.

Psalm 85 is a prophetic liturgy ... (A. B. Rhodes), taken from *Psalms*, published by SCM Press, 1960.

Psalm 86

This psalm is peculiar in many ways ... (G. Campbell Morgan), taken from *Notes on the Psalms*, 1946. © Control.

I want to pick up the themes ... (Ron Dale) © Ron Dale.

She (Mary, the Mother of Jesus) ... (J. Neville Ward), taken from *Friday Afternoon*, published by The Epworth press, 1976.

Psalm 89

Psalm 89:36 says 'I see his throne' ... (Colin Morris), taken from *The Hammer of the Lord*, published by The Epworth Press, 1973.

This psalm offers the fullest ... (John H. Hayes), taken from *Preaching Through the Christian Year: Year B*, published by Trinity Press International, 1992.

Psalm 90

This psalm thinks of three things ... (William Barclay), taken from *Seven Fresh Wineskins*, published by Labarum Publications Ltd, 1985. Used by permission of Mr Ronnie Barclay.

The main purpose of this psalm ... (G. Campbell Morgan), taken from *Notes on the Psalms*, 1946. © Control.

When I think about the concept ... (Ron Dale) © Ron Dale.

Psalm 91

How does the Christian conquer ... (Dietrich Bonhoeffer), taken from *Temptation*, published by SCM Press, 1955.

'If you desire,' writes Athanasius ... (James L. Mays), taken from *Psalms*, published by Westminster John Knox Press, 1994.

Psalm 92

This incident relates to a village . . . (E. R. Wickham), taken from *Encounter with Modern Society*, published by Lutterworth Press, 1964.

Psalm 92 is the only psalm . . . (J. Clinton McCann, Jr), taken from *Texts for Preaching*, published by Westminster John Knox Press, 1994.

Psalm 93

I see in the writer of this psalm . . . (Donald Coggan), taken from *Psalms 73-150*, published by The Bible Reading Fellowship. © The Estate of Donald Coggan.

Caesar entered Rome . . . (Anon) © Control.

Psalm 95

This psalm is an invitation . . . (William Barclay), taken from *Seven Fresh Wineskins*, published by Labarum Publications Ltd, 1985. Used by permission of Mr Ronnie Barclay.

He was sensitive to the fact . . . (John Travell), taken from *Doctor of Souls*, published by Lutterworth Press, 1999.

We pause here to note . . . (G. Campbell Morgan), taken from *Notes on the Psalms*, 1946. © Control.

Psalm 96

This psalm is a summons . . . (Donald Coggan), taken from *Psalms 73-150*, published by The Bible Reading Fellowship. © The Estate of Donald Coggan.

If we take Psalm 96:10 . . . (Walter Brueggemann), taken from *Preaching Among Exiles*, published by Westminster John Knox Press, 1997.

Psalm 97

Like Psalm 96, this text focuses . . . (John H. Hayes), taken from *Preaching Through the Christian Year: Year A*, published by Trinity Press International, 1992.

I wonder what sort of thoughts . . . (Ron Dale) © Ron Dale.

Psalm 98

This tremendous hymn of praise . . . (Cyril S. Rodd), taken from *Psalms 73-150* (Epworth Preacher's Commentaries), published by The Epworth Press.

Here is a well-known saying . . . (Colin Morris), taken from *Get Through Till Nightfall*, published by Williams Collins Sons & Co Ltd, 1979. Used by permission of the author.

Psalm 99

This is another enthronement . . . (Donald Coggan), taken from *Psalms 73-150*, published by The Bible Reading Fellowship. © The Estate of Donald Coggan.

By calling us, he (Christ) has cut . . . (Dietrich Bonhoeffer), taken from *The Cost of Discipleship*, published by SCM Press, 1962.

Beach Thomas tells us that . . . (A. J. Gossip) © Control.

Psalm 100

The Archbishop is right . . . (Leonard Griffith), taken from *Reactions to God: Man's Response to God's Activity in the Psalms*, published by Hodder & Stoughton, 1979.

Convictions is the title . . . (Donald Coggan), taken from *Convictions*, published by Hodder & Stoughton, 1975.

Psalm 103

One scarcely expects the Dean . . . (Leonard Griffith), taken from *God in Man's Experience: the Activity of God in the Psalms*, published by Hodder & Stoughton, 1968.

The experience of life not only . . . (A. E. Whitham) © Control.

Psalm 104

Enjoy this psalm! . . . (Donald Coggan), taken from *Psalms 73-150*, published by The Bible Reading Fellowship. © The Estate of Donald Coggan.

Psalm 105

Psalm 105 belongs among the . . . (A. B. Rhodes), taken from *Psalms*, published by SCM Press, 1961.

Who indeed knows . . . (Ron Dale) © Ron Dale.

Psalm 106

The writer cared deeply . . . (Donald Coggan), taken from *Psalms 73-150*, published by The Bible Reading Fellowship. © The Estate of Donald Coggan.

In 1938 a man died . . . (Anthony Bloom), taken from *School for Prayer*, published by Darton, Longman & Todd Ltd, 1970, 1999.

When I look back . . . (Ron Dale) © Ron Dale.

Psalm 107

We now begin the fifth and last book . . . (G. Campbell Morgan), taken from *Notes on the Psalms*, 1946. © Control.

The psalm lection for today . . . (Ron Dale) © Ron Dale.

Psalm 110

Happily for the preacher . . . (Peter J. Gomes), taken from *Sermons: Biblical Wisdom for Daily Living* by Peter J. Gomes, published by HarperCollins Publishers Inc., 1998.

In using the Apostle's Creed . . . (James L. Mays), taken from *Psalms*, published by Westminster John Knox Press, 1994.

Psalm 111

This is a hymn of praise . . . (Cyril S. Rodd) taken from *Psalms 73-150* (Epworth Preacher's Commentaries), published by The Epworth Press.

I am about to say a good word . . . (F. W. Boreham), taken from *Mushrooms on the Moor*, published by Hodder & Stoughton, 1976.

Psalm 112

True disciples are also the light . . . (Floyd V. Filson), taken from *The Gospel according to St.*

Matthew. Used by permission of Continuum International Publishing Group Ltd.

Identical acrostic structure . . . (A. B. Rhodes), taken from *Psalms*, published by SCM Press, 1960.

In one way and another . . . (Ron Dale) © Ron Dale.

Psalm 113

Three general considerations . . . (John H. Hayes), taken from *Preaching Through the Christian Year: Year A*, published by Trinity Press International, 1992.

It is true that the American . . . (Hans Kung) © Control.

Psalm 114

In the three-year Lectionary . . . (Elizabeth Achtemeier), taken from *Preaching Hard Texts of the Old Testament*, published by Hendrickson Publishers Inc., 1998.

Psalm 116

Latin American Christians . . . (Dorothee Soelle), taken from *Celebrating Resistance: The Way of the Cross in Latin America*. Used by permission of Continuum International Publishing Group Ltd.

Some grave peril . . . (William Barclay), taken from *Seven Fresh Wineskins*, published by Labarum Publications Ltd, 1985. Used by permission of Mr Ronnie Barclay.

In Judaism, Psalms 113-118 are . . . (A. B. Rhodes), taken from *Psalms*, published by SCM Press, 1960.

This is the fourth song . . . (G. Campbell Morgan), taken from *Notes on the Psalms*, 1946. © Control.

Psalm 118

The voice of the psalm . . . (Walter Brueggemann), taken from *Texts for Preaching, Year A*, published by Westminster John Knox Press, 1995.

Psalm Sunday is a juncture . . . (James D. Newsome), taken from *Texts for Preaching*, published by Westminster John Knox Press, 1995.

Psalm 119

John Ruskin, writing . . . (Leonard Griffith), taken from *God in Man's Experience: the Activity of God in the Psalms*, published by Hodder & Stoughton, 1970.

Psalm 121

This is called the Pilgrim's Psalm . . . (Ernest D. Jarvis) © Control.

Psalm 122

This pilgrim song may have been . . . (Cyril S. Rodd), taken from P*salms 73-150* (Epworth Preacher's Commentaries), published by The Epworth Press.

This is another of the psalms . . . (William Barclay), taken from *Seven Fresh Wineskins*, published by Labarum Publications Ltd, 1985. Used by permission of Mr Ronnie Barclay.

Generally the biblical sense of peace . . . (ed. Alan Richardson), taken from *A Theological Word Book of the Bible*, published by SCM Press, 1956.

Psalm 123

What a charming little psalm . . . (Donald Coggan), taken from *Psalms 73-150*, published by The Bible Reading Fellowship. © The Estate of Donald Coggan.

This psalm is a free composition . . . (A. B. Rhodes), taken from *Psalms*, published by SCM Press, 1960.

Psalm 124

There was a director . . . (Leonard Griffith), taken from *God in Man's Experience: the Activity of God in the Psalms*, published by Hodder & Stoughton, 1970.

This is characteristically the psalm . . . (William Barclay), taken from *Seven Fresh Wineskins*, published by Labarum Publications Ltd, 1985. Used by permission of Mr Ronnie Barclay.

Psalm 125

This psalm is one of a larger group . . . (Walter Brueggemann), taken from *Texts for Preaching, Year B*, published by Westminster John Knox Press, 1993.

Christianity, when it is true . . . (F. R. Barry) © Control.

Psalm 126

One man who certainly . . . (Henri Charriere), taken from *Papillon*, published by Haper-Collins Publishers.

This psalm has been selected . . . (John H. Hayes), taken from *Preaching Through the Christian Year: Year B*, published by Trinity Press International, 1993.

Psalm 127

A newspaper headline . . . (T. D. Meadley), used by permission of Mrs J. Meadley.

Psalm 128

The one who is rich . . . (Peter J. Gomes), taken from *Sermons: Biblical Wisdom for Daily Living*, published by HarperCollins Publishers, Inc., 1998.

The affinities between this . . . (A. B. Rhodes), taken from *Psalms*, published by SCM Press, 1960.

Psalm 130

The image is one of exquisite . . . (F. W. Boreham), taken from *Daily Readings from F. W. Boreham*, published by Hodder & Stoughton, 1976.

Out of the depths . . . (Leonard Griffith), taken from *Reactions to God: Man's Response to God's Activity in the Psalms*, published by Hodder & Stoughton, 1979.

Psalm 131

Modern man moves . . . (Leonard Griffith), taken from *God in Man's Experience: the Activity of God in the Psalms*, published by Hodder & Stoughton, 1970.

Psalm 132

This psalm, one of the 'royal psalms' . . . (Walter Brueggemann), taken from *Texts for Preaching*, published by Westminster John Knox Press, 1993.

Psalm 133

What community did . . . (Donald Coggan), taken from *Psalms 73-150: The People's Bible Commentary*, published by The Bible Reading Fellowship. © The Estate of Donald Coggan.

This short wisdom psalm . . . (Cyril S. Rodd), taken from *Psalms 73-150* (Epworth Preacher's Commentaries), published by The Epworth Press.

Psalm 136

In his remarkable book . . . (Leonard Griffith), taken from *God in Man's Experience: the Activity of God in the Psalms*, published by Hodder & Stoughton, 1970.

Psalm 137

If we ask what . . . (Elizabeth Achtemeier), taken from *Preaching Hard Texts of the Old Testament*, published by Hendrickson Publishers Inc.

Psalm 138

This psalm may be subdivided . . . (John H. Hayes), taken from *Preaching Through the Christian Year: Year A*, published by Trinity Press International, 1992.

Verse 4 – 5 of Psalm 138 . . . (Ron Dale) © Ron Dale.

Psalm 139

God pursues: A man who has never . . . (Leonard Griffith), taken from *God in Man's Experience: the Activity of God in the Psalms*, published by Hodder & Stoughton, 1970.

Psalm 143

This is the last of the seven . . . (A. B. Rhodes), taken from *Psalms*, published by SCM Press, 1960.

So far as the human situation . . . (G. Campbell Morgan), taken from *Notes on the Psalms*, 1946. © Control.

Psalm 145

There is scarcely a cloud . . . (Donald Coggan), taken from *Psalms 73-150: The People's Bible Commentary*, published by The Bible Reading Fellowship. © The Estate of Donald Coggan.

On the glorious majesty of thine . . . (F. W. Boreham), taken from *Daily Readings from F. W. Boreham*, published by Hodder & Stoughton, 1976.

Psalm 146

Put not your trust . . . (Leonard Griffith), taken from *Reactions to God: Man's Response to the Activity of God in the Psalms*, published by Hodder & Stoughton, 1979.

Psalm 147

This psalm consists of . . . (Cyril S. Rodd), taken from *Psalms 73-150* (Epworth Preacher's Commentaries), published by The Epworth Press.

There is a delightful story . . . (Leonard Griffith), taken from *God in Man's Experience: the Activity of God in the Psalms*, published by Hodder & Stoughton, 1968.

Psalm 148

And I heard every created creature . . . (William Barclay), taken from *The Revelation of John*, Volume 1, published by St Andrew Press, 1976.

Psalm 148 has been copied . . . (Artur Weiser), taken from *The Psalms*, published by SCM Press, 1962.

Psalm 149

From the fifth century . . . (Artur Weiser), taken from *The Psalms*, published by SCM Press, 1962.

Psalm 150

The content as well as the structure . . . (James L. Mays), taken from *Psalms*, published by Westminster John Knox Press, 1994.

Again and again in those psalms . . . (W. E. Farndale), taken from *The Psalms in New Light*, published by The Epworth Press, 1956.

Addresses of Copyright Owners

Augsburg Fortress Press, PO Box 1209, Minneapolis, MN 55440-1209, USA.

Cliff College Publishing, Calver, HopeValley, Sheffield, S32 3XG.

The Continuum International Publishing Group Ltd, The Tower Building, 11 York Road, London, SE1 7NX.

Cowley Publications, 28 Temple Place, Boston, Massachusetts 02111,USA.

Darton, Longman & Todd Ltd., 1 Spencer Court, 140-142 Wandsworth High Street, London, SW18 4JJ.

Epworth Press, Methodist Publishing House, 20 Ivatt Way, Peterborough, PE3 7PG.

The Estate of Donald Coggan, c/o Lee, Bolton & Lee Solicitors, 1 The Sanctuary, Westminster, London, SW1P 3JT.

HarperCollins Publishers, 77-85 Fulham Palace Road, Hammersmith, London, W6 8JB.

HarperCollins Publishers, 10 East 53rd Street, New York, NY 10022-5299, USA.

David Higham Associates, 5-8 Lower John Street, Golden Square, London, W1F 9HA.

Heinemann Educational Publishers, A Division of Reed Educational and Professional Publishing Ltd., Halley Court, Jordan Hill, Oxford, OX2 8EJ.

Hendrickson Publishers Inc., PO Box 3473, Peabody, Massachusetts 01961-3473, USA.

Hodder & Stoughton Ltd., 338 Euston Road, London, NW1 3BH.

Laurence Pollinger Ltd., 18 Maddox Street, Mayfair, London, W1R 0EU.

The Lutterworth Press, PO Box 60, Cambridge, CB1 2NT.

The National Association for the Advancement of Colored People, 4805 Mt Hope Drive, Baltimore, MD 21215-3297, USA.

W. Neill-Hall Ltd., Old Oak Cottage, Rope Walk, Mount Hawke, Truro, Cornwall, TR4 8DW.

The Peters Fraser & Dunlop Group, Drury House, 34-43 Russell Street, London, WC2B 5HA.

Robson Books, Bolsover House, 5-6 Clipstone Street, London, W1P 8LE.

The St Andrew Press, 121 George Street, Edinburgh, EH2 4YN.

St Mary's Press, 702 Terrace Heights, Winona, MN 55987-1320, USA.

SCM Press, 6-17 St Albans Place, London, N1 0NX.

Mr Bill Sykes, Senior Common Room, University College, Oxford, OX1 4BH.

Trinity Press International, 4775 Linglestown Road, Harrisburg, PA 17112, USA.

Westminster John Knox Press, 100 Witherspoon Street, Louisville, Kentucky 40202-1396, USA.